FANTASTIQUE

ABOUT THE AUTHOR

TONY EARNSHAW has been film critic for *The Yorkshire Post* since 1995. He has interviewed hundreds of film personalities while writing for such diverse publications as *Sight & Sound, Fangoria, Cinema Retro, Aesthetica, Flicks, Impact, Diabolique, Starburst, Film Review, .cent, Event,* and *Scarlet Street*. In the United Kingdom, he has appeared as a film critic on national television and radio and has lectured about film and film journalism at the University of Huddersfield, Sheffield Hallam University, and Leeds Trinity University. He was Head of Film Programming at the National Media Museum (formerly the National Museum of Photography, Film & Television) in Bradford, England, and was Artistic Director of Bradford International Film Festival from 2000 to 2011. He created the Fantastic Films Weekend and is currently Co-Director of Fantastiq, the Festival of Fantasy, Sci-Fi & Horror based at QUAD, Derby, England.

Earnshaw is the author of *An Actor and a Rare One – Peter Cushing as Sherlock Holmes, Beating the Devil – The Making of Night of the Demon, Made in Yorkshire* (with Jim Moran), *The Christmas Ghost Stories of Lawrence Gordon Clark* (Ed.), *Studies in the Horror Film: Tobe Hooper's Salem's Lot* (Ed.), and *Under Milk Wood Revisited: The Wales of Dylan Thomas* (with Mark Davis). He has edited monographs on Jack Cardiff, Om Puri, Eric Portman, Lawrence Gordon Clark, Peter Cushing and Stanley Baker.

In addition, Earnshaw has contributed to *Television's Strangest Moments, Bradford Chapters: Episodes in the History of a City, The Sorcerers, Dead or Alive: British Horror Films 1980-1989, '70s Monster Memories* and the forthcoming *We are the Martians: The Legacy of Nigel Kneale*. His debut piece of horror fiction, "Flies," was selected to appear in *The 11th Black Book of Horror*, published by Mortbury Press in 2015.

His work has also appeared under the pseudonyms Michael Black, Allen Faulkner, Chris Flanders, Julian Karswell, and Marcus Spiker.

Tony Earnshaw is married with two daughters and lives in Yorkshire, England.

FANTASTIQUE

Interviews with Horror, Sci-Fi & Fantasy Filmmakers

Volume I

Edited and with an introduction by
Tony Earnshaw

Foreword by Bruce G. Hallenbeck

BearManor Media
2016

Fantastique: Interviews with Horror, Sci-Fi & Fantasy Filmmakers
(Volume I)

© 2016 Tony Earnshaw

All Rights Reserved.
Reproduction in whole or in part without the author's permission
is strictly forbidden.

For information, address:

BearManor Media
P. O. Box 71426
Albany, GA 31708

bearmanormedia.com

Cover by Great British Horror
www.greatbritishhorror.com

Typesetting and layout by John Teehan

Published in the USA by BearManor Media

ISBN—1-59393-944-2
978-1-59393-944-1

Dedication

For
John Mosby
and
Peter Scott
"Can we have your tapes now, please?"

Table of Contents

Acknowledgments xi

Foreword xiii
    by Bruce G. Hallenbeck

Introduction 1

THE FILMMAKERS

Dialogue, Slow Pacing, and Silence 5
Alejandro Amenábar on *The Others*

Balancing Comedy and Horror 15
Paul W.S. Anderson on *Resident Evil*

Things of Today, Things of Tomorrow 31
Luc Besson and Jean-Paul Gaultier on *The Fifth Element*

Big Fear 47
Danny Boyle, Andrew Macdonald, and Alex Garland
on *28 Days Later*

Soaking up the Hammer Vibe 57
Tim Burton on *Sleepy Hollow*

Bringing the Monster into the Light 71
John Carpenter on *The Thing*

Third Act of the Über Film 77
Wes Craven and Neve Campbell on *Scream 3*

Emulating the Past 91
Roland Emmerich, Dean Devlin, and James Spader
on *Stargate*

The Supernatural in Realistic Terms 105
William Friedkin on *The Exorcist*

Giraffes on the Freeway 119
Terry Gilliam on *Twelve Monkeys*

Intuition and Girl Power, Silence and Stealth 133
Jon Harris on *The Descent: Part 2*

Gumby on Acid 145
Frank Henenlotter on *Basket Case*

A Case of Extreme Simplification 161
Peter Jackson and Philippa Boyens on *The Lord of
the Rings: The Fellowship of the Ring*

A Fairytale Gone Horribly Wrong 171
Neil Jordan and Stephen Woolley on *Interview with
the Vampire: The Vampire Chronicles*

Keeping the Cat in the Closet 187
Franck Khalfoun on *Maniac*

I Have the Power Now 197
George Lucas on *Star Wars: Episode I –
The Phantom Menace*

Entering a Narrative Hallucination 209
James Mangold and Cathy Konrad on *Identity*

Humans are the Scariest Thing 223
Neil Marshall on *The Descent*

The Antithesis of High-Budget Hollywood 237
Daniel Myrick and Eduardo Sanchez on
The Blair Witch Project

Texture and Reality 255
Christopher Nolan and Christian Bale on
Batman Begins

The Troll is Coming Out! 269
André Øvredal on *Troll Hunter*

Championing the Forgotten Monster 279
George A. Romero on *Land of the Dead*

"Look at the mess I became." 291
Eli Roth on *Cabin Fever*

Fear is the Unknown 303
M. Night Shyamalan and Bryce Dallas Howard on
The Village

Alien Movies are Hard to Figure Out 317
Barry Sonnenfeld and Will Smith on *Men in Black*

Don't Cast 'Em Unless it's Right 331
Quentin Tarantino on *Grindhouse: Death Proof*

People Like Their Bad Boys.. 341
David Twohy on *The Chronicles of Riddick*

Playing into Primal Fears 349
James Watkins, Jane Goldman, and Susan Hill on
The Woman in Black

Folding Genres Together 361
Ben Wheatley on *Kill List*

A Geek Conquest of the Universe 371
Edgar Wright, Simon Pegg, and Nick Frost on
Hot Fuzz

Filmographies 383

Sources 391

Index 395

Acknowledgments

FOR THEIR CONTRIBUTIONS to the preparation of this volume the editor would like to thank:

The filmmakers: Alejandro Amenábar, Paul W.S. Anderson, Christian Bale, Luc Besson, Philippa Boyens, Danny Boyle, Tim Burton, Neve Campbell, John Carpenter, the late Wes Craven, Dean Devlin, Roland Emmerich, William Friedkin, Nick Frost, Alex Garland, Jean-Paul Gaultier, Terry Gilliam, Jane Goldman, Jon Harris, Frank Henenlotter, Susan Hill, Bryce Dallas Howard, Neil Jordan, Franck Khalfoun, Cathy Konrad, George Lucas, James Mangold, Neil Marshall, Daniel Myrick, Christopher Nolan, André Øvredal, Simon Pegg, George A. Romero, Eli Roth, Eduardo Sanchez, M. Night Shyamalan, Will Smith, Barry Sonnenfeld, James Spader, Quentin Tarantino, David Twohy, James Watkins, Ben Wheatley, Stephen Woolley, Edgar Wright.

Interested parties: Vic Allen, Simon Ashbee, Lawrence Atkinson, Lee Benfold, Mike Best, Gareth Bevan, Kate Bradford, Zak Brilliant, Steve Burnip, Brian Burton, Phil Cairns, Jason at captainhowdy.com, David Castell, Natacha Clark, Leah Clarke, Chris Cooke at Mayhem, Alex Davies, Rob Deacon, Andrew Edwards, Jenny Erwood, Jo Fernihough, Zoe Flower, Lucette Fogarty, Allan Foster, Sarah Freeman, Ian Fryer, Gina Gilberto, Christopher Gullo, Marcus Hearn, Mark Herbert, Tim Hicks, Steve Hills, Annabel Hutton, Stephen Jacobs, Mark Jones, Mike Justice, N'Tashie Kane, Bill Lawrence, Kate Lee, Vicky Lewis, Tracy Lopez, Vicki Luja, Johnny Mains at allthingshorror.co.uk, Lorna Mann, Duncan McGregor, Cath Mercer, Rob Moore, Lizo Mzimba, Keeley Naylor, Amanda Nevill, CBE, Rob Nevitt at Celluloid Screams, Claire Newley, Suzanne Noble, Lucy Powell, Juliet Rees, Eric Roberts, Barry Ryan, Liz Rymer, Peter

Scott, Kenneth Peter Shinn, Nikki Soin, Danielle Soupe, Amanda Telfer, Jayne Trotman, Charlotte Tudor, Debbie Turner, MaryRose Upjohn, Andrew Vine, Tanya Von Moser, Jane Warham, Tony Watson, Mark Witty.

Fellow writers and broadcasters: Stephen Applebaum, Simon Barnett, Jason Best, Kevin Bourke, the late Anwar Brett, Stephen Brown, Dina Burgess, James Cameron Wilson, Jeremy Clarke, Eileen Condon, Van Connor, Maria Croce, Georgina Daly, Mike Davies, Andy Dougan, Rob Driscoll, Claire Druett, Al Dupres, Bob Eborall, Quentin Falk, Ashley Franklin, Jan Gilbert, Marianne Gray, Bruce Hawksbee, Sheldon Hall, Bryn Hamer-Jones, Danni Hewson, John Highfield, Liz Howell, Charles Hutchinson, Alison Jones, Bey Logan, Joanne Mace, Alison Maloney, Johnny Messias, John Miller, Alan Morrison, John Mosby, James Mottram, Tim Oglethorpe, Hilary Oliver, Elsa O'Toole, Martyn Palmer, Brian Pendreigh, Phil Penfold, Mike Polanyk, Andy Potter, Nigel Powlson, Steve Pratt, Joe Riley, Bill Russell, the late Robert Shelton, Anthony Sherratt, Bill Sims, Darryl Smith, Ian Soutar, Marcus Spiker, Siobhan Synott, Darren Vaughan, Kate Whiting, Ian Winterton, Graham Young, Neil Young.

At Great British Horror, Steve Shaw for his cover design.

At BearManor Media, John Teehan and Ben Ohmart.

And my colleague and friend Bruce G. Hallenbeck for his foreword.

Foreword

I'LL NEVER FORGET the time I first saw George A. Romero's *Night of the Living Dead*.

I was 16, and already a hardened horror fan. I had been weaned on the old Universal classics on *Shock Theater* and had grown up (or failed to grow up, as Forrest J. Ackerman had once reminded me) on Hammer horrors and Roger Corman/Vincent Price/Edgar Allan Poe movies. But nothing could have prepared me for Romero's bleak, brutal vision.

That December night in 1968, a friend and I found ourselves at the grand old Palace Theatre in Albany, New York, where Romero's movie was playing on a double bill with, of all things, *Dr. Who and the Daleks*. By the time *Night of the Living Dead* was over, my friend and I were in a state of shock. The gritty, black and white cinematography was a far cry from the glossy period horror films I was used to seeing. The modern setting made it more immediate. And there was the gore; it was one of the few films I ever found myself looking away from during some of its most powerfully-gruesome moments. A little girl stabbing her mother to death and then *eating* parts of her? Even then, I think I knew that Romero had changed the face of horror films.

George A. Romero is one of the twenty *genre* directors interviewed in this book, in this case discussing his fourth excursion into the mythology that he created, *Land of the Dead*. If you're a fan of all things dark and scabrous, however, you will find many of your other favorites in this wonderful tome, telling you, in their own words, about the creations of some of their most iconic films. Tim Burton will regale you with his thoughts on making his delightfully-Hammeresque *Sleepy Hollow*. John Carpenter will go on about his brilliant version of *The Thing*. The late Wes Craven, along with star Neve Campbell, will reveal to you all you've ever wanted to know (but perhaps were afraid to ask) about *Scream 3*. And William Friedkin will give you the supernatural details of his masterpiece, *The Exorcist*.

Tony Earnshaw is a lifelong gourmet of the *fantastique*, as he likes to call it, and it shows. He knows exactly the right questions to ask of these celebrity horror directors. He digs in (like a gravedigger) to find their cinematic influences, and he shares many of his subjects' interests. No one else could have written this book quite like Tony, and, once you've read it, you'll feel that you too have spent some time with these master filmmakers.

Keeping his finger on the pulse of the horror film, Tony has also included interviews with younger but no less potent filmmakers, such as Ben Wheatley, whose recent film *Kill List* has one of the most shocking endings I've ever seen; and Neil Marshall, whose film *The Descent* takes us straight down to Hell. Along the way, you'll hear from such disparate talents as Luc Besson, Terry Gilliam, Peter Jackson, and Christopher Nolan. The interviews encompass a virtual *Who's Who* of A-list filmmakers.

So find a comfortable spot, sit back, and enjoy this book. It may bring back memories of some of the most pleasurable frights you've ever had… and give you some idea of how the filmmakers caused those shivers to run up and down your spine.

Bruce G. Hallenbeck
Valatie, New York
September 2015

Introduction

TWENTY YEARS AGO, almost every regional newspaper in the United Kingdom could lay claim to its own film critic, reviewer, or cinema specialist. From Brighton in the South of England to Cardiff in Wales and Edinburgh and Glasgow in Scotland, the regional press corps was knowledgeable, informed, and highly experienced.

In 1992, I was a newcomer to the circuit, but I always had something to say. When it came to bagging a question at a press conference or roundtable interview, it was often a matter of grabbing the attention of the moderator. That and asking an intelligent question.

There were scores of regional writers and broadcasters in those days. Yet on many occasions it fell to just a handful to handle the interview. These were the people that could be relied upon to ask erudite questions, to engage with the talent, to be trusted to be professional, polite, punctual, and, above all else, prepared. I conducted interviews under the banner of *The Yorkshire Post*.

Two decades on, things have changed. Most of the old faces are gone. But the landscape has changed, too. Blogs and websites have largely replaced newspapers and magazines as the darlings of the film public relations world, and citizen journalism via Twitter and Facebook has become the norm when film companies seek a friendly quote for their advertising campaign. What price then the humble film critic? The evidence to the contrary is here in this book.

All of the interviews presented here took place over a twenty-year period. Several are borne of the traditional press conference. Others were conducted in intimate groups in what is known as the roundtable format. The remainder are exclusive to myself—the one-on-one style so desired by all self-respecting journalists.

Occasionally, however, one has to share. In the good old days, one could rely on one's contemporaries to cover much of the required ground. The questioning was precise, informed and uniformly excellent. It was a poor writer who couldn't extract a viable piece from those eclectic sessions.

For my part, being a member of that august press pack provided access to other journalists, some of considerable status. It was a learning curve and one that I relished. I relished also the opportunity to talk about old Hollywood with colleagues who had sat down for dinner with Bette Davis or who had sailed on Bogart's yacht off the Catalinas and for three days never took a sober breath.

Alas, those glory days were long past when I entered the profession. I have rubbed shoulders with remarkable people, though, among them some of the biggest stars on the planet.

There have also been encounters with an array of filmmakers—directors, producers, writers, cinematographers, composers, editors, special effects technicians, location scouts, and other equally vital denizens of the film set.

Some of them can be found within the following pages. They walk the world of the *fantastique* and they share a love of the genre. Perhaps most interesting is the tracing of the lineage—the films and directors that inspired them. You will find the same names and film titles appearing again and again.

The thirty interviews included in this volume—hopefully the first of many—are a personal selection. They include long-time favorites such as George A. Romero, William Friedkin, and John Carpenter, but also newcomers who, at the time the interviews took place, were just breaking through. Rising stars like Neil Marshall (*The Descent*) and Ben Wheatley (*Kill List*).

It is a fascinating exercise to talk with such individuals, to find common ground, to identify shared influences, and to swap stories of the beloved films of one's youth, and in doing so to gain a deeper and sometimes intimate understanding of the mechanics of filmmaking.

Some of these interviews go into considerable depth. Others are briefer. Some are laced with banter and laughter. Each and every one of them offers an insight into a classic film within the genre of horror, sci-fi, and fantasy. This is detail from the horses' mouths. I hope you find it entertaining and, more importantly, enlightening.

Tony Earnshaw
Yorkshire, England
September 2015

THE FILMMAKERS

ALEJANDRO AMENÁBAR
The Others

Discussions with the dead: writer/director Alejandro Amenábar and star Nicole Kidman during production of *The Others* in Spain. (Miramax/Manuel Outomuro)

THE OTHERS

Miramax, 2001

CAST: Grace, NICOLE KIDMAN; Mrs. Mills, FIONNULA FLANAGAN; Charles, CHRISTOPHER ECCLESTON; Anne, ALAKINA MANN; Nicholas, JAMES BENTLEY; Mr. Tuttle, ERIC SYKES; Lydia, ELAINE CASSIDY; Old Lady, RENÉE ASHERSON; Assistant, GORDON REID; Mr. Marlish, KEITH ALLEN; Mrs. Marlish, MICHELLE FAIRLEY; Victor, ALEXANDER VINCE; 2nd Assistant, RICARDO LÓPEZ; Gardener, ALDO GRILO.

CREDITS: *Written and directed by* Alejandro Amenábar; *producers,* Fernando Bovaira, José Luis Cuerda, Sunmin Park; *executive producers,* Tom Cruise, Paula Wagner, Bob Weinstein, Harvey Weinstein, Rick Schwartz; *line producers,* Emiliano Otegui, Miguel Ángel-González; *associate producer,* Eduardo Chapero-Jackson; *director of photography,* Javier Aguirresarobe A.E.C.; *editor,* Nacho Ruiz Capillas; *production design,* Benjamin Fernández; *music,* Alejandro Amenábar; *costume design,* Sonia Grande. Running time: 104 minutes.

> "On the secluded Isle of Jersey in the final days of World War II, a young woman waits for her beloved husband to return from the front. Grace has been raising her two young children alone in a beautiful, cavernous, Victorian mansion, the one place she believes them to be safe.
>
> "But they are not safe. Not anymore.

"When three new servants arrive to replace the ones that inexplicably disappeared, startling, supernatural events begin to unfold. Grace's daughter reveals she has been communicating with unexplained apparitions. At first, Grace is reluctant to believe in her children's frightening sightings, but soon, she too begins to sense that intruders are at large.

"Who are these numinous trespassers? And what do they want from Grace's family? In order to discover the truth, Grace must abandon all of her fears and beliefs and enter the otherworldly heart of the supernatural."

Dialogue, Slow Pacing, and Silence
Alejandro Amenábar on *The Others*

How did a young Spaniard, born in the 1970s, come to make a film set very specifically in the Channel Islands in 1945?

Alejandro Amenábar: I thought at the beginning about setting the story in South America. When my producers read the script, they thought it was the perfect Victorian ghost tale, so they thought it would be more organic taking place in England. Then the main problem to me was to integrate the Catholic stuff in the Anglo-Saxon context, so we found these islands, which have a Catholic church. Then I researched the story of the islands and I found very, very interesting the fact that they were occupied during the war, and I tried to integrate it in the story.

Did you discover a lot that you had not known about?

I didn't know the story of the islands beforehand. I wondered if someone had made a film about the real story of the islands, because I found the stories very moving and very interesting—what happened there.

Did you have to completely rewrite and rework your script?

Yeah, but it wasn't difficult. And my producers were right: it would fit very organically in the Anglo-Saxon context. So I changed the names.

Were you nervous about working in a different language?

That was my very first concern because I didn't speak any English at that time. So I took that challenge. To me, working in English and working with children were the two most difficult points. So I tried to learn English and tried to think how to face children and how to treat them.

You receive sole credit as writer and director. Did you receive help in terms of the Englishness of the script?

Yeah. Once you decide to do a project which is in not your natural language, what you have to do is rely on and trust people. We hired a very good English translator and she was working for months. I was very open to change things in order to make it sound very, very British. With the children, we hired a casting director. Then again it was very, very open. For more than half a year, we were looking for the little girl, because it was difficult. I had to make sure that these children could understand the complexity of the characters and who could endure shooting in Spain, because I insisted on shooting the film in Spain.

There was never any idea of shooting it in the Channel Islands?

We were thinking about shooting the exteriors in Jersey or in England. We went to Jersey and we found a very interesting house. Then we came here [to England] and we saw one hundred houses in a catalogue. Then someone in the office found this incredible house in the north of Spain and I said, "That's perfect."

How did you find working with Nicole Kidman?

She had to work in two films when she was working in our film. There were a few shots for *Birthday Girl* [2001] and *Moulin Rouge* [also 2001] [that she had to complete]. We were almost finishing and she got injured. She had to go back to the States and we stopped the shooting for one month.

How did you manage to attract Kidman to the role?

What happened is that before I wrote *The Others*, Tom Cruise got the rights of my second film *Open Your Eyes* [aka *Abre los ojos*, 1997] in order to do the remake, which will be *Vanilla Sky* [2001]. When I wrote the script, we translated it into English, my producers sent it to a few companies in the States including Cruise/Wagner and said, "This is the guy who did *Open Your Eyes*. Would you like to read the script?" They read it and they loved it. I guess that he gave the script to Nicole. We had this meeting where Nicole said she would like to play the role and I thought, *That would be fantastic*. It was very fast.

Where did Eric Sykes come from and when did he find out he was dead?

[Laughs] Actually I didn't know who Eric Sykes [was] when Jina Jaye, the casting director, suggested him. Then I realized that he was a kind of hero here [in the UK]. When I met him I [realized] he's almost deaf and almost blind. I thought that would be perfect for the character. He's a very funny man and I really had a great time working with him. I had a couple of meetings here [in the UK with Eric] and he was always really committed to the film. He really liked the character and the film—really loved it. We had several delays because Nicole was working in *Moulin Rouge*.

Given that the film is quintessentially English in tone, did M.R. James influence you in any way?

No. Considering this was going to be a ghost story, I tried to see any good ghost story from the '40s, '50s, and '60s. Obviously, in this case, there is not only the film based on *The Turn of the Screw*, which was *The Innocents* [1961], by Jack Clayton, particularly the use of silence as a form to create suspense. I found that very interesting. But then I can take things even from comedies—completely different films that I have seen. There is a film called *The Changeling* [1980], by Peter Medak, a Canadian film. I found it very scary. I particularly liked the use of music and sound without special effects.

And then any horror movie that I used to see when I was a child. The thing is, I was a very easily-scared child, but at the same time I enjoyed myself writing stories about ghosts and haunted houses. Then I did my first two films, which weren't about that at all. [*The Others*] was like going back to that period of my life.

What is it specifically about the English ghost story and films like The Innocents *that fascinates you?*

I would say that all the Victorian house elements from the Gothic storytelling [tradition] that come from England now belong to the world. It's something that you can feel really, really identified with. For instance, *The Haunting* [1963], a film that is very interesting to me—the old *Haunting*, not the remake—is American. In the case of English films, there is *The Innocents* of course and *Rebecca* [1940], which is an American film directed by an Englishman. There is also *To Kill a Mockingbird* [1962]. I find that film somehow terrifying and very, very moving. My childhood was very associated to England when I was a child because I used to read every single Agatha Christie novel. So maybe there's a kind of connection there.

It's a big project to write a script like this. What was your plan: to write a great ghost story?

I've been trying to think about the process when journalists ask me about it. It started from one single occasion. I wanted to have a bunch of good actors in one single location. That was when I was shooting my second film, which is completely the opposite [of *The Others*]. It takes place in many places in many periods of time. Then I started to include all the religious things. I read a story about these people who can't be exposed to sunlight, and I thought that was the perfect excuse to have all these people isolated in a house. Then I thought, *What if it was a mother with her two children and she's very severe? She's teaching them all this severe stuff about Catholicism. But then what if she discovers that she's a ghost and that makes her think about her whole situation in that worst moment?*

The posed photographs of the dead, which scared me somewhat, fascinated me. What makes you scared—and are there many of those photographs still in existence?

I wrote the script and then I think [I saw] a documentary or I read about it and I tried to include it in the story. Half of the photographs [in the film] are real and half are fakes. We asked for originals and we lost them. I appear in one of the photographs as one of the dead.

If the film is a success in America, will you go to Hollywood to make movies?

I'm very respectful with the Hollywood system and very reluctant, too. People like Tom Cruise and Nicole Kidman have been very supportive with me, and I really appreciate that. But I've seen so many frustrated directors who go from Europe to the States and end up doing a film they don't feel proud of. So I'm quite reluctant. It depends on the story. To me, keeping control and staying focused is very, very important.

Cameron Crowe is directing the American remake of Open Your Eyes. *Is it something you would have liked to do?*

No, not really, unless I wanted to change or remake things and make it different. But if it's about making the same film again, it's not worth it.

You appear to have built a reputation with this style of fantasy movie. Do you expect to continue in this genre or do you yearn to make a comedy?

When you finish a film and finally take it out of your mind, then it's a moment for me to think about the next one. Then I try to be as open as possible. After my first film, I started to write a comedy and I ended up writing *Open Your Eyes*, which is not a comedy at all. You never know. The truth is my three films are very different and at the same time very similar [in terms of] the questions that are asked. At this moment, I haven't thought about my next project.

Do you have any thoughts on the classification of the movie?

We're quite open in Spain about qualifications [sic] for the films. I've been told that in the States, many parents are taking their children to see the film. Of course, I wouldn't say it was a film for children. But there is a kind of naiveness [sic] in the story when I was trying to go back to that period of my life. I think it's quite an honest film. I wouldn't say it was a dark film in that sense. It's a story of redemption in a way. There is hope at the end.

Given that you also composed the music for The Others, *how important is it that you have control over the music as well?*

It's part of the process that I don't really enjoy, but I felt I had to do it. I always had a very clear idea of what I wanted. The only problem is that usually directors have these breaks between the editing of the film and the mix, and I still have to work on the music! To me, it helps to have a clear idea of the atmosphere. I always know when I'm writing if I'm going to need music [in a specific sequence] or not. Sometimes I've rehearsed with the actors listening to music, so it really helps to set the mood and the pace of the film.

Were you ever concerned that your big break in the States might be overtaken by the Cruise/Kidman break-up?

There was a lot of gossip and I felt a bit overwhelmed, especially in the release in L.A. and in New York. But I think the fact that the film has been in theaters and at first position at the box office for months now proves that the film stands on its own. They went to L.A. to the same premiere. I really appreciated that and I'm proud of them because I think it proves that they are really professional. What they promised always was that they would be devoted to and supportive of the film.

How has the film been received in the UK?

I always thought that [the UK] should be the natural market for this film. I guess here people should like it [and] so far it has been one of the warmest [reactions]. We had three test screenings—two in the States and one here [in the UK], and we got the worst results here in England, which shocked me!

With the success of The Sixth Sense [1999] *and this—and there is a slight relationship between them—there is clearly a public appetite for this sort of theme: confronting our worst nightmares. Do you see a connection, and why do you think there is such an interest in material like this?*

There have been many stories in the last few years about ghosts and children who see ghosts. I wouldn't say this film is influenced by *The Sixth Sense* because I wrote it more than three years ago, which is one year before *The Sixth Sense* was released. If I had to talk about influences, I would talk about *The Innocents*. The haunted house thing and ghosts in houses have much more to do with it.

If you were easily scared as a child, did you become less scared the more horror you saw?

I'm quite naïve with that. Actually I'm a very good viewer. I can get a scare with *any* film. One of the things that annoy me—because I consider myself a huge fan of horror—is the fact that many Hollywood horror pictures now are not even scary. That's unforgivable. You could expect from a horror movie to be damp, but not *boring*. Sometimes it's just a bunch of special effects. Nowadays I don't get scared in films. What I was trying to do when I wrote this was to write a story that I'd like to see in theaters.

Were you conscious of sharing an aesthetic with other films? Open Your Eyes *has similarities to* The Matrix [1999] *and this film shares themes with* The Sixth Sense. *In your mind were you trying to make them aesthetically different?*

No, not really. In my three films, there is a big twist at the end [of each]. That's vital. The audience is supposed to be surprised at the same time as the characters are because the connection is very close between the audience and the characters. That twist is vital. In this case, that change of perspective—I always had it in mind. When I start to write, I need to know how the story is going to end because I need to know the journey for the character. *The Innocents* was recommended to me, and then I saw it. Then you have *The Haunting*. And any Hitchcock movie. I have been very, very influenced by Hitchcock.

How did you break into the industry?

I was very lucky. I was starting a film at university [*Luna*, 1995], and a Spanish director saw it and called me in. He encouraged me to write a feature film. I was in my fifth year writing a script. I sent it to him and he decided to produce it. So I never finished my studies. The good thing is that he saw the film. That's important.

Do you see The Others *reviving the genre of* The Innocents *and films like it?*

I don't know. In this case, what makes this story new or fresh was trying to get many of the elements from the Gothic storytelling [tradition] and then trying to give entirely the opposite moral position. Many times, in the end, it's about this confrontation between good and evil. I wanted to do something more sophisticated. Instead of having this big monster at the end, it's just this change of perspective that helps the characters to think about their situation. Obviously, there is an influence of Gothic storytelling, but I was trying to do something a little bit fresh.

You were trying to make a better kind of film.

Yeah, exactly. From the formal point of view that was vital to me and very important. I was trying to feel all this contention and pacing. Nowadays, producers don't trust in dialogue and what the characters are saying. This film relies on dialogue, basically, and on slow pacing and silence. That was a risk when we decided to do it.

Given that Hollywood likes sequels, is there any prospect of The Others 2?

Of course not! I wouldn't be the director. I should see my contract to see if I can stop that!

2001

PAUL W.S. ANDERSON
Resident Evil

"It's the package of finding someone who's a good actor, who also looks right with a gun and can do the action scenes because a lot of actresses can't. And with somebody who looks as stunning as [Milla] does it's an amazing combination." – director Paul W.S. Anderson on finding his perfect zombie killer in *Resident Evil*. (Sony Pictures/Rolf Konow)

RESIDENT EVIL

Sony Pictures, 2002

CAST: Alice, MILLA JOVOVICH; Rain, MICHELLE RODRIGUEZ; Matt, ERIC MABIUS; Spence, JAMES PUREFOY; Kaplan, MARTIN CREWES; One, COLIN SALMON; Mr. Grey, RYAN McCLUSKEY; Mr. Red, OSCAR PEARCE; Ms. Black, INDRE OVE; Dr. Green, ANNA BOLT; Dr. Blue, JOSEPH MAY; Dr. Brown, ROBERT TANNION; Lisa, HEIKE MAKATSCH; Clarence, JAMES BUTLER; Mr. White, STEPHEN BILLINGTON; Ms. Gold, FIONA GLASCOTT; J.D., PASQUALE ALEARDI; Medic, LIZ MAY BRICE; Commando 1, TORSTEN JERABECK; Commando 2, MARC LOGAN-BLACK; Red Queen, MICHAELA DICKER. Uncredited: Doctor/Narrator, JASON ISAACS.

CREDITS: *Director*, Paul W.S. Anderson; *producers*, Bernd Eichinger, Samuel Hadida, Jeremy Bolt, Paul W.S. Anderson; *co-producer*, Chris Symes; *executive producers*, Robert Kulzer, Victor Hadida, Daniel Kletzky, Yoshiki Okamoto; *screenplay*, Paul W.S. Anderson, based upon CAPCOM's video game "Resident Evil;" *music*, Marco Beltrami, Marilyn Manson; *director of cinematography*, David Johnson, BSC; *editor*, Alexander Berner; *production and costume design*, Richard Bridgland; *visual effects*, Richard Yuricich, ASC; *make-up*, Hasso Von Hugo. Running time: 104 minutes.

> "Something terrible is lurking in the Hive, a vast underground genetic research facility run by the Umbrella Corporation, a faceless bioengineering conglomerate. A deadly viral outbreak occurs, and in response, the Red Queen—an immense supercomputer that controls and monitors the Hive—seals the entire facility to contain the leak, killing all the trapped employees. Alice and Rain

must lead fellow commandos to isolate the virus that has wiped out Umbrella's entire research staff. The team soon discovers, however, that the workers are… not… really… dead. They are now the ravenous Undead, *and they are prowling the Hive."*

Balancing Comedy and Horror
Paul W.S. Anderson on *Resident Evil*

What are the challenges associated with bringing this kind of iconic game to the big screen?

Paul W.S. Anderson: The main problem that you have is that you have a very, very strong core audience who expect a lot from a movie like this because *Resident Evil* is their favorite game and they've been playing it for seven or eight years. Now [they're frightened that] some asshole filmmaker is going to come along and mess it all up and ruin it. That tends to be the fans—that's what they think and what they're really scared of because they're very protective [of it]. They've played four *Resident Evil* games, they've spent hundreds of dollars buying them; it's part of their life. So you have to really be careful to make a movie that pleases them. But in pleasing your core audience you have to be sure that you then don't make a movie that's inaccessible to a more mainstream audience as well. Obviously, for a film like this, even if everyone who plays *Resident Evil* goes and sees it three or four times, it doesn't justify making a movie of the size of this film. And those things can be quite contradictory—pleasing a core audience *and* pleasing an audience that don't know *Resident Evil* from a hole in the head.

Was Milla Jovovich always your first choice for the role?

I didn't write it with her in mind. We had a two-page list of actors that we were going to meet for the leading role. Milla really chased after *Resident Evil*. She really, really wanted to do the movie, really wanted to come and meet me.

    She was the first person we met, at her insistence, and we never met anybody else after her. That's how perfect she was. I'd never met her before, so I didn't really know what to expect. She walked in and I thought, *Ah! That's it*. She *so* blew me away that we never met anyone else. We didn't need to look any further. We just kind of tore it up and threw it away. But she worked hard for it. She came back three times. She read three times—with Jason Isaacs, who was in Hollywood at the time. And we really put her through the mill. I was also worried that to commit to the first person that you see, you have to be really, really certain. It's one thing after you've seem a hundred actors to say, "Well actually the first person was the best," but after seeing her three times [it was clear to me] that she was really right for it.

It was exactly the same with Michelle Rodriguez. She was the first person we met for that role and the only person we met for that role. So in a way the casting was easy. I'd known Colin Salmon for a long time—not socially but just because I'd read him for every movie I've ever made. And I've never found the right role for him. This movie was just so right for him. I think very few people read for that role. Colin was very much the guy we wanted from the start.

So in many ways it was great. It was an opportunity for me to work with people who were very passionate about doing the movie and people who I felt very passionate about. It was one of the great things about making a gruelling action movie—because they're all difficult to make, especially when you're asking your cast to get knocked around as much as, say, Milla did in this movie—is when you have people who are passionate about doing the film. It makes a big, big difference. No one's there for a payday. They're all turning up because they really want to do *Resident Evil*.

What made Milla right?

Everything. It's the package of finding someone who's a good actor, who also looks right with a gun, and can do the action scenes, because a lot of actresses can't. They hold a gun and it just looks wrong. It's never going to look right. And with somebody who looks as stunning as she does, it's an amazing combination. It's rare in Hollywood to have someone who, lip-gloss or machine-gun, doesn't make any difference! When you find people like that, you've really got to grab onto them and hold onto them.

Did you play video games before making this film?

Yes. One of the games I particularly like is *American McGee's Alice*, which is a very twisted re-telling of the *Alice in Wonderland* story. *Alice in Wonderland* and *Through the Looking Glass* are my favorite books. I've always been looking for a way to do an *Alice* movie, and I think American McGee with that game really cracked it. Alice's house burns down and she sees her parents burned alive. The trauma of that makes her catatonic. You pick up with her ten years later where she's in a Victorian mental asylum. She's grown up, but she doesn't speak at all. She has to return to Wonderland, and because it is part of her own psyche, it's very twisted and dark. She's gone mad and so has Wonderland. It's a kind of ultraviolent, twisted, gothic retelling of the *Alice* story, and super cool.

Given that the game of Resident Evil *boasts an array of weird and wonderful creatures, why did you choose to focus on just two: the dogs and the Licker? Was that to not take the emphasis away from the zombies?*

The mutants of the day! It's everyone's favorite. The same with the dogs. When it comes to adapting it to a movie that's the advantage of me being a big fan of the games: it's obvious. If you know people who play the game, you've got to have the zombie dogs. They are the only creatures that are in all five *Resident Evil* games. They are just great and everyone hates them because they're really hard to kill in the games, so everyone has a real problem with them. It was obvious we had to have the dogs and also the Licker. His appearance in *Resident Evil 2: The Game* is one of the highlights of the whole franchise of games. For people who don't know *Resident Evil*, that's a really cool-looking monster. It's kind of humanoid with its brain exposed and this disgusting long tongue! It's one of the best monsters in the series of games to put on the screen. Along with the dogs, I think he's everybody's favorite.

How challenging is it to come up with new ways to stun people?

It's difficult to scare people, I must say, and especially with genre audiences because they've seen everything so they see everything coming. There is a lot of comedy in *Resident Evil* because there has to be. There has been a shift in the last ten years towards more action-horror/comedy rather than straight horror.

I went to see the re-release of *The Exorcist* [1973] a couple of years ago in Leicester Square. There was a young audience watching it and they were hooting and hollering. They thought it was the funniest film ever made, which was terrible. People were laughing so hard and then they walked out. They couldn't take any more. It's the way genre audiences have changed. I remember *The Exorcist* as being the scariest movie ever and I was still *terrified*. If you made *The Exorcist* again, shot-for-shot now but just with a modern cast, I don't think it would work. People don't take that stuff seriously anymore. People like to be scared, but they like some laughs with their scares as well. That's why in *Resident Evil*, there are scenes that don't pay off with a scare. You have the traditional lead up to where there should be a scare but there isn't because I think you have to play with the audience a little bit. Give them a scare when they're expecting and then not sometimes so it doesn't become too predictable.

Was there anything that you felt didn't work and that was removed?

There was surprisingly little cut out of *Resident Evil*. It was a very efficient film in that sense. The big scene shot that we changed was the ending. In the original draft of the script, we had the ending that is actually in the movie now. It was set in New York and one of the World Trade Centers was blown up. I'm so glad we didn't do it. And that was written, like, two years ago. Then we changed it to something that was a little more upbeat, and then we shot it. Then we thought, *We can't have this. Let's go back to everyone being dead!* It's what we always wanted to do, and at the end, the studio had some money left, as well. They thought, *Okay, let's go for it and blow it on the ending I really, really wanted.* So on the DVD there will be the original ending. It's a pretty cool ending.

The point where it changes is right after the viral tents: Max being dragged off, Milla restrained, and then we went to black. Over black there were footsteps and a voice-over and you pick up Milla walking into this amazing building, which is the Umbrella headquarters somewhere in Europe. And we shot it all in Berlin in the Daimler Chrysler Building, which has the largest set of doors in the wolrd—these fantastic, very gothic, huge set of doors, and this fantastic staircase in a triangular atrium which is all marble and reflective floors. She's wearing a completely different outfit. It's basically nine months later and she's come to Umbrella. She's looking for Max. She's raiding these Umbrella facilities and she walks up to the reception desk. As she does they do a retinal scan on her. It's quite interesting. We used real technology, this existing machine, and we just filmed it. They do have this camera that literally can do a retinal scan on you just as you walk through a lobby. And then they discover who she is—this wanted, anti-Umbrella terrorist. So all the guys behind the desk go for their guns and she produces this *huge* rocket launcher and fires this rocket. The rocket gets halfway to the guys, splits apart and there are mini rockets inside it. There is then this huge explosion, which you see reflected in her eye, and then her eye closes. That was going to be the end of the film.

The fans would like that. Every game ends with somebody getting shot with a rocket launcher.

It was very much like the ending of *WarGames* [1983], where you have the surviving characters go, "God damn you, Umbrella! We're gonna get you!" So it was very much like the game but it was nowhere near as cinematic, nowhere near as satisfying and nowhere near like *The Omega Man* [1971], which is one of my favorite films. So that was the big change: we shot a new ending.

How will you incorporate changes into any sequels, with characters carrying an obscene amount of artillery?

I'm two-thirds of the way through writing a sequel at the moment. It's more of an action movie. I'd love to see the franchise grow. The difference between *Alien* [1979] and *Aliens* [1986] was brilliant. What's wrong with that franchise is that they didn't make a similar jump between *Aliens* and *Alien 3* [1992]. But going from a tight, contained horror movie to more of an action/horror, the *Resident Evil* franchise needs to make that jump. We're not going to shy away from the obscene amount of weaponry. In the second movie, there'll be a lot more weaponry and a bigger playground as well, because it's all set in Raccoon City, which you kind of glimpse at the end of the first film. We explain the backstory. It's filling in lore from the game that isn't explained in the games. We're going to explain where the nemesis comes from and who he is.

How many times did you throw the joy pad on the floor in disgust after getting chomped on by zombies?

I actually did throw it at the screen at one point. I could never play cricket or anything like that school. I'm awful. So I missed it. I literally lost two to three months of my life playing *Resident Evil*, which is why I made the movie. I literally just sat there and played 1, 2, and 3 back-to-back. At the end of it I was just like, wow! We just have to go make a movie out of this.

It must be really hard, if you know the game, to decide what elements you use and what you don't because you have to discard stuff that you might really like from the games. Did you find that at all?

It was rich subject matter for sure, and that was one of the difficult decisions: which creatures do you put in, which do you leave out? I always viewed it as I wanted to make a trilogy of films, so in my mind at the end of the three it'll all have been done. It was tough to decide what to have and what not to have. I think when we came up with the idea of doing the prequel it was really key because it also got us around the problem of which characters to use and which not to use.

It's an interesting franchise in that unlike *Tomb Raider* [2001], where you always play Lara Croft, the characters in *Resident Evil 2* are completely different to *Resident Evil 1*. Even within the same game you play different characters. By having archetypes in the prequel and tied into the story and location of the games without the specific characters, we got around pissing people off who, if we'd done a straight adaptation of Number 2, would have been pissed because Jill Valentine or Barry Burton wasn't in it. You see it on the websites: some people just love Barry Burton to death and would be outraged if he wasn't in the film. So by having none of the characters in the film, I think we pleased the fans.

Are you going to go down that same route for the follow-up?

No. It'll be survivors from the movie meets survivors from the video game.

You mentioned The Omega Man *as an influence. What other films did you look at prior to making* Resident Evil*?*

I don't know if you've played *Resident Evil*, but I played it the wrong way round. I played the second one first. The thing that struck me was that it was just *so* John Carpenter. You're in an abandoned police station, and there's this Carpenteresque music playing. You're just in *Assault on Precinct 13* [1976], and it's great! But you're wandering through the abandoned city streets, which is very *Omega Man*. Then I played the first one where you're in a mansion in the woods, so it's very George Romero.

For me the touchstones for *Resident Evil* are early Carpenter: *Escape from New York* [1981], *Assault on Precinct 13*, *Halloween* [1978]. It's the Romero movies. And it's also Cameron's *Aliens*, which the game takes a lot from. The game is very cinematic and it really wears its cinema icons on its sleeve. So to do a successful adaptation that pleases the fans, you have to keep that for the movies. And those are not bad references: early Carpenter, early George Romero, and *Aliens*!

Resident Evil is probably the first major zombie film for seventeen years; the last one was Day of the Dead *[1985], directed by George A. Romero. What is it like reinventing a genre for a new audience whilst retaining elements of the movies that have gone before?*

There are undoubtedly a lot of nods to George, and for two reasons. I grew up watching his movies. When I was a kid the *Living Dead* trilogy, along with a lot of Lucio Fulci's movies, were the original video nasties [about which] your parents said, "You can't possibly watch those." A friend of mine had a videotape of *Zombies: Dawn of the Dead* [1979] so we did nothing but watch it. And also George had the advantage of having made three zombie films. The thing about zombies is that they're very slow. And it's difficult to make them scary. To suddenly have them appear - which is quite often the way that you shock people—George had to think of three movies' worth of surprises with zombies. They can't suddenly just drop from the ceiling or suddenly appear like the alien can [in *Alien*]. They are slow and lumbering.

When you start thinking, *How are we going to shock people with zombies?* it's almost impossible not to pay homage to him, because he's done it in so many ways and he's done it the best, really. And he had the advantage of doing three movies' worth of it. Some of the shocks in George's movies don't work and some of them do. Obviously, what we did was learn from the best ones. In terms of reinventing it, *Resident Evil* has already reached a much broader audience than George's movies ever have.

One of the reasons is it's a glossier movie that's aimed at a more mainstream audience than George aimed at. His movies were very gory pictures. In fact the level of gore that George could get away with seventeen years ago you couldn't even get into cinemas now. A lot of hard-core fans go, "Oh, it's not as gory as George's movies. That's a real disappointment." Well, firstly it never could have been. You wouldn't be able to see the movie. But also it's one of the things about George's movies: the reason why they're cult movies is a lot of people just won't buy people's bodies being ripped apart and the head still screaming while it's being taken off. We tried to make a slightly more realistic film than perhaps George was doing seventeen years ago.

Zombies walk a fine line between being scary and being ludicrous. How do you avoid the latter?

Resident Evil, like Romero's movies, has a lot of humor and that's a deliberate thing. After a while, the Undead stop being scary and they become funny. We limited the amount that they're in the movie. If you look at the structure of George's films, the zombies are there from frame one, and they stay there. And that's why halfway through, his movies become comedies. These things lurch and moan and they've been doing it for an hour. If you don't laugh *with* the movie, you're going to start laughing *at* the movie. With *Resident Evil*, what we did was deliberately delay the introduction of the Undead so that when they did appear, we had some chilling moments. They have a big impact, but if you count the minutes that the Undead are in the movie, you'll be surprised at how little screen time they actually occupy.

Do you agree that horror provides the biggest laughs?

Yeah. I talked to somebody today and she said, "I've never seen a horror film and I don't know anything about video games. And I really don't like science fiction," and I thought, *Wow! You're a good choice to come and talk to us about* Resident Evil! She'd seen it with an audience and was really shocked that people were laughing. Was I upset about that? No. They're supposed to! [Laughs] Yeah, I think you do get the best laughs. One of the biggest laughs I had in one of my movies was in *Event Horizon* [1997] where Laurence Fishburne, after just seeing the entire crew of the Event Horizon rip their own eyes out and fuck themselves to death, gives a big pause and says… "We're leaving." It gets such a good laugh.

How do you strike the balance?

There are a lot of similarities between horror and comedy. It's all about editing and it's all about timing. Telling a joke well and telling it badly is entirely about timing. It's the same with horror. You can tease a horror beat out too long and people get tired of it; they won't be scared. There are moments where people will find horror funny. Then they'll start laughing at the film rather than with the film if you drag the horror out for too long. So you do have to [be] careful about it. And that's when testing the movie is a positive thing. Some filmmakers hate the testing process, but if you're making a populist movie like this, it is useful to see where you're getting the balance of horror and comedy right, and how it plays.

Do focus groups play a part?

Not so much focus groups. I find the most beneficial thing is just watching the movie with three hundred people, sitting at the back. It's horrible. It's the most nerve-wracking bit of the filmmaking process because you spend the whole hour-and-a-half wanting to throw up. You're so nervous having spent a year and a half of your life [on this project], and suddenly it's in front of three hundred American kids who don't give a damn. They just don't care. And they didn't pay to come to see it so if they don't like it, they just walk out! That's the other thing you're terrified of, because you're always sitting at the back. You have people walk out and you think, *Are they coming back? Are they going to the toilet?* You become so aware of what every single person in the audience is doing because you really have very hyper senses. I find they're useful.

When you keep twenty people behind, focus groups are useful for the first couple of minutes and then everyone becomes a critic. After that people are transferring opinions but it's not really what you're after. You want what the broad consensus is. You can see in a movie what works and what doesn't just by watching it with an audience and especially in America, where they are lot more vocal than they are in Britain. They boo and they hiss and they cheer. If they don't like it, they let you know about it.

Are there other games you'd like to tackle?

Other from *American McGee's Alice*, I can't mention any other video games that I like because I'm just about to buy them. I'm paranoid that if I mention it, someone else will go and offer more money for it. But we're definitely in the business of adapting video games to cinema. Ever since the whole trend started, I've been a real advocate because I love video games and I've seen their importance in culture in general, which a lot of people in Hollywood have missed for a long time. It's just as valid now as buying a John Grisham book. I'm much more likely to go and play *Silent Hill* and go, "Whoa! That's a cool movie!" than read a John Grisham book and go, "Whoa! That's a cool movie!" Both have the same thing. They have an in-built audience that you can't piss off but then will come and see the film if it's a fair reflection. It's very, very similar. But just because of who

I am and because I'm more visually led, I'm more likely to adapt a video game than a book or a play.

Would you like to have a crack at Tomb Raider?

Tomb Raider is difficult because it's produced by friends of mine. I can't really talk openly about it. It's a great idea to make a Lara Croft movie and she's fantastic in it, but there were so many things that they didn't get right with the first one that hopefully they'll readdress with the second one. I think fans went to go see it. They went to go see the first film; it made a lot of money. It's like the first *X-Men* [2000] film. Everyone went, "It's okay. But the second one had better get it *right*." And I hope they do with *Tomb Raider*, I really do, because I'd like to see her adventures over the next ten years. I like franchise movies, I really do. That's why I'm really excited about doing *Resident Evil* as a series of films. It's cool to see how the characters evolve. When I don't like them is when they stay stagnant and end up being remakes of the first film over and over and over again but not so good.

How do you look back on your early movies?

For me, *Shopping* [1994] was a statement of intent when we made it. We wanted to make commercial cinema in Britain. I say "we;" I'm talking about my producing partner Jeremy Bolt. It's a movie I'm hugely proud of. It's a flawed film. I didn't know what the hell I was doing because I'd never made a movie before. And I didn't have the advantage that I'd come from the theater and had worked with actors before. I was making my mistakes in a very exposed way, because they were straight up on the movie screen for everyone to see. But there's a lot of really cool stuff about that movie that I think is great.

The critical abuse we got at the time was extraordinary. Things such as "Jude Law is too pretty to be an actor." I thought then and it's clearly been proved correct that that's a ludicrous thing to say. But the abuse we got just for having pretty people in the movie and daring to have a rock 'n' roll soundtrack and an album that might help sell the movie. There are a lot of things that we were doing that were deeply unfashionable at the time, and yet it was the first of many movies that led to a much more commercial British cinema. It's nice to see now when it shows on TV and it gets reviewed that the same people who slagged it give a lot kinder reviews—and no longer say that Jude Law is too pretty.

You might get the same comment about Milla Jovovich in Resident Evil.

Milla is a renaissance woman. With *Shopping* we went to Sundance, and American studios loved it for all the reasons that the British film industry didn't like it. It had really attractive leads that immediately got snapped up for American movies. I worked in Hollywood after that, and it's why I went to work in Hollywood. I was broke and I was sitting in Sundance thinking, *I can either go back to Britain where nobody likes me or I can go to Hollywood where people get what I'm trying to do.* So I went to Hollywood and I did *Mortal Kombat* [1995].

Having worked in TV and in film, what are the fundamental differences in scaring people on the small screen and the big screen?

Scaring people on TV is more about atmosphere. When you've got people in a cinema, you've got them. They're wrapped in a cocoon that is about sound and vision, and the screen is a lot bigger. To be scary on TV, you've got to be a little more unsettling. That's the main difference. You try to establish a little more unsettling vibe, I think.

Is a European co-production like this the way forward to challenge American movies?

Well, I personally [think so]. We did massive business in America. The fact that we opened at number two behind *Ice Age* [2002]—that's like opening opposite *Toy Story* [1995]; it's a really tough movie to beat—is telling. If we'd picked another weekend, we'd have opened as the number one movie in America. We beat the hell out of *Showtime* [2002], which was a typical, big, Hollywood blockbuster with Robert De Niro and Eddie Murphy. The movie has done spectacular business pretty much everywhere it's released around the world. We're really pleased with it. And it's a European movie which isn't a light romantic comedy and it doesn't have Hugh Grant in it.

There's no American money in the film. It was shot with an entirely European crew in Europe. All the visual effects were done in London. I would like to see more movies like this get made, for sure, because I think the profits from the film flow back into the European film industry. It's not like *Notting Hill* [1999], which looks like a British film, but all the profits go back to Universal. It's a terrible shame that *Tomb Raider* is an American movie because Lara Croft is a British character. The video game company is based in Britain. The movie was shot in Britain and it was a British director. Everything about that movie was British. But it was an American movie because too few producers in Europe have the balls to go out and option a video game property like that and make a big action movie. But I don't see why they shouldn't and I'd like to see them do it.

I think we got away with a lot of things in the film because it was a European film. We would never have done if it were an American studio movie. One of my favorite things in the movie is the end shot. I think it's a throwback to those '70s films that had rather bleak endings where you think, *The whole world is dead. Hurrah!* And there's no way you can do that. I've made enough studio movies to know that they'd say, "That's depressing! The whole world could be dead. We can't end like that." I think it's a super cool ending. We got away with things like that because it was a European movie with European sensibilities.

Will you do more or is it on a sequel-by-sequel basis?

I co-own and control the whole *Resident Evil* franchise, so I'll definitely be involved to some extent in all of them. I've always been frustrated with what happened to *Mortal Kombat*, because I always felt that should have been a great franchise in movie, although I had nothing to do with it after the first film. I felt like the franchise went "Blurgh." I've certainly learned from that, so I want to stay really closely involved with *Resident Evil*. I'd love to have the three-DVD box set around for a long time. I buy those things when I go to HMV. I like 'em and I keep 'em. I'd like one of those for me. I'd be really proud to have my name on three movies that develop a series of characters that live in this world and develop it in tandem with the computer games, as well.

It would be quite a compliment to learn in five years' time that they would like to base a game on one of your Resident Evil *scripts.*

It'll be interesting. We're going to have conversations with them. There have already been talks about [whether] they'll take some story strands from the movie. With the second one we're going to really bring the characters from the game and the movie together completely, so it'll really mesh the two. Then where we go from there will be really interesting.

Maybe by the third one we could actually do the video game and a movie combined.

What stage is the sequel at?

The script's coming very strong. It needs work in the character department. Paramount is still 100 percent behind it. When I go back, we're going to have script meetings with Cruise/Wagner and Impact Pictures, which is my company. I've got a large stake, as I'm one of the front-runners.

How useful is it to have Tom Cruise on your team?

I don't know if he's on my team or I'm on his team! [Laughs] It's exciting to be in the same arena as him, yeah. It's certainly a feather in my cap to have a Cruise movie in development, as it were.

When you do Resident Evil 2, *will it be a straight crossover like* The Lord of the Rings [2001]—*a continuation of the same story?*

No, it goes back in time. Actually, I don't know. I haven't finished it yet! The intention is that you see Raccoon City before the disaster overtakes it. Then you pick up after the first movie ends. If this is the timeline of the first movie, the second movie is kind of like that, there's a little bit of overlap and then it goes on. So you'll meet Milla and it'll be really cool, only she won't be in the start of the movie, obviously, because she's doing something else. You'll meet her twenty-five minutes into the second movie. I've already written that, and it's great. I've spent the budget of the whole first movie already!

2002

LUC BESSON and JEAN-PAUL GAULTIER
The Fifth Element

"Movies are made for you to sit down one day in the dark, big screen and – BOOM! – two hours of entertainment." – Luc Besson on the set of *The Fifth Element*. (Gaumont/Jack English)

THE FIFTH ELEMENT
Gaumont, 1997

CAST: Korben Dallas, BRUCE WILLIS; Zorg, GARY OLDMAN; Cornelius, IAN HOLM; Leeloo, MILLA JOVOVICH; Ruby Rhod, CHRIS TUCKER; Billy, LUKE PERRY; General Munro, BRION JAMES; President Lindberg, TINY LISTER JR.; Fog, LEE EVANS; David, CHARLIE CREED MILES; Right Arm, TRICKY; General Staedert, JOHN NEVILLE; Professor Pacoli, JOHN BLUTHAL; Mugger, MATHIEU KASSOVITZ; Mactilburgh, CHRISTOPHER FAIRBANK; Thai, KIM CHAN; Neighbour, RICHARD LEAF; Major Iceborg, JULIE T. WALLACE; General Tudor, AL MATTHEWS; Diva, MAÏWENN LE BESCO; Priest, JOHN BENNETT; Left Arm, IVAN HENG; President's Aide, SONITA HENRY; Scientist's Aide, TIM McMULLAN; Munro's Captain, HON PING TANG; Head Scientist, GEORGE KHAN; Head of Military, JOHN HUGHES; Omar, ROBERTO BRYCE; Aziz, SAID TALIDI; Mondoshawan, JUSTIN LEE BURROWS, RICHARD ASHTON, JEROME BLAKE, KEVIN MOLLOY; Mactilburgh's Assistant, BILL REIMBOLD; Staedert's Captain, COLIN BROOKS; Mactilburgh's Technician, ANTONY CHINN; Chief NY Cop, SAM DOUGLAS; NY Cop, DEREK EZENAGU; Flying Cops, DAVID KENNEDY, DAVID BARRASS, ROGER MONK, MAC McDONALD, MARK SEATON, JEAN LUC CARON, RIZ MEEDIN, JERRY EZEKIEL; VIP Stewardesses, INDRA OVE, NICOLE MERRY, STACEY McKENZIE; Stewardesses, RACHEL WILLIS, GENEVIEVE MAYLAM, JOSIE PEREZ, NATASHA BRICE; Check In Attendant, SOPHIA GOTH; Warship Captain, MARTIN McDOUGALL; Diva's Manager, PETER DUNWELL; Cops, PAUL PRIESTLEY, JASON SALKEY; Ruby Rhod Assistants, STEWART HARVEY WILSON, DAVE FISHLEY, CARLTON CHANCE; Diva's Assistant, GIN CLARKE; Human Aknot, VLADIMIR McCRARY; Mangalore Aknot, CLIFTON LLOYD BRYAN; Mangalore Akanit, ARON PARAMOR; Mangalore Kino, ALAN RUSCOE; Airport Guard, CLIFTON LLOYD BRYAN; Airport Cop, CHRISTOPHER ADAMSON; Tawdry Girl, EVE SALVAIL; Shuttle Pilot, KALEEM JANJUA;

Shuttle Co-Pilot, TYRONE TYRELL; Shuttle Mechanic, KEVIN BREWERTON; Ground Crew, KEVIN MOLLY, VINCE PELLEGRINO; Baby Ray, IAN BECKETT; Emperor Kodar Japhet, SONNY CALDINEZ; Princess Achen, ZETA GRAFF; Roy Von Bacon, EDDIE ELLWOOD; Fhloston Hostesses, YUI, LAURA DE PALMA; Hefty Man, MICHAEL CULKIN; Police Chief, LENNY McLEAN; Fhloston Commander, ROBERT OATES; Fhloston Captain, JOHN SHARIAN; Hotel Manager, FRED WILLIAMS; Zorg's Secretary, SIBYL BUCK; Scientists, SARAH CARRINGTON, GRANT JAMES, ALI YASSINE, SEAN BUCKLEY; Military Technicians, DANE MESSAM, ROGER MONK, NATHAN HAMLETT; CECIL CHENG; Lab Guards, SCOTT WOODS, LEON DEKKER; Staedert's Technicians, DAVID GARVEY, STANLEY KOWALSKI, OMAR HIBBERT WILLIAMS; Robot Barman, ROBERT CLAPPERTON; TV Stewardess, MIA FRYE; Power Operators, LEO WILLIAMS, KEITH MARTIN; Zorg's Men, J.D. DAWODU, PATRICK NICHOLLS, SHAUN DAVIS, ROY GARCIA SINGH, ALEX GEORGIJEV; Burger Assistants, MARIE GUILLARD, RENEE MONTEMAYOR, STINA RICHARDSON.

CREDITS: *Director*, Luc Besson; *producer*, Patrice Ledoux; *co-producer*, Iain Smith; *associate producer*, John A. Amicarella; *screenplay*, Luc Besson, Robert Mark Kamen, *from a story by* Luc Besson; *director of photography*, Thierry Arbogast; *production design*, Dan Weil; *editor*, Sylvie Landra; *special visual effects supervisor*, Mark Stetson; *costumes*, Jean-Paul Gaultier; *music*, Eric Serra. Running time: 126 minutes.

> "Every five thousand years, a door opens between the dimensions. In one dimension lies the universe and all the multitude of varied life forms. In another exists an element made not of earth, air, fire or water, but of anti-energy, anti-life. This 'thing,' this darkness, waits patiently at the threshold of the universe for an opportunity to extinguish all life and all light. Every five thousand years, the universe needs a hero, and in New York City of the twenty-third century, a good hero is hard to find."

Things of Today, Things of Tomorrow
Luc Besson and Jean-Paul Gaultier on *The Fifth Element*

Is it true that you got the idea for The Fifth Element *when you were just fourteen?*

Luc Besson: Fourteen? Come on! Only Mozart can do that. No, I was sixteen. The idea at sixteen, yes, but it's not the idea of the story of the film. It's just that I was so bored where I was. I grabbed a piece of paper and just wrote another world. I wasn't miserable, just sixty kilometers from Paris, in the forest, twelve kilometers from the next city, no cinemas, no TV, no VHS, no Walkman. So it was nice and very natural but to see a friend was such a deal, you know? My mum had to bring the friend or had to go into town. It was not an easy thing. So you just had to find [a distraction]. I was not very involved with stamps. [Laughs]

The original story was about a man on a journey. Did that come straight from your childhood?

Besson: Yeah. But that was more involved about the city of the twenty-third century and how it works. I tried to reinvent everything.

Did the forest inspire you?

Besson: No, not so much. *Métal Hurlant*—*Heavy Metal*—the magazine, and *Pilote*, the two French comic books, very well known. I worked [for *Heavy Metal*] a long time ago but as a screenwriter. I think I was seventeen. I didn't know I would be a director at all. I was just writing by myself. I don't know how it works in your country, but [in France] the funny thing is that you have two orientations. One is A, which is Littéraire and one is C, which is Math. And my autograph was so bad that they say to me, "Oh no, you can't be in literary. You have to be in science." It was so good to cheat at Math. I had a few good friends. I don't know anything about Math.

So how did you get from that point to a $100 million picture? Who did you convince?

Besson: I convinced nobody. I'm a bad seller. I'm not a good seller to sell things. So most of the time I write the script until I touch my own limit of intelligence and knowledge. I can't make the script better by myself, so if I want it better I need help. And when I reach this point, I go and see Gaumont and say, "This is what I want to do. Can you answer me next week?" That's it. And the funny thing is that they make the calculation [on whether] this is a good script. How can you say honestly five years before [a film is made], "You're going to make money with my movie?" I don't know if they're gonna make money.

But it's on its way to making money. Are you surprised?

Besson: Yeah, I'm surprised.

Will you get a chance to make Mr. Shadow, *the provisionally titled sequel?*

Besson: I don't know. It's too difficult to make.

Do you have any desire to make it?

Besson: Right now, no. A desire for holidays!

How do you go about setting clothes in the future without opting for the obvious futuristic look?

Jean-Paul Gaultier: First of all, I spoke with Mr. Luc and we spoke about what was his vision of the future. He gave me the directive that it was not supposed to be a vision that was futuristic. It was mixed with things of today and things of tomorrow but things that could be retro, like there is now. We see it all the time. One thing that was very interesting was that he told me something that I didn't even remark, for example there are some social people, like police, and their clothes go with their mentality. The military, they don't change. It's always the same thing, so we think they can go on and have the clothes almost like the ones they have now. It's something very obstinate, always the same thing. So it was very interesting. In reality I learned a lot of sociology with Mr. Besson, doing the clothes for the movie.

Has the film inspired you towards any designs that you might create for next year?

Gaultier: I am sure that it inspired me. I cannot tell you how or what exactly, or which clothes. But it's sure. When you are doing something like that, I am lucky because I have a big source of inspiration. That was a marvelous story. So to go into a story is a source of inspiration. A story can be in the street. You can see somebody walking there; it's a marvelous story. So all of that worked on the image and was a source of inspiration for everybody, I think.

Bruce Willis often wears a vest in his movies. Why did you choose that particular outfit for him in The Fifth Element, *and why orange?*

Gaultier: Orange because it was a color that was very visually strong. I don't know especially why.

Besson: At the end we chose it because of the color of Leeloo's hair. He made a few colors. One was orange; one was white, one yellow, and one silver.

Do you think we'll still be eating Big Macs in the twenty-third century?

Besson: Yeah, of course.

The McDonald's costumes were impressive. Would you like them to say, "Yes, this is what we'd like our staff to wear"?

Gaultier: It'd be nice if they'd do that. It would be good publicity. Maybe air hostesses, too, on Air France or something like that. More sexy, no?

Was there anything that you designed that either Bruce Willis or Milla Jovovich refused to wear?

Gaultier: No, no.

Besson: I protect him a lot. We discuss a lot together but when we finally agree on something, then they can't fight with him. They have to fight with us both. Bruce was happy in two seconds. Milla was very happy. The only one who was shocked was Chris Tucker, but then we had a trick together. Chris is a black man and he has a sense of *being* a man—about the girls and things. So he was a little scared about being a little too feminine—what are his friends in L.A. going to say about him now? So the trick was to show him the wildest one because what you see on a movie is not the worst; you can make it better. He designed a few and when I see the thing I was laughing. What was great was that even for the movie it was a little too much. But I used it to show to Chris, saying, "Here is what Jean-Paul designed for you." And he was like, "Oh my God! Oh my God!" And then slowly I say, "Okay, okay, maybe it's too much. What about *this* one?" And then we give him the one he wants.

Just a thing that's very important with costumes; that's why we work so long, and he was aware of that with the locations and what the designers do so he can be inspired by the buildings and the apartments and things. It's the fact that you always have the information that you get from the story and the dialogue, which is the direct information. Most of the time it's boring. Then you have the information you can give through the rest of it. So you can have six or seven layers of information in the same minute and costume, especially for the twenty-third century, are very, very important because you see the costume, and in two seconds you learn something. So it was very, very important and there is so much information that we can give through the costumes that I ask him to design hundreds and hundreds of things.

Why did you choose Jean-Paul?

Besson: He's the best. Always go for the best first.

Did he need persuading to do it?

Besson: One more time: I'm not a good seller. I just propose a thing: are you interested or not?

Gaultier: To be honest, he did not have to persuade me. It was more to the contrary. I learned that he had a project to make that movie and that maybe I should do the costumes, so I met him. But I wanted to completely. I was truly excited to be a part of it. When I met him to speak about the movie I was passionate and excited because *he* was passionate. When he was explaining the movie he was already *living* it, so his passion became a passion for me, too. So I wanted it even more. I should have been very disappointed [not to get it]. I said after, "If it is not me I'll kill the ones after!" And he said, "You'll do it!"

Will you get into film more or was it just about doing this project?

Gaultier: No. I'm a fashion designer, so I do fashion first. And, honestly, I have to love the director, what he does and his movie first of all, because it takes a lot of time. I have to love it, and I love *The Fifth Element*. There are not so many movies that I am doing, and I don't want to make a career of costume design or cinema. It was an adventure for me, an extraordinary opportunity that I didn't want to miss. It has to be like that. Maybe I will do more a bit later on, but for the moment, no.

It was a closed set for a long time. Did you think that would benefit the movie in the long time as expectations got higher and higher?

Besson: That's not my problem. I'm involved in the secrecy because I'm the one who imposes it. When I'm in my bathtub, I just close the door. You're all in the room and I'm in the kitchen. Don't come in the kitchen or you're never gonna eat! It's so messy and everybody shouts, you see Bruce Willis with the nice orange things but the rest is in shorts with tongs. It's like seeing a magician preparing the rabbit in the hat. It's not made for that. You have to be on the stage, music—ta-daah! He takes the hat, and—rabbit! That's the trick of movies. Movies are made for you to sit down one day in the dark, big screen and—BOOM!—two hours of entertainment.

But for months after you finished filming people were speculating about what the film was about.

Besson: Because you have to make a difference. The audience is very happy. They love that. The problem is most of the press who don't have the same goal: "I need this fucking movie because I have to sell my newspaper!" Well, I'm sorry. I don't care. I'm not here to sell your newspaper. I'm here to protect my movie. And I make the movie for people. I know some kid of sixteen years old, waiting for six months for some movie, will go on Friday at 2 p.m. and stand in line to see it. And that's so great. I've watched that, you know? I've come up on the line to see them and they are so excited. Sometimes some of them are disappointed. Some of them say, "Wow! I'll go again." And it's made for that. Honestly I'm sorry. I know the press hates me most of the time because of that secrecy. But they have to understand me also. A movie is not made to be eaten by all the media together before the guy who who's gonna pay to see the movie. I've seen so many movies with fifty [magazine] covers and you see all the pieces on TV and everywhere and then people don't want to see it anymore. They've seen everything on TV and in newspapers and they know the story by heart. They've seen all the tricks. Why are they gonna pay?

Your casting of Bruce Willis is interesting because we're used to seeing him in action movies. In the first part of The Fifth Element, *he's in a vest. Later he's in a dinner suit. Is that an in-joke?*

Gaultier: It was part of the script. It was a situation: he had to go to the opera. The only clothing there was the tuxedo, so it's why he has that.

Besson: Can I say something about that? Don't take it as if I'm blaming anybody. But I don't make movies by reference at all. Most of the journalists or critics, they see so many movies and as soon as they see one shot they say, "I've seen this shot in twenty-seven black-and-white movies." I mean, honestly, I don't even think about my guy for eight months because my guy's name is Korben Dallas, I'm in the twenty-third century, and I know the history of the guy. So when you have seen so many movies of course from my roots somewhere, you're gonna say, "I've seen this smile of Bruce's in another movie." Yeah, of course. Obviously it's the same guy. Sometimes it's gonna look like a shot that you've seen in a movie for sure. But most of the time I think he looks like Korben Dallas. He's an action hero but at the same time very shy.

Whose idea was it to dye Willis's hair blonde?

Besson: It was Bruce. We were talking about it and he said, "What about your hair?" [Laughs] "Yeah, yeah. Let's try that. It's good."

Did you find the politics of dealing with Hollywood actors different from dealing with French actors?

Besson: Honestly, no. The approach that they have as actors is a little different but the politics, no. There are really two different things. There is the star system and all these things, but when you are on the set it's like in a garage. It's made by hand. There are no stars on the set, just people who work and do their best. The camera is here, the actor is here and we have to extract everything we can from him to print it. It's very physical. The circle of the movie is five meters. There is the camera and five meters all around. That's it. And everything you print is in the five meters. You don't even notice if you have three managers and twelve bodyguards. I don't know and I don't care. What you have to take is here in front of you. It's a matter of him and me and how we can get it. That's it.

How did he adjust to your style of directing, which is very hands-on? You're behind the camera and very close.

Besson: I don't know if it's a style. I don't understand why a director is half-a-mile from the set with a video computer and says, "Action!" Then when he's watched the guy, "Cut!" Then, what? He takes the phone to call the guy? I don't understand.

Did the actors working with you catch on very quickly?

Besson: I mean, come on! It's so great for them. The director is three feet from there. Sometimes the camera is here and sometimes I grab the guy in the shot and push him in the frame. I say, "Say your line again. Okay, go. Breathe, breathe, breathe! You forgot to breathe. Smashing! More, more, more!" And you can talk to him and participate with it because you have emotion. You have the burst of emotion and the actor goes up, up, up. Then you arrive at a good level. Then you go down. It's like a muscle; you can't hold the things forever. If you're in the middle of it, you can push and use the emotion to try to extend it for fifteen or even twenty seconds. It's just that the guy or girl is ready to cry and you say, "Say your line again. Stay up! Say your line again. Push him. Push her. Caress her!" And then you use that.

Sometimes I do two, three, or four takes the same. When you feel that the emotion is going to collapse, then you say "cut." It's very hard for an actor. Can you imagine if you have to pump yourself up and go up and have the emotion and then go down? The director comes, talks with you for two minutes, you go back to the screen and then you have to pump up again. You can do that three, four, or five times, but after a while, especially if you have to be crying or emotional, it's tough. I've seen Milla where she has no more tears. It's not the fact that she doesn't *want* to cry. The water can't get out. You have to wait half an hour to refuel it.

What inspired you when designing for Gary Oldman, who plays Zorg? He's pretty distinct. Was that something you got from him or you created?

Besson: It was difficult.

Gaultier: We spoke and he was the one of [whom] I made the most sketches. I remember that the character was very precise: somebody very like a monster, very fascist, so Luc wanted a costume but from that time, classical. I did some but it was not the best image. I presented it and it was okay but he didn't like it so much. Little by little I had the idea to make him more like Hitler—not exactly but somebody like that. And with the rolled gold, which is something militaristic that goes with the fascism type, that was a little accessory that made him like a monster. He's a little strange, as if you don't know what happened to him, as if he was an apparition. So there was a mix of that. It was difficult to find that one.

Besson: Yeah, it takes time. Sometimes you say one word. And it takes a month to find a word that can help him [Gaultier]. I remember one day I came and I said two words. I said "Dandy" and "Nouveau riche" or nouveau romantic. Then he started to work again. The first approach that I asked for was too dark. He did it and did it very well, but when I saw it finally I said, "It's *too* dark. It needs a little something more. He's not just a Hitler replica. He's somebody else."

Did anyone ask to keep any of the costumes or outfits, and would you let them?

Gaultier: Maybe if they cried!

Besson: We made a catwalk in Cannes. It was funny to see all these costumes with a different face attached and especially to see "Bruce," because it was not Bruce! The funny thing was to see Milla watching [a model] in her outfit with red hair. She said, "Oh my God!"

Given that you pioneered skirts for men were you ever tempted to put Bruce Willis in a skirt?

Gaultier: I thought if you were driving a taxi it was probably not the best—or maybe a mini skirt or a micro skirt! I didn't suggest it to Luc. But it could have been—a micro one!

Is it true that the first time you met Bruce Willis it was to discuss making a film with his wife [Demi Moore]? And is that still a viable project?

Besson: We're still working on it, but very slow because we're both very busy. The problem with a project—and this is why I don't talk so much about it most of the time—is that you hire a writer and you never know. The guy might write for six months and come back with something very good or come back with something very bad. We were unlucky three times. It's still not good enough. So we'll just hire another [writer] and start again. It's very difficult to find good writers.

Did Bruce need to be persuaded to do this film?

Besson: No. He read the script in two hours and he said yes.

And had you spoken to Gary on the set of Leon *[the Professional, 1995] about this?*

Besson: No, not during *Leon*. Later. He's one of my best friends, so it's easy to keep in touch.

He always seems to commit himself totally to a part. Are you ever surprised at how far he goes for a role?

Besson: Gary is *so* good. People think that directors never say anything. The good thing with Gary is that he is totally focused on you and doing exactly what you ask. If you say, "Pale orange minus two" he's going to do it. That's Gary. The funny thing is when you sit on the set and say, "How are we gonna control that?" it's because he's one of the best actors in the world. Tomorrow he could play a sixty-five-year-old lady, black, in Harlem. *Tomorrow*. Without preparation. And he would be good. And on Monday he could be on stage with *Hamlet* and know it by heart. Do you know the story about *Hamlet*? We were in the office of Zorg and he was with Picasso, the animal. We were talking about Shakespeare and I said, "What is the part that you would love to play?"

[Oldman] 'I love Hamlet. I've played it a few times.'

"You love Hamlet? What a shame you have all this text to learn and that you learned ten years ago. Now, ten years later, you've forgotten it."

'No, I remember the text.'

'Come on. You played it ten years ago.'

'Give me a cue. Act II, Scene III.'

So I did and he'd just start. It's *amazing*.

You seem to have had a lot of fun with him on set. What was the funniest moment?

Besson: It's always fun. The funniest is when he can't finish a line because he is laughing. He'll start the line and then say, "Wait, wait, wait," because he knows that he can't finish it. That's very funny.

Do you think it's a challenge to give modern audiences something as hopeful as The Fifth Element?

Besson: I don't know. It's just something I want to do.

Was there any reason why you began the film on your birthday?

Besson: No. I just had to pick a date so I picked my birthday. At sixteen years old, the only thing you want to shout is, "I have a voice," but you have nothing to say.

Audience expectations are one thing. What about your expectations?

Besson: I have no expectations. The problem is that most of the newspapers have an expectation of what they're gonna sell, or they're gonna die. That's not my purpose. That's not my goal. I do the movie I want to do. I know it's very difficult to believe because it's so expensive, but I'm nuts. Three years ago, the movie was too expensive. They asked me, "Luc, you have make concessions," so I said, "Bye!" Then I did *Leon*. Because there's no point.

Why didn't you do the latest series of Eurotrash?

Gaultier: Because I'm doing fashion and it was too much work. It was a great experience, very funny with Antoine [de Caunes], he's great, and it was good because I'm a little less shy. It was a good souvenir. I'm not a presenter. I try to be the best at sewing buttons on. I prefer that.

Besson: We had the same problem. There is only twenty-four hours per day.

Is there someone that you would really like to dress or a movie you would have liked to design the costumes for?

Gaultier: It's more about when I am excited to do something with a director. So after the actor it's the character of the director. It's that which excites me. I would like to dress the movie of a director but not a special actor.

The directors with which you have worked like Pedro Almodovar have all been very strong visually.

Gaultier: Exactly. They touch me. Truly, for me it's an incredible experience that I've had with Luc because I learned a lot. I was completely admiring when he was explaining to me. At the last moment he could change a little thing because he had a new idea coming, and also how he creates the language. All that for me was those things that I couldn't imagine or couldn't know. But I must tell you something: to direct a movie is *incredible.* When you want like him to make a movie that's truly yours, everything has come from yourself. It's enormous, enormous work.

Do you harbor any ambitions to make a film yourself, maybe a documentary like Unzipped?

Gaultier: That's different. To make a movie is to make dreams, to invent images. It's creating. Documentaries are something completely different. They are not dreams. *The Fifth Element* was a marvelous experience for me because it was a dream.

Are there any comic books you would like to adapt for the movies?

Besson: No, not at all. I'm not influenced by comics; that's not the point. You have a script and everything is in the script. How do you go from words to the visual? You ask people and most are comic designers because they do that all day long. So I asked and there were eight of them. Moebius [aka Jean Giraud], [Jean-Claude] Mézières, and six new guys, very, very talented. Piece by piece they created the thing so the world that you see is not the world of Mézières or Moebius, it's really a piece of everybody altogether and it's one color.

There are some rules that you have in movies that are nothing with comics. In comics, it's always unfocused. In movies, you can't do that. And in comics, you can just read ten pages and go to sleep and come back the day after and spend half an hour on one design. On movies, it's just another proposition. You sit down and for two hours you can't escape. You can't just stop and go back. You really have to keep up the attraction and the attention of your moviegoer. So it's really not the same perception at all.

Comic books are, I will say, between the literature and the design, the painting. It's the mix of the two. Films are closer to music. One is visual and the other one is just with the ear but in fact they are very, very close. That's why we put music on films and why they put images on videos. And the funny thing is I've worked with Eric [Serra, composer] since the beginning and we're still working together, because between director and musician there is always a connection. Take Morricone with Sergio Leone or John Williams with Steven Spielberg or Nino Rota with Fellini. Hitchcock and Herrmann. It's true.

Some of the profound elements of the film only came to you five years ago. Was there anything real-life that reflected that and which brought that deeper feeling to the film?

Besson: Everything. Let's talk about people who sell weapons today. Where are they on Sunday morning, most of them? At church. So then you are not so far from Zorg and the priest. They say, "We are in the same business." And most of the people in the church say, "Oh, it's Mister X. He's such a great guy. He gives so much to the church." It's here, at your door. It's enough.

1997

DANNY BOYLE, ANDREW MACDONALD, and ALEX GARLAND
28 Days Later

"I'm on a crusade that [*28 Days Later*] isn't known as a 'zombie' movie, personally, because it isn't that. We wanted [the infected people] to move with lightning speed." – Danny Boyle on location for the urban apocalypse of *28 Days Later*. (20th Century Fox/Peter Mountain)

20th Century Fox, 2002

CAST: Jim, CILLIAN MURPHY; Selena, NAOMIE HARRIS; Major Henry West, CHRISTOPHER ECCLESTONE; Hannah, MEGAN BURNS; Frank, BRENDAN GLEESON; Activists, ALEX PALMER, BINDU DE STOPPANI, JUKKA HILTUNEN; Scientist, DAVID SCHNEIDER; Infected Priest, TOBY SEDGWICK; Mark, NOAH HUNTLEY; Jim's Father, CHRISTOPHER DUNNE; Jim's Mother, EMMA HITCHING; Mr. Bridges, ALEXANDER DELAMERE; Mr. Bridges' Daughter, KIM McGARRITY; Infected Kid, JUSTIN HACKNEY; Private Clifton, LUKE MABLY; Sergeant Farrell, STUART McQUARRIE; Corporal Mitchell, RICCI HARNETT; Private Jones, LEO BILL; Private Bell, JUNIOR LANIYAN; Private Davis, SANJAY RAMBARUTH; Private Mailer, MARVIN CAMPBELL; Featured Infected, ADRIAN CHRISTOPHER, RICHARD DWYER, NICK EWANS, TERRY JOHN, PAUL KASEY, SEBASTIAN KNAPP, NICHOLAS JAMES LEWIS, JENNI LUSH, TRISTAN MATTHIAE, JEFF RANN, JOELLE SIMPSON, AL STOKES, STEEN YOUNG.

CREDITS: *Director*, Danny Boyle; *producer*, Andrew Macdonald; *line producer*, Robert How; *co-producer*, Chris Symes; *screenplay*, Alex Garland; *music*, John Murphy; *director of cinematography*, Anthony Dod Mantle, DFF; *editor*, Chris Gill; *production design*, Mark Tildesley; *make-up*, Sallie Jaye; *special effects*, Richard Conway, Bob Hollow. Running time: 104 minutes.

> "A powerful virus is unleashed on the British public following a raid on a primate research facility by animal rights activists. Transmitted in a drop of blood and devastating within seconds, the virus locks those infected into a permanent state of murderous rage. With 28 days the country is overwhelmed and a handful of survivors begin their attempts to salvage a future, little realizing that the deadly virus is not the only thing that threatens them...."

Big Fear

Danny Boyle, Andrew Macdonald, and Alex Garland on *28 Days Later*

How did the project come into being?

Alex Garland: Initially it was talks with Andrew that started it off, but Danny got involved so soon after that initial process and such a long period followed, that it seems almost irrelevant. I think of it purely in terms of a collaboration from the beginning. In many ways, if Danny and Andrew had said, "Look, we feel we want to share the writing credit," then I'd probably have said yes.

What was said to you about what they wanted to see?

Garland: I'm not even sure it was as explicit as that. All three of us were, to an extent, figuring out what we thought the thing could be over a period of six months. There were maybe forty-five sets of revisions and rewrites. All of us changed our minds over that period. I can't really give a very coherent answer to that. It was very organic. That's just the truth.

Andrew Macdonald: I had a conversation with Alex about making a science fiction film. That's how it started. Various ideas went on about the virus. One of the first things was the concept about the twenty-eight days later, which was such a brilliant idea. And then picking up the story and imagining what had happened. That was there right from the very beginning.

You've said that by missing out the bit in the middle you saved millions on the budget. And also the decision to use digital video (DV). Was that made very early in the concept—to go that way technically?

Danny Boyle: It was a brilliant script because it's a big film and yet it wasn't about a missing nuclear warhead. It's about Britain and yet it had scale. So you had to find a way of doing that, and one of the ways was that Alex missed out those twenty-eight days. The bits that you did see [was via] footage right at the very beginning of the film, or we recreated very tiny little bits of it. The idea of approaching it with DV was to try and harness some of the strength of that. It's almost like technically they *could* have survived those twenty-eight days. You couldn't go filming with a camera because you couldn't develop it in a lab and all that kind of stuff but with DV cameras, all you need are batteries. We resisted the impulse of having Jim come out of the hospital, pick up a digital camcorder, and start filming, or look at the evidence of what had happened, which was one idea at one point.

I'd made a couple of digital films in Manchester. It's a fantastic freedom with them. They're less beautiful [than traditional film cameras] in many ways, although I think they have their own beauty. Certainly for the London scenes at the very beginning there was a huge problem. We knew—as anybody does who lives in a big city—that the chances of emptying those streets were going to be limited with our budget and also with the general attitude towards filming, especially in London. They are really anti-filming. So we thought, *We'll set all up these cameras and block everything for a few seconds. That will give us a chance to build a sequence.*

It's very effective seeing London's landmarks with no one around them. How did you clear the streets?

Boyle: We got up very early. We got up with the milkmen! The problem with London [now] as opposed to fifteen years ago [is that] there was a period between 4 a.m. and 5:30 a.m. when it was empty and there were only milkmen around. Now, because of the club culture, all the clubs are coming out and everyone is looking for something to do! It's genuinely a problem. We got a load of people to help us and to whom we paid a very small amount of money. We called them traffic marshals. In Britain, you can't close streets for filming like you can in New York. You literally cannot. But the police will give you permission to appeal to people—drivers, pedestrians—to wait. The police stand in the background, but they won't actually say it themselves. So we got all these students—my daughter did it—justy saying, "Please wait there." And they *did*. It was amazing. We were very lucky.

What were your reference points?

Macdonald: There are lots. *The Daytrippers* [1996], *I Am Legend* [Richard Matheson's novel, first published in 1954], *Survivors* [1975], the British

TV show. *On the Beach* [1959]. Lots of these films—not so much with *Survivors*—are all concerned with this idea of the bomb and after the bomb. There was one I saw on television not long ago. It was a black and white British film called *Seven Days to Noon* [1950], where they evacuate London because this guy has taken a bomb. It was all concern about that. It was great seeing the evacuation. Now things have changed; the concerns have changed. It's a virus and it's a big fear.

Garland: All of those sources that Andrew mentioned. I'd also add George Romero films to that, predictably. All sorts of stuff. There are certainly conscious references in the script to some of those films and also to some novels. The reason the lead character is called Jim is a respectful nod to J.G. Ballard, who wrote a great series of post-apocalyptic novels that took a premise and then built an apocalypse from that premise, [like] *The Drought* [1965]. But then also *I Am Legend* or *The Omega Man* [1971], that kind of thing. It's partly because of a theory I've got: a post-apocalypse [scenario] is constantly zeitgeist because there is always something that people are generally terrified of. But it's also a wish-fulfillment. Scenes like looting a supermarket or taking over a whole shopping mall, as in *Dawn of the Dead* [1979]. Or a scene that we didn't have, and I sometimes wish it had been written in: sleeping the night at Buckingham Palace. It becomes an open brief for fantasies.

Boyle: We borrowed stuff like that, as you do, and those things provided a bit of an engine at times for the script. But I just thought that a psychological virus was a brilliant original idea, and that moves it on. If you just did a zombie movie, like a Romero movie, they're dated now. They came from a different kind of fear to do with the nuclear bomb and what would it do to us. The obsession now, and what Alex opened up brilliantly in it, is that it's a psychological thing. The whole Iraq thing is a psychological nightmare at the moment. Who do we believe? Do we think [Saddam] can do it or not? You can feel it feeding away at our brains. The use of that—and especially this idea of rage—was a fantastic starting point for a contemporary film. That's what we like to try and do if we can: make something about the contemporary world.

Was it deliberate to have such an ordinary backdrop to your post-apocalyptic landscape?

Boyle: Yeah. It's an obvious thing, isn't it, because with any kind of post-apocalyptic thing, the most redundant aspect is selling it? So we left money scattered around the streets but it didn't last for very long! [It was] all the stuff that would be redundant, like advertising. I saw this amazing advert on Tottenham Court Road for Benetton, with these cheesy people smiling down at you as you're scurrying to work. So we had to have that.

The film has been given an "18" certificate in the UK, probably due to the use of the c-word. Are you happy with that, or will it preclude a lot of the potential audience that might relish the film?

Macdonald: It's such a big issue around gore and violence. I have to say I hadn't expected it and I hope it won't ruin it. I haven't seen [Ken Loach's 2002 film] *Sweet Sixteen*,* although I've read a lot about it. Paul Laverty wrote a letter to *The Guardian*. He said that *Black Hawk Down* [2002] was a "15." That's what annoys me. Or when *Jurassic Park* [1993] is a "U." It'll be interesting to see what happens.

Boyle: All I remember distantly from when I was fifteen is that there was nothing cooler than getting into an "18" film! We can only hope they're out there and they'll try! [Laughs]

The geography of the film is interesting. Why is it that particular corner of the M602 motorway? Is it anything to do with [Jorge Grau's] The Living Dead at Manchester Morgue [1974], which is also set in that sort of area?

Boyle: [Laughs] Ha ha! No, it's not, actually. I haven't seen the *Manchester Morgue*, film though everybody says that that's a really good one. Pretty unusual. No, we could only get this [particular] road to stage the scenes on.

Can you explain the nature of the title and the use of the number 28?

Garland: It rolls off the tongue, that's why it's twenty-eight days. It could be twenty-nine. It's arbitrary. The idea of it always was that the title was very

---

* *Sweet Sixteen* made headlines due to its constant use of the f-word. There are 313 uses of the word "fuck" during its 106-minute running time. The film, which was passed uncut in the United Kingdom by the British Board of Film Classification, received an "18" certificate.

unimportant. It was a caption. And so it sidestepped anything that might get in the way of a story, like a credit sequence or a title sequence. That was the original idea. It could even just say "Later." It's not a period film.

Your zombies are not the traditional type we see on film.

Boyle: We wanted them unlike zombies, and I'm on a crusade that it isn't known as a "zombie" movie, personally, because it isn't that. It's wrong and it would disappoint zombie fans, really, who come to see it. We wanted the opposite of that. We wanted [the infected people] to move with lightning speed.

These digital cameras have this technique—the way they capture motion in this very strange way. It's a bit like the shutter that you see used at the beginning of *Saving Private Ryan* [1998], though it's a slightly different technique in that, but it gives a similar impression. You appear to be watching a series of static images. Scenes appear to be captured and then frozen for a second, yet they're not, because they've gone and everything seems to be moving at the right speed. So it was a mixture of that and also rabies.

We got some photographs of what happens—and God forbid it ever does—when you get rabies and you go into this rictus state where you're frozen. It's the water fear that sets the time of raving. So it's a mixture of that and Ebola. We read this amazing book by Richard Preston called *Hot Zone* [first published in 1994], which is a great read if anybody fancies it, and which is about Ebola travelling from Africa to America. We just speeded that up. All that stuff of him throwing up the blood, there's a journey on an aircraft in that book where this guy travels from Africa to America, and he fills up six sick bags of vomit—of black blood. It came out of stuff like that.

Your casting is interesting—you have an Irish actor playing a cockney. Would it have been better to have had his natural accent?

Boyle: We didn't think so. We thought probably we shouldn't do that. We wanted Brendan because he was this huge, warm, avuncular [presence]. If you couldn't cast your dad, you'd want to cast Brendan Gleeson! And then we thought he probably wouldn't be right if he was an Irish taxi driver, because there aren't that many of them in London. But they love a challenge, actors. They love a voice coach! When you get the right person the original character—if it was an original character as such—sort of disappears and you think it is them anyway. They morph together, if you get it right.

I never wander around with regrets. It was quite late for us getting Chris [Eccleston] because we didn't think he was available. He came available for it quite late, so we were lucky to coincide with him.

How different was it to write a script rather than a book or an adaptation of a book?

Garland: It was totally different. I had to learn a lot. A lot of the early drafts would often have Andrew saying, "Look, just take all that out. It shouldn't be there," either because it was the kind of stuff you'd put in a novel or in prose, just to fill a page out. Not *just* filling, but kind of. But also stage directions. I was constantly saying, "The actor looks nervous," or "they blink," which is fucking absurd because you're completely stripping them of their job. It's daft. But I had to learn that. Lots of old habits died very, very hard. But they did die eventually. I bludgeoned them into submission.

Will it appear as a novelization?

Garland: Nah.

What happened to Alien Love Triangle?

Macdonald: It was made as part of a trilogy—three films, sort of like *Four Rooms* [1995]. The other was a film called *Mimic* [1997], which *was* made. Before they shot the half-hour script, they made it into a feature film. There was another film with Gary Sinise in it that came out through Miramax recently, and they made that as *Impostor* [2001]. That was meant to be the other one. *Impostor* they made as a half-hour film and then turned it into a feature. It wasn't very successful. So they were meant to be the three half-hour films. We made ours a half hour; it could never be anything else. It was sitting there, and despite every encouragement we give Miramax, they don't seem to have an idea what to do with it. We've suggested selling it on the Internet because it really is a very good film. We made it four-and-a-half years ago.

Are we likely to see it?

Macdonald: It's out of our control, unfortunately.

Boyle: I think if Ken Branagh's a big hit in *Harry Potter*, then that might wake Miramax up! I don't know. It's very difficult to tell.

Was there any one thing that you wanted to do but that the budget prevented?

Boyle: No. That's one of the great things about doing it: we had a finite amount of money. It's not low budget compared to some films, but I suppose in terms of our ability to raise money, we could have raised more, but that would have influenced the script in a different way. So we limited the amount of money we took, and it was a very good discipline for us. It made us dream up ways of doing it that were feasible. You've always got that pressure where you want to make a big film because it's got to be in the multiplexes with all the big American films. And it has to compete with them, so you want to make it big, yet you've got to do it with less money than they've got. That's a very good discipline for us.

Many filmmakers are talking about digital being the future. Will you eschew film from now on and stick only to DV?

Boyle: I think it will all come this way eventually. Unfortunately, celluloid is a very archaic process and incredibly time consuming. It's one of the most poisonous industries for the environment, supposedly, although it's on a very small scale. And it will die out. I'm not an apostle for it, and there is a danger with it. What [Steven] Soderbergh did with it is very dangerous, because he clearly calls it his private or semi-professional work. That puts this ceiling on DV films because there's yet to be a DV film that breaks through a kind of ceiling of just professionals watching it, or people who are interested in the media or these so-called experiments. This was not meant to be an experiment. This is meant to be a mainstream film for a mainstream audience—for as many people in Britain to go and see it as possible, which is where you guys come in.

2002

TIM BURTON
Sleepy Hollow

"Some actors are kind of the same from movie to movie but Johnny likes to be something different each time. I get a really good energy from that." – Tim Burton on his frequent collaborator, Johnny Depp. (Paramount Pictures/Clive Coote)

A TIM BURTON FILM
Sleepy Hollow

Paramount Pictures and Manderlay Pictures LLC, 2000

CAST: Ichabod Crane, JOHNNY DEPP; Katrina Van Tassel, CHRISTINA RICCI; Lady Van Tassel, MIRANDA RICHARDSON; Baltus Van Tassel, MICHAEL GAMBON; Brom Van Brunt, CASPER VAN DIEN; Reverend Steenwyck, JEFFREY JONES; Magistrate Philipse, RICHARD GRIFFITHS; Doctor Lancaster, IAN McDIARMID; Notary Hardenbrook, MICHAEL GOUGH; Hessian Horseman, CHRISTOPHER WALKEN; Young Masbath, MARC PICKERING; Lady Crane, LISA MARIE; Killian, STEVEN WADDINGTON; Beth Killian, CLAIRE SKINNER; Burgomaster, CHRISTOPHER LEE; High Constable, ALUN ARMSTRONG; Crone, MIRANDA RICHARDSON; Jonathan Masbath, MARK SPALDING; Sarah, JESSICA OYELOWO; Van Ripper, TONY MAUDSLEY; Lord Crane, PETER GUINNESS; Glenn, NICHOLAS HEWETSON; Theodore, ORLANDO SEALE; Thomas Killian, SEAN STEPHENS; Doctor Lancaster's Wife, GABRIELLE LLOYD; Dirk Van Garrett, ROBERT SELLA; Spotty Man, MICHAEL FEAST; Thuggish Constable, JAMIE FOREMAN; Constable #1, PHILIP MARTIN BROWN; Young Ichabod, SAM FIOR; Young Lady Van Tassel, TESSA ALLEN-RIDGE; Young Crone, CASSANDRA FARNDALE; Girl #2, LILY PHILLIPS; Little Girl, BIANCA NICHOLAS; Rifleman, PAUL BRIGHTWELL; Headless Horseman Stunt Players, ROB INCH, RAY PARK; Ichabod Crane Stunt Player, DOMINIC PREECE; Stunt Coordinator, NICK GILLARD. Uncredited: Van Garrett, MARTIN LANDAU.

CREDITS: *Director*, Tim Burton; *producers*, Scott Rudin, Adam Schroeder; *executive producers*, Larry Franco, Francis Ford Coppola; *co-producer*, Kevin Yagher; *associate producer*, Mark Roybal; *screenplay*, Andrew Kevin Walker; *screen story*, Kevin Yagher, Andrew Kevin Walker, based upon the story "The Legend of Sleepy Hollow" by Washington Irving; *music*, Danny Elfman; *director of cinematography*, Emmanuel Lubezki ASC AMC; *editor*, Chris Lebenzon; *production design*, Rick Heinrichs; *costume designer*, Colleen Atwood; *visual effects supervisor*, Jim Mitchell; *human/creature effects created by* Kevin Yagher; *special effects supervisor*, Joss Williams. Running time: 105 minutes.

> *"New York, 1799. Ichabod Crane, an eccentric and earnest constable with an avant-garde approach to solving crime, is sent to the small village of Sleepy Hollow to probe a string of murders, allegedly committed by a headless horseman."*

Soaking Up the Hammer Vibe
Tim Burton on *Sleepy Hollow*

Is Sleepy Hollow *your revenge on Disney—taking a Bing Crosby animated short and turning it into the blood-soaked slice of gothic?*

Tim Burton: Oh, I don't know. I love the Disney cartoon [*The Legend of Sleepy Hollow*, 1949]. I knew of it before I even read the story [by Washington Irving]. That was my introduction to it. In fact, that cartoon has probably inspired me for lots of things. I always liked how spooky it was: the movement [and] the way they could make the horseman elegant and strong. And the design of it was really beautiful. I like to try to mix all of that together.

American audiences seem to think Sleepy Hollow *is a bit too scary for children. Yet children have a voracious appetite for that creepy stuff. Did you have to stop yourself from going headlong into making it completely gruesome?*

I agree [it's scary]. It's hard for me to say [whether it's *too* scary]. We tried to make a movie like the Hammer movies that I used to watch on TV on Saturday afternoons. In making this I never wanted to cross the line. I always wanted to keep it in the spirit of one of those movies—like a fairy tale or a folk tale—that were often pretty grim or extreme. As a kid, I never liked shying away from that. That's why I liked what I would call these sort of "safe" scary movies. It's not really scary, not really real, but like a good fairy tale or folk tale, it taps into that sort of "safe" fear, in a way. I was obsessed that it got an "R" rating because I didn't feel that it was that kind of a movie.

Was there any controversy over your take on the original story?

It's funny. When I got involved with the project, I realized that in America everybody knows this story. But if you did a poll about how many people actually read it, then the percent would drop like a brick. You wouldn't believe it. So that's what fascinated me and made me realize that's what the story is: it's about the power of the image of the headless horseman. It's somehow in our consciousness, and yet nobody's read the story. And it's a short story.

Then I got the script and it had already had these changes effected in it. I thought it was fine. What I got out of the story was that I liked the names; I liked the tone and the feel of it. And then with the Ichabod character, we just tried to keep his eccentricities and his separateness and squeamishness and all of that. So we tried to be true to the spirit of it. But I didn't feel that we were taking a great novel and disregarding. I felt like we were taking a short story—a folk tale—and giving it a different spin.

Do you second-guess yourself?

I try not to, but it's hard to know where you can draw the line. I feel in some cases in my career I've been lucky. I've been equally surprised that the film is successful. It's nice when it connects with people. *Ed Wood* [1994] probably got the best reviews of any film I've ever done, and people tell me they like it. I get more verbal response to that, and yet it was by far [the most unsuccessful]. Probably the people that talk to me are the only people that saw it! So there's a distorting aspect to the whole process. The one that you feel has the most human contact you think will be the most successful. So it's hard to know. I try not to second-guess. All you can go on is what you're doing and hope for the best with it, because you just have to spend too much time with it. You can get too close to it and do things for those other reasons.

Can you afford not to think. "If this one doesn't work, it'll be harder to do the next one"?

Yeah, you do think that. You can't help it. There's reality to it. But in the overall picture, I realized fairly early on that you live and die with each film. You really do. It's like a birth and a death or a life and a death within a film. Then it's on to square one again. It's finding a thing and then trying to get it going. It's always that way. That's just the nature of film. There are so many people involved and so much money, even if it's a low-budget film, that it's not like doing a painting where you can just go off and do it. It requires that amount of trauma, I think.

Did you see The Blair Witch Project?

Part of it. I haven't got the full effect of it. Watching partially a film on a plane with turbulence is not the best way to assess it.

Might it affect the way big players like yourself make films in the future?

There are two ways to look at it. There's the positive way, which is to say the more open, the more different ways, the more opportunities, that's great and fantastic. The negative side, which I can see Hollywood do, too, is that it's one way or the other: "Oh, okay, now we'll do that," and put all your eggs in one basket. "Now we'll do this kind of a film." The way to look at it is to just to be more open. This feels like it's a good time right now. It seems like there's a lot of potential for every type of film, which is more positive for everything.

Sleepy Hollow appears to reinvent the Hammer vibe under a different banner. That must have been deliberate.

Yeah. It's really odd when an entity creates a thing, and at Hammer they really did create their own sort of vibe in movies: this sort of lurid beauty, the sexiness of them, the strength of them. They did something that was very specific and that was very inspiring to me. This is the first opportunity that I've ever had to do something that was more of a direct inspiration.

Is that also why you used Christopher Lee?

I love Christopher, so this was an opportunity to meet him. I've been lucky to meet people that have inspired me. Then they *continue* to inspire you. So I was very grateful that he did that. It was a good way to start the film—and to meet Dracula!

Was there ever a discussion that you might use him more than what you did?

Once Christopher did it, I thought, *God, it would be so great to have him in it more*. I was just so grateful that he did it. I thought it was a great way to start—the perfect person to send Ichabod on his journey. I love hearing his voice. It has such command to it.

Were there any of those wonderful old actors that you wanted to cast but couldn't?

I thought about that and thought, *This is great. This is perfect.* I felt really good about that. I kept looking at Michael Gough. He always thinks I'm laughing *at* him, but I'm not. I'm just thinking, *You were in* Konga [1961] *and* Horrors of the Black Museum [1959]—*all these great films*. It's always these guys who play villains that are the nicest people. Often people that play heroes are complete jerks in real life, but the guys that play villains as a generalization are usually some of the nicest, sweetest people. I was really lucky.

Would you like to remake a Hammer classic and give it that Tim Burton look?

Oh, I don't know. Part of what's great about those [films] is that they're of an era, and they really capture something very specific at a specific time. It's more of the Hammer idea rather than any one specific. I don't know which one I would even pick as a favorite. They all blend together in my mind.

Why are you drawn to this type of movie—the quirky and the creepy and the odd? Does it come from your childhood?

Probably. My parents told me [that] before I could walk or talk I liked monster movies. And I did. I loved watching them. Maybe as a reaction to the southern California environment, which is very bright and light and white and square and [with] not a lot of texture to it. I've often thought that maybe it was just as a way to get in your life [that which] what was sort of lacking. And then also like a folktale or fairytale, monster movies somehow spoke to me. They were symbolic to life or were metaphors about how people misperceive other people. I always thought monsters were never like the bad guys. They always seemed like they had the most emotional qualities to them. So it was just a combination of things. When you have a place that always seems sunny and bright, it was a way to experience other things.

Is that why you film on sound stages rather than on location?

It depends on the project. I was always drawn to films that were visual and monster movies—of all the genres—had the most potential for me to be visually striking and strong. Not all horror movies are that way, but a lot of the old Universal, Mario Bava, and some of the Hammers were.

Why did you make the film in England when it's such an American story?

To try and soak up a little bit of the Hammer vibe, it felt right to do it [in the UK]. New York is a very resourceful city, but on a design level, they're not set up for productions—in terms of film—on the scale of something like this. We originally looked upstate, but since it's a film that has such a heavy design element and we realized we were gonna build a lot of it, all of that made it more appropriate to do it in the UK. I worked here before ten years ago on *Batman* [1989], so it was an opportunity to work with some of the same people. And there are just really good artists here.

What's the attraction of working with Johnny Depp so often?

I like actors who like to transform, you know? Some actors are kind of the same from movie to movie, but Johnny likes to be something different each time. I get a really good energy from that. Each time I've worked with him he's done something completely different. And I just find when you're looking at one person and seeing them transform that way it gives it an extra energy and excitement, which I really like. We can talk about weird inspirations. That's what filmmaking is all about: hundreds of people trying to come up with something somewhat specific. He's a great collaborator.

Is it true that you were the one who threw the buckets of blood at him?

Sometimes! I had a big hypodermic needle. I'd sometimes squirt; sometimes we'd have paintbrushes. I'd sometimes roll the heads. You spend so much time talking to people at the studio that it's nice to get in there and fool around with it for real. That's what's great about Johnny, though: usually he wants to look worse than you want to make him look. He's really open to all that.

Could you envisage making the film without Johnny Depp? The two of you seem like quite a working entity.

I know Johnny can do almost anything. I've seen it and I see it. It's just a process. I remember on *Edward Scissorhands* [1990], same thing: in your heart, he's the guy. Everybody knows it. The thing that always amazes me about Hollywood is that they see somebody do one thing and then they think that that's what they do. So somebody like him, who really does change, sometimes makes people uncomfortable. They don't quite know what he's gonna do. I've had that same thing with myself. So together some people recognize that we do good things together, and then they get freaked out by that, too.

Was the casting of Christina Ricci straightforward? Does the studio now see her as an adolescent star?

We knew what we were making—sort of a fairytale. We just went for people that gave us that vibe. I look at her, and she's got a timeless quality to her. She could almost be of any age and in any age. She's got that young/old, weird fairytale quality to her. With everybody we tried to go for that. [Her casting] was pretty straightforward. There was no controversy there.

Did you and your cast find much time to spend together off duty?

It's actually hard for me because when I get to see the people, you get so used to them as characters that it gets disturbing seeing them otherwise. [On *Ed Wood*] I remember with Martin Landau, I didn't want to see *him*. I was dealing with Bela Lugosi, you know? It's not that I get that into Method, but you work such long hours, and it's mainly with the characters, that you just keep it in that zone. I didn't have much time for [relaxing off set]. Nobody did. I don't think the actors did, either. They were just in there, going for it. I like to keep seeing them as who they are.

Is it also a little odd when they have to go in and model for their heads?

I know Richard Griffiths had a little trouble looking at his own head! It *is* weird. It's shocking, in a way, especially when they're laying on the ground. It looked like the actors was on the floor below sticking their head up through a hole, they were so intensely real in that way. I think Michael Gambon said he was going to send his out on auditions. [Laughs] I don't know if anybody kept theirs. It was a little much for some people.

Did they make one for you as a souvenir?

Nah. We had a big budget but we tried to keep it down as much as possible.

You have created a Tim Burton repertory company: actors like Johnny Depp, Jeffrey Jones, and Michael Gough plus all these other people that you've worked with behind the scenes. Is it important to you to be able to work with people that you feel familiar with?

Yeah, sometimes, although you can't always do that, because films seem to take longer and longer to do, and you never know if somebody's gonna be booked up or whatever. But I particularly enjoyed this because it was a truly international cast and crew. You kind of feel like that when you're making the movie anyway. But there's something about the absurdity of filmmaking with a great international cast and hearing all the different accents or people from different places thinking differently. I really, really enjoyed that, and on this one especially. I like that aspect of it.

That's why we also tried to do as little blue screen as possible. We built all of the sets. In this type of a film, which is somewhat technical anyway, you can have the actors be there and make it seem more present somehow. We treated this movie a little bit like a silent movie—event though there was a lot of dialogue—in the sense of people who can kind of convey weird thoughts. I'm not sure *what* weird thought; I'm not sure you'd even wanna know what. But Chris [Walken] is so able to just look and stare at you and convey something, even though he's afraid of horses!

How did you get over his fear of horses?

By using fake horses. It's the first time I've ever worked with horses, and they're quite powerful. These Spanish horses are quite amazing. And they are scary so I can understand his fear. It was the magic of movies. There were a few people that were [doubling including] a rider, Rob Inch. To be riding at a full gallop inside a sound stage and doing all this stuff with these intense, hyperactive Spanish horses was amazing. I gotta hand it to him.

Did it all pass off without any injuries?

The stunt people on *Sleepy Hollow* were really amazing. Nobody really got hurt. There were a couple of cuts and bruises, but no, thank God. I was amazed and very grateful for that.

Wasn't Ray Park, who played Darth Maul in Star Wars: Episode I – The Phantom Menace [1999], *one of the stunt performers? Was he cast before that?*

He was done with *Star Wars*, but that hadn't come out, or we hadn't seen anything of that. Ray's great. Because your main character doesn't have a head—which you obviously look to for character in people—we wanted to try and give him an elegance and a strength. So between Chris and Ray and Rob, to try and give a sense of character through movement. They were all really brilliant at that.

Is there any other area of American folklore you'd like to explore after doing Jack Skellington [in The Nightmare Before Christmas, *1993] and now the headless horseman in* Sleepy Hollow?

I always try to think more from the inside out. What's good about those folkloric or fairytale images is that they seem abstract on the surface, but somehow they mean something. So I guess the question is: what says something to you? Working on a project like *Superman*, which didn't go anywhere, I felt a certain way. Then I'm presented with this character with no head and I could completely relate to it, immediately. So you have to know how you feel at any given time and let it take its course that way. I do like them for that reason. I like metaphor. I like the character that looks symbolic but can mean something.

Will Superman *see the light of day now?*

I'm sure they'll do it with somebody, but I don't think with me. I worked so long on it and it was so painful. I can't imagine going back to that circumstance.

How far did Superman *get? Did you and Nicolas Cage discuss the character?*

Oh yes. That's why I got involved in it. I like him and thought that Superman out of all the characters was the most iconic, but at the same time the least logical. Here's the big, strong guy who puts on glasses and nobody knows the difference. We thought that for the first time we could maybe make that more believable somehow. Nic would be really good at that—of feeling what it's like to be Superman. We got pretty far into it. We were doing costume tests and effects tests, location scouting. It was just, "Oh yeah, the script!" which is what always happens.

Do you think you might work together again on something?

I would like to. I think he's great. I look forward to working with him.

One assumes given the Superman *experience and despite everything that you've done that it's not got any easier for you to make films within the Hollywood system.*

I realized that pretty early on. I thought after the first couple were really lucky to have success, then it was gonna be easier, but in fact an opposite thing happens, which is there's more of a fixation and a focus. You do the first *Batman* and there's no talk of the word "franchise" or any of that. You don't hear those words. Then it becomes like this extra added thing and this expectation. Those are always better when you don't expect anything and then you're surprised. It gets harder to do in the world but that's exciting. That's certainly been taken away to a degree. And also the climate changes on a yearly basis. I haven't been in it that long, but it's changed quite a lot. It's become a lot more corporate. You deal less with individuals and more with nameless, faceless corporations, which does make it harder for everybody.

How have you managed to maintain your individual vision?

I'm just lucky. You work with a great group of people who try to get into the spirit of something. That's what it really comes down to. With all the arguing and stuff when you're there making the movie, that's where you really have the opportunity. Those are the people you feel close to—the crew right around you.

Do you have studio execs coming on set telling you what to do?

No. They were really good on this. It also helps being here [in the UK] and the studio's half the way around the world. That does help. [Laughs] It's amazing what that does for you!

What's the status of your Vincent Price documentary and also the remake of 1963's The Man with the X-Ray Eyes?

I keep reading that. I feel like I have some evil twin out there somewhere! [Laughs] And especially on the Internet. The funny thing about the Internet is that it's so intense. It's not even like gossip but because it's printed and even if it's hearsay all of a sudden becomes fact.

Do you ever feel you should put these stories right?

But that could be a full-time job. It is true that I was involved and maybe thinking about *X-Ray Eyes*. And it is true that I shot some of the last footage of Vincent Price and I have been working on a documentary, but I had some trouble with some of the clips and rights to stuff. It's gone on so long that I'm kind of reassessing what it is.

What problems did you have with the rights?

I'll give you the best example. After doing *Batman* I wanted to do a low-budget movie. I wanted *Edward Scissorhands* to be low budget. But because you do *Batman*, people think that you're only making these big movies, and you're trying to convince them that you're not. Then they know you're in the movie business, so then they think that you're lying to them, which sometimes people do. So you have to walk away from lots of things because it's impossible. You get this weird sort of penalization because they think you're making and have nothing but money. That's not the case a lot of the time. So sometimes these things turn into bigger deals than they need to, and that's what happened with some of that. Time has gone on so much now that I just wanna look at the footage and reassess it somehow.

There has been talk of sequels and the possibility of developing Catwoman.

I like that character. I just have to be careful. It's not that I shouldn't be doing sequels or anything like that; I don't think I do that very well. I'm actually trying to protect the studio by saying that even though I like these characters and the idea of exploring them further is a good one. [Sequels are] dangerous because exploring characters and finding new, weird avenues is not necessarily, from a studio perspective, what they want from a sequel! [Laughs]

2000

JOHN CARPENTER
The Thing

"I made a really gruelling dark film and I don't think audiences in 1982 wanted to see that. They wanted to see *E.T.*" – John Carpenter on *The Thing* (Universal/Kim Gottlieb-Walker)

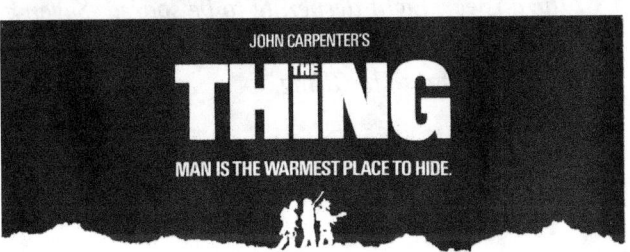

Universal, 1982

CAST: MacReady, KURT RUSSELL; Blair, A. WILFORD BRIMLEY; Nauls, T.K. CARTER; Parker, DAVID CLENNON; Childs, KEITH DAVID; Dr. Copper, RICHARD DYSART; Norris, CHARLES HALLAHAN; Bennings, PETER MALONEY; Clark, RICHARD MASUR; Garry, DONALD MOFFAT; Fuchs, JOEL POLIS; Windows, THOMAS WAITES; Norwegian, NORBERT WEISSER; Norwegian Passenger with Rifle, LARRY FRANCO; Helicopter Pilot, NATE IRWIN; Pilot, WILLIAM ZEMAN.

CREDITS: *Director*, John Carpenter; *screenplay*, Bill Lancaster, based on "Who Goes There?" by John W. Campbell, Jr; *producers*, David Foster, Lawrence Turman; *co-producer*, Stuart Cohen; *associate producer*, Larry Franco; *executive producer*, Wilbur Stark; *director of photography*, Dean Cundey; *production designer*, John L. Lloyd; *special make-up effects*, Rob Bottin; *editor*, Todd Ramsay; *music*, Ennio Morricone; *art director*, Henry Larrecq; *special visual effects*, Albert Whitlock. Running time: 104 minutes.

"*In the winter of 1982, twelve men are commissioned by the United States National Science Foundation to gather data concerning the physical and natural sciences in the Antarctic. What they discover is an alien being that fell from the sky and lay buried in the ice for one hundred thousand years. Soon it will be free and become one of us. Twelve men trapped in the Antarctic. Eleven discover the intruder. Ten battle the alien force. Nine agonize for the answer. Eight desperate to be spared. Seven consumed one by one. Six, five, four, three.... They will all die. Unless something, anything stops The Thing."*

Bringing the Monster into the Light
John Carpenter on *The Thing*

What did you like about the original film and why did you think it was possible to give it a modern spin for an '80s remake?

John Carpenter: The original film *The Thing from Another World* was made in 1951 and remains one of my favorite movies. It's a great science-fiction horror film. It was at least co-directed by Howard Hawks, one of my favorite directors, and it's got some of the greatest early scare moments in science-fiction movies of the '50s. I was offered to remake *The Thing* at Universal in 1981, and I thought long and hard about it because I didn't wanna compete with the old film, which was correctly loved by myself and many fans. So I went back to the novella [first published in the August 1938 edition of *Astounding Science-Fiction*] on which both films are based, *Who Goes There?* by Donald Stewart, otherwise known as John Campbell. And it's a vastly different story. So I thought if we just ignore the first movie and just ignore the science-fiction tropes of the time and the dated nature of it and go for a more literal reading of the novella, I thought we would be in better shape.

In scripting the film, how far did you think you could go?

In terms of scripting the film, I hired a young writer named Bill Lancaster. He had done *The Bad News Bears* [1976] several years earlier, and I was very impressed with him. He had a great take on the material and came up with some ideas for some great sequences, but as originally written, the monster was not delineated in the movie. There's this cliché [that] it's always better never to show the face of the devil. Never show the monster; always suggest it.

    I was struggling with that until I came upon Rob Bottin, who did the special effects. He suggested the secret of the movie, which was that the thing can look like *anything*. It doesn't have to look like one creature; it can look like every life form it has imitated throughout the universe because it's been on its travels for a long, long time. So there was a chance to create a monster that was design-based. And based on the movement we could give it, and based on some really crazy, offbeat ideas. I don't know that there has been a monster done like this. But Rob Bottin convinced me and that's the way we went.

Were there any specific challenges that you had to overcome?

The major conflict on the set was between the Director of Photography Dean Cundey and the Special Effects Creator Rob Bottin. Rob had done *The Howling* [1981] and generally felt that, of all the monster stuff, the thing emerging should be done in complete silhouette or backlight. Dean Cundey felt that if we were gonna go down this route with this creature, let's bring it out in the light—let's shine a light right on this creature and make it visible to we, the audience. This is a constant creative struggle.

The backdrop to the film is oppressively cold. What are your memories of shooting The Thing *and dealing with extremes of temperature and the associated conditions?*

The experience of making the movie was somewhat unpleasant in a number of ways. The first shooting that we did on the film was in the ice fields above Juneau, Alaska. This is essentially where all the weather begins in the United States. We went up there for a couple of weeks, and it was pretty grim. It was pretty grim not so much that it was cold, because it was actually warmish weather, but the sun would beat down so hard on you, and if you had an overcast layer of clouds, the light would bounce back and forth between snow and clouds. I got completely fried. I fried up my skin on *The Thing*. That's why I've had little reoccurrences of skin cancer ever since—because of that experience.

Then we moved down to Los Angeles and we shot the interiors. To get the idea of breath we refrigerated the stages down to about freezing. Actually it was a little higher than that—four degrees, maybe a little less. And you still had to push it. In other words actors had to drink coffee, really sell the breath idea. But it was nice. It gave a tactile sense to the sequences.

Then finally, after all this, we jumped up to Stewart, British Columbia. Halfway up the mountain, there's a glacier upon which we built the Antarctic station. It was extremely rural, and debauched, which I won't go into now. And finally there was the rest of the special effects shooting—the parts that we didn't do with the cast and crew. That was equally painful in its own way, but we finally finished it up and got her done.

The Thing is now rightly considered a classic. How was it received at the time you made it?

Over the years people have asked me about *The Thing* because on its release it was not particularly successful with audiences or fans. Years later, because of home video and so forth, it got to be known a bit better. My reaction? I was pretty stung by it at the time because I made a really grueling, dark film, and I don't think audiences in 1982 wanted to see that. They wanted to see *E.T.* [1982], and *The Thing* was the opposite of that. The thing that disturbed me about it was that the fans turned out hating it so much. There was a famous magazine back then called *Cinefantastique*, which was loved and hated by various directors. They had a cover story that said, "Is this the most hated film of all time?" which didn't do a lot to assuage my ego. I'm very proud of the movie. I've always loved it. It's one of my favorites of my own films. It still looks well.

2008

WES CRAVEN and NEVE CAMPBELL
Scream 3

"I was determined not to let it die." - Wes Craven, the erudite craftsman behind the *Scream* series. (New Line Cinema/Joseph Viles)

SCREAM 3

Miramax, 2000

CAST: Dewey Riley, DAVID ARQUETTE; Sidney Prescott, NEVE CAMPBELL; Gale Weathers, COURTENEY COX ARQUETTE; Mark Kincaid, PATRICK DEMPSEY; Roman Bridger, SCOTT FOLEY; John Milton, LANCE HENRIKSEN; Tom Prinze, MATT KEESLAR; Sarah Darling, JENNY McCARTHY; Angelina Tyler, EMILY MORTIMER; Jennifer Jolie, PARKER POSEY; Tyson Fox, DEON RICHMOND; Christine, KELLY RUTHERFORD; Cotton Weary, LIEV SCHREIBER; Steven Stone, PATRICK WARBURTON; Randy Meeks, JAMIE KENNEDY; Female Caller, BETH TOUSSAINT; "The Voice", ROGER L. JACKSON; Moderator, JULIE JANNEY; Student, RICHARD ARQUETTE; Maureen Prescott, LYNN McREE; Female Reporter, NANCY O'DELL; Male Reporter, KEN TAYLOR; Studio Executive, ROGER CORMAN; Wallace, JOSH PAIS; Stage Security Guard, JOHN EMBRY; Mr. Prescott, LAWRENCE HECHT; Studio Tour Guide, LISA BEACH; Silent Bob, KEVIN SMITH; Jay, JASON MEWES; Stan, ERIK ERATH; Office Security Guard, D.K. ARREDONDO; Waitress, LISA GORDON; Martha Meeks, HEATHER MATARAZZO; Bianca, CARRIE FISHER; Mr. Loomis, C.W. MORGAN.

CREDITS: *Director*, Wes Craven; *screenplay*, Ehren Kruger, based on characters created by Kevin Williamson; *producers,* Cathy Konrad, Kevin Williamson, Marianne Maddalena; *executive producers*, Bob Weinstein,

Harvey Weinstein, Cary Granat, Andrew Rona; *co-executive producer,* Stuart M. Besser; *co-producers,* Dixie J. Capp, Julie Plec, Dan Arredondo; *director of photography,* Peter Deming A.C.S.; *editor,* Patrick Lussier; *production designer,* Bruce Alan Miller; *music,* Marco Beltrami; *costume designer,* Abigail Murray. Running time: 116 minutes.

"In Hollywood, the production of Stab 3: Return to Woodsboro raises troubling questions about the events that terrified the town of Woodsboro and which continue to haunt Sidney Prescott. Three-and-a-half years after leaving Windsor College, Sidney has settled into a life of quiet seclusion in Northern California. But that uneasy peace is shattered when terror erupts on the set of Stab 3.

"TV personality Gale Weathers rushes to Hollywood, ready to jump on the Stab 3 story. But she's not prepared to discover old flame Deputy Dewey Riley in bed with Jennifer Jolie, the actress who plays Weathers in the Stab movies. Dewey and Sidney also find themselves dealing with their actor counterparts. Brat packer Tom Prinze plays Dewey, while wide-eyed ingénue Angelina Tyler is cast as Sidney.

"Veteran producer John Milton and hotshot director Roman Bridger are the masterminds behind Stab 3. Their cast also includes Sarah Darling, a starlet fed up with bimbo roles, and Tyson Fox, who's striving for dignity in his portrayal of a video store geek.

"LAPD Detective Mark Kincaid heads the Stab 3 investigation. Security expert Steve Stone is in charge of protecting the stars. Cotton Weary, now living with girlfriend Christine, has found fame and fortune with his Hollywood talk show '100% Cotton.'"

Third Act of the Über Film
Wes Craven and Neve Campbell on *Scream 3*

Scream 3 *is the first film in the trilogy that wasn't penned by the man himself. Was there any fear for the project when Kevin Williamson said he was too busy to take on that role?*

Wes Craven: I think we were in mortal fear that the project was dealt a deathblow. Certainly Kevin was always felt to be *the* writer to be writing the series, although beginning with the second one he was—not to tell tales out of school—already so incredibly busy with *Dawson's Creek* [1998-2003] that there was a lot of collaboration, let's say. By the time we got to the third, it wasn't that big of a leap to go with the direction that he had pointed us all in and find a new writer. We were extraordinarily fortunate I think to have access to Ehren Kruger. He was just completing work with John Frankenheimer on *Reindeer Games* [2000], so he was known to Miramax, and they literally said, "Well there's one shot we have. We have this young writer. He's a huge fan of the series—of *Scream* [1996]—and he wants to take a shot at an outline."

Over a long weekend, he came back with about eight pages that laid out the general course of the third film in a way that we were all very excited about. From there on it was a day-by-day collaboration working with him. He's in all of our understanding of the characters and where I wanted to take it, too. But it began with more than a moment of panic: "Oh my God! What's gonna happen?" I felt very strongly that the film deserved it and that the characters deserved to be taken to completion. I was determined not to let it die.

You did the first of the Nightmare on Elm Street *films in 1984, which later went off in a very strange direction…*

Craven: I did the last, also.

Does that mean you want to control these three yourself?

Craven: Yes, very much. I was talking about that a lot in the press. It was very gratifying to have control over three films like this. I enjoyed both that it was a trilogy and it had an ending and the fact that I was entrusted with the whole kit and caboodle.

Given that you had to watch the Nightmare *series take a wayward path after you made the first one, then is* Scream 3 *the final part? How would you feel about someone picking up the story for* Part 4? *Or has Miramax closed it all down now?*

Craven: I could say definitively, "There's absolutely no possibility," but I've just been alive too long. One can never predict entirely what a studio will do if their backs are to the wall, but my understanding is—and every conversation I've been a part of, and we have a pretty frank and lively and open relationship, myself and my producer and the studio—they always take a pride in the fact that they're doing a trilogy and we're not going to do sequels. At the same time, Bob Weinstein did say, "Look, in five years or four years, if there's a huge feeling that the audience would love to have another one, then we might do another and start with a whole new set of stories and characters." But as far as coming up next year or the year after and the year after that with another *Scream*, I see no indication of that. I can't speak for Neve except that I'd take a strong guess that she probably wouldn't want to do it. I don't want to do it either. I think it feels great to have done a trilogy and to stick with it.

What was different about Scream 3 *compared to the two movies that preceded it?*

Neve Campbell: The third one was less focused on the horror as much, although you still get a good amount of that. And it had a lot more black humor in it. It was suggesting itself about franchises and stuff like that.

Craven: This was unique in the sense of being a true trilogy and conceived as such from the beginning. As a director, the unique thing was that [it was] the third act of the über film, of the larger piece. In that sense it had revelations reflecting back through the second film to the first. It was kind of a summation of the character, the final movement. That made it different from the others just because it was that final piece of the jigsaw puzzle of Neve's character.

Was it a more interesting movie to make given that all bets were off, as it was a trilogy? Did it give you more room to have fun?

Craven: Certainly the threat of wiping everybody out! [Laughs] I think it was intriguing just because it was the summation. We did have to put our thinking caps on and say how best to summarize, not just plot-wise but stylistically and every other way we could think, of a three-film film. In that sense, it was exciting to be doing that completion.

Is it true that you don't actually like watching horror films? Will you actually go to see Scream 3 *if you haven't seen the first two?*

Campbell: I've seen the ones that I'm in. I don't have a problem with horror films; I think they're a lot of fun. I just have an issue with having nightmares if I do watch them. I saw one called *The Changeling* [1980] when I was twelve years old, and I had nightmares for two months. Have you seen it?

Craven: The Changeling? Oh yes. The little bouncing ball down the stairs....

Campbell: Exactly! The wheelchair?

Craven: I think I might have stolen from that one.

Campbell: But, no. Watching my own [horror films] is pretty easy because I know what's gonna happen.

So do you have a favorite horror film and, if so, what is it?

Campbell: I haven't seen that many. *The Changeling*, I guess. It's probably one of the two I've seen.

Craven: I'm never very good at this question because I don't have a favorite horror film. First of all and ironically, I don't go out of my way to see them, either, unless I hear that they're exceptionally good. I loved *The Sixth Sense* [1999] for a recent film. For a more exotic part of my repertoire—films that I love that are scary are probably three of Polanski's films, starting with *Rosemary's Baby* [1968], *The Tenant* [1976], and also *Repulsion* [1965]. But a lot of other films, too. *The Texas Chain Saw Massacre* [1974] I think is a great American wild and woolly horror film that is quite a classic. Also *Alien* [1979], *The Exorcist* [1973], and films of that sort, too.

When you're actually making a horror movie is it all acting or can any sense of fear be created on set?

Campbell: I find I have to create that for myself, so that it's realistic for the character and the audience will sense that. But you have eighty people standing around, and Wes doing doodles and crossword puzzles by the dozen, so you don't get too scared.

Is it part of your approach to a role to create a back-story to a character for your own benefit? Or have you found that it's a redundant process with these films because you're finding out lots of things with each successive script?

Campbell: No, because at the time I was doing the first or the second I wasn't thinking about the third. You have to create the present and the immediate, and the audience needs to belong to that film at that time and not have hints towards the third until that occurs. I do feel it's necessary to create a back-story no matter what because you're not gonna come across in a realistic way if you haven't created an entire character: if you haven't given her depth and a storyline beyond what's on the page.

Were there moments when you thought your back-story was better than the actual story they gave you?

Campbell: It's always better! [Laughs] No. Obviously, in your mind it's always richer, but you don't have the time to do that in two hours on film. And especially in a film like this. It's not about "What are her relationships?" It's about entertaining people with the horror and the comedy and keeping the picture moving. But you have to have it in your own mind so that people actually care about your character.

Wes, did you think at any stage that you might kill off the Sidney Prescott character, and Neve, if he did, how would you like to have gone?

Craven: I thought of killing her off quite often when she was being cheeky and it was just impossible to deal with. Actually even in *Scream 2* [1997], there was an original ending when Neve was virtually dead at the end. I'm trying to think. It passed through our minds with the threat of Randy saying—and it can be revealed because he's in the film—that all bets are off and anybody could die. And Sidney hearing that. In a way, the most severe step we could take with the plot would be to kill her or everybody. David Arquette actually lobbied for that. He addressed the camera once. He just felt that to be true, to go to the ultimate, we had to kill everybody in the final scene!

    I really felt—I don't know what it is, a growing maturity—that the character of Sidney Prescott deserved—and the audience deserves the right having gone through the odyssey with her—to win the right to be free. Her story is the serious part of the screen trilogy: this young woman moving from a traumatized childhood to an adulthood where she could leave the door unlocked and go and watch a movie with friends. She didn't know exactly what kind of a movie it was gonna be, but she trusted it was gonna be something that was good rather than bad. To my mind, it was never seriously considered. That was a long answer, wasn't it?

Campbell: If I did have to go? Extremely violently. I don't know. I had entertained the idea of Sidney being killed in the first ten minutes, like in the others films where Drew [Barrymore] went or Jada [Pinkett-Smith] in the second. I thought that could have been interesting and shocking to the audience. And kind of an interesting way to start it.

Craven: Cooler minds prevailed.

What's it like having another actress play your character in a film within a film? Was that a bit surreal on set for you?

Campbell: I never felt that it was someone else or anything like that. It's an interesting experience—to see who Wes would cast, and so I would get a concept of who he sees me as or the energy he was looking for. So that was cool. I thought Emily [Mortimer] did a great job.

When did Emily Mortimer—a very English actress—come on board the project?

Craven: She simply was the best that came through the door. In her audition, she simply had a vitality and a beauty that reflected Neve's and brought a very interesting dimension to it that was particularly her own. I fought quite hard for her. There was a fear on the part of the studio. I don't believe she had a work permit, as it turned out, or a right to be in the country working. Not until literally the morning of her first day at work.

We had to fly her to Vancouver and hope to get a judge there to give her the permission to come across the border and be officially a member of the working actors of the United States.

All the fictional characters have counter plots. Which were you: John Milton [played by Lance Henriksen] or Roman [Bridger, played by Scott Foley]?

Craven: I think there was a little bit of me in both. In fact, in a lot of the characters in the film. John Milton's office full of old props from his old movies is very similar to my office until very recently. Almost significantly in the past year I've started giving a lot of my old props away to charity auctions. There was a sad, almost bittersweet thing about that, but that love and affection for the films that you've done in the past certainly is there. I didn't throw wild parties in the '70s, though. That part of his character is more some other people that I won't mention.

Is it true that you were the only actor on set with a copy of the finished script?

Neve: I don't know if I was the only one.

Craven: Courteney and David were kept pretty much up on the writing, too.

Campbell: So I didn't have trouble with them. I didn't have the cast bugging me about it or anything. I was happy to have it, definitely. Courteney and David and Wes and I all really wanted to be on the same page and have an understanding of where we were going. But we were getting a lot of new pages. Wes was coming up with a lot of new ideas during the shoot. It was interesting. Normally, it could be annoying, except that with a film like this where Sidney is so confused in a lot of ways, and is lost herself, I didn't have to know everything.

How was the security this time after the ending of Scream 2 *made it onto the Internet?*

Craven: It was the actually the opening—the first forty pages arrived by fax in the morning, and it was on the Internet by the evening!

Was it 100 percent foolproof this time?

Craven: It was practically like a military operation. Everybody had to sign a non-disclosure pact. There were closed sets all the time. We never had a complete script on the set that I can recall except my personal copy. Neve, Courteney, and David had copies, but by and large we worked off of sides....

Campbell:... which we had to return at the end of the day.

Craven: They were collected by somebody who was assigned to collect them at the end of every day. Every way that, normally when you make a film, you never think twice about was followed through. [It was printed] on paper that couldn't be xeroxed. Even putting out misleading endings and so forth to Internet sources. Just pretty much doing whatever we could to keep it secret.

What happened to Laurie Metcalf's character [Debbie Salt] in Scream 2? *You don't really explain what happened there. You explain how the director goes back and influences the first set of killings but you don't tell us anything of what happens after that.*

Craven: Well, no, because principally we're talking about the final revelations about Sidney's relationship with and knowledge of her mother. I felt that was like the final tether to childhood—that mystery of the parent that we all go through when you reinterpret your own parents. You start to see them as human beings and try to get an accurate picture of who they are and, in some sense from that, who *you* are.

You've said goodbye to Sidney on screen but how difficult do you think it will be to leave her behind? Will you keep getting offered "Scream Queen" roles, and are you concerned about typecasting?

Campbell: People really stopped sending them to me after the first film. I was getting sent them, but I started to say in the press that I wasn't interested in doing any other ones beyond the *Scream* films, just because I didn't think it would be a smart move on my part.

She's a strong character. Will she be difficult to escape from in whatever you do next?

Campbell: I don't think so. I had that fear about Julia in *Party of Five* [1994-2000], and then I made a conscious choice to have a feature career, so I did *Scream* and then I did *The Craft* [1996]. Then beyond that, I did some comedies. I did *Drowning Mona* [2000] and *Three to Tango* [1999] and some independents like *Panic* [2000]. I'm producing and doing a whole bunch of stuff to avoid that. You're always known as whatever film you last did, basically. When I do a comedy and it comes out, all of a sudden all I get offered is comedies. Then I make sure I don't do a comedy. I do a drama. Then all I get offered is drama. So you've got to keep mixing it up.

So those films were clear decisions—to put as much distance as possible between you and Sidney?

Campbell: Absolutely. And from any of my other characters as well. I wanna challenge myself. I wanna grow as an actor. I don't wanna just play it safe and do what the audiences like.

Talking of Scream Queens, didn't you go on to work with Jamie Lee Curtis?

Campbell: I did, actually. She was in *Drowning Mona* with me.

Did she offer you any tips?

Campbell: No. She actually wanted her crown back. That's what she told me on the first day. She's a hilarious woman. She's a lot of fun. It's interesting: when the first *Scream* came out, I was being called "Scream Queen" and "The next Jamie Lee Curtis," and people asked me if that bothered me. I always said, "No. I think she's had a great career. She did a horror film, but she's done other things as well. She's done comedy, she's done drama. That's what I think we all should be trying to do: just expanding. I'd be happy to have a career like hers." So it was wonderful to actually do a comedy with her.

Party of Five brought you to attention but it also meant you had to turn down a role in Armageddon [1998]. Does it liberate you or are you sorry it's gone?

Campbell: It definitely liberates me. It's also bittersweet. They also feel like a family to me and they have been. I've been playing with them as my family for six years. So I'm gonna miss the cast members and I'm gonna miss the characters. It's strange when you stay with someone for that long, like Julia—she became a person to me. So it was very strange to read the last script and realize she wasn't alive. That was a strange experience. But I'm really happy now to first of all have a life, because it's been nine months or a year with fifteen or sixteen hours a day for six years, and that's a long time with movies on my hiatuses. So now I'll be able to do movies and then take a break, do the things I want to do [such as] spend time with family and friends.

Music of the Heart *[1999] was such a change of style for you. Have you got any more plans to change your accepted image?*

Craven: Just that general intent to do what Neve has been doing from the beginning and what I wasn't smart enough to figure out: broadening the kind of material that I do. The next probably will be a film version of the novel that I wrote last year, *Fountain Society*, and after that, I have two more films for Miramax Dimension. So probably one will be some sort of genre film, but not anything resembling the *Scream* type of films, probably some sort of thriller or murder/mystery. And then one more Miramax film. We're acquiring various novels and so forth. Perhaps I'll write something myself too. It's just the intent to keep expanding and growing having opened that door a-wedge now.

Did you see Meryl Streep's Oscar nomination for Music of the Heart *as some sort of a validation of your foray into a different genre? And did you invite her to the* Scream 3 *premiere?*

Craven: Meryl was dying to come. She just made me nervous. She kept wearing Freddy's claws. [Laughs] She's such a fan! No, I didn't invite her. She's terrified by scary movies and can't stand to watch them, even though her kids do. She's constantly having to hide in various parts of her house to stay away from it.

I certainly was extremely gratified to have that nomination—two nominations, actually, for things in the film. Meryl could almost read the phone book and people would think she's marvelous, because she is. She did give an extraordinary performance. It was a film that put her in virtually every scene but one that gave her a chance to stretch in a way that she hadn't had a chance in a long time. So it was a great feeling. It's always a great privilege to work with a great actress and, not to embarrass Neve, but to give my honest answer to this previous question, the sense in Hollywood very much is that Neve Campbell is a supremely gifted actress. All of us directors, I know, are thinking we'd be fortunate to work with her again in other ways and in just about any genre. I always speak of her in the highest terms as an actress. I'm making her sigh and twitch. Pay me later.

Campbell: Thank you so much.

You give the impression that you really enjoyed making the Scream *trilogy. How did you feel when filming the final shots, knowing it was the last time you'd get together under such circumstances?*

Campbell: I cried. I was sad. It's a bittersweet experience. It's been such a fantastic thing for all of our careers, first of all, but also emotionally. We've all learned a lot from each other on this—within all of these films. It feels like going to summer camp. So I'm sad that I'm not going back to summer camp. It's like growing up, in a sense. But it's also nice to open up time for further opportunities.

When it comes to horror, is it never say never?

Craven: Well, yeah. I've learned never to say never, but I do have a strong feeling like *Scream 3* marks the close of an era in my particular little neck of the woods. It would be foolish to go back to more of the same when I don't need to financially and I don't feel I need to emotionally or artistically. So it feels great to end on a high note and go on to different sorts of things.

2000

ROLAND EMMERICH, DEAN DEVLIN, and JAMES SPADER
Stargate

Roland Emmerich on the set of *Stargate*, a film that emerged from a 15-year period of gestation. (Carolco Pictures/Claudette Barius)

STARGATE
Le Studio Canal/Centropolis/ Carolco Pictures, 1994

CAST: Colonel Jonathan "Jack" O'Neil, KURT RUSSELL; Dr. Daniel Jackson, JAMES SPADER; Ra, JAYE DAVIDSON; Catherine, VIVECA LINDFORS; Skaara, ALEXIS CRUZ; Sha'uri, MILLI AVITAL; General W.O. West, LEON RIPPY; Lieutenant Kawalsky, JOHN DIEHL; Anubis, CARLOS LAUCHU; Horus, DJIMON; Kasuf, ERICK AVARI; Lieutenant Feretti, FRENCH STEWART; Nabeh, GIANIN LOFFLER; Lieutenant Freeman, CHRISTOPHER JOHN FIELDS; Lieutenant Brown, DEREK WEBSTER; Lieutenant Reilly, JACK MOORE; Lieutenant Porro, STEVE GIANELLI; Assistant Lieutenant, DAVID PRESSMAN; Officer, SCOTT SMITH; Sarah O'Neil, CECIL HOFFMAN; Barbara Stone, RAE ALLEN; Gary Meyers, RICHARD KIND; Mitch, JOHN STOREY; Jenny, LEE TAYLOR-ALLAN; Technician, GEORGE GRAY; Young Catherine, KELLY VINT; Professor Langford, ERIK HOLLAND; Taylor, the Foreman, NICK WILDER; Arabic Interpreter, SAYED BADREYA; Horus Guards, MICHAEL CONCEPCION, JERRY GILMORE, MICHAEL JEAN-PHILIPPE, DIALY N'DAIYE; Professors, GLADYS HOLLAND, ROGER TIL, KENNETH DANZIGER, CHRISTOPHER WEST; Companion, ROBERT ACKERMAN; Masked Ra, KIERON LEE; Voice of Mastadge, FRANK WELKER.

CREDITS: *Director,* Roland Emmerich; *executive producer,* Mario Kassar; *producers,* Joel B. Michaels, Oliver Eberle, Dean Devlin; *co-producer,* Ute Emmerich; *associate producer,* Peter Winther; *screenplay,* Dean Devlin, Roland Emmerich; *director of photography,* Karl Walter Lindenlaub; *visual effects supervisor,* Kit West; *editors,* Michael J. Duthie, Derek Brechlin; *production designer*, Holger Gross; *art directors*, Peter Murton, Frank Bollinger; *Yuma:* Mark Zuelzke; *special effects supervisors*, Trevor Wood, John Cazin; *special creature effects*, Patrick Tatopoulos; *costume designer*, Joseph Porro; *Ra's headdress/Anubis' & Horus' costumes*, Patrick Tatopoulos; *mechanical effects supervisors*, Wayne Beauchamp, Russell Shinkle; *make up artists*, Greg Nelson, Lisa Collins, Dennis Liddiard; *music*, David Arnold. Running time: 121 minutes.

> "Two very different men join forces to unravel a mystery which could reveal the origin of civilization. Tough-minded military man Colonel Jack O'Neil heads a top-secret team investigating a mysterious artifact unearthed at Giza. Daniel Jackson is a brilliant but unorthodox Egyptologist whose scientific curiosity clashes with O'Neil's secret agenda. But it is Jackson who identifies the object as a Stargate—a portal to another world.
>
> "O'Neil leads Jackson and a reconnaissance team through the Stargate, which transports them millions of light years from Earth, where they are stranded on a strange and alien planet. When Ra, the enigmatic ruler of this extraordinary world, discovers that the doorway to Earth can be reopened, he devises a deadly plot. Racing against time, O'Neil and Jackson must overcome Ra if they are to save Earth and find a way back home."

Emulating the Past
Roland Emmerich, Dean Devlin, and James Spader on *Stargate*

What's been the gestation of this project?

Roland Emmerich: It's really a long story, because I had the original idea in film school in 1979 or something like that. Then I was working on it off and on. In the mid-'80s, I had an attempt to do it. It was a different kind of movie, but it had the same basic concept and elements. But at that time, I was working mainly in Germany, and there was simply not the money available to do this kind of movie, so I abandoned it again. Then I met Dean [Devlin]. I hired him as an actor for my last movie I did in Germany. We hit it off pretty well and we started thinking about movies together. We discovered we had exactly the same kind of taste. Then we started to talk about *Stargate*.

At that time I was working for Carolco on another picture with Sylvester Stallone, which never got made. I prepared the movie for nine months. At one period a writer wrote a new script and it took two months. I turned to Dean and said, "A good time to write another movie!" We wrote the first draft of *Stargate*. Then we put it on ice again because we knew that nobody would give us the money. Then this other movie didn't happen, I did *Universal Soldier* [1992] for Mario Kassar and he said to me, "Look, you do *Universal Soldier* for me and help me here, and I will help you to do your own first project." The only problem was that when the time came, Carolco was not really existing anymore. It was in deep financial trouble.

We turned to one of the partners, CanalPlus. There was a young producer there, Mark Friedman, and he fell in love with the project. They then brought Mario in because he's a known entity in this world of films. So everything came together. It helped Mario, too. It also helped MGM. People forget with all the trouble Mario has financially that he has one of the best instincts in this business when it comes to big, mainstream event movie entertainment. He said to me, "It's amazing." It's the first year that he didn't do a movie either with Arnold [Schwarzenegger] or Sly [Stallone], and *Stargate*, which isn't with either of them, is a bigger hit than both of these guys' movies! So he's quite pleased about that because it tells a little bit about him.

What was the spur? Why the fascination with pyramids?

Emmerich: It was [from watching] a two-hour show documentary that showed all the hundreds of different theories about who and why they built the pyramids, from the traditional standpoint up to people like [Erich] Von Daniken. Recently there have been people who have shown how you can build them in a certain time. It was one of these things where I said, "Gosh, in just a couple of hundred years, people have been writing hundreds of books about the pyramids of Giza. This is like a worldwide symbol. They're building casinos in Vegas in the form of the pyramid. People crawl inside them for healing purposes. Why hasn't anybody ever done anything with that in a movie?" That was the original idea. Then I'm also fascinated by and I love Egyptian art. It's one of the most beautiful styles ever invented, and a very old language that is unique.

Judging by your back catalogue, you tend to go for action stars. You didn't do that with Stargate.

Emmerich: First of all, James didn't only play that part. The second thing is that James is a terrific actor and he has a very intelligent way of acting. We were looking for somebody who could really handle this part. James is pretty much running the movie; he leads us through. The public and Hollywood like to pigeonhole actors in a certain way. I think there's only good and bad acting. It's the same thing with directors. You have a certain period where you only make a certain kind of movie. That's because you like to do these kinds of movies. Then in ten years, you're in another period where you don't want to do that anymore. You're doing something else. And it's very hard to do that. Hitchcock did thrillers all his life, but he also did some of the greatest romantic comedies.

Dean Devlin: When we went out originally to set the movie up, the normal thinking in Hollywood when you do science fiction is that you cast absolute unknowns like they did on the original *Star Wars* [1977], or you go with someone like an Arnold Schwarzenegger or Sylvester Stallone for that big machismo approach. Roland and I had simple requirements: we just wanted the absolute best actors we could get and people that we admired. I'd been an actor for twelve years up to the point I started working with Roland, and James was one of the few actors I'd wanted to be! [Laughs]

What was the attraction of Stargate?

James Spader: I took this film because it *so* took me by surprise, you know? I hadn't heard anything about the picture ahead of time. I didn't even know it was out there. The script arrived in the dark of night, I read it, and it was so different from anything that I'd ever thought about doing, and an area that I really hadn't had much interest in [that] it intrigued me. I met with Roland the next day, and he just made it sound like it was going to be so much fun—actually making the picture—that I wanted to be there on the set. The only thing I'm equipped to do on a set is act, so I said, "I'd love to be in your film." I had a wonderful time.

After your performance in White Palace [1990], *you're very restrained in this, because you don't get the girl. But that would have taken the film off in a wrong direction.*

Spader: That'll be in the sequel. You have to save something. We didn't want to shoot our wad in the first one, you know? Metaphorically speaking. It's left a bit ambiguously on purpose. I think it's always a mistake in a film—and Roland and Dean can speak to this better than I because they wrote the screenplay—but as far as I'm concerned, and the way that it was played is that very often in films, you can hit someone over the head with something. Then you have the reasons for different things taking place in a film [and they're] all laid on thing like a relationship or a lesson learned. That gets a bit old, and I don't think it's true to life at all. It's always a series of events that lead to something larger. That's what happens in *Stargate*: it's a series of things that create the quite enormous ending to the film, one of them being this love story that takes place.

Did you find it easy working with special effects?

Spader: Yeah. On this film it was very easy, and I don't have anything to relate it to because I haven't done any films with a lot of special effects. On this film, it was quite easy because although the special effects are very spectacular and a big part of the film, in fact all they really were was sort of an enhancement of things that we were playing off of that were there alive and breathing on the set. Roland at great expense could have had three extras there standing in the sand in the backlot of Universal, and then we could have gone off in post-production and computer-generated those three people into ten thousand. Instead, we had two thousand people there on the set to play off of, we had enormous sets and we were out in a sea of sand. There was an awful lot there already—quite a spectacle to feast your eyes on, anyway. Then the special effects and post-production were simply a grand enhancement of that.

Were you influenced by the movies of the past when making Stargate?

Devlin: Movies like *Indiana Jones* [1981] and *Star Wars* are the films that we loved growing up. They've influenced us. But at the same time, *Indiana Jones* and *Star Wars* were emulating an old-fashioned style of movie, as we are. We were all reaching into the same pond. *Stargate* is an attempt to go back to a very old-fashioned style, including a love story. In the old movies, people would kiss and you'd pan up to the tree before anything else had happened. We dissolve to a sandstorm.

The old serials were [also] part of it, but also we were trying to emulate some of the old costume dramas—the ancient Egyptian epic type of films. Part of how this whole thing came about was we were watching a retrospective of movies like *El Cid* [1961] and *Spartacus* [1960]. Charlton Heston was the moderator of the event, and he said it was very important to have these retrospectives because these types of films can never be done again. They're simply too expensive. That was like a challenge to us. How could we a) sell that type of film to a modern audience, hence the science fiction aspect, and b) how on a technical level can you do a film that big and stay within a reasonable budget?

Did you actually go out to Egypt?

Spader: No! That actually was a cruel joke, sort of a piece of bait that was held out in front of us—that we were all going to go to Egypt and be shooting on location by the great pyramids. And then after we all agreed to do the film it got switched to Yuma, Arizona. So no, we didn't go to Egypt.

How badly were you affected by the heat and sand? You hear some real horror stories.

Spader: The heat and the sand.... The sand was an enormous problem all the time for the first two-and-a-half months of shooting. Then for the second two-and-a-half months, we were on stages. But for the first two-and-a-half months, shooting in the desert, movement from here to where you're sitting was a huge undertaking of equipment and people and so on and so forth. That was greatly due to the sand and not only the sand but the configuration of the sand—the fact that you're always going up and down steep inclines. And a lot of it on foot. A lot of the vehicles were breaking down or getting stuck or in the wrong place at the wrong time. For us, it wasn't as difficult as it was for the crew, who had to carry and lug everything. But the sand was everywhere. It gets in everything. In all the equipment. All over everybody.

We'd be out there on certain days, the wind would come up and it would kill us immediately. Any sort of wind and you'd just get sort of a sandstorm and you can't shoot. You can't do anything. Also, we were shooting scenes with thousands of people, and therefore if you want to move from here to there, [you must] move everybody through these huge sort-of snowdrifts. Not only that, but after every take, you've now ruined wherever it is that you've just shot because you've left footprints and drag marks all through it. It was all supposed to be virgin dunes. So you'd either have to move then to a new place, or we had a battery of sweepers that would be sweeping up after us. Resetting between takes took a tremendous amount of time and effort.

The heat was just something that you have to deal with. It demands attention. There was one day when we were shooting most of the scenes that were more demanding. We would try and shoot at cooler times of the day, but there was one day when we had to shoot something [and it] was probably the most demanding scene that we shot in the desert. We ended up, because of lighting problems, shooting it at the hottest time of the day. We were in this basin that got no breeze. It was just like a frying pan. I can remember in the scene, the way that we originally blocked it, literally I was just sitting on the side of this wall. Kurt [Russell] walks up and I stand up and start speaking to him. I didn't think there was a problem, but I stood up on the first take, started doing this scene, and I forgot a line. That's something that rarely happens to me. I didn't know quite what it was.

And then Roland came over to me and said, "Come here. You have to listen to this. What's the matter?" I said, "I don't know. Let me hear." I put on the headphones and listened to the take that they'd just done, and I'd stood up and immediately I was gasping. Myself and another actor were both suffering from heat exhaustion or sunstroke or something like that. You don't really know what it is but your mind starts to go. You become slightly delirious. So the heat was something that you constantly had to deal with. You had to make yourself drink a tremendous amount of liquids. You had to take potassium, nitrates, at a lot of bananas, do certain things and pay attention to it, or it was going to stop you dead in your tracks. It was 115 degrees some days that we were out there. Some days it was 120. A funny thing was on a day when it was about 115. Somebody actually registered the heat in the sand and it was about 130! It's like a big conductor, you know? It certainly affected everything that was going on, but you figured out how to make it work and move on from there.

How much did the film cost?

Emmerich: The exact budget is between 55 and $56 million. I can't tell you by the dollar. The movie was pre-sold worldwide very good, so everybody felt that when we hit the $50 million in America, we were doing just fine. We're doing well in foreign territories, too. It's the biggest opening movie ever in Taiwan and places like that. Then the money comes in. I feel very good about that because this movie was a risk to do. We knew it going in. It wasn't as big a risk as some people think, because movies are pre-sold to different distributors worldwide, so there's a certain security for the producers and the banks. I'm really happy that we recouped our money and that those people who gave us the chance to make this movie will earn money. All is good.

How was your character, Daniel Jackson, conceived?

Spader: I can tell you the genesis of where the character came from. In the first draft of the screenplay that I read, it concentrated mainly on the story and explaining what was happening in chronological order in terms of the narrative. Roland and Dean had both had the intention of putting their cast in place and then sitting down with them. The next pass was going to be character development. Daniel Jackson in that draft was a fairly straightforward, absent-minded professor. He was fairly anal retentive and a stumblebum. My biggest question about him was, "If that's what he was, then why would he go on this trip?" I just didn't think he'd go. If he really was as bookish and studious as that, then he might wait around and just find out about it once everyone came back.

The thing that I think we all felt about him—because he's the only one in that group that goes on the journey that is there by choice—was that he was a child in a man's body. A bit of a five or six-year-old. They have that inherent fearlessness and lack of regard for consequence and danger. They have a tremendously unadulterated enthusiasm and exuberance and curiosity for mystery. It's why you see Daniel sort of tripping over himself to be the first one over the next hill or the first one out of the door, diving headlong into whatever the next direction is.

I'll never forget when they were shooting the sequence when we're all passing through the stargate for the first time. It was funny: we shot it over the course of two days. Just endless shots of us walking through this rain. They had to shoot it from every angle so they could put in the opticals later. I arrived there on the first day and I said, "Oh my God! I haven't thought at all about this!" Here's this monumental moment where he's passing through the ring and I hadn't really thought about what would be going through his mind.

I watched the other guys, the soldiers and so on, who went ahead of me. They all looked like they were doing their duty: that they were willing at that moment to lay down their lives for the sake of the order of a superior. They all looked like they were preparing to die—crossing themselves, kissing their icons and all the rest. Not knowing what was going to come next. I stood there and watched the rehearsal of that. I looked at that big thing there and realized that for Daniel, it was a toy to be played with. That's how a child would react to it: something exciting, fun, and curious to be toyed with and to be played with. That's how he ended up passing through it: with an enormous amount of curiosity.

Was Jaye Davidson your first choice as Ra?

Emmerich: It was like this. First, we auditioned all the characters. Then we started to assign Ra when he first appears. That led us to a discussion that every picture of a pharaoh in Egypt is a young pharaoh. We were going through different casting choices of older actors. The more we talked about it, the more we thought it was a cliché to have the old, fat guy. Then we came to look for a young actor to do the part. We were mulling around all kinds of different names, and Mario Kassar came up with Jaye. We all immediately said, "But he doesn't want to do movies. He's said it openly." Mario said, "It's very simple. We can ask."

Spader: Make an offer that he can't refuse!

Emmerich: Exactly.

Spader: We stuck a horse head in his bed!

Emmerich: I said to Mario, "Yes, it's a good idea but I want to meet him." Then I met Jaye for two days, and we talked a lot about what his part would be. Then we made a decision. He brings a certain quality to it. I knew there must be an actor that brings an old quality to this part because it's not much of a part. A charisma. His biggest problem was the language. When he was reading his script, the dialogue was written in English so that people could understand it. The words were subtitled, so he wasn't really sure. "Do I speak English with an accent? What do I do?" Then we had to explain to him that we intended to do everything in the original ancient Egyptian language. That pretty much gave him the final push. Speaking English would have been terrible. It's always a big concern of people who finance movies: if they have fifty subtitled dialogue lines, will it still have broad appeal, or will it be considered a foreign movie? [Laughs] There was a rumor in Hollywood that we were doing a foreign movie.

Spader: A foreign movie that only one person on the planet was going to understand.

How did you cope with the complex scientific language?

Spader: I learned as little of it as I had to. I was able to get away with murder. I don't think I ever said more than about a second's worth of it at a time. There's an actor who's in the film. He had to spiel *reams* of the stuff at great volume and great speed. He'd be over at the side of the set holding his head in his hands. These sons of bitches rewrite a scene the same day and he would be over there painfully agonizing over new dialogue. They'd rewrite a scene of mine, but I'd always insist that if there was going to be a rewrite, and it involved that language, that I didn't mind them rewriting anything, as long as it was less! We had a very good technical advisor on the set all the time to help us with the language. He also happened to be an archaeologist, so he was able to give advice in terms of that.

Are you tempted to make more films like this or will you still pursue edgier roles in films like in The Music of Chance *[1993]?*

Spader: I'm not going to play anything but action/adventures from now on. It's all I'm doing! [Laughs] We'll just have to see what comes. I had a blast doing this. I really had a lot of fun. I'm wonderful at handling firearms.... [Emeriti laughs] I think I've got a future in it, you know?

It's hard for me to compare them because they were both a lot of fun to do. To be fair, they were both characters in an area in which I hadn't done much before. That's always going to be that much more fun and satisfying. I don't like to put too much of myself out there. It's probably the reason why I've played a lot of the bad guys: it's more fun to hide behind somebody else. That's the reason for doing *The Music of Chance*; you can put on a bunch of odd stuff, do dialect and something very different, and hide behind it. It frees you up to do whatever the hell you want and make a fool of yourself. That's great fun.

I've gone back and forth an awful lot, and I've been lucky to be able to have the opportunity to do that and want to continue. Funnily enough, I did *Stargate* and had a blast on it. Then the next film I did was something we made for a couple of million dollars, and it's an odd, little, quirky, strange role. I like to bounce back and forth between the two. There's a certain amount of sabotage for my career because it makes it hard to keep building in a certain direction. But I like to jump around and fool around with different things if I can.

That is a battle in itself in Hollywood, and for good reason. The average budget now for a studio picture is $28 million. If you're spending that on a film, you want to get the best possible person for every single position available on that picture. And for an actor or a director or a screenwriter the way you know you're getting the best person is to hire someone who you saw do that exact same thing in their last picture, and did it well. And it makes sense.

There's an inherent need in Hollywood to pigeonhole and hire people for the same thing for the rest of their career, conceivably. Everyone has to fight that battle. Directors and writers have to deal with that, and actors, too. You have to be willing to be patient, be willing to sit and say "no" and "no" and "no" again and again and wait for something. Beat people over the head. Sit in a room with somebody and say, "Listen, take a flyer. Hire me for this," or hope that someone has an imagination, like Roland and Dean, to say, "He's just the right guy. I know he can do this." Or you have to do what a lot of people do, which is go off and do a small picture with a first-time director who, frankly, because you say you're willing to play this Italian card player, he's going to be able to get his picture made. So maybe you won't screw it up for him. Then you get the opportunity to play that. But it's a battle for everybody to avoid pigeonholing. It is possible but you do have to be tenacious.

I understand Roland and Dean asked you and Kurt Russell to do the film separately and afterwards wondered if you would actually gel on screen. Did you share that view?

Spader: Not really. It's funny. I find that actors as varied and different as they are all have one consistency about them, and that is that they all know if they've ever done a film before, and if they haven't, then they learn very quickly that there isn't enough time for crapping about. You know what I mean? Very quickly you have to get down to the business of acting, and actors all become actors instantly. Personalities are left behind. There just isn't time for it—and no room for it. No matter who I've worked with, and they can be someone who's done one film or someone who's done seventy, like Kurt, eventually once we get in the room, all are down to the same business, which is getting from point A to point B in the scene. I had actually had a mutual friend of Kurt's and mine who before I left to go on location, I said, "So, tell me what sort of fellow Kurt is." And he said, "Oh, you're gonna *love* him."

Do you have a sequel or sequels in mind?

Emmerich: Yeah, it was always the plan to do more. When we talked in the beginning about that, I only made one condition, and I said, "It has to be something really original. It's can't be a rehash." So when we did it we were pretty well prepared. I'll wait and see what happens worldwide, but it would be fun to do another one. I liked the subject and the characters. And next time, we don't have to set up so much. There was an extreme, difficult period when we were still writing the script and it got changed. It was one of those movies where you have to set up so much. What you don't want to do is constantly make dialogue that explains all of the things that go on. So we had to trick ourselves through that to avoid constantly explaining things. It was always our biggest problem.

Devlin: It was.

Emmerich: And we got through *Stargate* without too much of that. I'm really happy about that. The next time around we can really explore the characters. We also created some characters on the planet, which are interesting and we will explore more.

1995

WILLIAM FRIEDKIN
The Exorcist

"The stories about 'the curse of *The Exorcist*' are just so much balderdash." – director William Friedkin dismisses the legends that surround one of the greatest horror films ever made. (Warner Bros./Josh Weiner)

Warner Bros., 1973

CAST: Chris MacNeil, ELLEN BURSTYN; Father Merrin, MAX VON SYDOW; Lt. Kinderman, LEE J. COBB; Sharon, KITTY WINN; Burke Dennings, JACK MacGOWRAN Father Karras, JASON MILLER; Regan, LINDA BLAIR; With REVEREND WILLIAM O'MALLEY, S.J., BARTON HEYMAN, PETE MASTERSON, RUDOLF SCHUNDLER, GINA PETRUSHKA, ROBERT SYMONDS, ARTHUR STORCH, REVEREND THOMAS BERMINGHAM, S.J., VASILIKI MALIAROS, TITOS VANDIS, WALLACE ROONEY, RON FABER, DONNA MITCHELL, ROY COOPER, ROBERT GERRINGER, and MERCEDES McCAMBRIDGE as the voice of Pazuzu.

CREDITS: *Director*, William Friedkin; *written for the screen and produced by* William Peter Blatty, *based on his novel; associate producer*, David Salvern; *directors of photography*, Owen Roizman, Billy Williams; *make-up artist*, Dick Smith; *special effects*, Marcel Vercoutere; *production design*, Bill Malley; *music*, Krzysztof Penderecki, Hans Werner Heinze, George Crumb, Anton Webern, Mike Oldfield, David Borden, Jack Nitzsche; *editors*, Jordan Leondopoulos, Evan Lottman, Norman Gay, Bud Smith. Running time: 117 minutes/132 minutes (director's cut).

> "In a quiet neighborhood, in a house with all the modern conveniences, an innocent young girl becomes afflicted. Her mother can't help her. Doctors uselessly test and attempt to treat her. In desperation—fearing her illness reaches beyond the physical and

into the spiritual—her mother calls a priest. But even he doubts that evil has come into their home, into her body. And the more he doubts, the more powerful it becomes. There is only one cause, and only one hope for a cure. 'It's an excellent day for an exorcism.'"

The Supernatural in Realistic Terms
William Friedkin on *The Exorcist*

The Exorcist has been described as a film very much of its time—a bleak film for a bleak period. Would you go along with that?

William Friedkin: I don't consider the film to be bleak *at all*. You can take the whole crucifixion story of Jesus and say, "That's a bleak story as well." On the other hand, it has tremendous power and uplift. I don't find *The Exorcist* to be bleak, nor do I find the '70s to be any more bleak than it is today, certainly in terms of what's going on in the world and back here [in the US].

Did you work closely with William Peter Blatty? How much is The Exorcist *your film and how much is it Blatty's?*

It's his novel and it's my film, but we worked very closely together. I felt that my role was to bring that novel to the screen as faithfully as I could. I really believed in it. I thought that it was an absolutely wonderful novel, and quite unique. And I felt that it would work as a film the closer I stayed to it. So Blatty and I actually spent several months working together on the screenplay, even though he had already written the novel. My role in preparing the screenplay was to underline passages of the book, hand it to him and say, "Bill, I want this scene, this and this." The novel has the ability in a single sentence to go from past to present to future. In a film, I felt that it was best if we just stayed with present tense with no flashbacks—no references back to anything or forward to anything. Just a straight-ahead telling of this story.

Linda Blair's performance seems as startling now [in 1998] as it did then. Could you describe the process by which you cast her and were you in any way protective of her when it came to the material?

I became a kind of a surrogate father to Linda and remain so to this day. There were literally thousands of young women who auditioned for [the part of Regan MacNeil]. I didn't see them all, but there were casting directors all over the United States trying to find her, and after a while, Blatty and I thought that it couldn't be done. We then started to look for a sixteen or seventeen-year-old young woman who might look younger. The young women that I was seeing—of twelve and thirteen years old—were obviously not going to be suitable.

And then one day Linda Blair came into my office. She was brought by her mother. She was actually represented by a casting agency that represented young boys and young girls. They had sent maybe twenty-five or thirty of the people that they represented over for us to see. They did not recommend Linda. Linda's mother brought her in on her own. Linda really hadn't done anything up to that point except some print advertising. But when she came in the room, I knew immediately that she was the one. She was intelligent, she was perceptive, she didn't seem to be bothered by the subject matter, and she understood it.

Then once I cast her—which I did after testing her with Ellen Burstyn, who had already been cast—what I tried to do was make it all a big game for her. Make it fun. And you'll see, if you look at the rushes of this film, that she comes out doing some of the most outrageous imaginable things, and then I would say, "Cut." And before the camera was cut, you'd see a stagehand hand her a milkshake and she'd start giggling and laughing. The whole thing was just made to be a big game for her. It was not taken seriously as far as she was concerned.

The audience wouldn't know that. How much was she doubled? For instance the famous masturbation with the crucifix sequence: was that her or was that a double?

It's certainly her face. The quick shot of the crucifix entering the vagina area is a double. Obviously it didn't have to be Linda, and so she wasn't even on the set that day. But it *is* her that you see sort of from the shoulders up: her face and when she's lunging the crucifix. There is a total of about twenty-six seconds in the entire film where a double was used, [mainly of] shots behind Linda. I remember we timed it once in the editing room to see how much we actually did not make use of Linda. There's a shot where I wanted her to throw a backhanded slap at this doctor, and the double does that. Everything else is her.

What was the key to locating that impressive ensemble cast?

The key to the casting was first of all to find Regan, and as I say, the movie gods delivered us Linda Blair. The next key to the casting would probably be Jason Miller, who had also never acted in a film, had done very little acting before he did this role. He was a playwright, but at the time he only had one play [*That Championship Season*, 1973], which was wonderful and had won a Pulitzer Prize over here [in the US]. But Jason was a journeyman actor doing supporting roles very far off Broadway. He was not known as an actor at all. I discovered him by pure chance as well.

So I guess the essential team was first getting Linda, then getting Jason, and then getting Ellen [Burstyn], even though I had Ellen first. Ellen was the first one I cast. I didn't know what I wanted for those three roles. There was no one I could go to and say, "I want this person" who had done work that I admire. Linda and Jason had never done anything on film, and Ellen was a very good supporting actress. But Max von Sydow is the guy I always wanted to play Father Merrin. He was on my wish list initially. There was no second choice.

How did actors like Lee J. Cobb and Mercedes McCambridge take to the subject matter? Did they buy into it or was it just another job?

Nobody who worked on the film took it as just another job. It was a significant piece of work for all of us, myself included. Mercedes McCambridge bought into it totally. She was a rather devout Catholic, and when she recorded the demon voice, which took us about a month to achieve, working every day, she had two priests with her at all times in the dubbing room.

Lee J. Cobb [as Lt. Kinderman] was a bit more cynical about the whole thing than some of the others. Lee would not necessarily buy into the story in terms of reality. But if you ask me my opinion, he gives the best performance in the film. He's one of the great American actors, one of the best we've ever had, and it was a great experience to work with him. So of the two people you mention, he was a bit more cynical about the subject matter, although he gave a very neat performance, very low-key for Lee J. Cobb.

The language in the film retains the power to shock even now. Was there a problem at the time getting that language passed?

It's really interesting. I believe that the only reason *The Exorcist* appeared with no cuts and with what we then called an "R" rating—which meant restricted; children of seventeen or under could not see the film unless accompanied by a parent—and not with an "X" rating, which would have meant it was restricted totally to adults was because of one person: Aaron Stern. He started the Motion Picture Code and ran the ratings board at that time.

It was his idea of how it was coordinated, and it was his decision to release the film that way. I believe that the present ratings board, and the ratings board that followed him, would have asked for a great many cuts, especially back in the '70s. The film would have probably not have been shown in its present form at all. It was only due to the mindset of this one individual that it went out the way it did. Certain other countries where the film was played should have followed the lead of the American ratings board.

After Stern retired, the board became very, very restrictive. It really operated as censorship. And Stern didn't believe in censorship. He believed in *caveat emptor*: tell people what it is, let them be aware that the content may be strong for children, and then it's up to them to decide if they want to see it or not.

Who were your inspirations for the look of the film? Were they painters?

Those films that I did give you a sort of Impressionistic overview of what was influencing me. The music of Stravinsky, the music of certain contemporary classical composers—excerpts from which appear in the film—like Hans Werner Henze, Krzysztof Penderecki, and George Crumb. Largely that music. Also the music of Shostakovich. The paintings of Magritte. There's a painting called *The Empire of Lights*, which totally inspired the image of Sydow approaching the house for the first time. No other film that I can think of. There was no precedent for this kind of a film. I'm not a big fan of horror films. There are several that I like, *Rosemary's Baby* [1968] being one, certainly. I had seen that, but it did not influence *The Exorcist* in any way other than both films attempt to portray the supernatural in realistic terms.

Why did you film The Exorcist *in Georgetown, Washington? And do you have your own religious beliefs?*

The original story took place in a little town called Silver Spring, Maryland, which is moments away from Georgetown. Blatty went to Georgetown and graduated from there with a degree in English Literature. He set his novel in Georgetown. As I said earlier, I wanted to be faithful to the novel. Georgetown itself has a wonderful atmosphere, a wonderful feeling. It's the feeling I get when I go into the East End of London, specifically Whitechapel, today. And as much as Whitechapel has changed in the hundred years since the Jack the Ripper killings, there is an aura that takes place when you walk down the streets of Whitechapel. It's true of Georgetown as well.

As for my own religious beliefs, I guess I could be called an agnostic. My definition of that is I believe that the power of God and the soul are unknowable. I don't believe that the revealed Word is given to any one religion over another. I think that there is a lot of beautiful ideas and thought in Catholicism as well as Buddhism and any number of other religions. I was brought up in the Jewish faith but I'm not a practicing Jew at all. In fact, I feel closer to the doctrines of the Catholic Church, although I couldn't call myself a Catholic. I don't feel that I would make the cut as a practicing Catholic. I do to this day consider myself an agnostic and very much a believer. I just don't know any more than I *believe*. I cannot define it any further for you.

There has been much talk of the curse that allegedly afflicted the film. What are your thoughts on that and have you experienced anything odd since you made the movie?

The stories about "the curse of *The Exorcist*" are just so much balderdash. I really don't know what that means. People talk about a number of people who died after the film was made, or relatives of certain actors who passed away while it was filming. It took about ten months to film *The Exorcist*, and the overall process took two years from its inception to the final cut to when it appeared on screens initially. And in a two-year period, you're gonna get a lot of people that, you know, die. I did a film [*The Night They Raided Minsky's*, 1968] back in the late '60s with Bert Lahr, the great music hall comedian. He died during the making of the film [and] before he could finish his role. No one was really talking about a curse back then. There were certain strange things that happened that had never happened on any film I did before or since, like the set burned to the ground for no reason. That was attributed, I guess, to some sort of a curse, but I don't put any real stock in that. Most of the things that happened were normal things that would happen over a two-year period.

You've directed almost all genres of movie, including comedies, musicals, and even a film from a Harold Pinter play. In terms of The Exorcist, *did you have to adopt a different approach to maintain the intensity that was required?*

Not really. The intensity comes from the script. I remember there was a great deal of intensity on the set of *The Birthday Party* [1968], which I did in England and which was written by Pinter. There was a great deal of intensity there and concentration on the material.

My recollection of the filming of *The Exorcist* was that it was a lot of fun. At times it was very difficult to bring off. There were no opticals in the film. Opticals hadn't even approached the capability that they have now with digital technology and computers. Most of the stuff would have been done on a computer back then. In those days, we had to do it live, mechanically. We had to achieve these effects as best we could, and so that part of it was difficult.

The Iraq shoot was difficult, simply because it was a political hotbed at the time. Iraq was at war on all of its borders and within the country with the Kurds. We were filming while all of this was going on. There was no diplomatic protection at all. We were in the hands of the Baathist Party that did then and does now [in 1998] rule Iraq. Having said that, I must say I loved being over there. It was a great experience and I made many friends. In terms of my contact with them, I found the Iraqis to be absolutely marvelous as a people.

How much religious preparation did you do for the film and what kind of involvement did you have from genuine priests?

There was no direct official cooperation from the Church. Many high officials of the Catholic Church in America and in Italy were aware of it and did help us but on an individual basis. There are two priests who played priests in the film, Father Dyer [played by William O'Malley] and Father Thomas Bermingham [who played Tom, the president of the university]. They were also technical advisers. They are both Jesuit priests and are now together teaching at Fordham University in New York. They were very helpful, and they act in the film. There was a Father John Nicola, who's passed away. He was a Jesuit and he was considered the foremost expert on exorcism in the Church in the United States at that time. He was on the set every day that the exorcism scene was filmed.

At the highest levels of the Catholic Church, the film was widely praised. The Cardinal of New York, the head of the Jesuit order in Italy, then Father Pedro Arrupe, was a very big supporter of the film. Obviously they realized that it was basically putting forward pure Catholic doctrines, and there were these cases. This was based on an actual case that is thoroughly and widely documented. It was in the newspapers at the time. *The Washington Post* in 1949 did three pages in one issue on this particular case that the film is based on. It's considered one of the few actual cases of possession in the twentieth century in America. So, yes, I had a lot of individual Church cooperation at some levels of the Church. A great many practicing Catholics took offense at it, far less than those who supported it.

Looking at the film today, are there any changes that you would make to it now?

Obviously, I've spent a lot of time looking at it over the last few months because I supervised the new print and the new video. No. It's the only film of mine that I've made where I wouldn't change a frame. I love the performances, I think that's what makes it: the people. The actors just embody their characters. I wouldn't have any other actors play any of these roles. If I could reach back into history or reshoot it in the present day and substitute another performance, I wouldn't do it. I can't say that at all about all the films I've made.

And for the most part, I'm like most other filmmakers, which is that I would *constantly* re-edit my films if I could. There's the famous story of Bonnard, the Impressionist painter, who was eighty years old, and his works were hanging in the Louvre. He went in with a little palette and some brushes and he was painting over one of his canvases. They grabbed him and arrested him and he said, "But I'm Bonnard! This is my painting!" and they said, "Sorry. It's hanging in the Louvre. It's finished!" Most film directors I know have a great affinity with Bonnard: we would constantly tinker with our work. I wouldn't touch a frame of *The Exorcist*, neither to add nor subtract.

You've been quoted as saying you didn't think the original could be improved upon. Is that an accurate quote?

Anything can be improved on. I feel that this is the best version of *The Exorcist*. It was never cut for censorship anywhere that I'm aware of, certainly not in the States. The version that you've just seen is the version that I cut, and the scenes that I took out of the film I took out for reasons of pacing, clarity—some of the scenes I felt were just redundant. So I took out about five or six scenes. I even asked to take them out. That was done mainly for pacing concerns.

Why haven't you restored the scenes that were cut from the film, specifically the scene where Regan crawls down the stairs like a spider, given that fans have long debated those sequences and want to see them in the film?

Tony, I just felt that the scene that you refer to was over the top. There was so much going on in the film in terms of the apparitions, the special effects; I just felt that that was one too many. It was a problem of the writing. We could never really resolve that easily and get to the next sequence. There are four or five other scenes. They are, by the way, all going to be put on a digital videodisc and on a laser disc when it's released as a separate chapter.

I'm not reintegrating it into the film. I don't feel that the film requires them. I didn't at the time. I cut them, as I say, either for reasons of redundancy or, in the case of the spider walk, [because] it was over the top. But people who are able to see the laser disc or the DVD will be able to look at them and decide for themselves. I don't know why the cut scenes acquired such a reputation, or how it even got out that these scenes were cut. I have no idea. But they were cut because I felt they were not necessary to the final edit.

What is your take on the controversy that surrounds the film twenty-five years on, and particularly in the UK, where we're unable to see the film on video?

It's hard for me to speak about the laws or the censorship of another country. I don't know why it isn't shown on video [in the UK]. I think it should be up to the public to decide if they want to see the video or see the film. I don't think the government should dictate that to people. I'm aware of the concern over young children seeing it, but again I think that's a parental responsibility or should be, rather than the responsibility of the state. I was surprised by the controversy. I always felt that the film was powerful and intense, but why it stirred so many emotions both positive and negative still escapes me.

After all this time, are you able to look at the film objectively?

Yes, I can, and it's not lost its power to move me, as well. I have more distance from it, of course, and I can now deal with it as a story quite apart from my own participation, but I do find it very intense and very powerful.

How would you feel if, at some point in the future, someone decided to make a new version of The Exorcist?

More power to them. I don't know whether you're aware of it, but there's some guy over here [in the States] who's trying to do a television series based on *The Exorcist*—the exorcism of the week or something. Then there's another producer who's planning to do a so-called prequel to *The Exorcist*, I guess not realizing that there *was* a so-called prequel made. It was called *Exorcist II* [1977], which was a load of rubbish beyond definition. *Exorcist II*, in my opinion, was a travesty, as was *Exorcist III* [1990]. But this is what happens when you do something that has a degree of success. They wanna do sequels.

I would have nothing to do with any sequel. I didn't then; I wouldn't now. Of course, anyone is welcome to remake it. If it's remade as *Psycho* [1960] has been remade, it means it's achieved a kind of classic status and it's sort of public domain. Why shouldn't it be remade for another generation? Although I think that the version that you saw this evening certainly is adequate for this generation and perhaps one or two beyond this. But it doesn't mean that it's not possible to do it better than I've done it. It clearly is.

Did you personally ever at any stage toy with the notion of doing a sequel to The Exorcist *or to* The French Connection? *Were you tempted? Were persuaders dangled in front of you?*

Of course, but it was not even a consideration. I wouldn't do a sequel to *The Exorcist* if they had offered me $100 million. Or *The French Connection* [1971]. It was of no interest to me whatever. I thought that the idea of a sequel would simply be to rip off the original. There was no reason for a sequel. Everything that needed to be said about *The Exorcist* is said in that film.

Look at the sequels that they've made. They're pathetic. The sequel to *The Godfather* [1972], *Godfather II* [1974], is a very great film. Francis Coppola had a vision for *Godfather II*, as did Mario Puzo. They could see a way to extend that story. The story in fact lends itself to extension—other, earlier generations. A film like *The Exorcist*—and *The French Connection*—is set very much in the present. You don't need a prequel and you sure as hell don't need a sequel.

I would have been no more interested in doing sequels to those films than in agreeing to let them put stills of *The Exorcist* on a cornflakes box. There's no reason to do it other than strictly to commercialize something. At that time and now, I really think that even though all of my films are not as good as this, and my work is probably very uneven, I think of myself as working in an art form. I don't think of myself as manufacturing bricks.

If you were making The Exorcist *for the first time now, would you be able to make that same film?*

It's not that my affections are for then as opposed to now. I'm simply giving you my opinion of how it was then and how it is now. The people who were at the head of the studios then clearly had more of the elements of showmanship about them, that is for sure. Today many of the studios are run by accountants, agents, executives, ex-accountants, and ex-lawyers.

Would that script have got green-lit in 1998?

I doubt it. It's hard to say, but I don't think so. I think it's still very much against the grain today. There was a lot of concern when we made it. The head of the studio, Ted Ashley [Chairman of Warner Bros, 1969-80] reluctantly green-lit *The Exorcist*. He was afraid of it once he saw it. He wasn't sure quite how to release it. And he didn't know if there'd be a posse coming after him, picketing his house and burning crosses on his lawn.

There was a lot of fear at that time because those films did not have a mass release initially. *The Exorcist* was initially released in the United States in twenty-six theaters in six months. It expanded to fifty theaters within those six months simply because they were literally breaking down doors to get in. They couldn't have put it in three thousand theaters even. There weren't mass releases then. You had *Jaws* [1975] a couple of years later. You had *The Godfather* a year later. That was released in eight hundred or a thousand theaters in America.

The Exorcist went out in twenty-six theaters because the studio was *terrified* of what the response might be. They wanted to release it, but they wanted to do it by just dipping a toe in the water, so to speak. I don't know if you could make it today. They've done some stuff that they call *Exorcist III* or whatever, and it's *nothing*. They're just using the title.

How much has Hollywood changed since the days of The Exorcist?

Compared to the way it was twenty-five years ago, it's brilliant now. In those days, at the major studios there was one person who made a decision. They usually made that decision by the seat of their pants. Because the costs were so much less in those days, it wasn't a disaster if you failed. Today the failure of one film could bring down the management of the studio! In the '70s and prior to that, they would make hits, they would make some films that didn't work, and the studios go on.

Today you have all these levels of executives—various levels of development people—before you get to the Head of Production. All of the major studios are owned by the biggest corporations in America. The kinds of films that you see have been largely sanitized so that the corporation doesn't offend anybody. [They] own and control what films are made, and that's why they license this drivel. We largely produce stuff that is forgettable. You walk out of the theater and you don't even remember what you just saw. In my opinion, most of this stuff is just not on, as far as I'm concerned. And I think that's one part of it. The old-fashioned showmen when I was making these films in the '70s, they're gone and forgotten.

Now for everything that they do, they'll take a poll. "What shall we do? How shall we do this story? What shall we cut? What shall we add? What should be in it? What shouldn't be in it?" Market research dictates American film.

They have what they call "synergy." I put quotes around that. Warner Bros., for example, that made *The Exorcist*, is now Time Warner with *Time* magazine and a whole bunch of cable stations and God knows what else. The only other business Warner Bros. was in at the time they made *The Exorcist* was a funeral parlor business. They were undertakers. So if they made a bad film in those days, they would just bury it. That was the only "synergy" involved then.

1998

TERRY GILLIAM
Twelve Monkeys

"I'd met Bruce Willis on *The Fisher King* [1991] and liked him enormously. I said, 'Yeah, let's do it.'" – Terry Gilliam (with Bruce Willis in costume as James Cole) on the Philadelphia location of *Twelve Monkeys*. (Atlas Entertainment/Phil Caruso)

Atlas Entertainment, 1995

CAST: James Cole, BRUCE WILLIS; Dr. Kathryn Railly, MADELEINE STOWE; Jeffrey Goines, BRAD PITT; Dr. Leland Goines, CHRISTOPHER PLUMMER; Dr. Fletcher, FRANK GORSHIN; Jose, JON SEDA; Young Cole, JOSEPH MERLITO; Scarface, MICHAEL CHANCE; Tiny, VERNON CAMPBELL; Botanist, H. MICHAEL WALLS; Geologist, BOB ADRIAN; Zoologist, SIMON JONES; Astrophysicist, CAROL FLORENCE; Microbiologist, BILL RAYMOND; Engineer, ERNEST ABUBA; Poet, IRMA ST. PAULE; Detective Franki, JOEY PERILLO; Policemen, BRUCE KIRKPATRICK, WILFRED WILLIAMS; Billings, ROZWILL YOUNG; Ward Nurse, NEIL JOHNSON; Fred Strother, L.J. WASHINGTON; Dr. Casey, RICK WARNER; Dr. Goodwin, ANTHONY "CHIP" BRIENZA; Harassed Mother, JULIET HARRIS; Waltzing Woman Patient, BRUCIE McDANIEL; Old Man Patient, JOHN BLAISSE; Patient at Gate, LOUIS LIPPA; X-Ray Doctor, STAN KANG; WW1 Captain, PAT DIAS; WW1 Sergeant, AARON MICHAEL LACEY; Dr. Peters, DAVID MORSE; Professor, CHARLES TECHMAN; Marilou, JANN ELLIS;

Officer #1, JOHNNIE HOBBS, JR; Anchorwoman, JANET L. ZAPPALA; Evangelist, THOMAS ROY; Louie/Raspy Voice, HARRY O'TOOLE; Thugs, KORCHENKO, CHUCK JEFFREYS; Teddy, LISA GAY HAMILTON; Fale, FELIX A. PIRE; Bee, MATTHEW ROSS; Agents, BARRY PRICE, JOHN PANZARELLA, LARRY DALY; Anchorman, ARTHUR FENNELL; Pompous Man, KARL WARREN; Lt. Halperin, CHRISTOPHER MELONI; Detective Dalva, PAUL MESHEJIAN; Wayne, ROBERT O'NEILL; Kweskin, KEVIN THIGPEN; Hotel Clerk, LEE GOLDEN; Wallace, JOSEPH McKENNA; Plain Clothes Cop, JEFF TANNER; Store Clerk, FAITH POTTS; Weller, MICHAEL RYAN SEGAL; Woman Cabbie, ANNIE GOLDEN; Ticket Agent, LISA TALERICO; Airport Detective, STEPHEN BRIDGEWATER; Plump Businessman, FRANKLIN HUFFMAN; Gift Store Clerk, JOHN S. DAWSON; Airport Security, JACK DOUGHERTY, LENNY DANIELS, HERBERT C. HAULS, JR; Impatient Traveler, CHARLEY SCALIES; Terrified Traveler, CAROLYN WALKER.

CREDITS: *Director,* Terry Gilliam; *executive producers,* Robert Cavallo, Gary Levinsohn, Robert Kosberg; *producer,* Charles Roven; *co-producer,* Lloyd Phillips; *associate producers,* Kelley Smith-Wait, Mark Egerton; *screenplay,* David Peoples, Janet Peoples, inspired by the film La Jetée by Chris Marker; *director of photography,* Roger Pratt; *editor,* Mick Audsley; *production designer,* Jeffrey Beecroft; *art director,* Wm Ladd Skinner; *special effects mechanical and pyrotechnic engineer,* Vincent Montefusco; *special effects project manager,* Shirley Montefusco; *on-set supervisor,* Anthony Simonaitas; *costume designer,* Julie Weiss; *make-up/hair design,* Christina Beveridge; *music,* Elliot Goldenthal. Running time: 129 minutes.

"The year is 2035 and humankind subsists in a desolate netherworld following the eradication of 99 percent of the Earth's population, a holocaust that makes the planet's surface uninhabitable, and mankind's destiny uncertain.

"In order to preserve their fate in this grave new world, survivors must rely on time travel as their only hope. Desperately hoping that the resources of the past might help them reclaim and rebuild the future, a group of scientists living beneath the once populous Philadelphia secure a volunteer to embark on an experimental trip back to the year 1996. There, they hope he can help mankind's

desperate efforts to unravel this apocalyptic nightmare before it completely erases humanity from the planet.

Cole is the reluctant volunteer who may or may not be the ideal candidate to complete this dangerous assignment. However, he possesses a significant trait that supersedes the scientists' doubts—his obsession with a haunting image from his childhood, a memory whose meaning cannot be understood, even though it replays itself endlessly in his tortured mind.

When Cole arrives in 1996, he meets Jeffrey Goines, the unstable son of a renowned scientist, and Dr. Kathryn Railly, a psychiatrist and author whose expertise lies in the study of madness and prophecy. Railly first diagnoses Cole as delusional; more simply, a madman. However, as their relationship grows, her alarm over his prophetic warnings of the world's fate turns to conviction, and she comes to believe that mankind may indeed be doomed.

While also questioning his own sanity, Cole struggles with Railly to unravel the mystery with his only two clues: the haunting childhood memory and a series of puzzling symbols from a group known only as The Army of the Twelve Monkeys."

Giraffes on the Freeway
Terry Gilliam on *Twelve Monkeys*

How do you begin to pitch a movie like Twelve Monkeys?

Terry Gilliam: We didn't have to; that's what was nice about it. They came to me. And the irony was it was Universal, the studio that I'd had this huge battle with over *Brazil* [1985] with. There's actually an Englishman working in Universal, Barry Isaacson, and he prides himself on being the fifth columnist. He slipped me this script, [whispering] "It's really weird!" I read it and as he said, it was weird and wonderful and intriguing. I'm a big fan of [screenwriter] David Peoples. *Unforgiven* [1992] is the last decent film that was made. And so I read it, but I was working on a couple of other projects. The strange thing was [that] in all the projects that I was working on—one was one of my own and the other was *A Tale of Two Cities*—in all cases, the hero dies in the end! It was like a magnet that was sucking dead heroes towards me! [Laughs]

So I read it and said, "Great. But I'm working on my own projects." But Chuck Roven, the producer, is a very tenacious man, and he just went on and on. And when my project collapsed and when *A Tale of Two Cities* collapsed—Mel Gibson [who was to play Sydney Carton] left and went off to be a director on *Braveheart* [1995]—I said, "I better work again. It's been four-and-a-half years since I was behind a camera." So off we went. And I said, "If I'm gonna come back to Universal, fine. But I've gotta have total control over this thing—final cut, all of those things."

I was originally trying to do it as low budget as possible so we could maintain total control because even with final cut, when you've got a lot of nervous nellies around—you still get into problem situations. And it went on. We started working on it and being as complex a film as it is, the studio wanted a star in it. There was a period when they started throwing names at me and I said, "Nah" and I walked away. Then Bruce's name came up and they said he was really keen to talk to me about doing it. I'd met him on *The Fisher King* [1991] and liked him enormously. We met in New York and talked and I said, "Yeah, let's do it."

It's only the second time you've not been involved in originating the screenplay. In this particular case you were given a screenplay. Did you provide input as it developed or did you leave it as it was?

That's what is so odd: people keep thinking it's *my* film and these are *my* ideas. It just happens that I'm sympathetic with all the ideas. I do [contribute] things, but it's pretty much the script they [David Peoples and Janet Peoples] wrote. Little details are changed. When you write about it, don't give away the ending, because that was the thing that attracted me the most to the film—the idea of a person seeing their own death. It was just extraordinary.

The film balances lo-tech with hi-tech. It's something you've done before. Is there a pattern to this approach?

No. It was a bit frustrating because I knew *Twelve Monkeys* would be compared to *Brazil*. I knew I was going to get this kind of question! [Laughs] But that's exactly what they wrote, the justification being that if people had to dive underground to survive, they would grab whatever technology from the twentieth century they could take with them and it would be that kind of place. There it was and there was no escaping from it: "Oh, it's *Brazil* again! Here we go." But I did like the fact that technology, as impressive as it is with time machines, is very imperfect. That's important as part of the story.

Assuming that the screenwriters drew their inspiration from La Jetée [1962] *for the script, did Chris Marker's film influence you at all visually?*

No, I've never seen *La Jetée*. I've seen pictures. And somebody spotted the hammocks that [the characters are] in at the beginning. Apparently they had hammocks in *La Jetée*. But it's actually almost a mistake. Some of the American critics have spent *pages* comparing *Twelve Monkeys* to *La Jetée*. I think that's a waste of time because we weren't making a remake of *La Jetée*. David and Jan saw *La Jetée*, the producer had bought the rights to do something with *La Jetée* and said, "We don't want to make a remake of this but there are some really interesting ideas [including] seeing your own death, time travel...." You could say *The Terminator* [1984] is as influenced by *La Jetée* as *Twelve Monkeys* is. I've watched many critics wax lyrical about this one. It shows how many films they've seen, but it doesn't really relate.

Given the complex back-and-forth nature of the narrative, did you have to take extra care with Bruce Willis and Madeleine Stowe so that they could always find their place in the story?

We helped each other because we all kept getting lost. We literally did. It was the most unenjoyable filmmaking I've ever done. I didn't like getting up in the morning. We were all very tense and uncertain. There's a scene with Madeleine and Frank Gorshin saying, "We're the new priests, psychiatry is the new religion, and I'm losing my faith." And we shot that. Then the next day Madeleine called me and said, "I think we made a mistake," referring to the emotional level of the scene. "We thought it was later on in the film," and I said, "It *is* later on in the film." "No, no, it's *here* in the film." And we constantly did this: got lost.

The making of it was very much like the film itself, and incredibly unnerving. We actually went back and reshot that scene with her taking her performance down. But the irony was that when we did the final cut of the film, we put the original wrong shoot in because the whole film had gotten up to a height that we didn't expect.

We kept asking, "Do we need to shoot this scene? Are we telling the story? Is there enough information? Are we being too obtuse?" And Mick Audsley, the editor, said, "Just pack a lot of socks because I'm coming back to England to cut this thing. Make sure you've got a lot of socks for the journey in the editing room!" There are really no scenes missing. Scenes have been cut down, but it is pretty much what it was.

Given that you weren't making films for four-and-a-half years and that your relationship with Hollywood has not been a comfortable one, what kept you going? Did you feel like quitting altogether?

No. It was success that fucked me up, basically. *The Fisher King* was a successful film, and suddenly I got all these offers. Being a greedy person, I started going, "That's really good. I'll make *that* film. Oh, *that's* a better one!" Before, by being the bastard I'd been with them, all the doors were shut except usually one at a time that I was trying to push open.

Then suddenly, I had all these choices. I would literally start on a project and then lose confidence in it or it wasn't moving fast enough, and I'd leap to something else that came along. I wasted—well, I didn't waste—but I spent four years effectively getting into the kind of development hell that I'd so smugly warned other people not to get into.

What's been so strange with this one is that I've been waiting for the other shoe to drop somewhere with the studios. But they were great. The marketing people were right there from the beginning on this film. At most I had one half-hour conversation with the head of the studio. He said, "It would be nice if he was a little more dynamic, if he saved a little bit more of the world but it's your film. Go with my blessing." So that was it. It was a surprisingly pleasant experience.

There is a clip from Hitchcock's Vertigo [1958] *in the film. Why are filmmakers so keen on* Vertigo?

I never even questioned it. It was in the script. And basically what was in the script was the section where it says "This is where I was born and this is where I die." I've just been in Paris doing interviews and I found out that apparently Chris Marker's favorite film was *Vertigo*. He spent a lot of time writing about it. I don't know if David and Janet had spoken to him or they knew that because to choose *Vertigo* of all films—well, there it is.

What was interesting about that scene, though, was that Mick Audsley, again the wise man that he is, started playing with it. There's more of a dialogue between the four characters than there was in the script. And then it grew beyond that. Because we had to have Madeleine in a blonde wig in the foyer of a cinema, suddenly we were in a Hitchcock film with a Hitchcock blonde. Now that wasn't planned, because in the script [Stowe's character], Railly was blonde and she wore a black wig, but because I cast Madeleine, it went this way. It was only when we were shooting it that I realized that all these things had come together. It's like we were in a Hitchcock film.

And it got even stranger. Having finished the cut—and we put that Bernard Herrmann music from *Vertigo* over the scene in the foyer—we had a problem with the sound because we were getting it from the original print and it was wowing. So we had to go back and get another copy of it. So we had to take the tape and try to find out where that bit of music came from. And this was not planned: it turns out it came from exactly the spot where Kim Novak is turned into a blonde and comes forward. The cuts are exactly the same rhythm, cutting from him to her. It was a very peculiar, strange, and mysterious moment when we discovered that. We leapt around a lot thinking, *there are obviously forces at work here*. [Laughs]

How did you come to cast Frank Gorshin?

Margery Simkin, the casting director, said, "I wonder what Frank Gorshin looks like these days." I don't know why she said that. And so I said, "Let's go and find out." So we called him in to play the part of the desk clerk in the seedy hotel. And he said, "There must be something bigger than this for me." And I said, "What do you want?" And he said, "I'd like to play Dr. Goines." I said, "Chris Plummer's playing that." "How about Dr. Fletcher?" And he read for it and he was brilliant. And I thought the idea of the Riddler [from the 1960s TV show *Batman*] being the head of a psychiatric institute seemed too good to pass up. He's actually a wonderful actor. He was trained as a serious dramatic classical actor, but unfortunately he could do impersonations and his whole career went *phffft* over there [in the US].

Sci-fi dramas like this have a habit of opening slowly and then building a head of steam. This one actually opened very strongly with audiences in the United States. Were you confident of that or did you think you'd have a cult film on your hands?

[Laughs] Being cursed with a cult film is the worst thing you can do to somebody! It just means you don't make any money and nobody sees it! No, I thought with Bruce Willis and Brad Pitt, one or two people would come on the opening day. It would be very hard to keep them away. But my fear was that they would come with the wrong expectations and then see *this* thing, say "Fuck that!" and then disappear.

But it hasn't happened. They're going again and again. I actually think the pendulum has swung in America, I honestly do, and that more intelligent, more demanding films are making their way through. Audiences have had ten years of formula and they seem to be changing. I think *Seven* [1995] is a case in point. It's not an easy film. Just because Brad is in it doesn't mean it's gonna be a big hit. And then they seem to be craving something. We're finding with the returns on *Twelve Monkeys* that they're going again and again. It's reaching a much larger and much less intellectual audience than I suspected. So it's clearly filling a need.

What was the route that Brad Pitt took to the project?

It was a very strange time where superstars were begging to be in this movie. Bruce convinced me he could do it. And then I kept hearing that Brad wanted to do this thing and I said, "I won't see him, because he's wrong." Eventually he came to London and saw me. He was *so* determined. In the course of the meal he convinced me that he could do it. He just wanted to prove that he could do things that were different and was trying to escape from the blonde, blue-eyed bimbo chap.

My real reason for doing it was I was feeling that I'd sold out by having Bruce—that I was suddenly making a commercial film. I thought, *Now here's a chance to really endanger this project if I was to put Brad in. He's going to take this character and make a hash of it!* And that's what I was feeling for several months having agreed to have him in it. I thought that was going to happen.

We got him together with a man named Stephen Bridgewater, [a private drama coach] who had worked with Jeff Bridges on *The Fisher King* to train Jeff as a DJ. He and Brad sat down together, and Stephen called me, I remember, at the end of the first session. He said, "What have I ever done to you to deserve this? He's incapable of doing it. He's got a lazy tongue. He can't hold his breath for more than five seconds. He has no ability to speak fast or enunciate properly." I thought, *Oh, that's a good start! Here we go.*

And then he started working. Little by little, he became more confident. Brad was supposed to be sending me tapes every couple of weeks of his progress, which he consistently failed to do and made me even more nervous. We were arranging for him to go to psychiatric hospitals and watch schizophrenics at work and talk to a lot of doctors. He even had himself interviewed by a psychiatrist, in character. He worked amazingly hard at it. He's a very diligent, earnest guy.

And then he arrived on the day to do it, and he *did* it. What you see there—that first scene where he's introduced—that's the first day's shooting. That's what he did the first day, and it's extraordinary. The trouble is that by the end of the day, he was this limp rag; he couldn't move. He'd been kicking, twitching, jerking all over the place, and he was completely destroyed for the next day's work. I'm really impressed with him. He's very cautious about this superstardom that's been thrust upon him, and he's determined to prove that he's an actor first and this star thing is secondary. The dark contact lenses with the skewed eye—that's all his idea. He did it. I just put the camera in the right place.

If the tide is turning and Hollywood is accepting things that aren't overtly commercial, do you think your relationship with them will get easier and that your projects won't cave in as they have done in the past?

I don't know. I think because this has done well, I'm good for six months of positive reaction from Hollywood. After that—they've got a short memory there. I don't trust any of it. I don't spend time there. A telephone and a fax are enough to keep in touch with what's going on. At the moment, things are riding high, so I'm going to try and take advantage of it, basically. After *Twelve Monkeys* bombs, I'll be back in the dustbin again. The irony is that I never wanted to work with stars. With all the earlier films, the film was the star. It was about getting the right actors. Then, for a variety of reasons, I seem to be attractive to stars now. They come knocking on my door, which, of course, makes the projects more likely. I'm not sure exactly how it's gonna work yet. I'm a bit confused at this point.

Given the success of the Peoples' script and the continued frustrations you have experienced setting up your own projects, would you ever give up that element and simply become a director for hire?

No, because I don't really get any pleasure out of it. The directing part is the unpleasant part. When we were actually shooting it, that was the hard work. If I'm not obsessed with the material, then I just don't care to do it. I get scripts all the time—literally several a week. All of them have been successful films and I haven't done them. *Roger Rabbit* [*Who Framed Roger Rabbit*, 1988] was one of the big ones. I tend to forget them. *The Truman Show* [1998], I turned that one down. I didn't turn *Cutthroat Island* [1995] down. I *wanted* to do that one! But Renny [Harlin] got there first.

What about A Tale of Two Cities?

I'm very sanguine about the whole thing. I spent a long time working on it with Don Macpherson, who's a local writer [from the north of England]. He wrote a really wonderful script. They'd spent, like, two years on this, seducing Mel Gibson into playing Sydney Carton. I was kind of intrigued because I thought of all the stars, he could actually pull it off. I think he's a good actor and he could do a decent English accent.

I was seeing it slightly different: Sydney Carton as a middle-aged drunk, rather than a twenty-eight-year-old or whatever he is in the book. Then they got me in. With Hollywood and films, it's always about assembling this house of cards. So they had Mel, they had a script, they had a studio, then they needed a director that Mel was gonna be happy with, and I became that person. So we had a house of cards that was standing for a moment, and then Mel changed his mind and said he wanted to be a director. So off he went. And then we were in a situation madly trying to get another star.

So we did the lists and ended up with finally with Liam Neeson. This was the time when he was nominated for *Schindler's List* [1993]. Now they would have done the film for $60 million with Mel Gibson playing it. We got the budget for the same film—same sets, same everything—down to $31 million with Liam, and they wouldn't go [ahead]. "Twenty-six for Liam," they said. And that was the end of the conversation.

You see, these things just fall apart. So my attitude is when they get the star and the money and it all looks good to me and I like the person that they've got *and* the money's solid, then I would consider it. But I think I have learned my lesson about getting seduced into these things. They're great fun in a sense. You're on the phone all the time, you're talking movies, and you're going off to see locations. You actually feel like you're making a movie. You get all this energy going, and I can see it—I can see the shots. And then the rug is pulled out from under you. It's just crushing. I don't know how most directors put up with it, but most of them do. They deal with it. Luckily, I've only had to spend the last four years doing that.

Movies invariably stop traffic on location. How did this one go?

Those opening scenes with Bruce wandering around the snowed-in, decayed city, that's Philadelphia City Hall. It's the dead center of the city. It has a great roundabout going round it. We shot on a Saturday, so we didn't actually stop traffic for more than three minutes at a time. We'd put all these snow blankets and things on the ground and we had a camera right on the ground. About forty feet out from the camera, where this roundabout was, we did a little lip that went up maybe a foot-and-a-half with the snow on. It was just enough with the angle of the camera, and so you could actually have traffic going through. The things we couldn't have going through were the buses. We had to step them. It was quite extraordinary.

Philadelphia is very film-friendly. The mayor—he may not be after he's seen this version of Philadelphia—is smart and he liked the idea. You go to Philadelphia and you drive around and you have people coming up saying, "Do you know where the stairs are that Rocky ran up?" And they probably ask where Tom Hanks died in *Philadelphia*. What we used for the air terminal is in fact a convention center that is built in the shed of the old train station. We got all that and we got these power stations. It's very nice to have a city that cooperates and helps, unlike London, unfortunately.

What about giraffes on the freeway?

Thank God for computer graphics! It was the same process as *Jumanji* [1995], but with more talent. [Laughs] That was monkeys, come on! Giraffes are really hard to do. The key thing is their mane. I think we almost succeeded. Unfortunately, too many people spot that they're CG. The flamingos are CGI too, but all the other animals are real and they're in the city.

There are two other projects with which you've been associated: The Defective Detective *and* Watchmen. *What's the status with them?*

Strangely enough, on my Christmas holiday, I took an old script of *The Defective Detective* away with me, and I read it and I liked it. That's one of the ones [for which] I'm trying to take advantage of this momentary success. I'm gonna push that one and see if I can get it [going]. Unfortunately it's fairly expensive, so we'll see.

    I actually did get a call from the now-owner of *Watchmen*. I don't know what to do with it. I think it's too hard to reduce that to two hours. That's what I thought before. I still feel that way. A mini series would be great.

What is likely to be next?

I don't know. I'm gonna try *The Defective Detective*—throw it into the system and see what happens. Then there's the possibility of a western, just to confuse things. And I think I've decided not to do *The Hunchback of Notre Dame*, which I kept reading about, because Disney have got a big animated version coming out, all-signing, all-dancing. [Laughs] It is! Esmeralda and Phoebus fall in love and ride off into the sunset. And Quasimodo has got three anthropomorphic gargoyles called Lon, Chaney, and Quinn. This is all true. And Bruce Willis's wife [Demi Moore] is the voice of Esmeralda. We were actually working on this project. Then I saw the [Disney] trailer and just said, "Nope. That one's dead!"

1996

JON HARRIS
The Descent: Part 2

"I don't really believe in auteurship," – editor-turned-director Jon Harris on the team spirit that led to *The Descent: Part 2*. (Celador Films/Oliver Upton)

Celador Films, 2009

CAST: Sarah Carter, SHAUNA MACDONALD; Juno Kaplan, NATALIE MENDOZA; Elen Rios, KRYSTEN CUMMINGS; Vaines, GAVAN O'HERLIHY; Greg, JOSHUA DALLAS; Cath, ANNA SKELLERN; Dan Shepherd, DOUGLAS HODGE; Dr. Roger Payne, DOUG BALLARD; Lynch, JOSH COLE; Ed Oswald, MICHAEL J. REYNOLDS; Nurse Lambert, AXELLE CAROLYN; News Reporter, JESSIKA WILLIAMS; Mayor Riley, MAC MACDONALD; Marie, KELLI KERSLAKE; Sam, MYANNA BURING; Holly, NORA-JANE NOONE; Rebecca, SASKIA MULDER; Beth, ALEX REID; Beanie-Hat Caver, SEAMUS MAYNARD.

CREDITS: *Directed and edited by* Jon Harris; *producers,* Christian Colson, Ivana MacKinnon; *executive producers*, Paul Smith, Neil Marshall; *co-producer*, Paul Ritchie; *writers*, J Blakeson, James McCarthy, James Watkins; *director of photography*, Sam McCurdy; *production design*, Simon Bowles; *music*, David Julyan; *costume design*, Nancy Thompson; *special prosthetics/creative designer*, Paul Hyett; *special effects supervisor*, Johnny Rafique; *visual effects supervisor*, Sean Wheelan; stunts coordinator, Jim Dowdell. Running time: 93 minutes.

> "Dazed, bloodied, and speechless with trauma, Sarah Carter emerges alone from the Appalachian cave system where the events of The Descent took place. Local Sheriff Redmond Vaines forces her back underground to help the rescue team, which is desperately searching for her five missing girlfriends. As the team moves

deeper into the caves, Sarah's flashes of fractured memory intensify, and she begins to realize the full horror of the would-be rescue mission. Only Sarah knows the terror that lurks in the shadows of the caves. But they are about to encounter a new tribe of Crawlers—inbred, deformed, and even more viciously feral than those Sarah faced before...."

Intuition and Girl Power, Silence and Stealth

Jon Harris on *The Descent: Part 2*

Having edited the first film, did you even contemplate a sequel, let alone consider that you might direct it?

Jon Harris: There was some talk of a sequel at the time. I think there was an awareness that it was potentially going to be quite marketable. For a small British film, there were possibilities. It was about a year after that was finished that I got a call one day from Christian Colson, who was the producer and who I got along with quite well. I'd probably confessed to him in a drunken episode that I'd once had ambitions to direct, so he called my bluff.

It was one thing to want to do it, but did the enormity of the task dawn on you when the job was offered?

It was obvious all the way that it was enormous. I had to break it down and think, *Okay, this is the offer of a first directing gig for me, which is not something I'm just gonna get handed in any other environment*, so that made it very attractive. But at the same time, I didn't want to just accept it because of that. I wanted to be sure that we could do something with it, that it was worth doing, and we could do it well. So we did have a good, long think about what to do and how to do it.

Had you ever directed actors before?

Yeah, I had. In short films. I had directed two or three short films twenty years ago when I was at college—at film school—and I had directed little bits of second unit on a lot of the things I'd done like *Stardust* [2007] and *Eden Lake* [2008]. You get brought in to grab extra stuff that's needed.

Did you find there was a big gulf between the edit suite and the studio floor?

I actually didn't. The gulf of moving from editing to directing is more about the physical difference. Having sat by myself in a room for fifteen years to suddenly be on the set with sixty people around me, that was the biggest difference. And getting up in the morning and all that sort of thing. Creatively it was almost seamless. I've always thought of myself as just a filmmaker because when I used to direct my short films, I used to edit those. For me, it's just a big, organic filmmaking process. And when you're editing, you're very, very closely tuned to what the actors are doing and thinking, and choosing takes when their emotions are slightly different here and there. So you're very used to thinking, *I wanna find takes where the actor is just a bit more held-in in this scene.* And so going from that process to going onto the set and asking them for what you want was great. I enjoyed it.

Did you have the freedom to mould the script, or was there the sense of protecting a franchise?

I have to say I was very free. There were two completely different scripts that had been done just on spec by different interested parties, and I didn't really like either of them. We took very, very tiny elements of them both and pretty much threw the rest away and started developing a story from scratch. Christian Colson had the plan of having me edit *Eden Lake* with James Watkins, and then while I was editing his film, he was writing mine. Over a period of two years, we worked together on both things, and that was good. We were pretty much left alone. They were *so* eager to get going on the sequel. Sometimes I thought it was too easy. What I didn't want was to be in a scenario where the makers of the film just wanted a trailer and a poster. I didn't want to be involved in that—if they said, "Look, it's the sequel. People will go and see it." That wouldn't have been any good for me and it wouldn't have been any good for the audience. I wanted to make sure that it was worth doing and doing well.

Given your work on Eden Lake *and now* The Descent: Part 2, *do you have a particular affinity for horror? And does being an editor give you more freedom to create your own vision for the film?*

As a young kid, I used to watch anything and all sorts. I did love horror as a kid. As I got older, I was more interested in storytelling, so the horror films that work for me are the ones that have a strong story and [in which] the characters hold up. I probably got more involved in it because of *The*

Descent, Eden Lake, and *The Descent: Part 2,* I certainly discovered more of a love of horror than I knew I had.

In terms of editing and directing the same film, to be honest, I probably wouldn't do that again. I now appreciate the energy that a new person brings into the room. I was properly exhausted after seven weeks of shooting, and I really could have done with a new person full of new energy. I'm totally happy with where we got to at the end of the day; it just took me a bit longer to get there. I don't really believe in auteurship. On all the other things I've done, I really am a strong believer in creative friction. I love it when there are three people in the room who completely disagree with each other because that way, every single idea gets tested to the full, and I appreciate that.

Including actors?

Yeah. The difference is that on the set there isn't as much time for sitting around and pontificating. That all happens later on in the edit room. That's where I like the creative friction.

Neil Marshall spoke of The Descent *as being almost a feminist version of* Dog Soldiers *[2002]. Was it a challenge to keep the women as proactive characters rather than victims?*

It was a little bit. I had a plan, a definite plan, from the beginning. It seemed fairly obvious that we couldn't go all female again. It wouldn't have been plausible. It would have seemed contrived. So I knew that we were going to have to have men in it, but I wanted to stick to the themes of feminine intuition and girl power, if you want to call it that. I wanted to be sure that by the end, it was the girls that survived and that the men pretty much killed themselves off by being loud, blustering, and macho. At the end of the day, it was the feminine intuition and the ability to understand silence and stealth that helped the women to survive. So in that way, I think we managed to keep that strand.

The first film had two different endings, with the UK ending rather bleaker than the US one. Did the American ending give you a way in to the sequel?

Actually, no. What happened was that the original [American] film ended with a sequence where Sarah, the last surviving girl, sticks a pick through Juno's leg. Then she gets out of the cave, jumps in a car, runs down the road, stops at the side of the road, and then suddenly the ghost of Juno appears next to her, and she wakes up back in the cave. She's dreamt the fact that she's got out. We pull back and reveal her sitting alone on the edge of a precipice with her imagined daughter next to her. And what the Americans did was they quite simply lopped off that last bit so that it ended with a scare, but that the inference was that she had got out but was a bit mad and would be forever haunted by this. But in actual fact there was a bit of an outcry, and they put the original ending back on when they released the DVD. So I think the majority of people who have seen the film in America have probably seen it with the original intended ending. This film carries on from the British ending, where she was trapped. She gets out. I know how she gets out—and we filmed it—but it was very much felt that if this new film was going to stand alone, we had to present her from the point of view of a mystery. She was a mystery to herself, she was a mystery to the cave rescue people, and she's a mystery to the audience. It was really the only way to set up this film so that it stood on its own two feet, because if we showed her journey out of the cave, it implied that she could remember, and it took credence away from her amnesia. So that's what we did and we stuck with it.

Will this be the US release version as well?

I think so, unless they start pulling the scissors out! It could always happen; you never know.

It's dark, cold, claustrophobic. Was it as gruelling for cast and crew as it looks on screen, or is it a different experience when you're filming it?

It's not cold because obviously we filmed it in the studios. It is dark. You don't see daylight all day long, so there is a bit of a sense of it. And pretty much everything that you see them doing: if they're crawling between little tiny spaces in the rocks, they are doing that and they're going underwater. They all got fairly bruised and battered. I don't think we could have filmed it in real caves. That probably would have been a bit restrictive.

Who did you recruit as your crawlers?

We looked at dancers, interpretive mime artists, and models. What we looked for were people who could just move. I spent a day with fifty people just crawling around the walls. [There was] one guy in particular—the guy who's in the shit pit [in the film]. After I'd met them all and described what the crawlers were able to do, I said, "These guys can climb up the walls and climb across the ceiling, but of course I don't expect you do that here." He saw a beam and was straight up it and across the ceiling! I was like, "Okay, we'll have you." Some of them are quite crawler-like even without the make-up. They have to completely wax and shave their heads. And they need to be quite petite, shall we say, because they're meant to be emaciated creatures. A lot of them had it down—the look.

Where did you make it?

The first film shot for about ten days above ground, and that portion was shot in Scotland, and then the cave sequences were all shot at Pinewood Studios. We shot all our cave sequences at Ealing, and the exterior we shot in Farnham, in south London. There's a certain area down there that is quite popular with filmmakers called Bourne Woods. If you've seen the opening scene in *Gladiator* [2000]—the battle set in Germania—you'll see this amazing tree line. It's just a spot in south London with very big woods. It seemed to do okay for us. We did go to Scotland to get the helicopter vistas.

Have you ever been caving or pot-holing—a hobby that's terrifying even without crawlers being present?

I used to go in caves a bit when I was young. I grew up in Sheffield [in South Yorkshire, England], so I used to go in Blue John Caves and Speedwell [in nearby Derbyshire]. I look back now and I can't understand how I was able to do that. I got stuck on the corkscrew at Alton Towers [a ride at a British theme park] when I was about twenty. We had gone round the whole thing, it was raining that day, and it shorted out. I was stuck in this thing. I'm quite tall so this thing was really restricting me. For twenty minutes I was stuck there. I literally had to talk myself down. And ever since that day, I've really suffered [from] claustrophobia. We went in a cave to meet the cave rescue people. We didn't go very deep, but I didn't really need to. I can just conjure that up. I can imagine what that's like. And I went in the Cenote [cave system] in Mexico, where you snorkel and it gets narrower and narrower and narrower. It's one of the things I brought to the film and what works in *The Descent*. What I know about claustrophobia is that I'm okay as long as I can retrace in my mind the way out. As soon as you lose track of that, that's when you start to panic. That's one of the reasons why in both the *Descent* films, you have to take quite a lot of time. I wanted the lift shaft to be very long and I wanted the journey through the mines to be long. You have to give a sense that they have gone a long, long, long way in. You can't just turn around and come out. That's a large part of claustrophobia.

How long did the composer get to work on the film, because his music dovetails perfectly with the mood? And can you talk about the sound design in general?

I really love sound design, and as an editor I'm always there, right through to the end. My first day on any film is the first day of shooting. And my last day is the last day of the final sound mix. I really like that process. The composer David Julyan was great. We'd normally bring him on three months before the end. [That's when] he would start thinking [of his score]. Obviously, in many ways, the look and sound of the film was very tried and tested. I wanted it to feel like an extension of the first film. There was not so much experimenting to do. It was more a matter of doing some of the same things without—hopefully—feeling repetitive.

Given that Neil Marshall invented the franchise, how close was he to this project?

Very, and in all good ways. He wasn't possessive or controlling. He was really supportive. He came to the set four or five times and hung out. I kind of imagined that he'd be standing there going, "I want to be doing this." And there were times when I would go to him in the middle of something and go, "Mate, I haven't quite figured this thing out. What should I do?" And there was a sense of him trying to hold it back himself, because he wanted to do it. And on the other hand he was thinking to himself, *You're the director. Get on with it.* But he was always absolutely supportive and on side.

The sequence where they replay the camcorder is an interesting story. We had two of the girls already, but we got all of the girls back from the first film and dressed them all up in their old costumes. And Neil directed those sequences that you see in the camcorder. It seemed like a good idea at the time. Ultimately, I think they all found it a bit odd; a bit like having a date with the girlfriend you broke up with four years ago. It was a nice little thing to do, and he kindly helped us out with that.

Does he get a credit for doing that sequence?

No. He didn't ask for one.

There's a story that came out years ago when Ridley Scott was shooting Alien, *that some of the cast members were so freaked out by the production design of the ship that they didn't like to go onto the set on their own. They completely bought into the idea of the horror. It's probably apocryphal, but I like the notion of it. Did anything similar happen on* The Descent: Part 2?

Well, yeah. It happened to me. You'd walk down the corridor and there'd just be a corpse! Honestly. If a person who'd never been on a film set before went onto a set—a lot of the clichés are true. You've got to be careful. You can't lean on anything because it's probably fake. On a *Descent* film, you don't know what you're gonna come across. There were dismembered corpses just lying about. The scary thing is that they were people that you know. Saskia [Mulder], who plays Rebecca, I know her very well. She's a friend of Neil's and Christian's. They built her entire head in order that the rat could come out. It's incredibly convincing and actually quite disturbing to see someone that you know very well lying abandoned and dead in the corridor. You never know what you're gonna come across.

On a film like this, how much of the effects work is done in camera and how much is CGI? You had tons more blood this time around. How much of it was real and how much was cleverly added?

The blood is probably 99 percent pretend-real, as in a practical effect. It was actually there. People were choking on it and gargling on it. That was all good fun. There was occasionally a shot—like where the crawler's head gets squashed. We added a little tiny burst onto that to make it more effective. But largely, the blood was practical and was there. People had wires all around them and pumps [for the blood]. You'd just see people carrying in buckets of blood and shit and saliva. You just didn't know where to put your hands.

Actors can be precious creatures. Were they game for this, or did they eventually say, "Enough!"?

Not really. They were really up for it. When you see them in water, the water for health and safety reasons has to be kept at quite a high temperature. So the people who are in the water are probably the happiest of all. There was a bit of localized chafing that went on after two days in the shit pit. They were wearing wetsuits underneath their clothes and when water gets trapped—you don't wanna know! It all starts to *rub*. So there were a couple of rashes there, but nothing really serious. Nobody reared up, as they say. Not at all. There were a couple of near misses with the crawlers, but that's another story. Shauna [Macdonald] in particular was always signed up to do a sequel, and so I felt a huge loyalty to her. I didn't want to let her down. I didn't want to spoil the experience of the first film for her by making her come back and do something she wasn't happy with. I brought her back very early, and we talked through the development that her character would go through. And by the time we got to the set she was absolutely great. The only time she got annoyed was when we wouldn't let her do a stunt. They did have stand-ins and doubles to do certain things, and she wanted to do everything.

The first film has an online following. Did you take on board any of the suggestions that the first film had generated or seek the advice of the existing fan base?

Yeah. One of the things that I was fascinated with from the first film was a lot of speculation about whether the crawlers existed or whether Sarah imagined them and killed all her own friends. There was a lot of talk about that. We certainly played around with the edit in the first film just to sort of tease that out a little bit. For instance, there's a bit in the first film where Sarah, who's by herself, lets out a blood-curdling scream. And then we cut halfway on that scream to the other people reacting. And on the cut you cut to the sound of a crawler scream, which is what they're hearing. It was just little things like that to have the audience think, *Wait a minute....* The stuff I liked best in the first film personally was when Sarah's thinking that she's seeing things and no one else is believing her. I liked that aspect—that she goes from the least trusted member of the party, and everyone thinks that she's mad, to suddenly everyone realizing that she's the only one that knows what's going on down here, and she's not about to help us. That was a dynamic that I was really fascinated with. So to answer the question: just that idea of the possibility that she maybe imagined them in the first film.

Is there talk of a possible Descent 3 *and, if so, how would you see a storyline developing on that?*

There hasn't been much talk of it. The thing to do would be to see if there was any appetite for it. Obviously, certain people are clearly dead at the end of this one, so they're not going to be in another one. But I think there's room for it. It would be quite interesting to maybe start to bring the crawlers above ground. I don't know how well they work because you have to keep them in the shadows and see them flitting around. But maybe stealing into people's bathrooms and coming up through the plumbing! Could be fun!

2009

FRANK HENENLOTTER
Basket Case

"I loved making films. They were basically self-indulgent. It was all my sense of oddball humor." – Frank Henenlotter with his creations. (Courtesy of Frank Henenlotter)

Basket Case Productions, 1982

CAST: Duane Bradley, KEVIN VAN HENTENRYCK; Sharon, TERRI SUSAN SMITH; Casey, BEVERLY BONNER; Hotel Manager, ROBERT VOGEL; Dr. Kutter, DIANA BROWNE; Dr. Needleman, LLOYD PACE; Dr. Lifflander, BILL FREEMAN; O'Donovan, JOE CLARKE; Duane's Aunt, RUTH NEUMAN; Duane's father, RICHARD PIERCE; Young Duane, SEAN McCABE; Josephine, DOROTHY STRONGIN; Detective, KERRY RUFF; Social Worker, ILZE BALODIS; Thief in Theater, TOM ROBINSON; Kutter's Date, CHRIS BABSON; Patient, MARIA T. NEWLAND; Nurses, FLORENCE SHULTZ, MARY ELLEN SHULTZ; Hotel Tenants, CONSTANTINE SCOPAS, CHARLES STANLEY, SYDNEY BEST, JOHNNY RAY WILLIAMS, YOUSEF ABUHAMDEH, LUBI KIRSCH, CATHERINE RUSSELL, MITCHELL HUVAL; Drug Dealer, NOEL HALL; Second Detective, BRUCE FRANKEL; Street Girls, PAT IVERS, EMILY ARMSTRONG; Casey's John, RUSSELL FRITZ. Uncredited: Belial, FRANK HENENLOTTER.

CREDITS: *Director*, Frank Henenlotter; *screenplay*, Frank Henenlotter; *producer*, Edgar Ievins; *executive producers*, Arnold H. Bruck, Tom Kaye; *music*, David Maswick, Gus Russo *special make-up effects*, John Caglione Jr, Ken Clark, Kevin Haney, Ugis Nigals; *director of photography*, Bruce Torbet; *editor*, Frank Henenlotter. Running time: 91 minutes.

"What's in the padlocked wicker basket Duane Bradley carries with him everywhere? Why does he feed it hamburgers and frankfurters? Why does he speak softly to it through the wickerwork and then occasionally turn it loose to wreak bloody havoc on unscrupulous doctors....?"

Gumby on Acid
Frank Henenlotter on *Basket Case*

Where were you in your career when Basket Case *came to you?*

Frank Henenlotter: Well, I had no film career. And in fact, I never really thought about doing films commercially. From the time I was thirteen and discovered my father's 8mm camera, I was making movies: regular 8, regular 8 sound, 16mm, 16 sound. I loved making films, but I was making them simply to make them. I never showed them, or very rarely. They weren't made to be seen by the public. They were basically—I guess you could say—self-indulgent. It was all my sense of oddball humor.

What sort of stuff were you doing?

Oh, very much the same thing like *Basket Case*. They had that feel—combinations of comedy and violence of some sort. I once had a friend say, "Every time you try to make a comedy it comes out like a horror film, and every time you try and make a horror film it comes out like a comedy." They were just weird mixes of that. I was in the middle of making a 16mm short when I met Edgar Ievins, and he said he'd love to produce one. "Why don't we make a commercial film?" And I thought, *Sure, why not? I'd love to.* It wasn't the direction I was going in, but, fine, let's do it. He said he could raise probably a hundred or a hundred and fifty thousand [dollars], and while he went off to raise some money, I wrote the script, I did the casting, and we even started building one of the sets. Then he let us know that he really wasn't able to raise a dime. Then it was *oh-oh*. So I said nevertheless, let's start shooting on the weekend, and I'll fund it with the $8,000 I had in the bank at the time. And then Edgar said he'll match it with $8,000 he's got. And then Edgar managed to get additional funding here and there—a piece from different friends—that gradually brought the budget up to $35,000. And that's what we shot it in.

How much would that money be worth now?

Not much! [Laughs] Listen, it didn't buy anything then. As much as I wanted to do it that way, what it meant to me was I really can't film the script as I wrote it. While I knew the premise of the script was absolutely ridiculous, I played it very straight. Now I really had—for all intents and purposes—no crew, no money for equipment, no nothing. I figured the one way I can do it is to really go over the top with the humor and go over the top with the blood and gore and to make that as comical as well. The other thing I knew was that back then, everything was theatrical. The home video was in its infancy, so you really weren't thinking about that. But back then there were a hundred times more theaters than there are now, and more companies. So if you had a film, you could always find some small distributor that only released shit to skid row theaters that would release your little shit film. So I knew we could get it sold. But I also knew that it would probably never get reviews and it'll probably never be seen. I figured in New York it'd play a week on 42nd Street and then disappear forever.

I'm playing devil's advocate here. If the film is never going to be seen or reviewed, why bother? What made you want to succeed?

I didn't. I just wanted to make a film. I said before: the films I was making I made because I enjoyed the process of making a film. In this case, even though we were taking people's money (including my own), I knew we could sell the film. So it wasn't like me just dismissing. In fact, what happened was it actually emboldened me to go a little crazier. I figured, "No-one's gonna see it. Let me have some fun with this." So I started putting in scenes that were making me laugh. I'm sitting on the set shaking my head going, "Oh my God, we can't get away with this! Let's keep it!" I think I would have been far more self-conscious if we had raised money and I did it a little more artistically. I certainly wouldn't have had the same film and maybe not the same success with it.

You'd have had a producer looking over your shoulder and tutting and saying, "You can't do that."

Well, that's true. Edgar, he never really cared. He left that all up to me. He was very supportive. He helped build the sets. Whatever we needed—if we needed another hand on the set—he was the first to jump in there and do it. We were enjoying it as a lark—having a good time making it, even though it seemed to never end. We were filming it on weekends, whenever we had money. If we had a little bit of money, we went up New York State to Glen Falls and filmed some scenes there. But we never had the money. There were long periods in between where [we said], "We gotta find somebody else that'll give us a coupla grand." Usually you have dailies where you can see what you shot the next day. We couldn't afford the lab bills, so I had monthlies where the film was still in the lab for a coupla months before we could develop it and see what we even had there! Everything about filming is, I think, a compromise. Whether you get freedom or not, there's always a give and a take away with every project. And you kind of just say, "Well, fine. It is what it is. Make the best of it." That's all.

Where did the idea come from? Was it something you'd had buzzing in your head for a long time?

No. No. I only have one film in my head right now that I wanna make. I'm always as surprised as the next one as what the next one's gonna be. I don't have a clue, all right? With the case of *Basket Case*, once Edgar said, "Let's do something commercially," we figured that back then, the safest bet would be a horror film because you could always sell those back then. So, okay: what kind of a horror film? I don't know. I was sitting around playing with titles in my head. I remember this one day I was coming up with titles like *Psychopath*. Oh, that's been done. *Homicidal*. That's been done. That kind of stuff. When I came up with *Basket Case*—as a crazy person; he's a basket guy—right away I had this image of a monster in a basket, and I thought, *Oh God, that is so visual and simultaneously so stupid it's hard to resist it.* That was just such an irresistible concept: this stupid image of a malignant jack-in-the-box, and whenever you open it this thing leaps out. It was *great*. I actually started writing scenes like that until it occurred to me that why would anybody walk around with a monster in a basket? It was just ridiculous. Why would anybody do that? I really couldn't lick it. Then one day I was in Times Square, where I used to live, practically for the films. I'd be there every evening. I'm in a Nathan's Hot Dog stand and all of a sudden, I thought, *Whoa! What if it's his brother?* The moment I thought of that, [I came up with] all of this imagery and dialogue and I started writing dialogue on my mustard-stained napkins. It's almost verbatim what's in the film; I didn't really change that dialogue at all. The dialogue I'm talking about is when Duane gets drunk and says to Casey, the hooker, "He's my brother. We were born like that, blah, blah, blah." Whenever I hear Kevin Van Hentenryck say those lines, I smell the mustard and I can taste the Nathan's hot dog! That's exactly what that was that night.

We all have to get our inspiration somewhere, and a hot dog is as good as anything.

Hell, yeah!

How quickly did you manage to turn the script around?

Very fast. I wrote that one surprisingly quick. I'm not sure why. Usually, scripts take a while to write, but that one [happened] very quickly. It kind of wrote itself. Once I figured out where the setting was gonna be—there's a monster in a basket at a flophouse killing doctors. It's almost a three-act concept right there. It was just variations on the same joke, quite honestly. So it really didn't take a lot of work.

But it has to be relatively simple, doesn't it, to sell the concept?

You mean the plot? Oh, absolutely. Absolutely. And that's why it worked, because that's all it was. It was a very simple visual: monster in a basket equals monster movie. That really was the plot.

When you were a kid were you inspired by those monster movies of the '50s and '60s? What were you watching as a kid growing up?

I was, but I was inspired by almost everything I've seen. I was a pretty lonely kid; I had very few friends. I guess I was an obnoxious little creep. So I spent an awful lot of time in front of the television set, and I would watch movies in spite of the fact that I may not even like the movie, care about the movie, or even understand the movie. I just liked watching the mechanics: people open a door, walk in a room, talk, the camera follows them. I was just fascinated by the whole process. So it didn't take much to impress me, I guess that's what I'm trying to say. When it came to horror films, most of the films I saw were monster movies as opposed to horror films. And I loved monster movies on television, too, because monsters are so funny. They are very seldom scary. They're goofy. They look like the weird kid we all think we are. I just never took monsters seriously. In fact, the moment you see a monster as a kid, the next thing I was trying to do was, "How are they gonna kill it now?" That's all I was looking forward to. Also back then in the late '50s and early '60s, there were tons of neighborhood movie theaters around me where I was able to go. As young as you are, they would have kiddie matinees where they segregated the kids, so you didn't have to worry about adults who shouldn't be there. For some inexplicable reason, over here [in the US] they thought that horror movies were great for the kids. [Laughs] You know? I was nine years old watching *Horrors of the Black Museum* [1959], which probably shouldn't have been seen by a nine-year-old kid, but, boy, it did wonders for me. Vividly I recall the effect that film had on me. The same with *Circus of Horrors* [1960] and *The Brides of Dracula* [1960]. I've just realized now: all three are British films, aren't they? I didn't realize that. But they were three of the films that had the most impact on me when I look back at it. And *The Tingler* [1959], believe it or not, William Castle's film. I saw that in a theater on Long Island that actually had the little joy buzzers under some of the seats.

So you got the whole show?

Yeah, I did. And I was *terrified*. First of all, I was too young and stupid to realize that the film was not meant to be taken seriously. So when they're telling me that we all have this little parasite in our spine that gets bigger, I was already like, "Oh GOD! I don't like this one." [Laughs] And when I was eight or nine, my memory now is that I was in a theater full of adults, but I couldn't have been. It was a Saturday afternoon. So it was probably a theater full of teenagers, which to my young brain looked like adults. And I remember when they turned the lights off, some of the "adults" would jump up, go "Aargh!" and start laughing. I didn't find that funny. I was *so* afraid. It didn't occur to me to look under a seat. I didn't know what they would do, and I didn't know how this was going to be done. I remember thinking, *If the guy behind me accidentally kicks my seat, I will drop dead*. I remember walking out of *The Tingler* just spent, just *exhausted*, and also thinking, *Boy, that was great. I hope there's another one like this next weekend*.

So childhood trauma led you into a career in exploitation movies?

Absolutely. It was fascinating how the realization of what I felt was almost ninety unpleasant minutes and I couldn't *wait* to go back. It was like the fear and joy of a rollercoaster. All of that stuff meant a lot to me, and when I was fifteen, I started cutting high school. I would take the train from Long Island, where I grew up, into Manhattan. I started going to the film theaters on 42nd Street when I was fifteen. And when I was fifteen too I looked like I was twelve. I never had any trouble. Sure, they were selling drugs, but if you weren't buying, if you were just here to see the movie, you were fine. So I had many, many blissful, ignorant, and happy days there. I grew up there. I always feel that way. I finally moved into Manhattan in the early '70s—why go anywhere else? It was right there. And if it wasn't on 42nd Street, I would be in Times Square. And if I wasn't there, well, New York at the time was blessed with tons of repertory theaters, so you seldom had to see a movie on TV. If there was something you wanted to see, you just waited for it to show up at one of these repertory theaters. So I was always going back and watching the films of the past, constantly.

What you're talking about represents paradise.

It was paradise. You wouldn't always [find the movie]. I'd read *Variety* and read what's playing down South at some Carolina drive-in and hope it comes to New York. And if it does, I hope I'm in town. Because there was no guarantee, especially on 42nd Street. Those theaters never advertised the movies, or very seldom. You really only knew it was playing by physically going to the street. Plenty of times, there would be a great double feature or a triple-bill, and it would play maybe one day or two, maybe three days. Sometimes no one went. Other times, it would be a filler waiting for something else to come in. In the mid-'70s, I remember going there. They had three black-and-white CinemaScope 20th Century Fox horror films made in the '50s or early '60s: *Curse of the Fly* [1965], *The Cabinet of Dr. Caligari* [1920], *The Alligator People* [1959], *The Day Mars Invaded Earth* [1963], and *House of the Damned* [1963]. And it was for one day! Twice that happened in the course of a month. Fox may have been clearing out their prints and offered them all three for a hundred bucks. And I was thrilled. They never showed on New York television. I was like, *Oh my goodness, I can actually go there and see them in CinemaScope.*

Describe the casting process on Basket Case.

The actress in the film who plays the social worker with the big hairdo was my girlfriend at the time, and she worked at the American Academy of Dramatic Arts here in New York. She had access, so she did all the casting. "What are we looking for in Duane?"

"Well, somebody who is normal but stands out a little bit. Maybe he's a little awkward."

And she went, "Oh, I know. Kevin. He'd be great. He's too tall, so he always stands out."

And he was. She did all the casting. I didn't do any of that. Which is excellent. Then I told her she's gotta play the social worker. We were up in New York state shooting that. Each day I told her I was gonna shoot her scene, knowing that I wasn't. I just loved seeing her in that high hairstyle. She knew that, too. She caught on really fast. Her name that she used in that was Ilze Balodis.

How lucky were you to have the freedom to do and cast exactly what you wanted?

I don't believe there is freedom, okay? Maybe I had that form of freedom, but the downside is I didn't have a cameraman who knew what he was doing, I had me. I wanted some stop-motion animator. I didn't have a stop-motion animator, I had me. That's why it's so bad. I didn't know how to light, I didn't know what I was doing. I could barely figure out how a camera worked or where the button was. The most common phrase on *Basket Case* was me walking around going, "Where's the camera? Where did I put the camera? Anybody know where the camera is?" It was embarrassing. I'd put the camera down and a minute later, it was covered with something and I couldn't find it. That's not how you make movies. So it didn't strike me as freedom at all. It struck me as what happens when nobody wants to be involved in making your movie! That's really all it felt like to me.

New York has always had the reputation as being a film-friendly city. Was this a case of guerrilla filmmaking at its most pure? Did you just go out there and do it, or did you seek permissions?

I never asked permission and I still don't. I have a new film that I'm editing now. I'm gonna have the final cut done probably by the middle of next week. I shot that all over Williamsburg, Brooklyn, and down in New Orleans. We only asked for one police permit because we had a generator we were gonna use for lights. Otherwise, I never ask anybody for permission. I don't think it's anybody's business. What do I have to ask them permission for? You know—fuck off! I'm making a movie; I'm holding the camera. I don't need permission for this. I think it would be different if you had a movie crew with vans and equipment and you have to light an entire street and you need it closed off. I thought I had a big crew with this new film, because I brought eleven people down to New Orleans with me—and that includes the actors. That, to me, is a lot of people. But to anybody driving or walking past us, they saw a camera, but they didn't figure we were making a movie. Probably a short or something like that. That's fine.

That has to work in your favor, too. People are going to leave you alone.

Absolutely. I don't post on Facebook. I don't let anyone know when I'm making a movie because I'd rather just very quietly go out and make it. Then when I get it done, then we can talk about it.

Was that the same with Basket Case: *you just went out and did it?*

Oh absolutely. I've done all of them like that. *Brain Damage* [1988], *Bad Biology* [2008], all of them. Whether I'm shooting in 35 or 16, I don't ask permission. I needed permission from the city for a subway for *Brain Damage*. That's about as close as we ever got to doing it legitimately, you know what I mean? In fact, there's a moment in *Basket Case* where Kevin Van Hentenryck is walking the length of 42nd Street. It's a beautiful shot and you can see all the stores as he's passing. One of the stores was a porn store. You can see all the way in. What you see in the film now is Take Two. On Take One, I'm camera operating and I'm sitting in the van. The side of the van is open. I'm so focused on keeping Kevin in the frame that I didn't realize what was happening until it was too late. Some guy from inside the porno store, I don't know where he came from, but all of a sudden, I realized he was running the length of the store, and in a split second actually dove into our van at us! Screaming he was gonna kill us and threatening all kind of stuff. We didn't even know what the hell's going on. Kevin calmed the guy down. I'm standing there thinking, *Shit! This guy's gonna murder us!* And Kevin's going, "It's okay. What's the problem?" And the guy thought we were a news van from a local TV station that was doing a story on the adult business or something like that. He thought we were the news. And then, as Kevin said, "We're just making a dumb little horror movie." I said to him afterwards, "That should be the title: *A Dumb Little Horror Movie*." The guy was instantly apologetic and very embarrassed. "Oh, I'm sorry. Okay." Then I said to him, "Listen, I didn't get the shot so we're gonna drive around the block and do it again. Is that okay?" "Oh, okay. Don't worry about it. I'm sorry, I'm sorry!" [Laughs] That's when you know you're doing it real guerrilla style. In fact, in *Frankenhooker*, at the very beginning, when Jeffrey is in his car driving around looking for where the hookers are, we show a bunch of hookers in the streets. And those initial shots are real hookers working the streets. We drove around the block and we got the shot once. But when we went back and drove around the block a second time, they were already savvy to it and were ducking and turning and hiding. Again, they probably figured we were law enforcement, news or something like that.

So not just exploitation but Cinéma vérité as well.

Yeah, somewhat. It's just a matter of trying to do the best in any circumstances. It's also a lot of fun to do it that way, too. "Let's go out and see if we can film some real hookers tonight. I know where the streets are well lit. That'll be fun," never realizing it could also look very good, too.

Tell me about the special effects with the monster in the basket. Your monster came about through circumstance and budget, or lack of it. Quite a bit of it is you with a glove on your hand. But it works.

I'm very heavy these days, but back then I was about as thin then as I'm heavy now. And I was so thin back then that I am inside the dresser drawers that are in that hotel room. They were hollow drawers, and I'm in there with the glove on my hand sticking out of the top. I'm squinting out from the holes of the drawers themselves at a mirror across the room that I had put there. I'm figuring out that I've got to do the opposite because I'm looking in the mirror. And I thought, *What if somebody walks on the set and wonders where the director is? They'll hear some disembodied voice saying, "Alright, turn on the camera!"* It's not exactly glamorous, you know what I mean? I wish we had footage of it, but think about it: how else could we have done it? We only had two monsters made. One was the large puppet that opens its mouth. If he doesn't open his mouth it's the other one. Originally, Kevin's face was cast as Belial and pulled on one side, but because it didn't have a skull, you don't see it on the Belial whose mouth opens. But when you see the Belial that doesn't move, if you look at it, you realize it's Kevin Van Hentenryck's face. And I kind of liked being able to use both of them intermixed. And I also inadvertently realized that there was a wire structure in the second Belial that didn't open its mouth, and I realized that I could use it to do very crude stop-motion animation. I am not the person who should have done that, because I have zero patience. I'm on a set completely by myself and the camera's across the room. I'm standing at the cameras, click-click, then I walk across the room, then down, move Belial a little bit, walk back to camera, click two frames. Well, ten minutes later, I'm moving Belial with my foot. Just kinda kicking it. So it's awful looking. It's dumb, jerky animation. When I saw the footage I got really depressed. I got very angry. I remember picking up the reel of 16mm—I was in my apartment watching it—and I just threw it across the room. It hit the corner and I let it lie on the floor. It was lying on the floor for about two months because I just wanted a reminder of how badly you can fuck up. And after about two months, I thought, *What can I do with this thing? Is there anything I can use out of it?* I put it on again, and this time I started laughing at it. *This is so cheesy and kinda wonderful. Maybe I can do something with it.* So I re-wrote the scenes and then added some more animation and turned the animated sequences into comedy. So when Belial's throwing a temper tantrum, running around the room doing that goofy stuff, suddenly it was funny. And I think that's why audiences are somewhat forgiving about it, because it's now a joke. I only saw the film twice with an audience when it was first released, and the first time I went there—and the film had been out for a coupla months—as soon as the animation came on, some guy yelled, "It's Gumby on acid!" And I thought, *Wow. That's exactly what this is. Thank you very much.* That was the most perfect description I've ever seen of those scenes. The rest of it was just [about], "How do you manipulate Belial?" Sometimes I needed the help of another person. How do you make something work when clearly it won't?

The feel goes back to the Hammer horrors of the 1950s and '60s. People talk about groundbreaking effects, but those guys had fifty cents and they had to create an effect, and they did.

Hammer's effects would work most of the time! I tried to do everything I could to reflect the fact that we weren't doing it right. A lot of that was comedy. A lot of it was, *Well, look: I'm killing this little Irish guy here. If*

I don't do it right, you're gonna see Ilze behind him. She's got one hand in the gloves. Or maybe both hands in the gloves, because I'm filming it. So let me throw a lot of blood on his face, because then you're gonna be looking at that and you may not look too carefully at where Belial's other arm is coming from. And then you shake the camera a little bit and go a little tighter. Then when you're editing it months later, you go, "Oh God. I can only use this much. Okay, fine." So it's like everything else: how much can we get away with before the audience rebels and kills us all?

How does it feel all these years later to be still on the festival circuit with Basket Case?

It's very surreal to me. Like I said, I thought this film would never be seen. Here it is, thirty-some years later. I was just this past weekend in Colorado at a horror film festival where they showed *Basket Case*. I saw the sense of surprise that the film wasn't just seen but became something of a little cult hit. So I'm still surprised over that. And I'm seriously delighted that so many people like the film, and they like it enough that it's still playing. There's five other theaters that are showing it this month in the US here. At the same time, I'm also embarrassed by it because I was very self-indulgent when I made it, because I thought it would never be seen. That self-awareness is also tempered with the fact that maybe if I had known it would be seen and I'd done it differently, I would not have a hit film on my hands. Everything about *Basket Case* kind of confuses me—the reaction to it, that it still exists and it still gets watched and people like it. I am the one guy sitting in the theater with the big question mark over his head going, "What the hell is this thing?"

You shouldn't be embarrassed by it. Look what it spawned.

I should be! I've seen the film! I've seen it many times! I've got a damn good reason to be embarrassed by it!

Sequels are one thing, but have you ever come close to a remake?

I get that all the time. I don't see any reason for a remake. Period. Okay? If there is, I wanna hear why it should be remade. I did have a fairly well-known actor who wanted to remake it and had a great take on how to remake it. It was a real nicer re-working of the original story, different enough that it could co-exist with the original, meaning that you could have two films called *Basket Case* with Duane and his Siamese brother. And you'd have two similar but wildly divergent stories. And I liked his approach very much, but his management team and lawyers must have figured—oh , I don't know what they figured—that I would give them everything for ten dollars and walk away. I have no idea. If the deal was even halfway acceptable, I would have done it. A lot of times, people involved in making films in Hollywood figure if you haven't made a movie for a long time, then you must be broke. Or if you're not in the film industry, then you're desperate for money. I don't know. But none of those things apply. And I still make money off *Basket Case* very nicely, thank you. So they had this great idea, this great concept, everybody in place, they had a director, a production house that wanted to do it—and you're offering me $89.95 for all the rights to everything? They very generously told me I was able to keep ownership of the original. I thought that was decent. That was the closest it's come to a remake. A lot of times, when I get asked about a remake for the film, they figure since the film was made cheap, we can do a cheap remake. And I think, *But I already made the cheap version.* [Laughs] Now it's time for the expensive version. I have no interest in it. If it's a good idea, sure. But I'm not just gonna hand it somebody and walk away.

2012

PETER JACKSON and PHILIPPA BOYENS
The Lord of the Rings: The Fellowship of the Ring

Peter Jackson shares a joke with Sean Bean, aka Boromir, during shooting on *The Lord of the Rings*. This sequence – the battle for Osgilliath – was cut from *The Two Towers* but would eventually appear on DVD in an extended edition. (New Line Cinema/Pierre Vinet)

New Line, 2001

CAST: Frodo, ELIJAH WOOD; Gandalf, IAN McKELLEN; Arwen, LIV TYLER; Aragorn, VIGGO MORTENSEN; Sam, SEAN ASTIN; Galadriel, CATE BLANCHETT; Gimli, JOHN RHYS-DAVIES; Pippin, BILLY BOYD; Merry, DOMINIC MONAGHAN; Legolas, ORLANDO BLOOM; Saruman, CHRISTOPHER LEE; Elrond, HUGO WEAVING; Boromir, SEAN BEAN; Bilbo, IAN HOLM; Gollum, ANDY SERKIS; Celeborn, MARTON CSOKAS; Haldir, CRAIG PARKER; Lurtz, LAWRENCE MAKOARE; Everard Proudfoot, NOEL APPLEBY; Sauron, SALA BAKER; Mrs. Proudfoot, MEGAN EDWARDS; Gil-Galad, MARK FERGUSON; Elendil, PETER McKENZIE; Bounder, IAN MUNE; Gondorian Archivist, MICHAEL ELSWORTH; Witch-King, BRENT McINTYRE; Rosie Cotton, SARAH McLEOD; Farmer Maggot, CAMERON RHODES; Gatekeeper, MARTIN SANDERSON; Isildur, HARRY SINCLAIR; Barliman Butterbur, DAVID WEATHERLEY; Hero Orcs, Goblins, Uruks & Ringwraiths, VICTORIA BEYNON-COLE, LEE HARTLEY, SAM LA HOOD, CHRIS STREETER, JONATHAN JORDAN, SEMI KURESA, CLINTON ULYATT, PAUL BRYSON, LANCE FABIAN KEMP, JONO MANKS, BEN PRICE, PHILIP GRIEVE, THOMAS McGINTY, KATE O'ROURKE; Cute Hobbit Children, BILLY JACKSON, KATIE JACKSON; Otho, PETER CORRIGAN; Mrs. Bracegirdle, LORI DUNGEY; Gaffer Gamgee, NORMAN FORSEY; Old Noakes, WILLIAM JOHNSON; Lobelia, ELIZABETH MOODY; Ted Sandyman, BRIAN SERGENT. Voice of the Ring, ALAN HOWARD.

CREDITS: *Director*, Peter Jackson; *screenplay*, Fran Walsh, Philippa Boyens, Peter Jackson, based on the book by J.R.R. Tolkien; *producers*, Barrie M. Osborne, Peter Jackson, Fran Walsh, Tim Sanders; *executive producers*, Mark Ordesky, Bob Weinstein, Harvey Weinstein, Robert Shaye, Michael Lynne; *co-producers*, Rick Porras, Jamie Selkirk; *associate producer*, Ellen M. Somers; *director of photography*, Andrew Lesnie A.C.S.; *production designer*, Grant Major; *editor*, John Gilbert; *costume designers*, Ngila Dickson, Richard Taylor; *music*, Howard Shore; *special make-up, creatures, armor and miniatures*, Richard Taylor; *visual effects supervisor*, Jim Rygiel; *conceptual designers*, Alan Lee, John Howe; *supervising art director*, Dan Hennah. Running time: 178 minutes/208 minutes/228 minutes.

> "Shy, young hobbit Frodo Baggins inherits a ring; but this ring is no mere trinket. It is the One Ring, an instrument of absolute power that could allow Sauron, the Dark Lord of Mordor, to rule Middle-Earth and enslave its people. Frodo, together with a loyal fellowship of hobbits, men, a wizard, a dwarf and an elf, must take The Ring across Middle-Earth to the Crack of Doom, where it was first forged, and destroy it forever. Such a journey means venturing deep into territory held by the Dark Lord, where he is amassing his army of orcs. And it is not only external evils that the Fellowship must combat, but also internal dissension and the corrupting influence of The Ring itself. The course of future history is entwined with the fate of the Fellowship."

A Case of Extreme Simplification
Peter Jackson and Philippa Boyens on
The Lord of the Rings: The Fellowship of the Ring

Most directors would run a mile from attempting a film of this size. You've made three in one. Are you mad?

Peter Jackson: Yeah! I don't know. I've always loved making movies. I wanted to when I was a kid. I just feel in a way that I'm the luckiest guy in the world. I don't really feel it's hard—even though it *is* hard. It's sort of what I love doing. So I just feel very lucky, really.

How did you get through it all?

Jackson: There are two answers. One is we had a lot of preparation. Normally on a movie, you would probably expect to prepare the movie for something between six and eight months before you started shooting. You put the crew together, find your locations, plan the schedule. And in this case, we had three years of planning, essentially, from the time we started writing the script. In that time, we also hired designers and had [special make-up supervisor] Richard Taylor working on things. We were looking for locations. We were doing a lot of work. And from that point, it was three years until the day we first started shooting. So we had sufficient time, I think, for something this difficult. A lot of the credit for the very smooth running of the film, it should be Barrie [Osborne, producer] taking that credit. I know that Barrie's first movie as a young production assistant was *Apocalypse Now* [1979], so I think he probably acquired a few of the lessons from what happened on that to make our shoot run so smoothly. Also, you don't really stop and think about the big picture too much. It's a psychological thing: you don't stop and say, "What have I got myself into?" You just look at the next day's worth of work and day after that and the next week, and you take one job at a time.

How tough is it to sit down and begin to write this script of a book that some people regard as the most important ever written?

Philippa Boyens: It was incredibly tough. When you read things like Professor Tolkien wrote in the period that these books were written in, you stand back a bit. It tends to get a little overwhelming. But it was a process of navigating the demands of the film and navigating the demands of the book. And always, we had Peter's vision and the contributing vision of the crew and the actors on our side. So it was a privilege and a great joy to do this. Fran [Walsh, co-writer], Peter, and myself approached this not so much with reverence as with a determination to succeed and fulfill the possibilities of what this film could be. That's what drove us.

What is it about you as a filmmaker and the era that we're living in that means The Lord of the Rings *could be made now as opposed to thirty years ago?*

Jackson: There's the obvious issue that technology with computer effects means things are of a standard now [which means that] anything that Tolkien put into his book you are able to show on screen. Literally, with computers, you can do anything now. It's really come to that in the last two or three years.

But the critical element to our approach is that we've done three movies rather than just one. Other filmmakers have looked at *The Lord of the Rings* over the years and tried to figure out a way to tell it as one single film. That's always been the assumption: take the book and make a film. And they have not been able to do that. We didn't take that approach. We've made it as a trilogy of movies to match the trilogy of books that originally was published. So I think that really has allowed it to happen because we literally have nine hours of screen time to be able to tell the story, and that's what it needs really.

We've seen the emergence of films such as Star Wars *[1977] and* Harry Potter *[2001] that have been shot in an episodic format. Would that be your preferred way of tackling classic books—to not try and truncate it into one movie, but to have the feel of a Saturday morning serial?*

Jackson: It's interesting. We're a little different to *Harry Potter* and *Star Wars*. Obviously, *Star Wars* originated from a single movie, but because it was successful it led to a series of sequels and the story expanded. *Harry Potter* was a series of separate stories. We've done something that is a huge risk, really, when you think about it. We're asking a cinema audience who are used to paying their money and seeing a film and having that complete experience [to take a leap of faith]. We're saying, "This story is too big for one film. In fact, it's three movies released over three years, and when you see *The Fellowship of the Ring*, you're not gonna see the end of the story," which is a risky proposition. From my point of view, it's the only way that *The Lord of the Rings* can be told.

There has been a history of other filmmakers at times attempting to adapt *The Lord of the Rings* into a screenplay. Everybody has tried to write a script. The Beatles tried it at some point. John Boorman had a go. But the key to why we've been able to make the film was that creatively, we decided if you were to make *The Lord of the Rings*, you had to have a certain expectation of how it was going to be. Secondly, it was the studio. New Line Cinema stepped up with the courage to go ahead and make three films at the same time without releasing the first one. You've got to appreciate what a huge, enormous amount of courage that actually shows. Hollywood today is a very safe, conservative place. It doesn't take those sorts of risks. It just doesn't. And this is quite extraordinary.

When you have been so immersed in a project like you were with this, are you able to sit down and watch it as a regular person would? And are you completely happy with it?

Jackson: No, I can't watch it. I have no objectivity, really. Maybe I will in ten years' time. The thing that I'm proudest of about the film just from my own strictly personal point of view in seeing the finished film is that it doesn't remind me of any other movie that I've ever seen. And I'm proud of that. That's something, because I think in this day and age, there's an industry pumping out big budget films, and to me this feels a little bit like the biggest independent film ever made. It doesn't feel like a studio film. And I am actually proud of that. It fits with the spirit. And the spirit that it was made in manifests itself in the film, which I think is quite rare. It was made by a cast and crew that worked together for fifteen months, working on material that they loved, becoming friends, and there's something of a spirit that we generated unlike anything on any other job. No films last that long. They *never* take fifteen months to shoot. But I think you can feel that coming across on the screen.

Was there ever a point during those fifteen months when you wondered whether you had bitten off more than you could chew?

Jackson: There are down times. There are definitely times when you think you'd rather be in bed! [Laughs] But often, they're not so much a bitten-off-more-than-you-can-chew moment; it's more just stress and depression at things that are happening, usually with the weather, actually. It's the weather that creates the worst time in filmmaking because you're sitting there when it's snowing or floods are washing the set away. We had everything over the course of the time it took us to film. Over fifteen months of shooting, we had every possible weather situation that you could imagine. That's tough. The secret with the preparation is that we had three years of planning. No film has ever planned for three years, but obviously, we're making three, so we made sure we had an adequate length of time.

On the first day that we started shooting, we had been totally immersed in this for three years prior to that, full time. So as difficult as it was, it was very, very well planned—like running a military operation.

A film of this size requires a sizable cast and some very significant names within the broad ensemble. Were you ever affected by actors' egos?

Jackson: We cast the film very carefully on two levels. Obviously, first and foremost, we wanted to find the best actors in the world to bring these famous icons to life: Gandalf, Frodo, Bilbo Baggins. These are favorites from the last fifty years—names that have entered popular culture. So we cast it on that level. But also, every time you are casting a movie you get to meet the actors. Obviously, you spend some time with them. We went round to Ian McKellen's house for two hours just to say "hi" to him and to talk to him about what we were doing. This was before he agreed to do it.

We met with everybody. And you're also thinking as you meet these people, in the back of your mind, *Can I work with this person for 15 months?* Because if we made a mistake and we cast an actor who was gonna be difficult, ego-driven, or precious, it would have been a nightmare. It would have gone off the rails very, very quickly, so because we had such an ensemble cast, we needed a very even temperament. We cast actors very carefully. This is going to sound twee but we just cast actors who were nice people because we wanted to work with nice people for fifteen months. And everybody was. They're funny, humorous, good-spirited, and they're not in the slightest bit ego driven, thank heavens.

Stuart Townsend, who was originally cast as Aragorn, has been vocal about being fired. What's your take on that?

Jackson: We certainly take full responsibility [because] I think Stuart is a fantastic actor. I really have a very strong desire to want to work with him. And in a sense, after he was cast, we tried so hard to cast the film in a way that felt totally authentic to the book. Stuart himself auditioned for Frodo, in actual fact. When he auditioned, he didn't audition for Aragorn. We liked his screen quality and his presence so much that we didn't think he was Frodo but thought it would make an interesting Aragorn. We just came to realize that it was a classic situation and we had miscast the role; he was just too young. He was only twenty-three or twenty-four. It's always a very difficult situation; it's very emotional and very upsetting to have to come to a parting of the ways like that. But he himself said, "You're crazy. I'm not Aragorn," and we said, "You are, you are, and you'll be great!" So we have a huge amount of responsibility to take. But I also believe in fate. I think there are many moments on the six years that I've spent on this film that fate has been kind to us. I think [on] the day that Viggo [Mortensen] joined this film, fate was playing an incredibly wonderful hand to us. I couldn't imagine anybody other than Viggo playing that role. We were immensely lucky.

There is an innate Englishness to the story that is apparent even though there are many different accents throughout the telling of it. How did you select how it sounded?

Jackson: I felt a very strong connection with J.R.R. Tolkien. He wrote this as an English mythology. He felt that England's mythology had been lost but that old stories existed in the spirit of the Norse sagas and Greek mythology. Presumably, those same tales existed, but the records had been wiped out by the Norman invasion. He set about trying to remember [these stories] from his country. There's no doubt whatsoever that Tolkien was imagining a very English story. We're basically a bunch of Kiwi filmmakers using American dollars to make an incredibly English story! And we did take that quite seriously. To tell you the truth, it's the sole reason why the world premiere is being held here [in the UK]. There's no other reason. It could be in New Zealand, it could be in Los Angeles, but we felt pretty strongly that England should be honored with the premiere.

You've crammed a great deal into the film. What did you have to leave out, if anything? And did you have to drop anything that you regret?

Jackson: It's inevitable. We've got some wonderful footage that didn't make it into the film, which will be in the DVD. And so you can look forward to seeing some more of *The Fellowship of the Ring* sometime next year probably.

Anybody that knows the book and who has seen the movie will obviously realize that there is an enormous amount of detail, of subplot, in some cases characters, that we had to leave out. From my point of view, in a movie adaptation, there is basically only one thing that happens, and that's simplification. And I think *The Lord of the Rings* is probably the most extreme version of adapting a book that had to be simplified. To make a movie, you have to really decide on your central plot—the storyline that's going to drive the film forward.

In *The Fellowship of the Ring*, the storyline is really Frodo and the Ring. It changes a little bit. There are other key storylines that come in in the second film and the third film, but in the first movie we really had a rule. Our focus [was on] Frodo carrying the Ring, what the Ring does to Frodo, and what the Ring does to people who become involved with Frodo [in terms of] how it affects them. Any material that didn't relate directly to that we'd look at very carefully as to how important it was for the film. That really was the simple way that we approached adapting the book.

Boyens: We worked very hard in terms of bringing to life the imagery. The world is so *there* and so *true*. Sometimes, what sits on the page can be very leaden and full of exposition. [Our duty was in] bringing it to life with a sense of immediacy, aided magnificently by our actors who took that on board. There was a constant note from Peter, not only to the actors but also to Fran and I, which was to keep it fluid and immediate. We did set out feeling that we had two audiences: those who know the book and those who don't. In the end, that divide sort of merges, because what you have is the film as its own story and own journey. Hopefully, it's just going to capture you. Even if you've seen it and you know the story, you just fall into it and go "wow!"

Jackson: I felt a very strong responsibility towards an audience who had never read the book. I don't know how that breaks down, but I've got a guess that approximately two-thirds of those who see it will not have read the book. I felt my primary responsibility, as a filmmaker, was to make an entertaining and enjoyable film that could be enjoyed by anybody. It doesn't matter whether you've read it or not read it. We wanted to make a film that was enjoyable and entertaining, even if you knew nothing about Tolkien.

The Fellowship of the Ring ends abruptly on a wonderful cliffhanger. Is there more of that to come? Is the best still to come? How are you going to match the film that comes first?

Jackson: [Due to] the way that the films have been written and shot, there is a certain expectation that you will be advised to see the first film before you see the second. We don't spend a lot of time mucking around in the second time going back over all the old myths again. We just get on with it. The story of *The Two Towers* begins twenty-four or forty-eight hours after this film stops. And then the third film will be remarkable because it's all climax. Several new characters are introduced in the second film, but by the third film [*The Return of the King*], there's nobody really new to be introduced, so it's all payoff.

    I haven't seen it, so I'm not talking from that point of view, but having shot the whole movie—the three films—I think the third movie is going to end up being my favorite. It has the benefit of being all payoff; there's no setting up anymore. We shot the third movie on the total expectation that everyone will have seen the first two, and so it is just wall-to-wall climax, which is interesting.

    It's weird, slightly, knowing that there are three films. The second cast and the second crew shot them at the same time. There's a really smooth flow to them. I've always been very aware that one day somebody's going to have a nine-hour DVD marathon at home, so they will play like a unified story. I think it'll be quite fun.

"Quite fun" is an understatement, I think.

Jackson: [Laughs] Thank you!

2001

NEIL JORDAN and STEPHEN WOOLLEY
Interview with the Vampire: The Vampire Chronicles

"It's a delicious irony: being offered exactly what you want, the greatest gift in the world, and finding yourself. I found that fascinating." – acclaimed Irish filmmaker Neil Jordan on what attracted him to *Interview with the Vampire: The Vampire Chronicles*. (Warner Bros./François Duhamel)

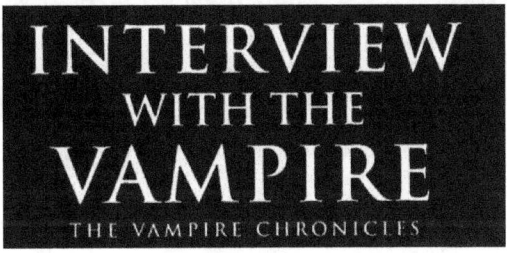

Geffen Pictures, 1994

CAST: Louis, BRAD PITT; Malloy, CHRISTIAN SLATER; Lestat, TOM CRUISE; Santiago, STEPHEN REA; Armand, ANTONIO BANDERAS; Claudia, KIRSTEN DUNST; Whore on Waterfront, VIRGINIA Mc-COLLAM; Gambler, JOHN McCONNELL; Pimp, MIKE SEELIG; Tavern Girl, BELLINA LOGAN; Yvette, THANDIE NEWTON; Widow St. Clair, LYLA HAY OWEN; Widow's Lover, LEE EMERY; New Orleans Whores, INDRA OVE, HELEN McCRORY; Plague Victim Bearer, MONTE MONTAGUE; Maid, NATHALIE BLOCH; Woman in Square, JEANETTE KONTOMITRAS; Piano Teacher, ROGER LLOYD PACK; Dollmaker, GEORGE KELLY; Creole Woman, NICOLE DUBOIS; Paris Vampires, MICHA BERGESE, RORY EDWARDS, MARCEL IURES, SUSAN LYNCH, LOUISE SALTER, MATTHEW SIM, FRANCOIS TESTORY, ANDREW TIERNAN, SIMON TYRRELL, GEORGE YIASOUMI; Estelle, SARA STOCKBRIDGE; Mortal Woman on Stage, LAURE MARSAC; Woman in Audience, KATIA CABALLERO; Mortal Boy, LOUIS LEWIS-SMITH; Madeleine, DOMIZIANA GIORDANO.

CREDITS: *Director*, Neil Jordon; *producers*, David Geffen, Stephen Woolley; *executive in charge of production*, Bonni Lee; *co-producer*, Redmond Morris; *screenplay*, Anne Rice, based on her novel; *visual effects supervisor*, Rob Legato; *directors of photography*, Philippe Rousselot; Paris: Rob Legato; *editors*, Mick Audsley, Joke van Wijk; *production designer*, Dante Ferretti; *art directors*, New Orleans: Alan Tomkins; San Francisco: Jim Tocci; Paris: Jean-Michel Hugon; *special effects supervisor*, Yves de Bono;

costume designer, Sandy Powell; *make-up supervisor and Lestat make-up*, Michele Burke; *vampire make-up*, Stan Winston Design and Co-ordination; *music*, Elliot Goldenthal. Running time: 122 minutes.

"*The vampire Lestat. Timeless. Ageless. World without end. Infinite life. Death without mortality.*

"*Lestat flows through the years on a river of blood, which sustains his existence. When he so desires, he awards his victims with immortality—whether they want it or not. Into Lestat's world, in the late eighteenth century, comes one mortal man, devastated by the loss of his beloved wife and infant daughter: one Louis de Pointe du Lac. Amid the torpid heat of a delta settlement near New Orleans, the air thick with portent and promises of unearthly desire and unspeakable horrors, Louis encounters Lestat.*

"*Two hundred years later, in late twentieth-century San Francisco, Louis decides to tell his story—a vampire's story of desire, love, yearning, grief, terror, ecstasy—to a young reporter, weaving the history that has come to be known as* Interview with the Vampire."

A Fairytale Gone Horribly Wrong
Neil Jordan and Stephen Woolley on *Interview with the Vampire: The Vampire Chronicles*

Were either of you familiar with the source novel before you became involved in the film of Interview with the Vampire?

Neil Jordan: I didn't know the book. John Boorman had told me years ago that he'd been asked to do it. That's all I knew about it. I wasn't aware of the huge reputation the book had or of its cult following. I did enjoy the book when I read it. I thought it was overwritten, but it brought up some fascinating things that I felt would make a great movie. It's not *War and Peace* [1869].

Stephen Woolley: No. Neil gave me the book after [producer] David Geffen asked if he was interested in directing it. It's still a bit of a cult book in Europe. It's much more of a bestseller in America; it's a huge bestseller over there. It really is up there with *War and Peace* in terms of sales. In Europe, it seems to be much more of a cult book. So I'd sort of vaguely heard about it, but I always thought it was something to do with Woody Allen! Did he ever do a skit where he was interviewing a vampire? When Neil gave it to me, I was a complete virgin to it. I thought it was really good. I enjoyed reading it. It's very melodramatic, sort of Barbara Cartlandish, in a way. Really enjoyable.

The book was published in 1976. Other than John Boorman, had there been many other filmmakers involved with it over the years?

Jordan: Apparently so. More producers, I think, than filmmakers. I know that they'd asked Brian De Palma, Steven Spielberg, Roman Polanski, and various other people. It's a difficult book to make into a movie. If you read the book, [you'll notice that] it's difficult initially to see the film in it because it's told from the point of view of one person. A lot of it is an interior monologue that obscures the movie that's there, in a way. The fact that a story was being told from the point of view of the vampire—with the possibilities of that whole idea and relationship—gave rise to something interesting.

Given that a lot of people have walked away from the project, what made you think you could do it? Was it just Celtic arrogance?

Jordan: No. The minute I read the book, I knew the context from which it had come. I could see that this girl had been taught by the Sisters of Mercy. I could see there were young nuns from Tipperary stuck in New Orleans who taught this strange little girl about St. Anthony and bleeding hearts and all that sort of stuff. I could relate to it immediately for that reason. Honestly, I'm serious.

Was it crucial for you to have a writing input? One assumes that there were scripts floating around.

Jordan: Yes. They showed me Anne Rice's script, and I showed it to Stephen as well, but I had to do my own work. There were areas of it that were fascinating, but it was very melodramatic—even more so than the book.

Woolley: Anne Rice's script also had [in it] bits of the other books flashing back and forth [along with] characters and scenes from the books that she wrote afterwards. When Neil wrote his version of the book, it was much closer, in fact, to the book.

Jordan: She wasn't faithful to her own novel, really.

Woolley: She wasn't at all, no.

How were you able to concentrate on the work in hand given that Anne Rice said, "Tom Cruise is no more Lestat than Edward G. Robinson is Rhett Butler." How do you divorce yourself from all of that?

Jordan: Well, in a strange way, maybe the controversy helped. We had to have a closed set when it all blew up because there was no way we could let any foreign body onto the set. So it kind of closed us off from everything—[including the] studio as well and the normal pressures that a movie like this gets. It's strange: everybody was saying, "It's becoming a typical Hollywood project," but the opposite was the case. They absolutely left us alone and said, "Go ahead and make your film."

Was there a sense of bonding?

Jordan: Totally. There was a sense of being underwater in a very strange glass bubble for six months.

Given that Anne Rice was positive about you as director from the outset, did her comments on Tom Cruise come out of the blue?

Jordan: Totally. Totally out of the blue. I actually called her and said—because I heard she was unhappy through somebody within the Geffen Company—"Look, this is the reason why we're doing this. From the point of view of the vampire, there are aspects of Tom that you've never seen before." And she said, "Oh, I understand. That's interesting," and we had a nice conversation.

Woolley: She was promoting her book *Lasher*, and so in a way, by saying all these things, she was getting headlines. Here [in the UK], you wouldn't have noticed it so much, but while we were making the film in America, it was appearing everywhere. *People* magazine, the arts pages just kept regurgitating all of her comments. It was throughout the whole filming, and I think Tom got a little hurt by it. Things kept going on. I think a lot of it was the press repeating what she'd said.

Jordan: It was.

Woolley: And it was quite upsetting, I think.

Did you have any misgivings about casting Tom Cruise as Lestat?

Jordan: No. Everybody seems to have an impression of Tom—they seem to think he's this paranoid man who exerts control over the set by these unseen advisors or something weird like that. I didn't know the guy. I thought, *Okay, if this is true and if he is somebody who tries to change things into other things and not commit himself to the part, it won't work.* All I wanted to know was: would he commit himself absolutely to it? And after meeting him, I knew he would, so I didn't have any misgivings. But to be fair to Anne Rice, I think her criticisms were genuine from her point of view. It's just that she's a particular kind of woman. I do think she was appalled at the fact that I'd cast Tom! [Laughs]

Woolley: Also, this is her most personal novel. The character of Claudia was written after the death [in 1972] of her own child, and so of all of her work—and she's really churned them out; she has loads of books in her own name and other names or pseudonyms—this is the one book that is very personal to her. It meant an awful lot to her. And so I think her approach to it was not a professional approach but very much an emotional feeling.

Given that the international press received her statement, was there perhaps some pressure on Anne Rice to produce that as a result of the first thing?

Jordan: I'm sure there was. I'm sure the studio would have done anything to get her to back the film, but there's nothing you can do to change that woman's mind. Believe me, I know that. If she had seen the movie and hated it, you would have known about it. You'd be still hearing about it now!

The death of River Phoenix, the original casting for Malloy, the journalist, came as a tragic shock. How did Christian Slater feel about taking on the role?

Woolley: It was really quite upsetting for all of us. We were shooting nights in New Orleans. I couldn't believe it when I heard the news, [which was] first thing in the morning. I got a phone call from my wife in London who said, "River's died." And I said, "That's wrong." And suddenly, floods of calls came in from Los Angeles, from the other film, from his family and his agent. I really just couldn't believe it for days after.

We'd cast River quite early on. He was one of the first people we originally cast. The film that he tragically died on, which I was executive producing, called *Dark Blood*, was completely closed down and has now been shelved. It will never be completed.* We hadn't started working with River, so on a practical level, there was no immediate effect to our production other than emotionally. We were all very, very upset, especially Tom and Brad, who were both looking forward to working with River.

---

* *Dark Blood* was shelved in 1993, following the death of River Phoenix. It was eventually completed by original director George Sluizer, who bought the rights to the project after a long period of negotiation. The film was premiered at the Netherlands Film Festival on September 20, 2012. Sluizer died exactly two years later on September 20, 2014. He was 82.

They were both big fans of his. They were all very upset and quite moved by his tragic death, but it didn't make a physical change other than we had to re-cast the movie.

Obviously, we really miss River not being in the film. Although I think Christian is absolutely fantastic, River would have done something very different. I think it would have been wonderful. What Christian did in terms of the short preparation he had to play the part [was impressive]. And also he had to shoot the San Francisco ending two or three months before he actually did the interview because that's the way the schedule dictated it. So he had to make himself available and managed to do that. He also donated all of his fees to River's charity.

How was it for Christian Slater having to step in under those circumstances?

Jordan: He found it very difficult to step into a role intended for somebody who'd died.

Was Slater the first choice?

Woolley: No. We discussed various actors at the time, but it was very hard to concentrate on it immediately. It took us some time, and we talked to lots of different people. In the end, Neil chose Christian and it was a great decision.

Is it true that Kirsten Dunst was worried about a moment in the film where she had to kiss Brad Pitt?

Jordan: Yeah, I think so.

How did that difficulty arise and how did you get around it?

Jordan: [It was] the scene where he's lying on the Paris balcony and they're saying a final goodbye to each other. I said, "Kirsten, you should kiss him here—but like an adult would. Not like a little girl." And she *begged* me—she just couldn't bring herself to do that. She found Brad's lips too big or something! [Laughs] But it just showed to me what a little girl she was, really, because the idea of her kissing men was yucky. I said, "Okay, I'll say 'cut' just the minute that you touch his lips," and the last take was the best and I didn't say "cut"! She was really angry!

I wasn't being wicked. She didn't *kiss* him—she didn't have to put her lips on top of his. I found it consoling because I was worried about a girl so young going through this experience. And when I realized that she still is a little girl and the idea of boys is "rats and snails and puppy dogs' tails," and that she still saw them that way, I thought it was great. She hasn't been damaged at all by the movie.

You don't receive a writing credit on the film. Is that just modesty on your part?

Jordan: It's pure humility on my part! [Laughs] What I had to do was reintroduce lots of aspects of [Rice's] own novel into the screenplay. As a director and a writer, the Writers Guild has a certain prejudice against you. So if you're a writer/director and you come onto an already existing project, you've got to prove you've written 50 percent of original stuff. In this case, it was impossible because what I was doing was using her writing to make this into a screenplay that I wanted. I did write some scenes myself. A lot of the humorous scenes are mine, but it's impossible to say that I did fifty percent of this work. So they decided not to give me a credit.

Was there a certain style of humor in the book?

Jordan: There's no humor at all in the book. Have you read her book? It's the most humorless book ever written. [Laughs]

Woolley: It is, actually.

Jordan: Isn't it? Even the stuff where she debunks the vampire legends. It's not funny. It's more ironic.

Was it crucial when working on a big Hollywood project to have a strong right arm in the form of Stephen [Woolley]? Would you have gone ahead without him?

Jordan: No, I wouldn't have. Stephen and myself have done three films together [*The Company of Wolves* in 1984, *The Crying Game* in 1992, and *Interview with the Vampire*]. For one thing, if you've got a $60 million budget and a Hollywood studio, you need partners on your side. We understand the way we work. Stephen knows how I work and I know how he works. And it was the way of making it as an independent movie—a European movie within the Hollywood system.

Was it a daunting prospect?

Woolley: It was very exciting. I love cinema. Budgets don't really mean a thing to me when I see a film. Whether it's a Kieszlowski film or a Mike Leigh film, a Steven Spielberg film or a Mike Nichols film, it doesn't really matter. A film is a film is a film. And I think that many of us in Europe get tarred with this brush [that] we only make independent or low-budget films: "Of course they can make *The Crying Game* or they can do *Mona Lisa* [1986], but they can't make the step up." And so I was really excited by the idea of being able to make the film with Warner Bros. and with David Geffen, because it really proved that as Europeans—Neil, myself, Dante Ferretti, and Sandy Powell—we would bring a sensibility to the movie that is really not Hollywood so much and yet making a film within the Hollywood system. And the final point is that we had the challenge of making a film that would have to bring in the bucks, which the film has done.

So it was not daunting at all. It was a real challenge and really exciting and, to me, a great experience. People always say that working with studios is an awful experience and they'll interfere—they'll do this and do that. It didn't happen. They're very, very passive in terms of their involvement in the shooting. They loved the dailies. They only ever said, "It's great. It's going in the right direction. Carry on." They were incredibly sympathetic to all the problems of what we had to do in terms of our schedule, which was quite tight [along with] the budget and everything else. The post-production period was never painless, but it was always a collaboration and a discussion. No one ever dictated anything. [They said]: "This is what we'd like you to do. This is what you're doing. This is how we see it." And if Neil didn't agree, it was fine. It was hands off.

Jordan: And it worked out cheaper. If this had been done with Hollywood's producers, it would have cost probably $120 million. It's the kind of film that does nowadays tend to get out of control.

Woolley: We wouldn't spend any more money. The schedule we had in New Orleans was a killer. It was gruelling. We worked incredibly hard, we worked to a deadline, and we got out on that deadline. We shot what we needed to shoot in San Francisco within schedule. We shot in Paris within schedule. It was a very well-controlled film. And so Warners really didn't have to be involved inasmuch as we weren't out of control. And the quality of the material was very good. And to be honest, it's a very odd subject for a major studio to make. I think they realized that they would need people that were a little strange to make this kind of film. In the end, they went, "Well, they seem to know what they're doing," and they left it in Neil's hands. It was a good experience.

Last year we had Mary Shelley's Frankenstein [1994]. *Now, just eighteen months later,* Interview with the Vampire. *What's the motivation for big stars to suddenly appear in mainstream pictures within the horror genre?*

Jordan: I just think it goes in waves in Hollywood. About ten years ago, they were all talking about sword and sorcery, weren't they? Now they're all talking about pirates. A couple of years ago they were all talking about Robin Hood. It's a big machine that's constantly looking for a new sensation. I think probably a lot of it was to do with the success of Coppola's *Dracula* [1992].

Woolley: The Silence of the Lambs [1991] was also quite significant. Up until then, most horror films had not been treated with respect. You don't think about *Frankenstein* [1931] and remember Boris Karloff accepting the Oscar. Or even films like *Psycho* [1960]. I don't think anyone won any awards for that. But when *The Silence of the Lambs* suddenly hit Oscars, finally people woke up to the notion that the genre—whether it's horror or suspense or whatever you want to call it—had suddenly grown up. Then a film's made about somebody enjoying eating other people and it was really nasty. That was a watershed for the acceptance of horror—or however you want to phrase it—as being mainstream.

How much pressure did you come under from the studio to tone down the book's very strong homoerotic element? Were they very wary about that?

Jordan: They were a bit nervous of it, yes. In terms of mainstream filmmaking, it's unusual, but I got no pressure whatsoever. I was asked—once—"Don't you think this is a bit strong?" and I just had to say, "Well that's the story." Maybe that's why it hasn't been made for so long: people were a bit scared. I didn't see it as a homoerotic thing. I just saw it as an erotic thing. I think the book does get a little bit turgid and obsessional about certain things, you know what I mean? And a bit tired. I just made as sexy a movie as I could see it. Maybe I'm not that sexy! [Laughs]

What were the things in the story that fascinated you?

Jordan: It was the idea of creating a new creature. The way that you've got a guy [Louis] who's in pain, in emotional turmoil. He wants that turmoil to end, so this other man enters his life and says, "I'll make you live again. You'll never feel pain again. You'll have absolute power." He agrees to do this and then his life is hell. It's a delicious irony: being offered exactly what you want, the greatest gift in the world, and finding yourself. All three characters find themselves in different kinds of isolation. I found that fascinating.

Some observers have admired the acting, the casting, the writing, and the direction, but have been troubled by the violence in the film. Was that necessary?

Jordan: That's the nature of the book, and that's what attracted me to the book in a way. Where you would normally see passionate relationships, blood and bloodletting is a substitute for that. I was attracted to that subject matter. It's not everybody's cup of tea. You could see it as distasteful or not. What interested me was when you take characters with such extremes of behavior and this obsessional relationship between Lestat and Louis, or between Louis, Lestat, and Claudia [Kirsten Dunst], and you create a mirror image of a little family, and you can show unfamiliar things in absolutely unfamiliar and grotesque lights. That's what attracted me to the thing, actually.

You can construct a story and a movie that is a bit like a fairytale gone horribly wrong. All those things you say are reasons why I was attracted to doing the film. I think this is an extremely moral movie because it's about moral issues.

The central question in the film is what happens to Louis when he gives up all contact with normal parameters of morality? What is he left with? He's basically left with a longing for punishment. Punishment never comes and that's an even greater punishment than if it *did* come. That's the way I saw the film.

If this was a turgid and overwritten book, why not do something original yourself?

Jordan: I didn't say the book was turgid and overwritten. I said I loved the book. I said parts of it were humorless. I said there's not a lot of humor in the book and parts of it are turgid and the book is somewhat overwritten. But I loved the book; otherwise I wouldn't have done the bloody movie. Don't quote things that I've half said. Quote what I've said, please. There's no humor in the book at all, but there's no humor in Marcel Proust, either. And I like Marcel Proust. Humor is not a guideline for something that's good or bad.

You have something in common with Bram Stoker in that you're both Irishmen.

Jordan: What I loved about Anne Rice's book was that she situated these vampires in Paris, in the center of European culture. To me it was a great relief, because the entire thing that Bram Stoker invented has become a visual cliché now: stakes through the heart, garlic, and the cross.

How much work was involved in setting up the panning shots in the theater of the vampires?

Jordan: We had to plan them, really. It was a combination of real sets and computerized matting techniques that went into them. So we had to plan everything very carefully. We had it storyboarded. There's a lot of areas where this computer work is used where you're not aware of it. To me it was a revelation because you could use scanning and computer painters to enhance the particular environments that we shot in. But we had to plan it very carefully.

And Stan Winston was brought on to the project early on?

Jordan: Not so much in that aspect of it. He was more involved in the make-ups. We had to re-design the make-ups. Actually, he was involved.

Woolley: It was partly his company that did all the computer-generated effects. He also introduced us to people who physically put the effects on. People like Rob Delgado, who was part of Digital Domain, which was the company that Jim Cameron and Stan Winston established, was the person who supervised all that aspect of the film.

Over the last ten years as you've established yourself as a director, you seem to have forsaken novel writing. Was that a conscious decision?

Jordan: Not really. It's just the way it happened. I needed a producer, which was Stephen, to whip me into making a movie. But I had nobody to stimulate me to finish a novel.

Your writing style seems to be very concise.

Jordan: The style of my writing never used to be that concise. [*Sunrise with Sea Monster*] is the most spare book I've written, and maybe it's that spare because the last time I wrote a novel was in 1984 [*The Dream of a Beast*], and in between I've written a lot of screenplays and one tends to be very spare in the description of scenes in a screenplay. Let the story dominate the proceedings rather than the use of language. So maybe that's what happened. I just hadn't written a novel for so long because I probably couldn't think of anything to write a novel about, in a way, and hadn't had the time to sit down and think about it, you know?

What satisfaction do you get out of writing?

Jordan: Writing a novel is a very private thing. It's exhausting—far more exhausting than making movies. I started writing books. I started with words and delving into language, and for me to get back to that and rediscover it was very important to me personally.

Why?

Jordan: Films are very difficult things to make and very difficult things to feed their own life into, and every movie I make, I often wonder whether I've done it or whether I've failed. Do you know what I mean? Whereas with a book, the final responsibility is absolutely yours. You stand or fail by how much you've given to it. There's great pleasure in the making of it. When you've finished it, you have people criticize it or take it this way or that way. I always see more thoughts in it that people at large do—or maybe different thoughts—because you never know whether you've finally succeeded or not.

The sea has a very specific and strong role in your fiction. What's the significance of that for you?

Jordan: It's a deeply neurotic thing. I've always lived by the sea. I grew up in Dollymount on the north side of Dublin. I was born in a little seaside town called Rosses Point, in Sligo. I bought a house in Bray. I've always lived by the sea. And when I first started writing fiction, I could only ever finish the stories if in some way I got the characters into the water somehow. [Laughs] It's a strange thing, you know? It just gives me great pleasure to write about it and to describe it. I don't know where it comes from apart from how I grew up.

Are there elements of your early life and your relationship with your father in your writing?

Jordan: Kind of, yes, there are. The fishing, definitely. My father died in 1984, and because he always told me ghost stories, I always believed I would be haunted some day, and I was profoundly upset when I wasn't!

What does Anne Rice think now?

Jordan: Well she's written another book, which begins in Paris. It's a very complicated book. People are talking about it, obviously, but I'd have to see if a script could be gotten out of it first [before deciding whether I want to direct it].

But the ending—you've got these two guys, and they're both given eternal life. For one of them, it's eternal hell, and for the other, it's eternal pleasure. Louis says, "Isn't this *dreadful*, we have to kill people to live?" And Lestat says, "We're not monsters. Aren't we great? Nobody punishes us." So I wanted to end with the second principle rather than the first, just for reasons of my own satisfaction.

Is it true that David Geffen was so pleased with the film that he gave you carte blanche to make the Michael Collins *project?*

Jordan: I wouldn't call it carte blanche. You never get that. But within reason, yeah. I've had this project for years, and various people have wanted to do different versions of it. One was with Michael Cimino, and then Kevin Costner wanted to do a version. They've [now] said, "Let's do it." I think various things have happened that have made it possible, not least the peace talks. Perhaps there could be some objectivity around the whole area now and it might be possible to make a film that would not be as inflammatory. I wrote the script a long time ago. I'm rewriting it at the moment and trying to get it down and into a manageable shape where it can be made. It's not going to be a big budget film.

What kind of man do you think Michael Collins was, and what was his attraction for you?

Jordan: What do I see him as? It's hard to say. He's a genuinely tragic figure. He's somebody who set up a military machine to achieve a certain end, which at the time was to make British rule in Ireland unworkable, and then tried to dismantle that machine. Having built it, he found he couldn't dismantle it. To me it's a story about the use and the consequences of the use of political violence.

The shock ending of your film of Interview with the Vampire *augurs very much towards a sequel. Did that stem from studio pressure?*

Jordan: Well, I wrote that. They didn't. And when I wrote it and I presented them with the first draft of the script, they said, "Look, we love this, but we think the ending is a bit too Hollywood!" [Laughs] That's the truth, so it's my fault!

Was there a sequel in mind?

Jordan: No, it's nothing to do with the sequel. One enjoyed the character of Lestat so much, I wanted to end the film with him.

1995

FRANCK KHALFOUN
Maniac

"Somebody came out of the movie and said he felt he'd seen his puppy get run over." - director Franck Khalfoun on working with Elijah Wood on the remake of *Maniac*. (Canal +/Daniel C. McFadden)

La Petite Reine/Studio 37/Canal+, 2012

CAST: Frank Zito, ELIJAH WOOD; Anna, NORA ARNEZEDER; Jessica, GENEVIEVE ALEXANDRA; Rita, JAN BROBERG; Lucie, MEGAN DUFFY; Judy, LIANNE BALABAN; Martin, JOSHUA DE LA GARZA; Frank's Mother, AMERICA OLIVO; Jason, SAMMI ROTIBI; '80s Man, BRIAN AMES; Man in the Alley, AARON COLOM; Puppeteer #2, ALEX DIAZ; Young Frank, ELI DUPONT; Waiter, LUIS FERNANDEZ-GIL; Clubber Boy, DAN HUNTER; Saleswoman, DEVRA KORWIN; Pharmacist, AKBAR KURTHA; Police Chief, SAL LANDI; Officer Burton, BRYAN LUGO; Puppeteer #1, MIKE McCARTY; Policewoman, DELE OGUNDIRAN; '80s Man #2, PATRICK ORR; Clubber Girl, STEFFINNIE PHROMMANY; Officer Norton, RON REZNIK; Old Man, MIC RODGERS; Dancer #2, ROCHELLE RUDOLPH; Walker, GREGORY TAIEB; Dancer #1, LAUREN EMILY VAUGHAN; Frank Double, STEVEN WILLIAMS.

CREDITS: *Directed by* Franck Khalfoun; *producers*, Alexandre Aja, Thomas Langmann, William Lustig; *screenplay*, Alexandre Aja, Grégory Levasseur, based on the motion picture Maniac by William Lustig; *co-producer*, Emmanuel Montamat; *executive producers*, Antoine de Cazotte, Daniel Delume, Andrew W. Garroni, Alix Taylor, Pavlina Hatoupis; *associate producers*, Justine Raczkiewicz, J.B. Popplewell; *music*, Rob; *editor*, Baxter; *director of photography*, Maxime Alexandre; *production design*, Stefania Cella; *costume design*, Mairi Chisholm; *art director*, Dooner; *special make-up effects*, Greg Nicotero, Howard Berger; *SFX supervisor*, Eric Coon; *visual effects supervisor*, Jamison Goei. Running time: 89 minutes.

"Just when the streets seemed safe, a serial killer with a fetish for scalps is back and on the hunt. Frank is the withdrawn owner of a mannequin store, but his life changes when young artist Anna appears asking for his help with her new exhibition. As their friendship develops and Frank's obsession escalates, it becomes clear that she has unleashed a long-repressed compulsion to stalk and kill."

Keeping the Cat in the Closet
Franck Khalfoun on *Maniac*

It's a brave man who remakes a classic. It was always going to be contentious, wasn't it? What made you want to do it?

Franck Khalfoun: A brave man or a total idiot! One or the other! I knew when [producers] Alex Aja and Thomas Langmann first approached me that it was a classic of the genre. I was reluctant and I was very clear that we come up with some concept—they were open to some concepts—that was different [otherwise] I don't think that I'd be willing to be involved. I knew how badly remakes get panned and [are] hated by the core audience. That being said, I also know the core audiences are real cinephiles; they like all kinds of movies. I was willing to give them a movie that stood on its own. We didn't make a movie for the sake of milking a brand. We actually came up with a film that was decent, that was good and that stood up by itself and that could be appreciated.

It's faithful to the source material—the Bill Lustig original. Was that important to you?

We go off of a story, you know? My whole thing is [that] many stories are the same. It's really from what point of view you're telling them. It's a story about a man who scalps women—a photographer. In that sense, it's the same. Some things were the same. My job really was to adapt it to a more contemporary audience and to try and have the kind of sensibility that an audience can appreciate today, more so than reinventing the story.

Alexandre Aja and Grégory Lavasseur are giving you a chance. How big a challenge or opportunity did it represent to you?

We've done a bunch of things together. They've produced one for me before. Obviously, it's difficult to get a movie made, and we were uncertain whether this one would be a gift or whether this one would be very difficult to pull off because of the fact that it's a remake and it's a loved film. But we've got a long-standing collaboration. It's certainly wonderful to be included and have them call on me to work on projects with them and direct things, certainly. So it's nice. We have a really great pool of creativity between the three of us. When I got the script, it wasn't really written for the point of view [of the central character], so I had to spend a lot of time re-adapting the script for the concept. It was a real creative partnership.

Were you nervous of the challenge, or did you think "bring it on"?

Oh totally, bring it on! It's kinda funny. You read about what people are saying immediately when you say you're doing *Maniac*. It's just a challenge. My niche, if you will, was [that] I knew if we came up with a good movie, the genre audience would not be turned off. They respect films, and they're not just going to hate for the sake of hating. I understand the genre audiences have had a real hard time with some of the remakes, because a lot of them have just been a way for producers to exploit a brand. I knew that if I remained true and tried to do something creative, that they would forgive me, and I think that was the case.

What came first: the film or Elijah Wood?

The film came first. Obviously, when you have an actor like Joe Spinell, who is really the most remarkable thing—for me anyway—in the original film, you're looking for someone who is his contemporary, who is similar.

There's nobody like Joe Spinell.

There's nobody. That's the first point. But in terms of silhouettes and what he looks like and the way that he is in that movie, when we started talking to Elijah, it didn't seem like it would work at first, and then we saw the total benefit. For me, one of the main things—as much as I love Joe Spinell—was that I had a hard time in the original film with the love story. It seemed that this guy was such a horrific and awkward [individual] that I had a hard time believing that a fashion model would fall for him. I'm sure that today's audiences might feel the same way today, especially as today, women are a lot smarter, there's much more information out there, and people are really more cautious about who they let into their lives. With Elijah's boyish charm and kind eyes, I felt that could definitely add to the film. To this version of the film, anyway.

No more typecasting for Elijah Wood after this. Was that part of the attraction for him, and were you concerned about the baggage he brought with him?

I think it's the first time that I've worked with an actor where I've felt the baggage could work to our advantage, you know? You consider in most of his movies—and he has played some tough parts—for the most part, he is loved as the heroic and kind and fair character. That's the baggage he came with. I thought how much fun that would be for me to break that—turning this kind character into an evil monster. It was very interesting to play it in this very disarming and charming manner and soft-spoken way. It really benefited us, and it was really truly terrifying. Somebody came out of the movie one day and said he kinda felt he'd seen his puppy get run over. I thought that was a great quote.

So he came in to break the bubble of that typecasting.

More importantly, he was really intrigued by the idea of doing an entire movie in this manner. And I think also—which I didn't know before—he's a huge horror fan and he's become [via] travelling the world, going to all the Fantastic fests, and seeing the huge array of genre and horror films. He is a cinephile in the genre. He knows horror movies really well; he loves 'em.

It's a no-holds-barred performance from Elijah Wood. Did he need encouragement or did you have to rein him in?

No. At first, I was questioning a little bit of the shyness, if you will, of the character. But he really played it well. A wonderful thing about the character, and I've heard it mentioned before, an awful lot of the filming process and then later on when we were doing voice-overs and ADR, he continued to bring things because he wasn't on screen. So later on in the movie, he could continue working on the character and could continue adding lines. Some of the lines and some of the things he said, he's off camera. And some of those things he said much later. So I think the whole process was really interesting for him, and that's why he was so drawn to the project.

Given the backdrop to the film, was the gore all in the script, or did you ramp it up even more when you shot it?

I'm thinking it was all on the script. What we ramped up obviously was that we were a lot closer to it because we were seeing it in a point of view. We were focused in on the gore aspects of it, you know? It was then drawing the line between going too far and maintaining the audience's attention and keeping them in. I didn't want it to be the type of movie that made you laugh, in a way—where the gore became so over the top that it became ridiculous and it was ridiculed. It was a big part of having the character be real. Everything should function on a more realistic level. I didn't want it to look fake or to pull the audience out. So it was a real balance of "How much gore do we give them, and how much do we pull back?" For instance, [there was the issue of] the head in this film, the Tom Savini effect where a head explodes, which was big at the time. I felt that one should be left alone. It was cool at the time, and there are some things you don't wanna mess with. And I think that maybe that would have been too much for this audience. We're taking you out of the character way too much.

I agree. Straight horror should be horrific. Why ham it up?

Right.

Are modern audiences ready for a film like this, or have they been insulated against it via films of recent vintage?

In terms of the way it was shot, audiences are ready for this type of film. In terms of the horror, I agree with you. If you're laughing at it, you're being pulled away from it. Given that some of the laughter is kind of nervous, then it flips you out and you're not participating in the film any more. You're defeated in the process of making a horror movie. Horror for me should remain visceral and heartfelt. That's what I wanted out of this one. People go, "Oh, its super gory and violent," but it's not as gory as the majority of the horror films that are out there. I think it's the fact that it's so visceral and you're so close to it and it's so serious that perhaps it seemed that way. Does that make sense?

Opting for point-of-view was a brave move. It keeps Frank anonymous and makes the audience complicit. Talk about that and the decision to not show your very famous star on screen.

That was a big debate, and obviously there are a couple of tricks that I put in there for the audience to be able to see the actor. They're all justified within our concept, so I'm okay with it. At the very most when you make a movie it's not that big a challenge, really. Technically it was in two parts. Moviemaking is about feeling empathy for your character—you wanna follow them on their journey. And if you don't see the character, [then] that's a real challenge. The idea that I wanted to do a suspense movie/horror movie without the techniques, without all the tools that I need to cover everything—the change of angles, the construction of time—I'm not able to do that because everything is seen from one point of view. So I'm stripped of all the tools that are required. What I did have was the audience's complicity. I was able to make things look beautiful, to sound beautiful, and to trap an audience into this man's existence. And if somehow you felt that you couldn't get away from all of the things that he's doing, then you were able at the same time to feel something of the inevitability of what he's doing: the inability to remove himself, the inability to stop himself, which is his disease, his major problem. He tries not to kill Anna, but you know that she's doomed regardless. The audience is trapped in the same way that he is. So I didn't need the trickery that you see in horror films—the cat jumping out of the closet, if you will. So it was a completely different technique to horrifying and scaring people. It was a lot more enjoyable and a lot more personal, I felt.

What was the female perspective on the movie? What kind of a reaction did you get from your actresses?

You mean the females who have watched the movie or the actresses that are in the film?

Both.

A few females have used the word "misogynist," but for the most part I'm certainly not trying to glorify the violence. For the actors, it was strange for them to have to act into the camera. Elijah was gracious enough to be with us every day, because I think he understood that a great deal of his character would live through the eyes of the other performers. So he was there every day to ensure that they got eye lines and the right emotion from him. I think it was exciting for them; it was a new experience. Actors today are often acting with green screens—with nothing—so this was a little bit like that.

It seems that there is a touch of Peeping Tom [1960] *about* Maniac. *Was that in the back of your mind when you were making it?*

It wasn't so much in the back of my mind, but I felt comfortable with the idea. This movie in a way went back to the origins of horror, and to me, *Peeping Tom* is one of those great films that started it all. It made me feel good that this movie might be mentioned in the same sentence.

Well if it's good enough for Michael Powell, I guess it's good enough for you, too. Is that fair?

[Laughs] I take that as a compliment. Thank you.

2013

GEORGE LUCAS
Star Wars: Episode I – The Phantom Menace

"There's a lot of people who don't get *Star Wars*. That doesn't really bother me at all. There's a lot of critics that hate it." – George Lucas, creator of *Star Wars*, on the legacy of his phenomenon. (20th Century Fox/Ralph Nelson Jr)

STAR WARS EPISODE I
THE PHANTOM MENACE
20th Century Fox, 1999

CAST: Qui-Gon Jinn, LIAM NEESON; Obi-Wan Kenobi, EWAN McGREGOR; Queen Amidala/Padme, NATALIE PORTMAN; Anakin Skywalker, JAKE LLOYD; Senator Palpatine, IAN McDIARMID; Shmi Skywalker, PERNILLA AUGUST; Sio Bibble, OLIVER FORD DAVIES; Captain Panaka, HUGH QUARSHIE; Jar Jar Binks, AHMED BEST; C-3P0, ANTHONY DANIELS; R2-D2, KENNY BAKER; Yoda, FRANK OZ; Chancellor Valorum, TERENCE STAMP; Boss Nass, BRIAN BLESSED; Watto, ANDREW SECOMBE; Darth Maul, RAY PARK; Sebulba, LEWIS McLEOD; Wald, WARWICK DAVIS; Captain Tarpals, STEVEN SPEIRS; Nute Gunray, SILAS CARSON; Rune Haako, JEROME BLAKE; Daultay Dofine, ALAN RUSCOE; Ric Olié, RALPH BROWN; Fighter Pilot Bravo 5, CELIA IMRIE; Fighter Pilot Bravo 2, BENEDICT TAYLOR; Fighter Pilot Bravo 3, CLARENCE SMITH; Mace Windu, SAMUEL L. JACKSON; Palace Guard, DOMINIC WEST; Rabé, CRISTINA da SILVA; Eirtaé, FRIDAY (LIZ) WILSON; Yané, CANDICE ORWELL; Saché, SOFIA COPPOLA; Sabé, KEIRA KNIGHTLEY; Republic Cruiser Captain, BRONAGH GALLAGHER; Republic Cruiser Pilot, SILAS CARSON; TC-14, JOHN FENSOM; Fode, GREG PROOPS; Beed, SCOTT CAPURRO; Jabba the Hutt, HIMSELF; Jira, MARGARET TOWNER; Kitster, DHRUV CHANCHANI; Seek, OLIVER WALPOLE; Amee, JENNA GREEN; Melee, MEGAN UDALL; Eeth Koth, HASSANI SHAPI; Adi Gallia, GIN; Saesee Tiin, KHAN BONFILS; Yarael Poof, MICHELLE TAYLOR; Even Piell, MICHAELA COTTRELL; Depa Billaba, DIPIKA O'NEILL JOTI; Yaddie, PHIL EASON; Aks Moe, MARK COULIER; Yoda Puppeteers,

KATHY SMEE, DON AUSTEN, DAVID GREENAWAY; Voice of TC-14, LINDSAY DUNCAN; Voice of Darth Maul, PETER SERAFINOWICZ; Voice of Rune Haako, JAMES TAYLOR; Voice of Daultay Dofine, CHRIS SANDERS; Voice of Lott Dod, TOBY LONGWORTH; Voice of Aks Moe, MARC SILK, Voice of Tey How, TYGER.

CREDITS: *Director*, George Lucas; *screenplay*, George Lucas; *producer*, Rick McCallum; *executive producer*, George Lucas; *director of photography*, David Tattersall, BSC; *production designer*, Gavin Bocquet; *editors*, Paul Martin Smith GBFE, Ben Burtt; *costume designer*, Trisha Biggar; *sound design*, Ben Burtt; *music*, John Williams; *design director*, Doug Chiang; *visual effects supervisors*, John Knoll, Dennis Muren ASC, Scott Squires; *animation director*, Rob Coleman; *live action creature effects supervisor*, Nick Dudman; *chief make-up artist*, Paul Engelen. Running time: 136 minutes.

> "Senator Palpatine, an influential politician, is quietly making moves to consolidate his position in a time of unrest throughout the Republic, during which the government has been weakened and turned into a bureaucratic nightmare. A specific incident within this framework places Palpatine at the center of a conflict between the gigantic, commercial Trade Federation and the small, peaceful planet Naboo. Naboo is threatened by the might of the wealthy corporate powers, which begin to disregard the constraints of the weak galactic government. The young queen of Naboo finds herself faced with difficult decisions. Committed to peace, she must choose whether to sacrifice her ideals when war descends upon her people. Sent into this crisis to negotiate a settlement are two Jedi Knights, the guardians of peace and justice in the galaxy. Prepared for a political dispute, the Jedi Master, Qui-Gon Jinn, and apprentice, Obi-Wan Kenobi, discover that the Trade Federation is about to unleash its mighty forces in open combat against Naboo. Unless the two Jedi can succeed, the planet's fate is grim. In the course of the their adventure, Qui-Gon discovers a young boy, Anakin, who is a slave on the desert planet Tatooine. Qui-Gon senses that Anakin is the individual destined to bring balance to the Force, and makes a fateful decision to train Anakin as a Jedi Knight. At the same time, Anakin begins a friendship with the Queen of Naboo."

I Have the Power Now

George Lucas on *Star Wars: Episode I – The Phantom Menace*

Did you ever feel over the years, with the Star Wars [1977] *phenomenon mushrooming and growing to a massive extent, that you had created a monster that you would never be able to control?*

George Lucas: No. There's not much you can do about it. Once it takes on a life of its own, you either go with it or you don't, but it's not going to stop it from continuing to happen. I've tried to go with it as much as I can and keep it in check as much as I can. A few years ago, I came to the realization that this is probably what I'll be known for whether I like it or not. I spent ten years of my life before doing it and I'll probably spend ten years of my life now doing it. So twenty years of my life will have been spent doing these films, and that's a significant amount of time. I just have to live with the fact that at some point in your life, you realize that that's what you are.

What do you think you've tapped into with this phenomenon? Why do people react as they do?

Ultimately, it's because part of the experiment I was playing with when I started it was to take mythological motifs and move them into a more modern format. I think ultimately that the ancient fears and emotions and psychological drives in people haven't changed that much. They're still the same as they were during the Greeks or during Shakespeare's time.

What is it about the Jedi and the Force that inspires fans to adopt that language and turn it into an almost cult?

If Francis said that, he was probably saying it in jest, because he was contemplating political aspirations at that point. A lot of the fans, no matter what you do, become obsessed, in any form. It's interesting that fans become less obsessed in the film medium than they do in the record medium. There are a lot more obsessed fans. Why it is I'm not completely sure. You get that sort of thing no matter what you do. The film isn't a religious film or anything. It's a film that contemplates spiritual matters and the mystery of entities and powers beyond our knowledge, which *all* mythology has done throughout history. Most of the most powerful mythology is based on that. So you have to build a sort of cosmology that fits the universe that you've created. In this case, it's kind of a generalization and metaphor for all kinds of religions.

Do you ever lose patience with the fans' obsessiveness?

No, no. I don't have that much contact with it, so there's not much I can do about it. I know it comes with success. Any time there's anything successful, or sometimes even things that *aren't* successful, they become cultish. It's especially more prominent now with the Internet, because it's much easier to find another person who believes the same things you believe. As soon as two people believe the same, you've got a cult.

You've been very smart in retaining control over the things you've created. In doing so, in essence is there no limit to your vision? You're not restricted by what other people have written in the Star Wars *canon—you can expand out because you wrote it.*

Well, yeah. It's something that I've created and therefore I've worked very hard in terms of the cinematic processes to keep control of the work and not have studios or any outside people try to change the vision to make it more conventional or more marketable or anything. And as a result, it's fine. You never really know in film what's gonna happen. The next film is a love story. It's the next sequel. It'll probably drop down considerably. And the third one is a very dark film and probably will not do even close to what the other two have done.

But I have the power now to do that: to say, "Yeah, I know this won't make that much money, but I'm gonna do it anyway because it's part of the story that we're telling. And the story is more important than how successful it is in terms of each individual film." I think of it as six films. I think of all six films as one film. It's accepting all six films as one, not each one individually as it gets released.

Would it be your first nightmare to lose control over what you create? Does that keep you awake?

Well, I think that is a driving force for most creative people. Nobody likes to do something—and art is very elusive—and have somebody else come in and muck around with it a little bit here and there. I don't mind talking to friends of mine, contemporaries who are also artists and who I respect. But to have businesspeople come in, or marketing people, or something like that—it's very arbitrary and it's destructive and nobody has ever liked it.

You got yourself out of that loop at the right time. Perhaps no one like you could ever come along again, because the film business is so corporate now.

Oh, I don't know. The independent American film industry now is bigger than it's ever been, and 25 percent of the films released now are independent films. So actually, that part of it has grown substantially from the way it used to be.

Do you think that's a good thing?

Yeah, I do think it's a good thing. Being a San Francisco filmmaker, I've never been very pleased about the dominance of Hollywood over the American film industry. We need more diversity. I'm very pro-regional filmmaking in the United States, like in New York and Chicago, Austin, Texas, and San Francisco. We exist, too. I've lived in San Francisco all my life. There are three or four little studios up there. And I think in the end, because we're not part of the studio system, we're able to make more interesting films.

The special effects, once you've figured it out, then you think, *How in the world are we gonna do this?* What it was is I had an idea. When I started out in college, my father was very discouraging towards me becoming an illustrator, which is what I wanted to do. So I went into the social sciences and primarily majored in anthropology. One of my classes was on mythology. In that class, one of the professors was saying that one of the last mythological genres that's left is the Western. Then I got into film school, I studied film, I started making movies. In the meantime, in the film world, I began to realize that most of the films had become very realistic and gritty. A whole different kind of film had evolved. After I did my first film, I was looking around for ideas, and one of my ideas was to do one about growing up in high school, cruising and that sort of thing. Another one I had was to try to make a modern myth, to sort of continue that tradition that had been left off with the Western and put it into the format of a Saturday

Matinee Serial: all action/adventure, but basically using the same psychological underpinnings and motifs that existed for thousands of years. It was out of that that the whole thing started. It went back on the shelf for a while. I went off and did *American Graffiti* [1973]. After that I came back and thought, *I'm gonna do this*, and then started writing it.

At the beginning, I was pretty stung by it. Now it's part of my life, I guess.

This is the first time you've directed since 1977. What put you off directing and what brings you back?

I'd always wanted to go back to directing, but one thing sort of led to another. When I finished *Star Wars*, I had to pull my companies together to deal with *Star Wars* as an entity. I had licensing, and there were a lot of things that suddenly didn't exist before and that I didn't even think about. Suddenly, I had to cope with if I was going to take advantage of what this opportunity presented to me. ILM [Industrial Light and Magic] was just for one movie, but now that we were doing more movies, I had to build that into a real company and I had to oversee the entire movie. So I wanted to make sure that I could oversee and control everything, rather than be locked into working [on] directing a movie, because you sort of get out of touch for four or five months at a time.

So I became an executive producer, and also at the same time, I had a couple of ideas on the shelf that I was toying with. I mentioned one to Steve Spielberg, the Indiana Jones film [*Raiders of the Lost Ark*, 1981], and he said, "I wanna do that." So suddenly, I was producing that picture. I just found myself a producer. So I finished all the *Star Wars* films and started a family. And I wanted to spend more time with my family and raise them. I didn't really want to do any more *Star Wars* films at that time because I was kinda burned out on the whole thing. So I spent time raising my family and trying to progress the technology that I needed to make the kind of films that I had imagined and that I hoped *Star Wars* would be.

Were you ever tempted back to directing?

No. I don't miss it at all. Directing is a lot of hard work.

Bob Hoskins said it was like being pecked to death by pigeons; everyone's asking you questions.

That's right. That's *exactly* what it's like. And you have to get up early in the morning.

Didn't you do some second unit stuff?

Yeah. I kept directing. It wasn't like I'd stopped. I actually directed second unit, and as an executive producer, I'd oversee productions rigorously. It wasn't like a normal picture in those kinds of situations. But I had a lot of different things that I wanted to do. There were a lot of films I wanted to make that weren't *Star Wars* films, and I wanted to push this technology forward. Again, I could imagine *Star Wars* being something, and then I'd always have to cut it way, way, way down in order to make it. All three films were done that way, so I said, "I'm not gonna go back and do *Star Wars* until I get the technology to where if I can imagine it, I can do it. I'm not stuck with compromising by putting people in rubber suits that don't work and all that sort of stuff."

So I continued to develop the companies, develop the technology, raise my family, make offbeat kinds of movies that I wanted to make, and did the TV series. Then when I'd finished all that and we had the technology and my kids were old enough, I decided to come back and do the next *Star Wars* and direct it myself because it was going to be using techniques and technology that nobody had ever used before, and I wanted to try and learn it while I made the movie and figure out how it actually works. That's why I came back to directing. And now I'll probably stay directing, because I've done the executive producing thing, so I can go back to directing again.

You mention six films in the Star Wars *series. Perhaps the only thing comparable to it is* Star Trek, *which is at about ten films now. Could you ever foresee a time when you've completed the* Star Wars *sextet, but you might come back and do a completely separate story with new characters which aren't specifically related to Luke Skywalker, Han Solo, and the whole mythology that you've created?*

I'm sure I will come back after I've finished the *Star Wars* series to do a lot of different kinds of movies. But I doubt if any of them will be in this kind of science-fiction mood. There are too many other films I'd rather make, and there's not enough time to actually make them all.

On the back of that, do you feel that you have been pigeonholed too much with Star Wars?

No. I chose to return. I could have *not* come back to this. I knew it was a ten-year commitment. I knew it was a lot of work, a big chunk of my life. I guess I resign myself to the fact that this is probably what I'm going to be known for. I like *Star Wars*, and it was the chance to actually make them the way I envisioned them, the way I could imagine them—was too strong a lure, really. That's what brought me back: the fact that finally I could do it without all these chains around me. That was actually the most fun part of the movie, just being able to not have to figure out how to get around a problem. If I wanted to tell a story, I could just tell it, and tell it straight. I didn't need to figure out how I was gonna get the droids into the ship because there were stairs and not a ramp.

All that kinda stuff. You spend all your time figuring out around problems: "I can't shoot this character too close because there's a rubber mask and the eyes don't work too well." I didn't wanna have to face all that stuff. I wanted to be able to have alien characters that could actually act and perform and be funny and run around and be like anybody else. That was something I was striving toward. And to be able to have locations where I could say, "We're on a landing platform in Coruscant," and do it. Before, with *Star Wars*, I couldn't even conceive of doing something like that. It would have been beyond any capability that I had. So that was fun.

To many people, Star Wars *is the film of the millennium. But what do you say to those people who just don't get it? And if you had to sit someone down to explain the whole* Star Wars *thing, where would you begin?*

Interestingly enough, I think that only about 30 or 40 percent of the world has ever seen or heard of *Star Wars*, so in the grander scale, it's something I'm used to. Obviously, nobody makes a movie and thinks that everybody in the world is gonna see it. More people see television shows than see movies, and obviously *Star Wars* has been on television, so it's been allowed to expand its market a little bit. But even so, it doesn't get seen by everybody. So that doesn't really bother me at all. And there's a lot of people who don't get it. They don't like it. There a lot of critics that *hate* it. There are a lot of people, especially kids, who have never seen the other films. This is the first one they've seen. So they'll get to see it in order, which I think is good.

People talk about the film using words like purity, spirituality, and sincerity. Others ask how that fits with merchandising and Qui-Gon Jinn on a lollipop. Did you think carefully about that element?

The films are very separate from the merchandising. I don't have a lot to do with that. I make the movies; the company then takes it and exploits it. The reason that happens is that it's very hard to make money-making movies, even *Star Wars* movies. And I'm a San Francisco company, so we don't have the resources that they have in Hollywood. We don't have a giant studio. We're a real small entity compared to the major studios. So we have to use everything we can to sustain ourselves.

I was fortunate that merchandising grew up around *Star Wars*. It grew up because kids liked to take the fantasy of the movie and play with it in their ordinary daily lives. That's actually how that whole phenomenon got created. And I don't think that's a bad thing. It's great for kids to have fantasy lives; it's great for kids to play. A lot of people think that it's somehow a sin that children should play. I think that's completely wrong. We live in an economic world, unfortunately, and as I said, in San Francisco, the joke is that there are three big studios there—four, really, but Pixar is new—but the old three that have always been there are Saul Zaentz's company, Fantasy Films, which did *The English Patient* [1996] and *Amadeus* [1984]. He's actually a record company, and they make records in order to make movies. And then Francis [Ford Coppola] and American Zoetrope. He actually sells wine in order to make movies. And I sell toys in order to make movies.

In a real world, you can't exist as a movie company. It's not financially viable, no matter how successful you are. So you have to figure out another way to get a revenue stream to keep yourself going for those times when you make movies that aren't successful. It's a very expensive medium to work in. What I've been trying to do is struggle to make it less expensive to work in so you can also make more esoteric movies with grander themes. So the world of children and the world of art and the world of commerce are all sort of mixed together in the real world. You try and separate them out and say, "In the most perfect world, children will all be given toys for free and nobody will have to pay to go to the movies," which would be great if somebody would feed those of us that have to do the work.

Do you watch movies to relax?

I like movies. I go to movies a lot, actually. I don't know what the last one is I liked. [Laughs] That's a tough one. Old-time favorites? I like *Seven Samurai* [1954] and *A Hard Day's Night* [1964] and *Dr. Strangelove* [also 1964]. I like lots and lots of movies. I enjoy films just like anybody else does. In fact, probably more than most people, which is why I'm doing it.

1999

JAMES MANGOLD and CATHY KONRAD
Identity

"There's a great Everyman quality about John." – director James Mangold on his *Identity* leading man, John Cusack. They are pictured together on set. (Sony/Suzanne Tenner)

IDENTITY

Sony, 2003

CAST: Ed, JOHN CUSACK; Rhodes, RAY LIOTTA; Paris, AMANDA PEET; Larry, JOHN HAWKES; Dr. Malick, ALFRED MOLINA; Ginny, CLEA DUVALL; George York, JOHN C. McGINLEY; Lou, WILLIAM LEE SCOTT; Robert Maine, JAKE BUSEY; Malcolm Rivers, PRUITT TAYLOR VINCE; Caroline Suzanne, REBECCA DE MORNAY; Defense Lawyer, CARMEN ARGENZIANO; District Attorney, MARSHALL BELL; Alice York, LEILA KENZLE; Assistant District Attorney, MATT LETSCHER; Timmy York, BRET LOEHR; Judge Taylor, HOLMES OSBOURNE; Detective Varole, FREDERICK COFFIN; Bailiff Jenkins, JOE HART; Naked Businessman, MICHAEL HIRSCH; Bailiff, TERENCE BERNIE HINES; Frozen Body, STUART BESSER.

CREDITS: *Director*, James Mangold; *screenplay*, Michael Cooney; *producer*, Cathy Konrad; *executive producer*, Stuart Besser; *associate producer*, Dixie J. Capp; *music*, Alan Silvestri; *director of cinematography*, Phedon Papamichael; *editor*, David Brenner; *production design*, Mark Friedberg; *art direction*, Jess Gonchor; *costume design*, Arianne Phillips; *special make-up effects supervisors*, Greg Nicotero, Robert Kurtzman. Running time: 90 minutes.

> "What if every choice we ever make is already made for us? What if there really were no coincidences in life, and our destinies were already predetermined?

> "Ten strangers with secrets are brought together in a savage rainstorm: a limo driver, an '80s TV star, a cop who is transporting a killer, a call girl, a pair of newlyweds, and a family in crisis. All take shelter at a desolate motel run by a nervous night manager.
>
> "Relief in finding shelter is quickly replaced with fear as the ten travelers begin to die, one by one. They soon realize that, if they are to survive, they'll have to uncover the secret that has brought them all together."

Entering a Narrative Hallucination
James Mangold and Cathy Konrad on *Identity*

Audiences might think they can spot lots of influences in Identity. *Where did the story come from?*

James Mangold: It was from an original screenplay that Cathy found by Michael Cooney.

Cathy Konrad: I'm a Sony-based company. I produce other movies other than my husband's, and a common occurrence in Hollywood is agents sending out spec screenplays. Basically this script went out, it came to my company, I read it and quite liked it. I loved the mystery/puzzle movie—the idea of something that had this kind of grand twist at the end. So I sold it initially—without Jim attached to direct it—to Screen Gems, which was a counterpart to Sony. I took it home for the weekend and said, "This is a script I've just got." He read it and said, "I want to do it!" I sold it on a Friday. He read it, said he wanted to do it on a Sunday, and I called the studio and said, "I think we should move this over to Sony proper now because Jim's interested." So it came together very quickly.

Mangold: What attracted me to it when I read it was that I'm a big fan of a sub-genre that I like to call "the single location thriller" or "the claustrophobic, circumscribed location thriller." That for me encompasses so many of my favorite films, like Hitchcock with *Lifeboat* [1944] or *Rear Window* [1954] or *Rope* [1948]. Or coming forward, *The Others* [2002]. In between, *The Shining* [1980], *Knife in the Water* [1962], *Dead Calm* [1989], *Alien* [1986], John Carpenter's *The Thing* [1982]. I could keep going! They're all about how somehow an ensemble is fenced in. What interests me is not only thematically what happens, but that you have all these people stuck in a place, confined and battling, and trying to figure out what the predator is around them.

But there's another aspect that I love about these films, which is that they tend to be more visually daring. That flies in the face of conventional wisdom about movies, which is that whenever someone is taking a play and making a movie out of it they say, "You've got to open it up and make it take place in nineteen different places instead of just this parlor." One of the great things about these confined films is that somehow the limitations upon the filmmaker make the movies more cinematic, not less so. I very much looked forward to that when I read this: the idea and challenges of trying to stage something that way.

Did Michael Cooney remain involved?

Konrad: Michael had written a very good script that needed work. He was very collaborative with Jim and I. We had very specific notes. The one thing that Jim and I really focused on was enhancing the characters in the script. Michael wrote a wonderful, structural puzzle box of a movie that had a great beginning, middle, and end, and the characters were very intriguing. One thing that I'm very proud of in the movie and that Jim and I worked at was the cast. I think it's splendid for this kind of movie. We really wanted to raise the bar by bringing that kind of quality into the movie. So we worked very hard with Michael to give each one of these people in this movie a distinct personality, if you will. They each had to represent a piece of the whole, which comes together in the end. That was something that we worked really hard at establishing in a very short period of time because the movie doesn't afford you a lot of time to talk or get to know these people. It happens very quickly in the first act, and then you have to be on the journey. We paid a lot of attention to that kind of detail.

Did you bring much of your own original writing to the script?

Mangold: I did some work on the script, but Michael designed this house, the architecture of this place, this journey. What I really wanted to do—and tried to do in working on it—was in the way Cathy's talking about the cast. I couldn't do what Michael did. I never could. As a writer, I'm not a structure person. When I see a movie, I see moments or feelings or characters, and scenes. This movie is kind of a magic trick. It's got construction. It's like one of those boxes you put a girl in and then you put the things in. I would never build one of those. That I can't honestly say I contributed much to.

[Instead I was] trying to put flesh on those bones. We were even working when we were shooting. Like that scene where John [Cusack] talks about his past as a cop. Things like that. The ink was barely dry from our trailer working on [such scenes] when we'd come flying out to shoot them. Sometimes that can be the sign of two things on a movie. One is that you're not sure where you're going, but thanks to Michael's thing, we always knew. The truth is that there was such great camaraderie among the cast and us all working on it that ideas were coming all the time. How to try and do things efficiently. Sometimes when you're on the set with the actors, you figure out new ways to communicate something, really with great economy. Sitting alone at a typewriter, you might take thirteen times as much ink to figure out how to say it.

Working with an ensemble, do you experience different relationships with each of your actors in terms of how much they want to know about the story?

Mangold: Interestingly, one of the things that I found when I started the movie was that this was a film where everyone was playing the end. I almost sent out memos, not just to the cast but also to a lot of the collaborators that we'd worked with in the past on movies, [warning against] playing the dreamscape of a movie too much. Everyone could come up with clever ideas.

    I remember the art department had in every room a painting of a state that was the last name of the person that happened to be staying. Well, a couple of rooms. We took them down in a couple. But it was like everyone was playing the punch line, as opposed to the moment of real. That was something that not only were the actors but everyone was very focused on: play yourself. Don't play yourself as a piece of a puzzle of Malcolm's mind. Play Ed. Play Paris.

    The reason being, frankly, is that when you read any literature about split personalities, what makes them so fascinating is that they are fully realized people. They're not half-people or symbolic people or sketches. These are full people who could sit and converse with you about where they've been and what they've seen, [but] coming out of the mouth of someone who's lived another life at the same time.

Konrad: When we were doing research for this, we found a book on the Internet called *Serial Murder*.

Mangold: I'm sure I got myself on some list [from] ordering it!

Konrad: Yeah! It comes in the mail and it's like a bible! It's black and it's called *Serial Murder*. You start opening it up and it has *amazing* stories. The one that was really intriguing and that we were excited by—only in its relativeness to the movie—was the Hillside Strangler case, which was a split personality case. There were all the interviews with Ken Bianchi and his psychiatrist talking to both Ken and "Steve."

Mangold: It was a very interesting case because they arrested this guy Ken Bianchi for multiple murders. And this was by way of research: trying to hang some meat on the bones of the incredible twist that Michael had installed in this thing. Anyway, even though blood evidence and eyewitnesses put him at these murders [and] he was irrefutably the murderer of these people, Ken Bianchi had no recollection of it whatsoever.

What vexed the detectives was that not only did he proclaim his innocence, but he did so in a way that they had never seen before. It was like he *hadn't* done it. It wasn't like he *had* done it. It wasn't the sort of strident, nervous, proclaiming of innocence that they had seen before. It was really unnerving for a lot of the people working on the case. They called multiple psychiatrists out and the last one, who was a specialist in multiple personalities—they didn't know Bianchi had it—came out and hypnotized him. And on the third or fourth hypnosis—when he was in the trance the hypnotist would always say, "And who am I speaking to?"—Ken Bianchi answered, "Steve."

"Steve?"

"Yeah."

"Well, where's Ken?"

"He's not here."

"Why not? You couldn't have committed the murders."

"Yes, I did."

And he told them all the details about it and how he didn't tell Ken and how he hates Ken and he hopes Ken gets put away for it! It's an *amazing* transcript to read. It reveals to you [that] these are completely discrete beings living within one person [and] they have their own ideas about each other. In a sense, they're like neighbors and they resent each other like the people upstairs. There's a kind of wild relationship. It's very interesting.

Audiences might not necessarily identify an actor like John Cusack with a movie such as this. How did he come on board the project?

Mangold: We just thought he was a great idea, so we sent it to him. I'm not normally the guy you'd think of making a movie like this either, so I don't tend to think of casting actors "in genre." There's a great Everyman quality about John. Man or woman, you like him. There's something about him really appealing regardless of the dark. He's played hit men [in *Grosse Pointe Blank*, 1997] who were appealing. He's a really interesting combination because not only is he a magnificent actor, on a par with our best actors in our country, but he also had this kind of really wonderful magnetism. It occurred to us that the character of Ed could be really well served by him.

With an ensemble cast, you run the risk of ego clashes on set. What did you experience on Identity?

Konrad: I wish this movie could have been more scandalous, because it would be more interesting for you to write about! Most of my films have been ensemble films, and I quite enjoy them, more so than just one star or dueling stars. In this case, it's about the acting, and all of the actors had tremendous respect for one another. Certainly, there are moments when someone's not there and two others are waiting, but by and large, it was one of those cases where everyone was just so in love with each other. It was like, "Oh my! God, I can't believe it! Alfred Molina!" There was this great quality all around. They all loved each other and hung out together independently of the film. The actor John C. McGinley, who plays George, is best friends with John Cusack. They would sometimes come to set together or host softball games inside the sound stage. It was a really good vibe on this one.

That's the producer's version. What's the director got to say?

Mangold: She's right. *Cop Land* [1997] and *Girl, Interrupted* [1999] are very much ensemble films. Even *Heavy* [1995] I call an ensemble film. For me, it is one of the things that are the responsibility of the producer and the director—to set a stage for everyone to get along. That is a big deal. One of the best ways to ensure that is to hire good people. I can think of moments in the first week or two on the set where Cusack would lean over to me, referring to Clea Duvall, and say, "She's *good*." And those moments happened over and over again. Ray [Liotta] would lean over to me after doing a scene with John and feel like he got the ball hit back to him really well. Ultimately there is a very simple equation here, which is that everyone loves acting. They all *love* it. They're not celebrities first, they're actors.

Konrad: I also think that Jim, to his credit, is really good in terms of setting rules. It's about defining—you do have to set the rules as the parents of the house. It's like, "Here's the deal. There are gonna be days when it's not about *you*. But you're gonna be here because it's about *them*. There's going to be days when you need to be here for off-camera for him and even if [it] means you're going to be on screen for two minutes, you've got to stay here for eight hours. And that's what you're gonna do." And of course all of the stars in a firm but clear way get why they're there. The crew of this film has done six other films with me. They're part of my family, so there's a shorthand that evolves when I work with them. We like to lay it out there and hopefully people follow us.

Have you ever deliberately and blatantly copied anything from other movies, or been inspired to borrow a moment, a shot, an angle from another director's work?

Well I couldn't, because I didn't *per se* develop each of these sequences from the core. I know when we were working on the script that it's more of the rules you learn. From the literature of film you learn rules, which can, when you follow them, bring you back to something familiar.

One of the ideas I came up with was there was a different depth for Lou in Michael's original script. In fact, I don't think Lou and Ginny were the same characters as much. One of the things I was fascinated by with the hotel was doors. One of the things I encouraged Michael to try and come up with—and it was this quick idea I had—was that they were a fighting couple. So why not have that classic situation of the fighting couple, with the door closed between them, yelling through the door—only something horrible happens to one person on the other side? At least, in my film buff's head, I'd never seen that before, but as realized on screen, it certainly has a kind of resonance with something I know I saw in *The Shining*: a feeling of Shelley Duvall—that same last name—in a bathroom screaming her head off.

Sometimes those things just happen because you're making a movie of this genre and you're in a bathroom and someone's on the other side of the door. But I was coming at it from another direction. Certainly though, when you're making a confined movie, that happens to take place in a motel on a roadside....

Konrad: There's not a lot of them.

Mangold:... you've got to be aware that there's a kind of resonance with other films. I've always felt like John Carpenter's *The Thing* was inspiring or guiding me, no matter how many Hitchcockian references anyone makes. More than anything, that was guiding the way I saw we had to make the film, although there are no strange spaghetti beasts in this film!

And when I made *Girl, Interrupted*, *The Wizard of Oz* [1939] was guiding me, not Milos Forman's movie [*One Flew Over the Cuckoo's Nest*, 1975]. I have very strange guideposts that lead me through the day. That's more of what I had in my head. I would never want to come out for a day and do what Gus [Van Sant] did with *Psycho* [1960]. I wouldn't sit down and go, "For the next five minutes, we're gonna replicate this scene from another movie with our actors." It would be a bore.

Was the weather and the storm always an integral part of the story? Were you tempted to make it too big?

Mangold: I think we both were concerned that the storm had to be big, or else the movie would fall down. The storm had to be almost biblical in its proportions, or else you'd ask, "Why didn't they leave?"

You mentioned Knife in the Water *and* Dead Calm, *both of which are set on water. Directors often say directing on water is a nightmare. This film has so much water in it. Was that a nightmare?*

Mangold: It was tough. But the thing that made it doable on a reasonable budget and with reasonable control was that our feet were on land. We were on a sound stage, and 95 percent of the movie is on one huge set. It's one of the biggest sound stages in the world and, in fact, where the Emerald City was in *The Wizard of Oz*, on what was the old MGM lot. We'd built this entire motel, parking lot, swimming pool, the desert around it; the cars could pull in and out. All this action took place on this stage. All the spigots were controlled from above. The chill was taken out of the water. I could rain on you but not us. I rain on us but not you.

Konrad: Our special effects guy should win an award for the tower he designed. It was just fantastic. It could go at different speeds. Rain is very hard to film. It comes off many times looking like mist, and he designed these rain bars so that water would spin in multiple directions and the raindrops would actually fall farther apart so that they would read on film. It was an elaborate situation.

Mangold: It would hurl the water upward and let it fall in very large drops as opposed to a sprinkler coming down.

Konrad: I know that sounds ridiculous, but if you've ever stood under a rain tower, normally it just feels like you're getting misted with Evian or something.

How did you achieve the sense of shock that this genre demands? Was that done in the editing, or did you have a sense of vision during the shooting?

Mangold: There were times I'd turn to Cathy and she would have a great idea about how to stage something. There were times I had an idea. I was excited about how to pull something off. There were times with the actors, and the way they just moved through this space would reveal to you the way to shoot it or feel it. We didn't storyboard that much or plan it anally in advance. It was much more [about] feeling this space.

A lot of times the best way to make sure you come up with those moments or opportunities is in the staging. It's in the moment when you realize, "Well, I've got my back to this direction. I could just come sweeping in with something." It's very physical. You need to put the scene on its legs sometimes to feel the opportunities. Sometimes you can script one, and then you get to a place and you go, "Well, it *reads* great, but no one would be shocked by this. The way the set's built, there's no way someone would be surprised in here," so you reconfigure it in some way.

Given the multitude of twists, did the cast know what the ending was going to be?

Mangold: By and large, the actors understood what was going on in the movie. If anything, I was concerned that they *not* play the ending but that they play themselves as fully realized people. I think they were all very aware of where we were headed.

Was there any aspect in terms of logic that took the actors by surprise or that didn't gel?

Konrad: There was one. Clearly one of the most challenging moments in the movie—we always hoped it would work, and it did for most people—was where we played the twist in the third act, when you became aware of the multiple personalities. That's part of the twist in the movie, and yet the movie continues in the hotel with these people who you now know are personalities. There was always this idea, and we were very excited to put that in front of an audience initially. Were they invested in these people as characters even now they know they're not real flesh and blood? It was a great moment. It was very rewarding to find out that they still cared about them and almost forgot that they weren't real and rode the film out until the end.

Mangold: And, of course, the interesting aspect when you actually start, as we did, talking about this endlessly is that you realize they're not really *real* to begin with. Most people sitting in this box watching it are already semi-aware of that and are already investing in it.

Konrad: But they forget it!

Mangold: They do! So everything's within these brackets. Like, "I've entered a certain narrative hallucination where I believe these people are real. Then in the narrative, they tell me they're *not* real! Am I still gonna stay with it?" I think it's one of the more interesting components of the movie.

Konrad: The thing that really attracted John Cusack—and actually most of the actors—to this movie was the originality of that ending. To him, it came down to that one scene, that one moment. He'd never seen that before. And I'd never seen it before. Sometimes when you haven't seen something in a town where you feel like you've seen everything a hundred times, you go to what's fresh.

How do you manage to retain the twist and the various plot points when you're describing the film to people? And do audiences abide by that, too?

Konrad: It is a movie that can be reduced to one line, but I think it wouldn't do it justice. The rewarding thing about this movie when we had the junket in the States [was that] everyone came out of feeling blown away by it.

They'd thought it was one thing and it was completely something else. The reaction from the public has been pretty much the same. The movie's had tremendous legs. It's a movie that's been discovered and it keeps playing. I kind of like the idea of that word of mouth, with a little bit of withholding, teasing people, and getting them excited. That is challenging, but it's got benefits.

The moment you mention multiple personalities, the bubble bursts.

Konrad: For some people. It is an odd thing. The prologue sequence in the movie kind of gives a lot to people.

Mangold: I still wouldn't advise anyone writing a review with "multiple personality" in it. [Laughs] Because in the movie, it seems like it's all about a character. I don't know how you'd phrase it but there's a chance to blow it. You have to make several leaps, as Cathy was saying. It takes a few sentences to articulate what's happening in the picture.

Have you had any feedback from people who have watched it twice, and whether their perception of the film has changed?

Konrad: In this computer age, you can live online and get instant feedback from people who have gone to the cinema and are writing about their experiences. That's happened a lot with this movie in a really fun way.

Mangold: There are people who are doing all this analysis of the film. In a way, all the work we've put in and even sometimes what we *didn't* put in is becoming turned into great flights of imagination. People breaking down who all these personalities were in Malcolm's childhood, how he was raised in a motel.

Konrad: The frozen body is the shell.

Mangold: That was one of the more beautiful things: the frozen body in the refrigerator is the shell of Malcolm—who he would have been had he not fractured into all these pieces, which we'd never even thought of. I thought that was genius! [Laughs]

Konrad: The other good one was via Jim's mother's doctor, who called her and said something that was *so* brilliant.

Mangold: Oh yeah. It was that the doctor, Molina, never knew about the kid because the kid never speaks. So he could never have talked to him.

Konrad: We're like, "Wow!"

Mangold: That was great! I wanted him to be mute because I thought it would be cool. I thought his line would be more powerful at the end.

Konrad: We thought it would be one less character to give dialogue to. We have eight already!

Mangold: I thought you wouldn't buy it if the kid was friendly and chatty through the movie, and suddenly he turns demonic. I thought if he were a little cloaked, he would be [more plausible]. Also, at least in my experience, whenever you're doing something right, it produces resonances and bounces around. People find different angles to come at you from. It invites you in and brings other people's minds into it. That's really a rewarding thing.

2003

NEIL MARSHALL
The Descent

"Horror is a really essential part of British film history. Somewhere along the way we seem to have forgotten that." – Neil Marshall (far left) and key crew filming *The Descent*. (Celador Films/Alex Bailey)

THE DESCENT
Celador Films, 2005

CAST: Sarah, SHAUNA MACDONALD; Juno, NATALIE MENDOZA; Beth, ALEX REID; Rebecca, SASKIA MULDER; Sam, MYANNA BURING; Holly, NORA-JANE NOONE; Paul, OLIVER MILBURN; Jessica, MOLLY KAYLL; Scar, CRAIG CONWAY; Crawlers, LESLIE SIMPSON, MARK CRONFIELD, STEVE LAMB, CATHERINE DYSON, JULIE ELLIS, SOPHIE TROTT, TRISTAN MATTHIAE, STUART LUIS, JUSTIN HACKNEY.

CREDITS: *Director*, Neil Marshall; *screenplay*, Neil Marshall; *producer*, Christian Colson; *executive producer*, Paul Smith; *co-producer*, Paul Ritchie; *associate producer*, Ivana MacKinnon; *director of photography*, Sam McCurdy; *production designer*, Simon Bowles; *art director*, Jason Knox-Johnston; *costume designer*, Nancy Thompson; *make-up designer*, Tanya Lodge; *special make-up & effects designer*, Paul Hyett; *special effects supervisor*, Johnny Rafique; *visual effects supervisor*, Leigh Took; *editor*, Jon Harris; *music*, David Julyan; *stunt coordinator*, Jim Dowdall. Running time: 99 minutes.

> "In a remote mountain range, six female friends meet for their yearly adventure, a caving trip into the arteries of the earth. The leader of the trip is Juno, tough, compelling, and dangerous. Along for the ride are Scandinavian half-sisters Rebecca and Sam, wild base jumper Holly, and English teacher Beth, who has reluctantly come to look after Sarah. Sarah is still recovering from a total mental breakdown after the deaths of her husband and child one year previously, and needs this trip to reclaim the life she once had.

"It soon becomes clear that Sarah is not fully recovered, and that the hallucinations and memories that have dogged her for the past year are still very much hovering over her. But Juno shrugs off Beth's worries—Sarah is her best and oldest friend, and she is going to make this work.

"Together, the group make their way through the remote cave system, enjoying the hazardous but beautiful surroundings. Then, deep inside the cave, disaster strikes when their route back to the surface is blocked by a rockfall. When they learn that Juno, always pushing herself a little further, has brought them to an unexplored cave, and that no one is coming to rescue them, the group starts to splinter. But left with no option, they push on through the cave, praying for another exit.

"The women battle through this harsh underground world, pitting their strength and determination against each new challenge. But there is something else lurking under the earth, a race of monstrous creatures hidden from the light, devolved to perfectly live in the dark. As the women realize they have become prey, they are forced to unleash their most primal instincts in order to survive."

Humans are the Scariest Thing
Neil Marshall on *The Descent*

Were you surprised just how successful Dog Soldiers [2002] *was?*

Neil Marshall: Yeah, very pleasantly surprised. It did okay at the box office when it was originally released, because it was quite difficult. It was the week after *Spider-Man* [2002] and the week before *Star Wars* [*Episode II – Attack of the Clones*, 2002], so it was up against some pretty big competition. For a very small, unknown British film, it did two-and-a-half million, which is not bad at all. I was very pleased with that. But it really found its audience on DVD because essentially it's the classic post-pub movie: you sit down with your mates and a few beers and have a good laugh. That's really what it's designed for. I'm amazingly proud of the whole experience.

Was it a fairly rapid turnaround between putting the script forward and shooting the movie?

For *Dog Soldiers*? Six years! I wrote the first draft of *Dog Soldiers* in 1996, we didn't film it until 2001, and it didn't get released until 2002. So it was quite a long turnaround. At the time, the British film industry wasn't interested in horror at all; they uniformly turned their noses up at it. It wasn't until Christopher Figg, the producer of *Hellraiser* [1987], came aboard, and David Allen, the spirits billionaire, who funded the whole thing, that it got made. We went round every possible source of finance to get the money for that film, and they all said, "It's not our cup of tea." Meanwhile in the States, at that time, *Scream* [1996] had opened and basically started the wave that continues now of the resurgence of popular horror. We just didn't see it. Our industry was [saying], "Horror? We don't wanna do that. That's not for us," forgetting that it's a really, really essential part of British film history. Some of the greatest horror films of all time have come from Britain. Somewhere along the way, during the '80s and early '90s, we seem to have forgot that. Now they're finding that it's a really good thing to do and shouldn't be looked down the nose at.

Were you bombarded with offers once the film had become a success?

Yeah, I got a lot of that, but it was a question of taking my time. I didn't just wanna rush into the first film that came along. There were a few offers made, [but] nothing particularly great. When I was in development on *The Descent*, I was offered a BBC drama called *Messiah* [2001], and it was a really difficult decision. It was going to be seven or eight months' worth of work, a lot of money, and I had to say no [to] concentrate on the *Descent* script. That's what I want to do: feature films. I don't want to do TV drama. That's a discipline in itself, and that's not something that I wanna do. So I did have to turn down some lucrative offers just to concentrate on getting this one made.

Was there pressure for you to do Dog Soldiers 2*?*

There was a lot of interest. I wouldn't say there was any pressure as such. *Dog Soldiers 2* may or may not happen, but I have no involvement in it.

Through choice?

Through contractual issues more than anything. In order to get the first film made, I had to sell my rights in it to the financier, so he owns the project. He can do whatever he wants with it. The *Dog Soldiers* sequel at the moment seems to hang on whether Kevin McKidd's involved. Like I say, it's got nothing to do with me now.

Did you have a number of projects on the boil and The Descent *just came up as the most viable option?*

I've always got a number of projects on the go. What is it they say: numerous projects in various stages of development? We took a couple of ideas to Celador Films. They'd just established themselves, really. *Dirty Pretty Things* [2002] had come out and had done very well [and], we knew they had a pot of money. It was a unique setup in that it was basically one guy, a whole bunch of money, and he wants to make films. So we took a few ideas to them, and the issue they had was that in order for them to make business sense, they put a ceiling on their budget of £3 million. They didn't want to go over that because that enabled them to make something good and potentially make a profit from them. Paul Smith, who runs Celador, is very much a smart businessman, and that's what he's in it for—to make good films but also to make his money back. So with that feeling in mind, a lot of the projects we had simply couldn't be done for that, so we had to come up with something a bit tighter, a bit smaller, no less ambitious but more manageable on that kind of budget. It was coming back from that meeting that I came up with this idea of a pot-holing horror film. My business partner Keith Bell came up with an idea, which he threw into the mix, which was, "Why don't we do it with an all-female cast?" With those two elements together, the story came from there. We took it back to Celador and they jumped on it. That was two years ago. We've developed the script for two-and-a-half years, gone through lots of drafts of getting it right, then went into production and shot it at the beginning of last December [2004].

What were your influences?

I'm thirty-five. I was born in 1970, so I grew up through the beginning of the blockbuster era with *Jaws* [1975], then the video nasty [period]. The first horror film I ever saw was when my dad let me stay up late one night to watch *Frankenstein* [1931], with Karloff, which was on TV. I was only about five or six. That absolutely stuck in my mind—that whole gothic darkness. I love it. It was a mixture of that, a mixture of the video nasty period when I was about eleven or twelve. The first videos I ever saw were *I Spit on Your Grave* [1978] and *Zombie Flesh Eaters* [1979], stuff like that, which certainly had an effect on me. I don't look on them and think, *Weren't they great films?* but I think the blood and guts must have had some sort of an effect on me. If anything, they probably taught me to not make films like that and to strive for something better. Also watching films like *Deliverance* [1972], *The Shining* [1980], *Alien* [1979] for the first time—the impact that they had on me at an early age has really stuck in my mind. Every so often, you see something that's absolutely remarkable, particularly the ones from the '70s. Seeing *The Omen* [1976] for the first time, *The Exorcist* [1973], *The Texas Chain Saw Massacre* [1974]. They've got an edge to them. They dare to take themselves seriously. They've got a really sharp edge to them, a sharp visual style.

Which filmmakers do you admire and do you try and incorporate ideas from their work into your own?

Definitely. I'm the biggest Spielberg fan going. I grew up with Spielberg movies, and I think the one thing that Spielberg does best but which he shies away from for some reason, is scare people. Think *Jaws*, think *Close Encounters* [*of the Third Kind*, 1977], some of the *Raiders* movies. When he sets his mind to it, he's great at terrifying people, yet he's never done a traditional horror movie. My lifetime ambition was to do *The War of the Worlds* on film, since reading the book and growing up listening to the Jeff Wayne musical version. I was desperate to do it, and I was *gutted* when Spielberg did it. I thought, *There's no chance of that now*. In terms of other obscure things, I'm a big fan of Westerns—Peckinpah, Howard Hawks, and the like. There's loads of Howard Hawks in *Dog Soldiers*—*Rio Bravo* [1959] and *Only Angels Have Wings* [1939]. That tight grouping in a very small place thing, trying to get overlapping dialogue and fast action stuff going on. I love all that, so I put loads of that in *Dog Soldiers*. With *The Descent*, I was much more paying homage to films like *Deliverance* [1972]—there are loads of little subtle in-jokes to *Deliverance*, *The Shining*, and *Alien* in there.

You seem to be leading a full-scale British horror movie revival. Do you see that, or is it something the fans have imposed upon you?

I think [it's an imposition]. That's the way I see it. I'm not setting out to "lead" anything at all; I'm just making films. I just wanna to make the best films I can possibly make. And I don't necessarily wanna do horror all the time. I'm really quite interested in doing something that's not a horror film because I don't want to get pigeonholed. I love horror fans. They're great, incredibly supportive, and I'm not gonna disappoint them by deserting horror for ever. But there's still an inherent snobbery in the British film industry, and if you're "a horror film maker," then that's what you're seen as, and you're never really gonna be taken that seriously by the Establishment. So, just to open a few more doors and provide a few more opportunities, I'd like to do a non-horror film, maybe next. That would be great. And then return to the genre further down the line and do something different again, just to see what other way I can go within it. I never wanna get tired of horror or of scaring people. That's why I'd like to take a break from it, do something different, and then come back.

Your re-invention of the genre with Dog Soldiers *led to you being compared with the likes of Wes Craven and John Carpenter. Would you embrace that?*

Oh, definitely. I'm a massive fan of John Carpenter, particularly. I grew up with *Halloween* [1978] and *The Thing* [1982] and *The Fog* [1980]. Great films. Unfortunately, he's lost it a bit lately, but I'm still hoping one day he's going to turn around and give us another great film. Wes Craven, again, they have great track records these guys. I'd be honored to be put up next to them somehow. I've got a long way to go.

You have terrific monsters in The Descent—*the crawlers. Where did the idea for those come from?*

The idea behind them was just to create this colony, this civilization of cavemen who have stayed in the cave. When the rest of us came out of the cave and evolved over millions of years, these guys, for whatever reason, stayed in the dark. They've adapted and evolved to be perfect within that environment. They've lost their eyesight because it's pointless having it down there. Their hearing has improved, they've got this sonar thing, like bats have, to hunt and kill and move around. They're the greatest free-climbers, going up walls and stuff like that. There's nothing supernatural about them, they're a stage in evolution like the missing link. I thought, *I want something down in a cave, but I don't want it to be aliens or slugs; I want it to be something human* because, for me, humans are the scariest thing. So therefore, making them more human, making them a colony—there are female crawlers and a baby crawler in there—was just playing with that whole idea. One version of the story could be that you've got this very happy colony of crawlers living underground who get attacked and invaded by this group of women who brutally kill them! [Laughs] That's one way of looking at it. So I wanted to make them interesting and get performances out of them as well. I hired a bunch of Northeast-based actors who I'd seen on stage before and had worked with on *Dog Soldiers* in the past. I knew they were incredibly physical but could also bring a level of performance to it—the make-up allowed them to still be incredibly expressive.

Who did you go to for the make-up effects?

A guy called Paul Hyett. He hadn't done a huge amount before—he had done another low-budget film called *Cold and Dark* [2005], which my DoP and the production designer both worked on, and they recommended him. He came in and it was a great meeting. He made us laugh so much. His portfolio was superb, but what he was constantly referring to was "Killin' and stabbin' and mutilatin', bleedin', choppin'." That became our tagline as soon as he left the room: "Killin', stabbin'." He's just great. He's got a great team around him, and he just delivered. They just worked so hard. Whatever hours we were doing, they were doing twice as many to get that done on time.

Did they go off and find ways to kill people?

We worked on it as a group, actually. We had some workshop sessions with the crawlers. We were looking at the way animals kill people, conjuring up the idea that they would go for the neck in the same way that lions and tigers do—rip out the neck first just to disable whatever you're trying to kill. They kind of jump up onto you and cling to you and bring you down that way, with their weight. It was all to do with pack hunting and that kind of thinking. I just wanted to bring as much reality to it as possible. It's also pretty nasty when you're faced with a predator that thinks that way.

You ration the gore, but when it comes, it's unflinching and relentless.

I specifically went for things that I knew just had that instant cringe effect: the rope burn across the hand, the leg break with the bone sticking out, the fingernails coming off—it elicits a very specific response from everybody. You can *feel* it. It doesn't take much to imagine the pain on that one. Then it escalates through the film: we start off small and then just get bigger and bigger and bigger until you end up in the crawlers' lair, which is kind of like an abattoir, a version of hell on earth full of corpses and blood, and all the blood has run down into this gathering pool at the bottom. Poor old Sarah ends up falling into it. For her it's a baptism—she's reborn when she comes out of it. She's completely lost her mind, and you probably would under the circumstances and what she'd been through in the film. It was just a question of taking it to a different level. I just wanted that level of intensity: it's brutal, savage, visceral, primal. When your heroine ends up smashing some creature's brains in with a bone, it's getting bad.

Let's discuss character development: Juno is complex.

She's kind of misguided. She won't acknowledge the fact that she's done something wrong or that she makes mistakes. She just keeps on digging the hole deeper and deeper with every mistake she makes, rather than acknowledging the fact that she's wrong. It's just a flaw in her character. She's not an evil person; she makes mistakes like the rest of us. She's just not very good at acknowledging them. That's her fault. It's kind of tragic, especially for Sarah. She loses everything that matters to her in her life along the way, and Juno is just another part of her life that falls apart. I was interested in this character of Sarah and specifically Juno's as being a non-villainous villain. She's just doing what she thinks is right.

How did you come up with the others?

Beth comes out of it as being grounded in reality. We just wanted somebody who would be speaking to the audience. Her main character trait is that she's basically looking after Sarah all the time. She knows that Juno can't really be trusted. Beth is Sarah's closest mate, she's been there through the worst of what Sarah's had to go through. She's solid. She's her backbone, her rock. The rest of them, Rebecca and Sam are sisters, an older sister/younger sister dynamic going on there. Holly is the pretender to Juno's throne, really, the new hotshot in the group. I got a really interesting little dynamic in the group.

But what I wanted to do was make an all-female ensemble film, an action horror film, a very physical film. It had never been done before, certainly not in a British film, and it's not about being an all-female film. That's not what the film's about. It's not a "chick flick." It's about as far removed from a classic "girl film" as you can get. I just wanted to treat them as a bunch of characters, and that's what they are. It didn't matter that they were boys, girls, or whatever. Most people come out of it not even aware that they've been watching an all-female cast until it dawns on them half an hour after the film: "Bloody hell, there were no blokes there." I don't think you question it. At least I *hope* you don't question it.

You didn't throw in a shower scene for the boys, which seems to suggest that you're taking it a little more seriously than other filmmakers might.

There is a shower scene. It's brief! I'm not interested in that. It cheapens the experience. If people want to see tits, they'll buy a copy of *The Sun* in the morning. That's not what I'm interested in in this film, and it's not what the actresses were interested in doing.

How did the girls react to the gore, the action, and the violence?

They got into it. I think they were a little bit apprehensive at the start, but once they got into it [they were fine]. Both Shauna [Macdonald] and Natalie [Mendoza] were just so gung-ho about the whole thing, they were brilliant. Natalie spent a day thrashing around on this builders' sand—we couldn't get any nice fine sand, so it was builders' sand—which is absolutely lethal. Her and the crawler at the end were completely covered in lacerations, but they did it. They laid into each other constantly in order to get that fight sequence. It achieved everything I wanted it to, which was just raw brutality. I didn't want it to look choreographed. I didn't want it to look nice and tidy in any way. I wanted it to be messy. It's about two people—a person and a crawler—definitely trying to kill each other. And I think that's what we achieved. Shauna was equally a trouper on the day when she had to spend the entire day in this vat of blood, constantly submerging into this red stuff. She was a trouper. She just did it all day.

You have an array of gory injuries in the film, including a compound fracture, a slashed throat, and an evisceration. Did you have a list of things you wanted to put on screen?

Not really. I just tried to find out how the crawlers would work. In some places I did have specific things [in mind]: I wanted to put in the rope burn in, the fingernails. The bone through the leg thing is a little bit of a nod and a wink to *Deliverance*. So there were a few things in there. You just conjure up these ideas: how do we kill somebody [in a fashion] that hasn't been done before? It's weird, though. Somebody like Holly, when she gets killed—she gets her throat ripped out and you think she might be dead, then she comes back as a corpse for quite [a] bit. Then she gets eaten in front of somebody's eyes. Then the [other] character uses her clothes and stuff that's on her body to make a torch. I just thought that was *icky* in itself. This is your friend lying dead and you've gotta fumble through all her belongings with her entrails hanging out. It's a bit harsh! I wanted more stuff to get under people's skin and make them squirm. [Laughs]

What are your favorite moments in The Descent *and* Dog Soldiers*?*

Watching the film now, my favorite moment is the first attack and what happens after it with Beth. That is total manipulation, in that we get the audience totally on Juno's side—they're rooting for her, she's fighting back for the first time, we know what kind of a character she is, we think she's totally capable and she'll deal with these guys. She does, you're absolutely rooting for her, and then we turn it totally on its head. Every time I watch it now it, gets a gasp out of the audience, and I'm so chuffed with that. That's really rewarding. In *Dog Soldiers*, it's probably Spooner [Darren Morfitt] and the werewolf in the kitchen; the fistfight in the kitchen is always great fun to watch.

I also love the little bit where Emma [Cleasby], playing Megan, takes her hat off for the first time and her hair comes down. Kev [Kevin McKidd] just looks up and her and goes "Hmmm." It makes me laugh every time I see it. "Sausages" is always a good line as well. That's pure Sean [Pertwee], that is. There's another little bit where Emma lets her hair down and Kev's just playing with this salt cellar. I just came up with it on the spot, and I had the producer saying, "What's he doing with the salt cellar? What is that about?" and I said, "It's not about anything. He's just playing with the salt cellar." It just gave him something to do, but I was determined to have it in there.

Future projects include Outpost, Eagle's Nest, *and* Battle of Hastings. *Can you talk about them?*

Outpost is another horror film, and it's probably more in the tradition of *Dog Soldiers* than *The Descent*. It goes back to being outrageous. It's zombies on an oil rig. It's full-on, over-the-top mayhem and chaos with some ludicrous sight gags and some crazy violence in it. That one's on the cards, but I don't know when we're gonna do it. I'm working on a new draft of the script at the moment, but we have a deal with Pathé to do that one at some point. *Eagle's Nest*, the pitch that we're telling everybody is *Die Hard* meets *The Remains of the Day*. I wanted to take the Merchant/Ivory formula and just turn it on its head. Actually it's a WWII action thriller set in a country house about a Fifth Column unit trying to rescue Rudolf Hess after he parachutes into Scotland. Fingers crossed, we might get to do that one next. The *Battle of Hastings* is a comedy about battle re-enactment societies and about the anniversary re-enactment of the Battle of Hastings, where the guys playing King Harold and his army decide that they're fed-up of losing all the time and want to win. It's mainly about their journey—the Northern Saxon Society journey—from up here [in Newcastle] down to Hastings and the French coming over on the ferry. Everybody's trying to get there and getting lost on the M25 and all that kind of malarkey. They end up calling in reinforcements for the final battle of [other] re-enactment societies like stormtroopers, WWII [groups], and whoever else happens to be around. It's a riotous comedy, and I'm the process of writing that at the moment. I've got a few things on the go.

You seem to have a good relationship with Pathé. Will that continue film-on-film?

Like I say, we've got a deal in place to do *Outpost* at some point in the future, not necessarily next. I love working with them; they're a great bunch. It's the same people we were dealing with on *Dog Soldiers* a few years ago, and I'm more than happy to work with them again. But I'm quite keen to work with other people as well.

Will you stay in the North?

I'll wait and see what goes along, but I have no desire to live in London or go to L.A. It just doesn't interest me. I love the buzz of the industry down in London, and it's been great working there on this film but I don't see the reason to live there. Celador paid for me to have a flat down there for the past five months, which is great, so why would I want to spend huge amounts of money getting a flat down there myself when the production company can put me up somewhere? It does you in after a while. I've put on so much weight living down in London—too much socializing, too much drinking, eating out. It's nice for a short period of time, but what will it do to my health? Nah. I like the peace and quiet of Cumbria. It's better to write there; there's less distractions. I want to bring the industry out here; I don't wanna conform. Everybody else does that. I wanna do something different.

What were you doing prior to Dog Soldiers *that got you an entrée into the business?*

Editing more than anything. I was editing for eight years. I did a short film for Tyne-Tees [a British regional TV station], a little thing called *Dog Eat Dog* [1994], which is a bit obscure. Then I made the short film *Combat* in '99, which pretty much led straight into *Dog Soldiers*. It used a lot of the crew, some of the cast. It was a lot of the same people involved. And that was it, really. It was incredibly trusting of the people involved in *Dog Soldiers* to say, off the back of that, that they'd give me a feature.

So the next gig will be Eagle's Nest?

Potentially, fingers crossed, that's what I'd like to do, but there's nothing set in stone. That's what I wanna do, but there's no deal signed. I'm writing it. Give it a few weeks, wait until [*The Descent*] is released, and then put it on people's desks and see what some of the feedback is.

Will it be another three years?

No, I'm not gonna wait that long. No way. I want to be filming by the end of the year. I'm determined. I can't wait three years.

Will you make it in England?

Ideally, yeah. It's very expensive to shoot here but, if we can, I'd much rather shoot it here than have to go to Romania. You get more for your money out there, but it's just not the same. Great crew here, absolutely brilliant crew. So that's what I wanna do.

2005

DANIEL MYRICK and EDUARDO SANCHEZ
The Blair Witch Project

Writing/directing duo Eduardo Sanchez (left) and Daniel Myrick were film students in Florida when they conceived what would eventually become *The Blair Witch Project*. "Those old documentary shows really creeped us out as kids. We thought it would be cool to make a horror movie based on that same format." (Artisan Entertainment/ Stefanie Decassan)

THE BLAIR WITCH PROJECT
Artisan Entertainment, 1999

CAST: Heather, HEATHER DONAHUE; Joshua, JOSHUA LEONARD; Michael, MICHAEL WILLIAMS; Interviewees, BOB GRIFFIN, JIM KING, SANDRA SANCHEZ, ED SWANSON, PATRICIA DECOU, MARK MASON, JACKIE HALLEX.

CREDITS: *Written, directed, and edited by* Daniel Myrick and Eduardo Sanchez; *producers*, Gregg Hale, Robin Cowie; *co-producer*, Michael Monello; *executive producers*, Bob Eick, Kevin J. Foxe; *production design*, Ben Rock; *art director*, Ricardo R. Moreno; *director of photography*, Neal Fredericks; *music*, Tony Cora. Running time: 81 minutes.

> "On October 21, 1994, Heather Donahue, Joshua Leonard, and Michael Williams hiked into Maryland's Black Hills Forest to shoot a documentary film on a local legend, 'The Blair Witch.' They were never heard from again. One year later, their footage was found, documenting the students' five-day journey through the Black Hills Forest, and capturing the terrifying events that led up to their disappearance."

The Antithesis of High-Budget Hollywood
Daniel Myrick and Eduardo Sanchez on *The Blair Witch Project*

What came first: the ghost story or the method of using home movies?

Daniel Myrick: The story came first. We were going to film school at University of Central Florida in Orlando, and Ed and I were taking classes together. We were sitting in his apartment one night talking about horror movies, and then we got onto the subject of those old documentary shows like *In Search of...* [1976–1982] back in the '70s and another feature called *The Legend of Boggy Creek* [1972] that really creeped us out as kids. We thought it would be cool to make a horror movie based on that same pseudo-documentary format, but contemporize it for a modern audience. That's where it really started, back in 1992.

So we came up with the premise of the three filmmakers getting lost in the woods. Then we needed a reason for them to be shooting. Why are they out in the woods and what are they shooting? So we came up with this Blair Witch legend and the folklore and all that behind it. It just kind of grew and evolved from there.

But with that in mind, we needed absolute realism. We needed it to look like a real documentary. Some of the documentaries that we've seen in the past had flaws, like you could tell it was an actor acting, or you could tell somebody was reading off a script. We didn't want any of those problems. We thought we would construct a process with the help of our producer, Gregg Hale, and shoot this in a real-time, totally immersive environment for the actors. So that came about later on.

Talk a little bit about the shoot.

Eduardo Sanchez: The shoot was eight days from the moment that Heather [played by actress Heather Donahue] starts in her house to the end in the decrepit old house. And it was a twenty-four-hour-a-day shoot for us. We basically let the actors loose into the town and into the woods. They shot the whole film and they improvised all the dialogue. We've said before [that] we were after complete realism, and so we thought that this was the best way to get this. We'd direct them with directing notes that we'd leave at certain checkpoints at certain times during the day. And then we would play the Blair Witch. We would come out in the middle of the night and scare them, shake their tent and then do all kinds of things to them. We basically tried to make the actors go through what the characters were going through. At the end of this shoot, we limited their food to a power bar and a banana a day. And so they were actually hungry and tired and they were very sick of sleeping in the woods. I think that added to the performances.

Myrick: Our objective in the film was for absolute realism, meaning that when you see the actors on screen, every frame of film had to look convincing—like it wasn't an actor and it wasn't scripted. With Gregg Hale, we devised a process that would allow the actors to roam free throughout this whole eight-day shoot basically unaware of the filmmaking process. So we gave them a global positioning system handset and we had one ourselves. We scouted out the woods in advance, marked all their locations, tent sites, where the stick men were gonna be, and marked those into the GPS system. So they were able to utilize this GPS system and navigate through the woods unaided by anybody.

We directed them at each one of these checkpoints with a series of directing notes, which we ingested their characters based on feedback that we received from the tapes that she shot each day, and also observing them in the woods. It was like a military operation: we were in full camouflage, watching them, and we didn't want them aware of our presence. So we felt that they would give us performances, the prime directive being real and "shoot everything and we will sort it out in the editing process." In a nutshell, that's how we shot the movie.

So you were watching unseen?

Sanchez: Yeah, we were the Blair Witch! We would come out in the middle of the night and scare them, shake their tent and then do all kinds of things to them. We basically tried to make the actors go through what the characters were going through. And they didn't know what was gonna happen next. We wanted to keep it as real as possible. So we would make the directions vague enough so that we wouldn't give any surprises away but distinct enough that they would get to the location and they would do what we needed them to do. Most of the time when they see something in the, film that's the first time they're seeing it. At the end of this shoot, we limited their food to a power bar and a banana a day. And so they were actually hungry and tired and they were very sick of sleeping in the woods. I think that added to the performances. Like Dan said, we were after realism.

You were clearly slave drivers for your poor actors. Have they come out of this experience very well?

Myrick: You'd have to ask their agents. It was tough for everybody. Like Ed was saying, it was a 24/7 shoot for us because we had to stay ahead of the actors—make stick men and hang them in the trees, put piles of rocks outside their tents at three in the morning. There was no one else to do that but us. So keeping this eight-day play moving along in real-time and staying one step ahead of the actors. But what you're looking at in the movie is eighty-two minutes of the most intense footage of twenty hours' worth of raw films. There's a lot of walking through the woods and seeing leaves and them smoking cigarettes and having a good time. When it was all over, everybody was really drained and tired, but we were all glad that we went through it, and learned a lot. I think they learned a lot as actors and we learned a lot as filmmakers. Even if none of this had happened, I think we wouldn't have changed anything. It was a really bonding thing for everybody.

The pair of you share the credits all the way down the line, but how did the tasks divide themselves? Did you have specific tasks or was it a totally collaborative thing?

Sanchez: It was pretty much totally collaborative. We wrote the script together, [although] I think Dan wrote more of the script. We did the outline together. Dan wrote the script. I broke it down. I wrote most of the directing notes. And we took turns going through the footage and observing the actors so that we could talk to each other before we did the directing notes. And in the editing, it was completely collaborative. He would come in on one shift, I would go in on the other, and we'd pull each other's shots out or add and argue over them and then come to a consensus. It was pretty collaborative. We didn't have any big problems until the very end. That was that originally we thought we were going to make a documentary. We had shot all this "Phase 2" footage: interviews with the parents, newsreels from the 1940s, interviews with the Brickwoods searchers and detectives. We were trying to add that in and make it more like a documentary, and it just wasn't working. I was trying one technique, he was trying another, and we were just butting heads. So finally we just decided to throw all that stuff away and go with the footage of the filmmakers. It seems to be have been the right decision.

Has that Phase 2 footage been used or will it be used?

Myrick: Yeah, we did a special for the Sci-Fi Channel in the States and in a comic book, so we were able to use a lot of that third-party material in those tie-ins. It has worked out pretty well.

The Blair Witch Project *has exceeded everyone's expectations. What is it about the Blair Witch that has grabbed the imaginations of American audiences, certainly, and has them screaming in their seats? Also, are you devotees of the horror genre and, if so, which movies gave you the creeps?*

Myrick: Ed and I have the same roster of films that have creeped us out in the past, like The Exorcist [1973], The Shining [1980], the Omen series [starting in 1976], and more recently Henry: Portrait of a Serial Killer [1986] was another one on the list. Mainly, it's psychologically-based horror, which has always really affected us more than just fun films like Scream [1996] or I Know What You Did Last Summer [1997].

But there are a lot of answers to how people are responding to the movie. It's operating on a lot of different levels for different people. Number one, it's scaring people. It's a movie that has a pretence of fear, and it's really delivering for a lot of people. It's the video generation now. I don't think this movie would have worked ten or fifteen years ago with everybody seeing shows like Cops [1989]. Young audiences in particular are really identifying with the movie. And we've all got video cameras now, so if we see something on video, we're conditioned to think it's real. So it's operating on that level as well.

And they're real people. You identify with the people. It's not Jennifer Love Hewitt and Freddie Prinze, Jr. These are three people that could be your next-door neighbors. So there are a lot of things that are affecting people. Overall, it's a movie that's approachable. We're a rags-to-riches story; everybody loves to root for the underdogs, so you've got that factored in as well. And it's the antithesis of high-budget Hollywood, which everyone is rallying around, too.

Sanchez: It's also the whole thing about the repeat viewings. We hear from a lot of people where they go see the film and then they go and don't tell their friends anything about it but just take them to the theater and play the joke on them—and watch them as they experience this for the first time. We hear a lot about that. But I think it has a lot to do that. It's kind of a film where, ever since from the beginning, people have kinda like played along with it.

Some people in the States have been sick seeing the film. Have you been amazed by the reactions?

Sanchez: Yeah. When Dan and I came up with the idea, all we wanted to do was make a scary film. It's just a dream come true to set out to do something like that and have that kind of reaction. We're just very fortunate. We set out to do a completely different kind of film, and I think the thing we learned as filmmakers is that you have to let the film become its own monster, and that's exactly what we did with *Blair Witch*. I think if we hadn't done that—if we had stayed with our original vision—it definitely wouldn't have been as successful. We're amazed by how people are feeling about the film; at the same time, there has been a lot of nausea in the American screens. When we were selling out [in cinemas across the United States] there was a report that pretty much every showing had somebody getting sick. We'd like to apologize to all the ushers because it must have been *terrible*. The film is hand-held, and that does cause a certain amount of nausea if you're really close to the screen, so we tell people to try and sit as far away from the screen as you can and you should be all right. It's really cool that all these things are happening around our film.

What type of release, if any, did you anticipate the film would have when you were shooting it? And was there a moment when you realized it had become this whole other thing, this phenomenon?

Sanchez: When we were shooting, we were thinking of a video release or a cable deal. The big dream was having maybe an arthouse run, where you have one or two cinemas in each major city in the United States, maybe a little bit of foreign, but I think we first realized that it was gonna be huge when the numbers of the theaters [went up]. Artisan kept saying, "We're gonna do two hundred screens. We're gonna do four hundred screens." Then there was talk of nine hundred screens. And this was before the release. We were all going crazy. As a dream, we thought, *If it gets released in thirty or fifty screens, man, that's gonna be incredible*—to have a film in the theaters. Just having it in the theaters was gonna be amazing. But once that third weekend—and it came out in 1,100 screens and we did $28.6 million then—we started to realize that we had something that was just way beyond anything we had expected.

What was the budget?

Sanchez: When we shot the film, we left the woods of Maryland spending about $22,000. Then editing—we didn't keep track of the budget because basically we were using a machine that we were leasing. We were doing Planet Hollywood videos on the side to keep our rent paid and keep the Avid and the Media 100 going. Then, once we got into Sundance, we spent probably another ninety to $100,000 to get it to film to get it to Sundance. Once Artisan took over, they have a figure of about $300,000 that they've spent. So including all our deferments that we paid once we sold the film, I think it's fair to say that it cost about half-a-million dollars.

Has it made you rich?

Sanchez: Yes!

Did anything really inexplicable happen when you were making the movie?

Myrick: No one got killed.

Sanchez: Yeah, that was the big one.

Myrick: So much of this film was serendipity. It's just amazing. All the things that could have gone wrong. When you hand your camera to three actors that are inexperienced filmmakers, and you're in the middle of the woods, and you're doing a whole Method approach where you're reading them on their own. You're opening up the world to problems, you know? We didn't really know what we were doing. We thought it was an experiment. We thought it would generate a few moments of realism, which is what we were going after. And we had no idea if it was going to work or not. Just by virtue of that, a million things could have gone wrong.

If I had to put my finger on one thing, and it's what Ed was describing before, where we had this original vision of the film being a normal documentary, and the film just took on a life of its own. It really forced us to jettison that original vision and adapt it ourselves to what the film was really telling us what it needed to be, and that was a process I wasn't expecting. To this day, it's kinda hard to describe when and how it happened.

I meant anything supernatural.

Sanchez: When we first starting thinking about the movie, and then thinking about the fact that we were gonna shoot it in the woods in October, and it was gonna be cold and it was around Halloween—you put all these things together, and we're shooting a film basically about the supernatural and about this legend, I thought *something* was gonna visit the set. I thought we were gonna get a feeling of something but it was very much on the contrary. I think something was actually out there, but kinda looking out for us, making sure the actors didn't get hurt.

This film for some reason has been blessed. Everything that we could have dreamed of happening with this film has happened. We got it financed just in time. We had just barely enough money. We found three brilliant actors. We were able to shoot it without anybody getting hurt. We got into Sundance. We were able to edit it at our own pace with our own equipment. We sold it at Sundance. We went to Cannes. Dan and I were on the cover of *Time* magazine. It's completely ridiculous! We've just been blessed. Artisan cut us a good deal and at this point, if we manage our money right, we won't have to do anything for the rest of our lives.

How much if anything of the film was factually based, and did you delve into local legends and myths to find the legend of the Blair Witch?

Myrick: The only fact in the film really is that Burkittsville is a real place in Maryland. Everything else is just crap! It was founded in 1824 and is called Burkittsville. That's where it ends.

Sanchez: We didn't take anything directly from any legends we had heard of. We kinda made sure that it sounded like a real legend, you know? There could have been a lot of crazy ideas. We actually threw around a lot of crazy ideas about the myth. We just kept it vague and creepy enough to be believable as something that happened a hundred or two hundred years ago.

Myrick: There's a Bell Witch in Tennessee, and there are a lot of civil war ghost stories around that time. It's like Ed said: we just kept it vague enough to intermingle with people's recollections of factual events or factual folklore.

Did you take anything from events from history?

Myrick: No, not really. We just made sure they *sounded* like history.

When you came up with the title were you aware that we in the UK have a Prime Minister called Blair? Has the use of the name in that respect been advantageous?

Myrick: Blair was just a perfect name, you know? I came up with it. I was writing a treatment for the film early on in '96, [when] we were trying to get financing. We had to name the witch. We called it *The Woods Movie* for a while, but that wasn't gonna work. So my sister had gone to a high school called Montgomery Blair High School, and the county I live in, and where we shot most of the film, is called Montgomery County. Basically, the name just popped into my head. I said, "We'll use *Blair Witch* for now," and it kinda stuck. But it's fine. Early on, before the film went everywhere, I would type in "Blair" on the search engines and come up with all this Tony Blair stuff! [Laughs] I couldn't believe it. I said, "God, there's nothing for *Blair Witch* yet!"

Your names are on the credits as directors, but how much credit should the actors have, given that they are filming? And have they participated in the film's riches?

Myrick: They have points in the movie.

Sanchez: We ripped them off pretty good! [Laughs]

Myrick: [Heather Donahue, Joshua Leonard and Michael Williams] are incredible actors. Ed and I auditioned for over a year and saw over two thousand actors in New York. We knew we needed three people to improvise all these performances. They also needed really good instincts and to look real and also willing to be treated....

Sanchez:... like crap.

Myrick: ... like POWs for a week. So it took a long time to cast these people. Most of the direction of this film was done in the casting process and in the edit process. It was by design that in the eight days that we were actually shooting that we would allow them to run wild, with the hopes of getting absolute realism and a few moments of really good performances. That was how we planned it, and they deserve all the credit in the world because they're just very, very talented actors. The fact that people ask us, "Were they really scared or really not scared?" is a testament to how effective they were. But it's a mixture of them playing from their real emotions, which we were trying to invoke, and also their innate talent.

The sound is very discomforting. This could have been your [version of] Orson Welles' 1938 radio production of The War of the Worlds. *Was sound something else you concentrated on?*

Myrick: Originally, this was recorded off the high-8 microphone, and we were pretty surprised how well it sounded. It was pretty amazing, the fidelity that we got. Again, in the essence of preserving realism, we didn't want to process it too much. Ed and I found out later on, when Artisan picked up the movie, they encouraged us to broaden the sound, make it more of an immersive experience, and put some sound effects in there. Ed and I were pretty resistant at first to do that, but with Wilshire Stages in L.A. and Harry Cohen who was the sound supervisor showed us that you can be subtle with the sound and sound reinforcement. A lot of the wind noises that you hear in the film are all afterwards. Some of the sound effects of the branches cracking in the woods are extra.

Sanchez: A lot of that night stuff—like when you see a lot of black—we had a lot of options. Actually, we had a lot of options to play with the sound throughout the film because you rarely see anybody actually moving their lips. It's always somewhere else. On the night shots, where the scary stuff happens and in the house, we played a lot with the sound. But like Dan said, we were always after the realism. We didn't want to put anything in there that sounded too processed.

The War of the Worlds *generated massive fear in 1938. Sixty years later, a lot of apparently intelligent people think that the events of your film actually happened—that this is a* real *documentary and that cinemas show "found* snuff." Does that give you pause to consider the gullibility of your fellow Americans?

Myrick: The fact and fiction issue has always been an issue, and there still people in America who think it's real. We get emails every day from people asking us, "Is it real?" or "Is it not real?" "Is it based on a true story?" or whatever. We worked pretty hard to make it *look* as real as possible or to *feel* as real as possible. But if you do any research at all on the website or read any article that Ed and I have ever done, you know it's fiction. The goal for us was to keep it as real as possible when you watched it and before you went it. We thought that that would add to the fear factor. But still people are totally convinced that it's real and don't know what portion is real or not.

Sanchez: When Dan and I first came up with the idea, we were thinking that it would be great to make a film that looks completely real, use the actors' real names and not even credit anybody. Just put it out there and see what people do. Don't show anything, even in the credits, that's it's a fictional [piece]. We kinda changed our minds pretty quickly when we showed an eight-minute segment on *Split Screen*, which is an American show on cable. This was back in April of '98.

The *Split Screen* website kind of exploded with people really digging the idea, but also a controversy about whether it was real or not, and with people getting really angry about the fact that they thought we were trying to fool them. They said, "If it is real, then they should be ashamed of themselves because they're exploiting the deaths of these three people. And if it's not real, then they should be equally ashamed of themselves because they're trying to fool us."

So there was a certain backlash, and we felt that if we did that all over the place—completely lied every time somebody asked if it was real or not—then there'd be a certain backlash. People would go into the theaters with a chip on their shoulders to prove that this film wasn't gonna affect them: "I'm gonna prove to them that this doesn't look real to me." So we just wanted people to enjoy the movie. Then Artisan, when they took over, went with the whole marketing strategy of dulling the line and making it really ambiguous as to whether it was real or not. But in every interview that we've ever done, if anybody asks us whether it's real or not, we've always tried to tell the truth.

What has been the reaction to the film from any real witches you may have encountered, or pagans?

Sanchez: We had one witch, an actual real witch that interviewed us on our press tour, and she loved it! [Laughs] She thought it was a cool film. She was spreading the word via her website that this was a film to go see. On the other end of the spectrum, we were pretty much almost sued by a witch organization. They wanted us to put a disclaimer at the beginning of the film that said we didn't mean any harm to witches in any way. It's a little bit foolish because the film's not really about witches at all.

How did you fuel the website yourselves?

Sanchez: We started the website in June of '98, before Artisan was in the picture, before Sundance, before we had even finished editing the film. I had had some prior experience in a previous job building websites, so I just took over the website. I started putting up mythology and all this stuff that we had created, scanning pictures in, film cans and tapes, and just coming up with this story for the background. Everybody helped. The popularity of the website was incredible. One of our fans during Halloween got on the air on a real popular syndicated talk show in Los Angeles and told the host, "Hey, you gotta go check out this website." And then went on the air.

That day we doubled the amount of visitors we'd ever had. That really generated such a momentum going into Sundance that it made the film one of *the* films to see. I think it was partly responsible for our quick sale. And then afterwards in April, once Artisan bought the film, they took over the website and basically revamped it a little bit—started from scratch from where I had started building it. They put up something new every week until they released the film.

But we created it. They kinda just copied us, but they took it a lot further because they had a lot more resources than we did. I think without the website, the film wouldn't have done even half as much business as it's already done, so it was crucial.

Are you prepared for the film to go even further?

Myrick: We're still getting over Sundance right now. It's just been so amazing, so far beyond any of our expectations. Like we said before, to be able to seriously consider buying a car was such a change for us. So now we're just trying to get caught up with the rest of our friends who've been working real jobs for the last ten years, buying a house, getting a car, stuff like that. We just wanna make movies. We just wanna try to make the movie that we wanna make on our terms. *Blair Witch* is hopefully giving us the opportunity to do that. That's why we're staying in Orlando, so we don't get sucked into the L.A. mix and hopefully retain our autonomy. That's our goal for the future. Just keep doing in the future what got us here now. That's the plan.

Given the success of the movie, have your lives changed, and what will you do next?

Myrick: Well, we're in England! Never been here before and glad to be here, it's cool. It's changed in a lot of ways. We can fill out a credit application and not laugh. That's a nice change. But the main thing is that we can seriously call ourselves filmmakers now for the first time in our lives, and have an opportunity to make more movies. Where do we go from here? Ed and I are writing a comedy called *Heart of Love*. We figure it's a 180-degree turn from *Blair Witch*. There's no way we're gonna be able to duplicate *Blair Witch*, so we're gonna go in the exact opposite direction with a comedy and fully embrace the sophomore slump. That's our goal.

Given the great response to the film, what offers have you had?

Myrick: We don't even know how many doors have opened. All we do know is that we're being taken more seriously now to do projects that we want to do. The key for us right now with the explosion of *Blair Witch* in the States is to be patient, not jump onto anything too soon, stick to our plan that we've had laid out for quite a while, and try to do it on our terms. In the long run, we're gonna be a lot happier if we stick to that plan than jump on the first thing that comes along.

Sanchez: We were offered the next *Exorcist* film. We read the script and we wanted to make some changes, but they were kind of just looking for a director to plug in to this production because it was already rolling. I think they're shooting it now or they're about to start. We've been offered a lot of things. A lot of people just send us scripts and ask us what we think of them. Some things have gone further than others, but we just decided that we didn't want to do another horror film, especially the kinds of scripts that they were sending us, because they were these hackneyed, really crappy scripts. And we didn't wanna do another horror film. We were completely horrored out and we still are. We've been offered a lot of garbage at this point.

Myrick: When we got back from Sundance and we were touted as the next horror duo, every producer in Hollywood dusted off those bad old horror scripts, sent 'em to our agent, and we got 'em! I agree with Ed: we've been living in the dark side of our brain for the last three years, so we're really looking forward to doing a comedy next.

Sanchez: A lot of things have been offered to us, but we didn't really like anything that was offered to us. After Sundance, we got a lot of horror scripts from L.A. It just got to the point where we couldn't even finish reading most of the scripts. So we decided that we weren't gonna do a horror film as our next film. But now that *Blair*'s made so much money, Artisan is really wanting to make a sequel—to make some other kind of *Blair* film. We told them, "We don't wanna make a sequel" as the next *Blair* film. We think it'd be a mistake. We have ideas for prequels, but right now they're doing a market study to see how the idea works.

Right now we're excited about doing *Heart of Love*. If we can come to an agreement with Artisan about when we can shoot the prequel, and if the idea comes together and if it's solid, if it's not garbage, then we'll do another *Blair* film. It's mostly up to Artisan right now and whether we can fit it into our production schedule. We want to do *Heart of Love* next.

Would you spend the same amount or would you have more money on the next one?

Sanchez: That's a big thing. That's what the agents continue to tell us: "Do you guys know how much money you're turning down if you don't do a sequel? Do you understand?" And the thing is that *Blair* has given us more money than we thought we were ever gonna make, so to tempt us with money right now is ridiculous.

What did you feel when you got your first paycheck, and what did you buy with it?

Sanchez: I paid off our credit cards, and then I bought myself a bunch of *Star Wars* toys. I hadn't been able to afford them until now. I just went to Toys R Us here and spent a bunch of money. I've spent probably close to two or three thousand bucks now on toys. But, you know, I hadn't bought any toys in all my twenties, so I deserve it.

Myrick: I bought a bunch of stupid robots. I had those when I was a kid, and I've always wanted to get into collecting them. It's not something that you really choose between—your rent or buying robots—so I haven't had the opportunity. So one of the first things I bought was that stuff. As a matter of fact, I was just with Ed at Toys R Us and I bought a few. You have some good robots here in the UK!

1999

CHRISTOPHER NOLAN and CHRISTIAN BALE
Batman Begins

Christopher Nolan pictured on location for *Batman Begins*. The IMAX camera underlines his love of large-screen, hi-def filmmaking. (Warner Bros./David James)

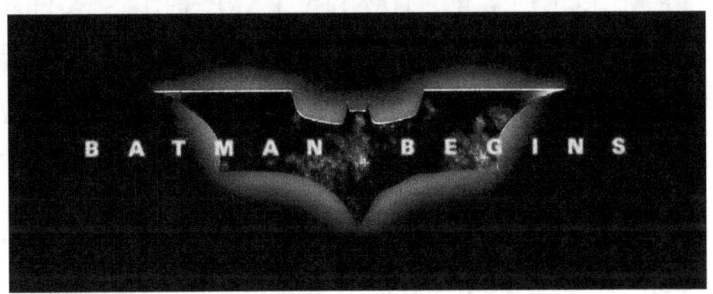

Warner Bros., 2005

CAST: Bruce Wayne/Batman, CHRISTIAN BALE; Alfred, MICHAEL CAINE; Ducard, LIAM NEESON; Rachel Dawes, KATIE HOLMES; Jim Gordon, GARY OLDMAN; Dr. Jonathan Crane, CILLIAN MURPHY; Carmine Falcone, TOM WILKINSON; Earle, RUTGER HAUER; Ra's Al Ghul, KEN WATANABE; Flass, MARK BOONE JUNIOR; Thomas Wayne, LINUS ROACHE; Lucius Fox, MORGAN FREEMAN; Finch, LARRY HOLDEN; Judge Faden, GERARD MURPHY; Loeb, COLIN McFARLANE; Martha Wayne, SARA STEWART; Bruce Wayne (Age 8), GUS LEWIS; Joe Chill, RICHARD BRAKE; Homeless Man, RADE SHERBEDGIA; Rachel Dawes (Age 8), EMMA LOCKHART; Jessica, CHRISTINE ADAMS; Blonde Female Reporter/Assassin, CATHERINE PORTER; Fredericks, JOHN NOLAN; Courthouse Reporters, KAREN DAVID, JONATHAN D. ELLIS; Faden's Limo Driver, TAMER HASSAN; Uniformed Policeman #1, RONAN LEAHY; Old Asian Prisoner, VINCENT WONG; Bhutanese Prison Guards, TOM WU, MARK CHIU,; Enormous Prisoner, TURBO KONG; Chinese Police Officers, STUART ONG, CHIKE CHAN; Himalayan Child, TENZIN CLIVE BALL; Old Himalayan Man, TENZIN GYURME; Stocky Chinese Man, JAMIE CHO; Jumpy Thug, DAVID MURRAY; Dock Thugs, JOHN KAZEK, DARRAGH KELLY; Dock Cops, PATRICK NOLAN, JOSEPH RYE, KWAKU ANKOMAH; Police Prison Official, JO MARTIN; Wayne Enterprises Executive, CHARLES EDWARDS; Female Restaurant Guest, LUCY RUSSELL; Male Restaurant Guest, TIM DEENIHAN; Maître D, DAVID BEDELLA; Restaurant Blondes, FLAVIA MASETTO, EMILY STEVEN-DALY; Gotham Dock Employee, MARTIN McDOUGALL; Arkham Thugs, NOAH LEE MARGETTS, JOE HANLEY, KARL SHIELS; Arkham Uniformed Policeman, ROGER GRIFFITHS; Arkham Lunatic, STEPHEN WALTERS; Arkham Chase Cop, RICHARD LAING; Gotham Car Cop #3, MATT MILLER; Captain SIMONSON, RISTEARD COOPER; Older Gotham Water Board Technician, SHANE RIMMER; Younger Gotham Water Board Technician, JEREMY THEOBALD; Gotham Society Dame, ALEXANDRA BASTEDO; Farmer, SOO HEE DING; Monorail Driver, CON HORGAN; Transit Cop, PHILL CURR; Little Boy, JACK GLEESON; Narrows Bridge Cop, JOHN JUDD; Mrs. Dawes, SARAH WATERIDGE; Basement Club Manager, CHARLIE KRANZ; Bad SWAT Cop #1, TERRY McMAHON; Liquor Store Owner, CEDRIC YOUNG; Victor Zsasz, TIM BOOTH; Valet, TOM NOLAN; Pedestrian, LEON DELROY WILLIAMS; Hazmat Technician, ROGER YUAN; Narrows Teenager #1, JOE SARGENT; Barbara Gordon, ILYSSA FRADIN; Uniformed Cop #2, ANDREW PLEAVIN; Driving Cop, JEFF CHRISTIAN; Arkham Lunatic Cell Mate, JOHN BURKE; Arkham Asylum Nurse, EARLENE BENTLEY; Arkham Asylum Orderly, ALEX MOGGRIDGE; Asian Man/Ra's Al Ghul, JAY BUOZZI; African Boy in Rags, JORDAN SHAW; Felafel Stand Vendor, OMAR MOSTAFA; Opera Performer #1 Faust (Bass), PATRICK POND; Opera Performer #2 Margaret (Soprano), POPPY TIERNEY; Opera Performer #3 Mefistofele (Tenor), RORY CAMPBELL; Caterer, FABIO CARDASCIA; League of Shadows Warriors, SPENCER WILDING, MARK SMITH, KHAN BONFILS, DAVE LEGENO, RUBEN HALSE, RODNEY RYAN; Narrows Cop, DOMINIC BURGESS; Additional Restaurant Guest #1, NADIA CAMERON-BLAKEY; Male Restaurant Guest #2, MARK STRAKER; Crane Thugs, T.J. RAMINI, KIERAN HURLEY; Narrows Teenager #2, EMMANUEL IDOWU; Bridge Cop, JEFF TANNER.

CREDITS: *Director*, Christopher Nolan; *screenplay*, Christopher Nolan, David S. Goyer, based upon characters appearing in comic books published by D.C. Comics; *story*, David S. Goyer; *producers*, Emma Thomas, Charles Roven, Larry Franco; *executive producers*, Benjamin Melniker, Michael E. Uslan; *director of photography*, Wally Pfister, ASC; *production designer*, Nathan Crowley; *editor*, Lee Smith, A.C.E.; *music*, Hans Zimmer, James Newton Howard; *visual effects supervisors*, Janek Sirrs, Dan Glass; *costume designer*, Lindy Hemming. Batman created by Bob Kane. Running time: 140 minutes.

"How does one man change the world?

"It's a question that haunts Bruce Wayne like the specter of his parents, gunned down before his eyes in the streets of Gotham on a night that changed his life forever.
Tormented by guilt and anger, battling the demons that feed his desire for revenge and his need to honor his parents' altruistic legacy, the disillusioned industrial heir vanishes from Gotham and secretly travels the world, seeking the means to fight injustice and turn fear against those who prey on the fearful.

"In his quest to educate himself in the ways of the criminal mind, Bruce is mentored by a mysterious man called Ducard in the mastery of the physical and mental disciplines that will empower him to fight the evil he has vowed to destroy. He soon finds himself the target of recruiting efforts by the League of Shadows, a powerful, subversive vigilante group headed by enigmatic leader, Ra's al Ghul.

"Bruce returns to Gotham to find the city devoured by rampant crime and corruption. Wayne Enterprises, his family's former bastion of philanthropic business ideals, now rests in the hands of CEO Richard Earle, a man more concerned with taking the company public than serving the public good.

"Meanwhile, Bruce's close childhood friend Rachel Dawes, now an Assistant District Attorney, can't secure a conviction of the city's most notorious criminals because the justice system has been so deeply polluted by scum like crime boss Carmine Falcone. It doesn't help that prominent Gotham psychiatrist Dr. Jonathan Crane bolsters insanity defenses for Falcone's thugs in exchange for nefarious favors that serve his own devious agenda.

"With the help of his trusted butler Alfred, detective Jim Gordon—one of the few good cops on the Gotham police force—and Lucius Fox, his ally at the Wayne Enterprises' Applied Sciences division, Bruce Wayne unleashes his awe-inspiring alter-ego: Batman, a masked crusader who uses strength, intellect, and an array of high tech weaponry to fight the sinister forces that threaten to destroy the city."

Texture and Reality
Christopher Nolan and Christian Bale on *Batman Begins*

When was a decision reached to go back to the beginning?

Christopher Nolan: For some time, the studio had been thinking about ways to reintroduce the character into cinemas. They were looking for a fresh approach. It seemed to me that to tell the origin of the story would be pretty fascinating because it's a story that's never been told on screen and hasn't definitively been addressed in any of the comics. It's always been treated in montage and flashback in the past. We wanted to flesh that out and tell the whole story.

How difficult is it to move and act in the Batsuit?

Christian Bale: I probably had the easiest time of any actor apart from Adam West [the star of the 1960s *Batman* TV series]; that looked like a pretty flimsy outfit he had there. But [I had] an easier time than any of the other [actors] in the feature films. [Costume Designer] Lindy Hemmings and the other designers came up with the lightest-weight Batsuit so far, and with the most mobility as well. I don't know if people noticed, but our Batman was actually able to turn his head, which has never been done before. [It's] always been very robotic [before now]. It's hot and it's sweaty and it gives you a headache and everything like that, but I didn't complain about it; I'm getting to play Batman, you know?

In the past, the villains were always more charismatic than the hero. This is the first time that Batman has been more than a guest star in his own movie. Was that the attraction to both of you?

Nolan: For me, Batman is the character [I'm] most interested in in the film, and I felt that it would be perfectly possible to have interesting and colorful villains who wouldn't overshadow the focus of the film. It shouldn't get in the way of the focus of the film and overshadow Bruce Wayne and Batman himself. In my mind, I was thinking somewhat of the best of the Bond films, where there have been some wonderful villains—criminal masterminds—but they've never got in the way of the focus of the story. I felt we could do something similar here.

Bale: I felt similarly that I'd never actually realized, from seeing the other movies, just how interesting Batman was because I was so fascinated with the villains. In many ways, it felt like treading water when Batman arrived. And it wasn't until reading the graphic novels—and the first one I read, because I'm not a comic book fan, was in 2000—that I was really surprised at just how interesting the character Batman could be. I wasn't sure why that had never been seen in a feature film.

How hard was it for you to get back to physical fitness again after the extreme weight loss that you endured for The Machinist *[2004]? Did any scenes have to be postponed until you were fit and able to do them?*

Bale: I don't believe that we had to postpone anything, unless these guys weren't telling me anything! But I think my heart was wondering what the hell was going on. It was a great deal of weight that I did have to put on, but you know, it was something necessary for the character. He has no superpowers whatsoever, so you have to really believe that he's capable of it. I think probably I knew that I'd be able to do it. I think probably Chris was worrying far more than me, because we were speaking. I spoke to him one time on the telephone whilst we were doing *The Machinist*, and he did say to me, "Well, you know, how are you looking these days?" It was, frankly, pathetic. I was 121 pounds and [couldn't] do a single push-up. Hmmm… maybe not the guy you want to cast as Batman! But we had enough time. It was a pretty arduous journey to get there, but I just managed to get into appropriate shape by the time we started filming. [Actually], I went *way* too big. There certainly there were some Fatman comments made at me when I first arrived on the set.

For a long time, people thought that comic book movies were the poor relations of Hollywood movies: lots of money spent, but not a lot of character. Did you have any preconceptions about that?

Bale: We'd seen what a comic book movie could be with the last two Batman movies, and very definitely we were trying to create something completely different. I like to think of this as being a graphic novel-based movie, much more than a comic book, but also more than that. I think Chris took it beyond the realm of the graphic novels, even. And so it's a finely made movie just in itself. Quite apart from having to be any fan of comic books whatsoever which, you know, frankly I'm really not—other than Batman because of playing him—I got quite obsessive about researching him in the graphic novels. Other than that, I've never read a single graphic novel.

There are so many great characters in the film played by so many great actors. As director, how do you deal with all of those different personalities? Do you require a schizophrenic frame of mind to deal with all these people, or is it just part and parcel of being a director?

Nolan: Interesting. For me, part of being a director is trying to figure out what an actor you're working with requires from you, because I think every actor is different and has unique requirements, really. As far as this film goes, it was a very large film with a lot of things going on, and the actors would come go—other than Christian, who was there the whole time and had to be in everything. People would come and go and do a few days here and there, which was quite nice and refreshing for everybody. Michael [Caine] would turn up and raise everyone's spirits a little bit, and then Morgan [Freeman] would come. It keeps everybody going to have a lot of different personalities coming and going.

The thing I've always noticed from great actors—and I've been very fortunate to work with a lot of great actors—is how naturally and easily they accommodate one another's needs. Even though their performing styles are maybe very different and the way you would expect them to approach a scene might be very different, they seem effortlessly to be able to mesh with the other performers. I think that's part of their talent. So I found it very helpful to have so many great creative allies on the set because the other thing a great actor will do—and we were working with a lot of great actors on this film—is have an entire life for their character off-screen. They've worked out their character's place in the world of the story as well. They become very, very useful creative allies for me and make my job a lot easier.

Why was the decision made to shoot the film in Britain as opposed to the United States or Canada?

Nolan: There are a lot of different reasons. From my point of view, I'd always talked to the studio about achieving a degree of texture and reality to the film and doing a certain amount of location shooting in an American city and then studio work elsewhere. The model I'd been looking at, that I first discussed with Warner Bros., was the 1978 *Superman* that Richard Donner made. They did a certain amount of location shooting in New York for that film, but everything else was done over here at Pinewood Studios. So we created a model of the idea of shooting at Shepperton Studios and certain London locations and then going to an American city. It turned out to be Chicago, which is a city I knew from having lived there as a kid. That, for me, was the jumping-off point. I was looking back to a great era of blockbuster filmmaking from the late '70s, where I think Hollywood films were doing some really marvelous escapist entertainment on a grand scale. All of those films were done over here—*Raiders of the Lost Ark* [1981], the first *Star Wars* [1977], *Superman* [1978]. So for me it was fairly natural to just look at that model of doing things.

Batman channels some of the anger that he feels for what happened to him as a child. You had a fairly nomadic life as a child, and there [have been newspaper] reports of you being bullied at school. Did that help drive your anger?

Bale: I've no idea what that's about—[being] bullied in school. You know, having a nomadic childhood certainly helps with doing this job: living in a different place for every single job. I liked that and I kind of need that because that is a normalcy for me. But as for any kind of correlation between anger as a child, I don't think there's a person alive that doesn't have some kind of anger stemming from their childhood. But I can't say that I ever really consider my own history particularly when I'm playing and creating a new character.

You've stated that you wanted to ground this film in a more realistic look. We're talking about a guy who disguises himself as a bat to fight terrorism. Why did you feel that need to give the film a realistic look, whereas the story is just a comic book?

Nolan: Well, to say the story is just a comic book is to miss the whole point, really. But, excepting that point, and say the story is just a comic book, when you talk about realism in films, you're talking about issues of texture and look as much as anything more substantial. For me, really, the idea of grounding the film in reality is about making the audience believe in the events of the story more. I think that the more people are invested in the story, both in terms of character and in terms of the actual events and the physicality of what's going on, if those things can be believed in, I think the narrative effects of the story are amplified. So it's all really about creating the most involving experience possible.

Why did you choose Christian? What makes him different to other young actors?

Nolan: I chose Christian to play Batman based on the idea that in trying to create a realistic version of the story, you need an actor like Christian, who has sufficient intensity and focus in his eyes to make you believe in the idea that somebody without superpowers—and Bruce Wayne has no superpowers—could through sheer force of will change himself into a superhero. From his other performances and then meeting him in person, it was very clear to me that Christian has the ability to project that kind of intensity and that's why I asked him to do the role.

What was your experience of working with the veteran members of the cast?

Bale: It was fantastic getting to work with Michael and Morgan and Gary [Oldman] and Liam [Neeson]—everybody involved in this movie. It was a wonderful thing to see that this caliber of actor was interested in the movie. [They] showed a great recognition that here we had a good filmmaker who they knew they could trust and who was going to be making an original and smart movie. Also, that this was a great story, which I think is really essential to remember here because that gets forgotten so much in large movies with lots of special effects and explosions and everything. Often storyline goes out of the window and, I think, with Chris, that could never happen at all. Working with people such as these wonderful actors makes it so much easier because it just happens, it flows. You can feel when things are right. It's a tough time when you're working with bad actors! That's when you're really having to bust your ass trying to make it work, and that wasn't needed on this movie at all.

Will you be in for the sequel and, if so, how you see the character progressing?

Bale: I could sit here and toy about whether I was going to be back for the sequel. I'm signed up for the next one. Whether anybody else is going to be back for it is a different matter, and that's what I keep asking them! But it is certainly something that I'm more than happy to be back for, if people embrace this movie and, and enjoy the style [and] the vein in which Chris has made it. If they enjoy my portrayal of Batman, then very much I'd like to reprise the character. I think it's kind of limitless with this superhero, unlike others, because he is so contradictory, he is so complex, and he has so many demons and issues. I think there are many things that can be done further and there would be no point in making a sequel if there was not going to be anything new seen. I don't think it would make any sense to return to what we've seen in the past, where suddenly Batman is sidelined and the villains are the interesting ones again. We've established that Batman is just as interesting and, in my mind, a more interesting character than the majority of villains. I would hope that that would continue.

Is there scope to do something grittier for a DVD release? Will there be two versions?

Nolan: No. The film you've seen up on screen is exactly the film that we made. There really isn't anything that I was forced to take out, put in, all the rest. As far as tonally, I always knew that in making a *Batman* film, I wanted it to appeal to a wide range of ages, not the youngest kids, obviously. I think what we've done is probably a bit intense for them, but I certainly didn't want to exclude the sort of ten to twelve-year-olds because as a kid, I would have loved to have seen a movie like this. We never really shot anything that would be alienating in that regard, so there isn't anything to put on the DVD. We managed to get pretty much everything we'd shot into the structure of the story.

If the Donner version of Superman *was a model in terms of your shooting plan, was it also a model in terms of the casting great actors all the way down to the smallest part?*

Nolan: Yeah, very much. I spoke specifically to the studio about coming up with what we talked about as an epic cast. We wanted the film to have an epic treatment other than big sets and big explosions. What really makes a film have that marvelous scale is a wonderful cast of the finest actors and recognizable faces playing even some of the smallest roles so that there's a life off-screen for all of these characters and a scope to the story. [In *Superman*] Richard Donner had Marlon Brando, Gene Hackman, and Glenn Ford. It was an extraordinary ensemble. That was very much what we were aspiring to. We dared to ask some of the finest actors to take on these roles, and I was able to put together a dream cast. I like to think we've actually almost passed that ensemble, which is kind of a fun thing and no less than *Batman* deserves, really.

Batman Begins represents a complete departure from your previous films. Might you return to smaller films next, or can we anticipate more blockbusters?

Nolan: I really haven't been able to focus on what I'll be doing next yet because, frankly, the release of this film is very overwhelming. It's a much larger film than I've ever done before. So this is a very new process to me. I think in the future I'll be interested in doing all sorts of films, really. I've enjoyed making a film on this scale. So I would absolutely be open to it again, but at the same time, I have various projects with different sizes of story, if you like. I hope to do a variety of things in the future.

How did you create the Batman *voice? Did you lower your voice or did you get technical help, like Darth Vader?*

Bale: When we were filming, it was just my voice, and we had a gentleman there who was kind of helping me out so that I could speak the next day. We did try a few different things in ADR. My understanding is that a couple of those things did work and Chris, I believe, used some effects on a couple of occasions but, to be honest, I'm not exactly sure where they were.

Nolan: Basically the voice Christian did in production was very powerful, and we found, when any attempt was made to over-manipulate that, it becomes very obvious and doesn't really work. We did a certain amount of re-recording of dialogue and tried that. As we were analyzing the voice and the way Christian had used it, [it becomes clear that] there is a degree of performance that, frankly, just being in the suit and adopting the character onset, lends the voice that [makes it] incredibly impressive. So we wound up using that very much as the basis of it.

Did you ever assume a different identity in order to achieve something?

Bale: I'm an actor; I do that every day of my life just to get through the day, I think. I don't have any specific phobias like Batman had. I was a bit of an odd kid, actually; I liked scary movies. [They] were certainly my favorite kind of movies. I enjoyed going walking in the woods at night time and walking down dark alleyways and things, just to purposely get the hair on the back of my neck standing up and trying not to run. So I always enjoyed toying with my own fears.

What was the attraction of using Mill Hill Medical Research Institute to [double as] the asylum?

Nolan: It *is* a very imposing building and very, very out of place up there in Mill Hill. We had a fantastic location manager, Ben Rimmer, and he looked high and low for an Arkham Asylum. We had very specific requirements because we needed a front courtyard, and we really looked at a massive number of buildings, but that building up in Mill Hill, with its sort of triangular courtyards and all the rest, is very unique and it was wonderful. The people of Mill Hill made us feel very welcome.

Were you worried about your health when you lost so much weight for The Machinist? *How far would you go for a movie role?*

Bale: You don't have the energy to feel worried about anything when you're that skinny. I had a fair amount of time to get ready for that movie because nobody wanted to give us any money for it, so I had a lot of time for preparation just in the hope that we would eventually get the money. It's not very interesting how somebody diets. You just don't eat very much. I did another movie called *Velvet Goldmine* [1998] in which I had to lose a certain amount of weight. I was running a lot and doing that, and my mom looked at me and said, "Well, this was the glam rock era, wasn't it? How do you think they lost weight? They weren't out running. They were just doing a lot of drugs. Why don't you do it that way instead?"

But how far would I be willing to go for a movie? I have to say that I do look back on *The Machinist* and I'm very proud of it. I very much like the movie. It's absolutely one of my favorites. I can look back now and see that I was crazy but I certainly didn't feel that at the time. With each and every project, you become obsessive about it. However, nothing is worth doing permanent damage to yourself [for], although the idea can sometimes be kind of tempting.

The film's final sequence hints that we might see a film with the Joker. Are you intending a remake of the 1989 film with Jack Nicholson?

Nolan: With respect, you're probably over-thinking it a little bit. The appearance of that device is very much intended as a dramatic effect for *Batman Begins* and for the end of it. As far as where sequels might go from here, I think that the tone of the film is very, very different to previous films, and so it doesn't stand as either a sequel or a prequel to any of the films that have come before. It is a separate thing. As far as what might be addressed in future films, if they were to be made, is just as the Batmobile, the Batcave, [and] Batman himself have all been reinterpreted in a fresh way, that [also] applies to the Joker [and] any other villains. This film really is a different tone to the previous films and so those elements can be reinterpreted.

2005

ANDRÉ ØVREDAL
Troll Hunter

"I wanted to make a movie about a heroic character like Indiana Jones but done with a very Norwegian sensibility – very droll and taking everything seriously. To a degree it's almost like *Monty Python and the Holy Grail*; it's very serious even though it's ridiculous."
– writer/director André Øvredal on the roots of *Troll Hunter*. (Momentum Pictures/Erik Aavatsmark)

Momentum Pictures, 2011

CAST: Hans, the Troll Hunter, OTTO JESPERSEN; Thomas, GLENN ERLAND TOSTERUD; Kalle, TOMAS ALF LARSEN; Johanna, URMILA BERG-DOMAAS; Johanna, JOHANNA MØRCK; Finn, HANS MORTEN HANSEN; Polish Bear Hunter, ROBERT STOLTENBERG; Manager, Electric Power Company, KNUT NÆRUM.

CREDITS: *Director*, André Øvredal; *screenplay*, André Øvredal; *producers*, John M. Jacobsen, Sveinung Golimo; *visual effects and post producer*, Marcus Brodersen; *director of photography*, Hallvard Bræn, FNF; *production designer*, Martin Gant; *editor*, Per Erik Larsen; *visual effects supervisor*, Østein Larsen; *sound designer*, Baard Haugan Ingebretsen; *animation supervisor*, Nina Bergström. Running time: 103 minutes.

> "The government says there's nothing to worry about—it's just a problem with bears making trouble in the mountains and forests of Norway. But local hunters don't believe it—and neither do a trio of college students who want to find out the truth. Armed with a video camera, they trail a mysterious "poacher," who wants nothing to do with them. But their persistence lands them straight

in the path of the objects of his pursuits: trolls. They soon find themselves documenting every move of this grizzled, unlikely hero—The Troll Hunter—risking their lives to uncover the secrets of creatures only thought to exist in fairy tales."

The Troll is Coming Out!
André Øvredal on *Troll Hunter*

Troll Hunter is a highly unusual and unique movie. It avoids being self-referential and does not use in-jokes, which makes it more accessible to non-Norwegians. Where did the initial idea come from?

André Øvredal: I wanted to make a movie about a heroic character like Indiana Jones but done with a very Norwegian sensibility—very droll and taking everything seriously. I loved the trolls from when I was a kid, and I found them to be completely underused in modern culture in Norway. So I thought, *Okay, why can't it be a story about a troll hunter? That would be great.* Then I realize, *Okay, how can I actually make a film like this?* If I was shooting it like a documentary, it would have quite a few things. It would fit in and both make it possible to shoot in terms of production and technical reasons, and it will also help emphasize the idea that this is all real, so that it becomes even more absurd and more humorous when we take everything seriously. To a degree, it's almost like *Monty Python and the Holy Grail* [1975]; it's very serious even though it's ridiculous.

Every country has its folklore. Ireland has leprechauns, Eastern Europe has vampires and werewolves, and we're all familiar with that. But most of us outside Norway are not familiar with your country's history of trolls and the associated legends. How much were you looking to use that backdrop to introduce Norwegian folklore to a wider audience?

We were constantly joking about it, that if this film becomes successful, it will be responsible for introducing trolls to a worldwide audience—if it gets a release in other countries. It seems like it's doing a little bit of that, so that's fantastic. But I was making a film for the Norwegian audience initially, with the knowledge that if it becomes a nice film, hopefully other countries will want to show it as well.

Were you always eager to retain that Norwegian sensibility in the hope that the film would go much wider?

Yes. It contains universal themes of the characters and monsters. You put a specific Norwegian spin on it and you have something that might be exotic *and* universal—and potentially worldwide. I was thinking of that mix, absolutely.

Otto Jespersen is a huge star in Norway but less well-known outside Scandinavia. How and why did you cast him as Hans, the troll hunter?

Initially, I wanted to have unknowns in all the roles, but we were going, "Okay, we've got to signal to the audience and make sure they understand that they are allowed to laugh." And also to broaden the attraction level of the film. There was a question about whether or not trolls would be an interesting movie [subject]. We were quite confident—the people inside the production—but some other people were questioning it. So we added the idea of a star to the lead role, and he was one of the first names we thought of because he was the right kind of guy. He had the right sense of humor. He can play both low-key and he has this kind of rough comedy to him. He's really good at doing these kinds of rants against something in his stand-up routines—he does it against something in society that annoys him. He can really do these negative attitude rants, and they're really funny.

That comes through clearly. He's been doing the job too long. He's fed up, he doesn't get a decent pension, and his entire working life is spent killing trolls.

Yeah, and that to me is the big trick of the whole movie. You have this kind of plain point of view on a worker, but the fact that his job is so crazy in a way in keeping the trolls at bay. That contrast, at least to me, becomes very interesting. You can play with it so much.

The film hints at a huge government conspiracy. Here you have an ordinary man, far from a superman, plus these mythical beasts. It's a crazy backdrop yet it grounds the film.

Yeah, definitely. I wanted to get away from the American superhero image as much as possible but still have a character that had a little bit of it—he still has these amazing adversaries, but I definitely didn't want to make a big American superhero movie.

I felt like there were elements of The Blair Witch Project [1999], Razorback [1984], Dog Soldiers [2002], *and* Jurassic Park [1993] *in the film. The trolls are absolutely convincing. How did you dream up their look? Is it based on folklore and fairy tales, or is it entirely a creation of the filmmakers?*

No, it's actually based on the art from this book of fairy tales that we have. I made an early decision that we cannot go too far away from the way Norwegians expect trolls to look. Sometimes there have been trolls in movies and you think, *These are not Norwegian trolls.* They're fine, they're trolls, but they're definitely not Norwegian trolls. I didn't want to end up in that trap. I wanted to make sure that we stayed close to that, and I'm thankful that we were actually able to do that because everybody in Norway said, "This is really Norwegian trolls."

One assumes that the actors were acting against nothing and their imaginations were running wild.

Yeah. Everything was digital, so we had nothing on set for them to play against other than a thin pole that was eight meters tall, and I said, "That's where the eyes are going to be!" To me, when it comes to acting in situations like that, I do find that as an actor you have to use your imagination, whether you're talking about something that is deeply heartfelt or it's a monster standing in front of you, so you are scared for your life. It's all [about] how you see it in your head. You have to invent all this stuff anyway and emotionally build upon that invention. To me, yes, it's technically a little bit of a challenge to make it right physically, but emotionally you're doing the same thing.

Is it true you were enthusiastic in assisting the actors by stepping in and doing some of the trolls' sounds?

Yes! Me or the first AD or whoever. I ended up doing a lot of standing around, doing a lot of screaming and yelling. Basically sometimes saying out loud what is going on because the actors appreciated having simple, factual information. I would stand there and yell, "Okay, the troll is coming out!" the most silly thing you would ever say on a set, but actually the actors wanted it, and they worked. I would have to show them the trample—of how quickly the troll would come out. Whether it comes out charging or if it comes creeping out slowly.

Did you have free rein for your concept of the trolls? Could you make them as frightening as you wanted them to be?

Yes, absolutely. We all decided this had to be taken dead seriously. Everything in the movie had to be taken completely seriously. The producer was in on it, I was, and we wanted to make it as frightening as possible. We didn't want to make violent, anti-family scenes with grueling attacks. We didn't want that. We wanted to hit broadly. But outside of that, to make them as frightening and in a way as fun as possible.

Was Theodor Kittelsen the classic artist of Norwegian trolls?

Yes, him and a guy named Erik Theodor Werenskiold. They drew the art for this book of fairy tales [*Norske Folkeeventyr*, or *Norwegian Folk Tales*], and everything else had to compare to that, in a way. All other depictions of trolls come afterwards. It was always a reference to that.

In watching Troll Hunter, *I was reminded of a classic British movie called* Night of the Demon *[1957].*

I just saw that, like, a month ago! That's so funny. The idea of showing the monster reasonably early—I think some movies might be making a minor mistake not showing what you're up against fairly early. I think particularly in *Night of the Demon*, I think I've read that that was done in post-production. That was a decision that was made very late in the process. It wasn't really the plan. I think even the producer may have taken that decision on his own, more or less, to put the major shot of the demon at the very beginning. My model basically would be *Jurassic Park*, where you're building suspense or anticipation for the creature. But you have to deliver fairly early because you want to play with it, you want to show how it behaves, you want to tell the story of the monster you have, obviously in our case a troll, instead of keeping it hidden. I wanted to build a mythology. I wanted to talk about the trolls instead of keeping it in the shadows.

Is it about humanizing them and giving them personalities? They have their own community, their own way of life. Humans are the latecomers. Do we have the right to destroy them because they've been here much longer than us?

Oh, definitely. There is a whole point like that in the film. They're a thousand years old and they're part of our country's past. It becomes almost like an animal rights topic in the film. I didn't want to deal with it on the surface, but it's there as an undercurrent.

You were shooting in bad weather and on challenging locations. What was the biggest challenge for you in delivering this movie?

The biggest fear was that we were not going to be able to even shoot this film in twenty-eight production days. Fortunately, I had a fantastic DoP, line producer, and producers who were really helping to put this production together and push it forward so we could keep the schedule. But that was integrated into the project by doing a documentary because you don't have to shoot coverage; you only have one angle on anything you shoot. So as soon as you've shot the thing from that one angle you can actually move on to the next scene instead of shooting it from three or four different angles. So that really made it possible, but definitely our biggest challenge was being able to finish our production days and not lose time. We ended up having one extra shooting day, but that was mostly because weather screwed us up. Weather was definitely an issue, yeah.

The final sequence with Hans fighting the huge troll is an epic piece of filmmaking. Did you achieve everything you wanted to?

I'm extremely happy with it, and that is down to us being able to shoot that stuff and also down to the effects people being able to make these scenes come alive. We were thinking, *Okay, we want to drive between the legs of the troll. How are we going to do that?* I'm very proud of the whole movie, but if you're talking about this sequence then, yeah, I'm very proud that we were able to do it. Of course, I could have extended it more and made it longer and even more exciting, [but] I really think it achieves everything I wanted it to achieve.

Do you have a favorite moment?

You know, I don't really have a favorite moment. I do really enjoy seeing the troll with an audience. There are so many moments. I do enjoy the Muslim jokes. Obviously I'm a big fan of all the troll scenes, but, I don't know. I don't really have a favorite scene. I couldn't say that.

Could there be a sequel or follow-up movie in the same tradition?

The producer and I are already talking a lot about it. Six months ago, we were talking about jumping straight onto a sequel because there is tons of material for it. I've been involved in quite a few other projects recently. I decided I wanted to do something else other than another troll film before possibly going back to it so I don't get pigeonholed with trolls for the rest of my life. [Laughs]

Will there be an American remake?

It has already happened. We sold the remake rights to Chris Columbus' company and they're going to do it. As far as I know, they're hoping to shoot it next year [2012], so they're doing the American version, but I'm hoping they will do it in Norway. That's kind of what they're indicating. That would be great fun for everybody, I think.

2011

GEORGE A. ROMERO
Land of the Dead

John Leguizamo (playing Cholo) looks on as veteran zombie wrangler George A. Romero gives directions on the set of *Land of the Dead*. The film brought Romero back to the walking dead for the first time in 20 years. (Universal)

GEORGE A. ROMERO'S
LAND OF THE DEAD

Universal, 2005

CAST: *Riley Denbo*, SIMON BAKER; *Cholo DeMora*, JOHN LEGUIZAMO; *Kaufman*, DENNIS HOPPER; *Slack*, ASIA ARGENTO; *Charlie*, ROBERT JOY; *Big Daddy*, EUGENE CLARK; *Pretty Boy*, JOANNE BOLAND; *Foxy*, TONY NAPPO; *Number 9*, JENNIFER BAXTER; *Butcher*, BOYD BANKS; *Tambourine Man*, JASMIN GELJO; *Mouse*, MAXWELL McCABE-LOKOS; *Anchor*, TONY MUNCH; *Mike*, SHAWN ROBERTS; *Pillsbury*, PEDRO MIGUEL ARCE; *Manolete*, SASHA ROIZ; *Motown*, KRISTA BRIDGES; *Brubaker*, ALAN VAN SPRANG; *Chihuahua*, PHIL FONDACARO; *Mulligan*, BRUCE McFEE; *Roach*, EARL PASTKO; *Sutherland*, JONATHAN WHITTAKER; *Cliff Woods*, JONATHAN WALKER; *Styles*, PETER OUTERBRIDGE; *Dead Teenage Girl*, LARA AMERSEY; *Dead Teenage Boy*, MICHAEL BELISARIO; *Knipp*, GENE MACK; *Kaufman's Security Guard*, MATT BIRMAN; *Lieutenant*, PAUL JERRICO; *Young German Soldier*, EDWARD KALINSKI; *Brian*, DEVON BOSTICK; *Gus*, JASON GAUTREAU; *Barrett*, CHRISTOPHER RUSSELL; *Veteran Soldier*, CHRISTOPHER ALLAN NELSON; *Female Soldier*, DEBRA FELSTEAD; *"High Noon" Soldier*, TINA ROMERO; *Guards* at the "Throat", COLM MAGNER, SCOTT WICKWARE; *Hobo*, RON PAYNE; *Steele*, RICHARD CLARKIN; *Bettor*, DARRIN BROWN; *Deke*, ELDRIDGE HYNDMAN; *Weapons Storage Guard*, TED LUDZIK; *Arena Policeman*, DAVID SPARROW; *Number 9's Victim*, BRIAN RENFRO; *Grenade Soldier*, JAMES BINKLEY; *Fiddler's Green Promo Announcer*, ROBIN WARD; *Topless Dancer*, DAWNE FUREY; *Kissing Woman*, SANDY KELLERMAN; *Kissing Woman*, DONNA CROCE; *Dead Tuba Player*, WILBERT HEADLEY; *Dead Trombone Player*, ROSS SFERRAZZA; *Cheerleader Zombie*, ERICA OLSEN; *Zombie Mother*, LIISE KEELING; *Zombie Daughter*, SONIA BELLEY; *Refrigerator Zombie*, CHAD CAMELLERI; *Policeman Zombie*, GINO CROGNALE; *Fence Fry Zombie*, SHANE CARDWELL; *Photo Booth Zombies*, SIMON PEGG, EDGAR WRIGHT; *Arena Fight Zombies*, KEVIN RUSHTON, NICK ALACHIOTIS; *Child Zombie*, JAMES CANTON; *Clown Zombie*, ERMES BLARASIN; *Hillside Zombie*, JAKE McKINNON; *Bridgekeeper Zombie*, GREG NICOTERO; *Temperance Street Zombie*, SUSAN WLOSZCZYNA; *Legless Zombie*, DAVID CAMPBELL; *Machete Zombie*, TOM SAVINI. *Uncredited: Voice of Puppeteer*, GEORGE A. ROMERO.

CREDITS: *Director*, George A. Romero; *screenplay*, George A. Romero; *producers*, Mark Canton, Bernie Goldmann, Peter Grunwald; *co-producer*, Neil Canton; *associate producers*, David Resnick, Silenn Thomas; *executive producers*, Steve Barnett, Dennis E. Jones, Ryan Kavanaugh, Lynwood Spinks; *music*, Reinhold Heil, Johnny Klimek; *art director*, Fred Carter; *director of cinematography*, Miroslaw Baszak; *editor*, Michael Doherty; *production design*, Arv Grewal; *art direction*, Douglas Slater; *costume design*, Alex Kavanaugh; *special make-up effects supervisors*, Howard Berger, Greg Nicotero. Running time: 93 minutes/97 minutes (director's cut)

> "The walking dead roam an uninhabited wasteland, and the living try to lead 'normal' lives behind the walls of a fortified city. A new society has been built by a handful of enterprising, ruthless opportunists who live in the towers of a skyscraper, high above the hard-scrabble existence on the streets below. But outside the city walls, an army of the dead is evolving. Inside, anarchy is on the rise. With the very survival of the city at stake, a group of hardened mercenaries is called into action to protect the living from an army of the dead."

Championing the Forgotten Monster
George A. Romero on *Land of the Dead*

You started almost as a guerrilla filmmaker, making movies for almost no money and having tremendous success. Land of the Dead *is a studio movie. Was there a huge difference?*

George A. Romero: Not much difference at all because we weren't rich. This movie was half the budget of the *Dawn of the Dead* remake [from 2004], less than half, and it was much more ambitious. It was big! Big sets, the truck, and all that stuff. So it was not that different. It was still guerrilla filmmaking. I feel that I have a bit of an advantage having done commercials and little "industrials"—little films with no money. You know what you need to do and you try to figure out the shots and how to spend the money. That's what it's really all about. So it wasn't that different. The big difference was that, for the first time, I had to deliver an R-rated version for US MPAA, so I used some tricks there. In the end, we wound up walking zombies in front of a green screen so that we could overprint them and put them on top of the gore shots and take out frames. We could then take them off for the DVD.

Some of the MPAA stuff is a bit ridiculous. They won't say, "Cut that scene," because then they're afraid of being censored, but they'll tell you, "Cut nine or ten frames out of that." So we were able to do that with these walk-bys that we did. Then consciously, we did a few things that were meant to escape the MPAA's wrath. We did a scene in smoke where they pull a hand apart, and we did a scene in silhouette and shadow where a guy's neck gets pulled off. We did some things like that in order to squeak by the censors. It's funny, because people say that this film is gorier than the others, but I don't think it is. You can see exactly what's going on but if you count it frame-by-frame I don't think it is. Maybe it's been a while so people think, *My God, this guy's NUTS!*

It wasn't easy to get off the ground. Was that a 9/11 thing and changes that you made to the script?

I have this conceit: *Night of the Living Dead* [1968] was the '60s, *Dawn* [1979] was the '70s, *Day* [1985] was the '80s, and I wanted to do the '90s.

I just missed it. My partner and I got hung up in Hollywood in development deals and we had a housekeeping deal with New Line for a while and never made a movie. Then we got involved in these development deals on films that never happened. Out of frustration, I fled and made a little film financed by CanalPlus called *Bruiser* [2000] that nobody has ever seen. So I missed the '90s.

Immediately after finishing *Bruiser*, I started to write a script for this. It was much more about homeland problems—homelessness, AIDS, the vanishing middle class—although a lot of the imagery [such as] the truck and the idea of a city protected by water was in that script. When I finished it and sent it around, it was literally before 9/11 and nobody in Hollywood anyway wanted to touch it. They wanted to make soft, fuzzy, lollipop movies. So I stuck it on the shelf.

A couple of years later, I took it down and put in some obvious references to this "new normal" in America now, but some of the things were there. They're more poignant now: the idea of an armored vehicle going though a little village and mowing everybody down and then wondering why they're pissed off at us! That scene was in the original script; it just meant more. The tower was made a taller, bigger building and one of the lines—"We do not negotiate with terrorists"—is *too* on the nose. It always gets a laugh, so maybe it works.

Night of the Living Dead had a subtlety to it, whereas Land of the Dead is more overt in its shocks. Do audiences expect that now?

I think that maybe my fans expect it of me. I think *Day of the Dead* had really the most graphic effects—[the ones] that Tom Savini did. I think probably there are a couple of moments in *Day of the Dead* that are much more graphic and much more gory than anything in *Land of the Dead*. But I think they expect it of me. I enjoy doing it, I grew up on EC comic books, I am not bothered by it. When I see gore scenes in someone else's horror films, I giggle, I don't cringe. Again, it's another conceit. It's sort of like a slap in the face. You see the original film version of *M*A*S*H* [1972] by Robert Altman and you're laughing your ass off for ninety minutes. And occasionally there's an operating room scene where there's blood all over the place, and it's a slap in the face. It's a wake-up call or something. I have sort of justified it that way, and maybe it is a justification, but I am also not bothered by it.

What was it about EC comics that influenced you as a young man?

In the days before the "comics code," when I was buying comic books as a kid, there were EC comic books, there was *Mad* magazine, but there was also *Tales from the Crypt*—that whole series of EC horror comics with the vault-keeper. I *loved* that stuff. They were horror tales, but also sort of morality tales. The bottom line is that they were always moral. When we did *Creepshow* [1982]—which Steve King modeled after those books—he wrote a tagline saying, "A Laurel comic is a moral comic." The bottom line is that the bad guys also got their comeuppance. Peppered here and there throughout, there was some social satire and social criticism. They were beautifully drawn—the great artists that drew for *Mad*, Wallace Wood, Jack Davis, and all those guys, were beautiful. I grew up on that, and then all of a sudden they said, "Wait a minute! Forbidden!"

Your career appears to have enjoyed a wholesale resurrection on the back of the Dawn *remake and via* Shaun of the Dead *[2004] over here. Now here you are making a new film. How ironic is that for you? Is it something you have to embrace or do you laugh in the morning when you're shaving in the mirror?*

You have to embrace it. I have to. I don't feel any anger. My ex-partner [Richard Rubinstein] had the right to do the *Dawn* remake; he told me he was doing it and I said, "Fine." I didn't have a problem with that. I don't think I would have had a problem getting this film financed. Initially, when I first took it back off the shelf after 9/11, Fox wanted it right away because they were in negotiations for *28 Days Later* [2002]. I think they were about to open and they wanted to develop their own franchise. The problem was that we wound up in negotiations with Fox for over a year. They wanted to own the franchise. They wanted to call the film *Night of the Living Dead*. It was ridiculous, typical sort-of studio stuff. We were resisting and resisting and resisting, and in the end that's really what helped us.

Then Mark Canton, one of the producers of this film, serendipitously was having lunch with my agent. He said, "What's going on with that project?" David Kersh, my agent, said, "The deal hasn't closed yet." Mark said, "I want it. I will have a deal within weeks." And he did. From that day, it was five weeks and we were off and running. That's really what happened with that. I think I could have always financed it. I wasn't even resisting it. I had written a script. By the time I got it finished, 9/11 happened and nobody wanted to touch it. I wanted to change it to reflect that and, again, it was better served having it come a couple of years later because I could be a bit more reflective.

I'm a guy who lives in Pittsburgh. I'm not a Hollywood guy. What the general public doesn't realize is that I'm working all the time. Often projects don't happen. But in that longish period before *Bruiser*, I made more money than I've ever made in my life—writing scripts, re-writing this and that. But it's a very frustrating process because all of a sudden there's three million bucks against a property and you can't make it. It becomes cast-dependent and they don't know whether I am a big enough guy. So it's frustrating. You develop something—it might even be your own material—and then somebody rewrites it. Or I rewrite it.

We had a project called *Before I Wake*, which was at New Line, went to MGM, went to Fox. At Fox, it was with Chris Columbus' company 1492, and at that time, he was a five hundred pound gorilla. He basically said, "Anything I wanna make gets made." He requested a few rewrites. We did them. It already had a lot of money against it at these other studios, and then all of a sudden, it needed A-list cast because there was so much money tied up in it.

You were going to do The Mummy [1999]. *What happened?*

This project *Before I Wake* killed *The Mummy*. I was under contract to MGM, and literally there were twelve days left to run on the contract. MGM said, "No, no, we are going to make this movie. This movie is happening. Forget about it [*The Mummy*]." They wouldn't let me off the contract. Universal had actually green-lit *The Mummy*—it was a "go" picture, not at all like the *Mummy* that they eventually made. It was much more old-fashioned. [Laughs] But they had green-lit it and MGM didn't let us out.

You've openly admitted that in your zombie movies you've been happily ripping off Richard Matheson's I Am Legend.

Well, I happily did in the very beginning. The first film [*Night of the Living Dead*] basically was a rip-off of *I Am Legend*. I mean unabashedly, except they were vampires. I needed something else, so I went with ghouls. I never called them zombies, I didn't even think of them in that way. I thought of them as ghouls—flesh-eaters. Our original title was *Night of the Flesh Eaters*. The word "zombie" never even popped into my head. Zombies in those days were those guys from Haiti.

So where did zombie come from, because you are so linked with that genre? Mention "zombie" and people say your name. It's automatic. How did it become part of your culture?

I think it worked for the second film. Well, no. Actually, when *Night of the Living Dead* first started to get noticed as something more than a "penny dreadful," some people that wrote about it called them zombies. That sort of woke me up, and I said, "Gee, maybe they are." I get credit for reinventing the zombie, but I didn't realize I was *doing* it, so I don't know if I deserve credit for that or not. In my mind, they were ghouls. Ghouls are really the forgotten monster, right? There was *The Mad Ghoul* [1943] and those old Universal flicks. That was the way I thought of them.

How and why did you cast Asia Argento in Land of the Dead? *Was it the connection with her father, Dario?*

Of course, but I always wanted to work with her. We were talking to her about another project that almost happened called *Diamond Dead*. Some of the people that did *Rocky Horror* [1975] were involved. Richard Hartley had written a score—it was a spoofy movie about a dead rock band. I called Asia because I thought she was perfect for the lead in that, and I said, "Would you like to do it?" We sent her the script and she loved it, so we started to talk. Then all of a sudden, this Mark Canton thing happened. I called her back and she said, "Is the movie happening?" and I said, "No, but there's *another* one!" So it happened like that. But I've known her obviously ever since she was little, through Dario. I think she's great, and I really wanted to work with her, so I'm glad she said yes to it.

How do you feel about people deconstructing your films and finding political motives that might not have been there when you wrote them? Are you trying to make political statements, or are you trying to make horror movies?

No, no. I'm not trying to incite. I think of the films more as a reflective of the times in which they were made. They are little snapshots: here's what's happening now. I'm not trying to answer questions, but I love the idea that it's a reflection of what's going on. It's important to me. Even when I wrote the first version of this film before 9/11, what it was about in my mind was ignoring the problem. That's what it seemed to me we were doing in America: ignoring big problems. That's what it was about.

Some of that holds over into this. Okay, now we're threatened. We thought we were protected by water. We're not. Don't worry about it. I've got all these soldiers. You're safe. Keep doing what you're doing. Stay down there in the taverns. We'll give you some vices. Don't come over here near me, up in the Halliburton office! So to that extent it's intentional. I don't try to put it right in the center, but it's important to me.

When I first went in to pitch the original version of this, I said, "It's about ignoring the problem," and they said, "Yeah, but what's the story?" I could build fifty stories. Why do you need a story? It's zombies. There's humans. It's about ignoring the problem! Nobody gets it. You can't pitch it that way. So what I always wind up doing is writing the script instead of trying to talk somebody through it.

To continue the political angle, your leading actor in Land of the Dead, *Dennis Hopper....*

Republican bastard! [Laughs]

... is very pro-Bush and vociferously so. I suspect you're not. That might have been an interesting mix in the workplace.

Well, it was. I remember at Cannes, we were sort of throwing pies at each other, you know? But openly. He's very cool about it. He doesn't proselytize. He just says, "That's where I'm at. Not him," and then he points at me. I didn't know Dennis before this film. I met him through Mark Canton. Dennis came in, he read the script and liked it, and wanted to play the character [of Kaufman]. The first thing he said was, "You know, usually when people want me to be the villain, they want me to go hysterical, go over the top and be histrionic. This guy is Donald Rumsfeld." That was the first thing that he said to me, and I said, "Dennis, we're gonna get along!"

Your films feature genre-busting casting, often with black actors. You've continued that in Land of the Dead.

Well, in *Night of the Living Dead*, Judy [played by Judith Ridley] was running around. She yelled, fell down, did all of these embarrassing things that women in horror movies did. I apologized [for that notion] in the remake of *Night* [in 1990], the Savini version. I wrote that script and made her strong, and I have tried to stay with that. Back then, during *Night*, I sort of just fell into that pattern: the woman was the weak one, catatonic, falling down, unable to do anything. I've felt bad about it ever since.

The other thing [is that] Duane Jones, the lead guy in *Night of the Living Dead*, was just the best actor from among our friends. The script wasn't written with any description of race. When we decided to use Duane, we did talk about changing the script, and we decided, "Don't change the script." So if there's any credit that's deserved for that, it was that we *didn't* change the script. It was not that it was intentional from the pop. And I'm now wondering if we shouldn't have. I think we might have missed a bet there.

Maybe we should have acknowledged it and it should have had some argument or should have addressed it somehow. Nonetheless, that happened. And then again, it became a conceit. I hate to keep using that word, but that's why you make movies, right? So I used an African-American lead [Ken Foree as Peter] in the second film and in the third film. This time, I sort of switched allegiances and made Big Daddy the African-American guy, hoping that people might notice.

In your early films, you had the cheeky habit of borrowing other people's cars and then wrecking them. Is that still part of the game plan?

Obviously, sometimes you have to do something to correct a problem. In the original *Night of the Living Dead*, it was Russ Streiner, one of the producers'—who is actually Johnny, the guy that goes to the cemetery at the very beginning with his sister—mother's car that we were using. We shot a couple of scenes with it, and then his mother hit a tree or something with it and dented the door. So we couldn't shoot it from that angle. I said, "Wait a minute. Maybe we can use this," so when she runs down the hill she runs into a tree, and then you see this crunch and the crease is there. So we took advantage of that situation.

You also took advantage of another car company when you used all those cars in the shopping mall in Dawn of the Dead.

We didn't actually wreck any, though. We just drove 'em around in there. We didn't wreck any, did we? Maybe when I wasn't looking!

There is a story from Dawn of the Dead, *which is probably apocryphal, that you sent a telegram to Tom Savini that said, "Start thinking of ways to kill people."*

It wasn't a telegram. It was a phone call.

Did the producers on the new film expect you to follow that tradition by including some really serious visceral gore, or was it left to you to deliver what you'd put in the script?

It was pretty much left to me, and a lot of the things were in the script [such as] the headless priest, where the head flops over. That's one that we couldn't pull off. We tried three times and just couldn't make it happen with puppets because it always looked like puppets. With CG, it looks like CG to me, but it was the only way we could pull the effect off. The idea works well enough, so you can actually get past it. But that was in the script. Many of those things were in the script. But I did say to Greg Nicotero the same thing that I said to Tom: "Can you come up with anything?" When you start working on something like this and you're sitting there puzzling or you're in the shower thinking what you can do—I just called Greg and said the same thing: "Can you think of other ways to kill zombies?" He came up with a couple of pretty good ideas. A couple of them never came off. It's just too difficult to do it mechanically, and we found that several of them didn't work. There are a couple that are on the DVD—and we put on the DVD a couple of failed attempts—to say, "Look, we tried to do this. It didn't quite work."

Do you have to embrace technology?

You know, as a filmmaker you have to appreciate that computers allow you to do things that you couldn't think of doing if you were working smaller or in the old days. But I don't like using it. I'm a Ray Harryhausen fan. I would have much preferred if we could have done it all mechanically. That would have been amazing. Like in *Day of the Dead*: that thing that Savini did of pulling the guy's head out, which is fabulous and seamless, the way he did it. You can see it's a live shot, a real shot. You can see the difference.

The scene that I'm talking about with this head, it's CG. It's obviously CG, at least to me. Maybe general audiences don't feel it or don't recognize it as readily as we do, but it bothers me. I'd rather it be amazing. I'd rather be David Copperfield: "Here he is! Live and in person!" You'll figure it out. So I much prefer trying to do it that way. And we really tried. Greg tried his damndest. There were just a couple of things that we couldn't do.

Your films have been giving us sleepless nights for forty years. You grew up on EC comics. What movies scare you?

I'm old enough that I saw the Universal films. I didn't see them in the '30s—I'm not *that* old—but on re-release. I saw *The Thing from Another World* [1951], the Christian Nyby version, if he's the one responsible. That was scary to me. But the stuff that scared the most out of me—I was a Hispanic kid in the Bronx getting beat up by the Italian guys—were the blackouts at the end of the Second World War. Then I remember [US news commentator] John Cameron Swayze telling me personally out of that whole boob tube that the Russians had the bomb! That scared me. It was reality, the shit goin' on around you, that scared me the most.

Stephen King contributed to the anthology Book of the Dead *[1989], which was based on your world. Would you consider handing over your legacy to other people, either by remaking your movies or by extending the series to books?*

I don't think about that, no. My work is my work. And Stephen, the first thing he gets asked is, "How do you feel about Hollywood ruining your books?" And he always says, "They're not ruined. Here they are right now, on the shelf. Nobody ruined 'em. They're not touched." I guess that's really the way I feel. I don't look too much at other horror films. I'm not a student that way. I'm doing my own thing and I don't particularly care what goes on around it. Maybe it's not a very scholarly attitude but that's my attitude.

2005

ELI ROTH
Cabin Fever

A horror movie obsessive since childhood, Eli Roth always knew he wanted to be a movie director. (Lionsgate)

Lionsgate, 2003

CAST: Paul, RIDER STRONG; Karen, JORDAN LADD; Bert, JAMES DeBELLO; Marcy, CERINA VINCENT; Jeff, JOEY KERN; Old Man Cadwell, ROBERT HARRIS; Tommy, HAL COURTNEY; Dennis, MATTHEW HELMS; Fenster, RICHARD BOONE; Andy, TIM PARATI; Lemonade Boy, DALTON McGUIRE; Lemonade Girl, JANA FARMER; Shemp, DANTE WALKER; Fake Shemp, JEFF RENDELL; Ray Shawn, BRANDON JOHNSON; Cadwell's Crush, CHERIE RODGERS; Happy Wednesday Band, BILL TERRELL, RICHARD TERRELL, JEFF EVANS, MIKE HILL, J.K. GODBOLD; Deputy Winston, GIUSEPPE ANDREWS; The Sheriff, RICHARD FULLERTON; Evil Deputy, PHIL FOX; Shooters, GABRIEL ROTH, DONALD LEE HALL, JR, JEREMY A. METCALF; The Hermit, ARIE VERVEEN; The Hog Lady, CHRISTY WARD; Shotgun Casey, MICHAEL HARDING; Beautiful Wife, JULIE CHILDRESS; Justin, DAVID KAUFBIRD; Dr. Mambo, ROCK; Guitar Man, NOAH BELSON; Harmonica Man, DOUG McDERMOTT; Troubadour, MATT CAPPIELLO; Winston's Date, JESSICA MASSERMAN; Underage Girl, PAIGE HUNTER; Cerina's Brother, GINO VINCENT; Rider's Brother, SHILOH STRONG; Shiloh's Girlfriend, DARCY JO MARTIN; Sir Chug-a-Lot, JAY AASENG; The Bad Influence, MATTHEW SCHWARZ; Cat Hat Girl, JESSICA SHORTKOFF; Shocked Guy, MARK MORSE; Shocked Girl, HEATHER SIMMONS; Mr. Mom, DEAN MASSERMAN; Doctors, SAM FROELICH, TOM TERRELL; The Bunny Man, WE WILL NEVER TELL; Helpless Bystander, EVAN ASTROWSKY; Dennis Double, LUKE BLACKWOOD; Hospital Attendant, MARK SCHWARZ; Hospital Hottie, SHANA SCHWARZ; Killer, JOE ADAMS; The Happy Bald Guy, ADAM ROTH; The Victims, JEFF HOFFMAN, DEAN MASSERMAN,

JOHN NEFF, NANCY NEFF, MICHAEL REARDON, GLENN WEISBERGER, ROY WOOD.

CREDITS: *Director*, Eli Roth; *screenplay*, Eli Roth, Randy Pearlstein, from a story by Eli Roth; *producers*, Eli Roth, Lauren Moews, Sam Froelich, Evan Astrowsky; *executive producer*, Susan Jackson; co-*executive producer*, Jeffrey D. Hoffman; *associate producer*, James Waldron; *director of photography*, Scott Kevan; *editor*, Ryan Folsey; *music*, Nathan Barr; *special make-up effects supervisors*, Robert Kurtzman, Gregory Nicotero, Howard Berger; key *special make-up effects artist and set supervisor*, Garrett Immel; *production design*, Franco-Giacomo Carbone; *costume design*, Paloma Candelaria. Running time: 93/98 minutes.

> "As a last hurrah after college, friends Jeff, Karen, Paul, Marcy, and Bert embark on a vacation deep into the mountains. With the top down and music up, they drive to a remote cabin to enjoy their last days of decadence before entering the working world. Then somebody gets sick. Karen's skin starts to bubble and burn as something grows inside her, tunneling beneath her flesh. The group is so repulsed, shocked, and sickened watching their friend deteriorate before their eyes; they lock her in a shed to avoid infection. As they debate about how to save her, they look at one another and realize that any one of them could also have it. What began as a struggle against the disease soon turns into a battle against friends, as the fear of contagion drives them to turn on one another. The kids confront the terror of having to kill anyone who comes near them, even if it's their closest friend. The survivors have to find help before they're all killed by the virus, or by the local lynch mob out to destroy anyone who may have come into contact with it."

"Look at the mess I became."
Eli Roth on *Cabin Fever*

What is it about American filmmakers and the woods? There seems to be an obsession with unpleasantness in the pleasant rural areas.

Eli Roth: I think that there is unpleasantness everywhere. When I think of my favorite horror movies in the late '70s, early '80s, they are about a bunch of kids going into the woods and getting into trouble. One of my favorite films is *The Evil Dead* [1982], and one of the great things about the woods in America is that you can get very lost very easily. Like in *Blair Witch* [1999]: you go deep into the woods and can get lost for days. I wanted to put the *Cabin Fever* kids in a situation where they could not get help easily, and the woods seemed perfect.

Do you think that the horror genre is coming back?

Yeah. I think that the horror genre is coming back. I think that movies like *The Ring* [2002] and *The Others* [2001] really help it out.

It seems you have been a horror nut since you were a child, making home movies, etc. What can you tell us about this?

I have always been a nut! But when I was about six years old I saw *The Exorcist* [1972], and it traumatized me. When I was eight I saw *Alien* [1979], and I actually vomited in the theater. That was a big thing for me. I started going to see horror movies regularly and I would just puke in the theater. My parents were very upset and tried to ban me from horror, and each time I would be like, "No, this time I will be fine." Then I'd go and see a movie like *Outland* [1981]. I'd see exploding heads and I would just puke everywhere.

When I was thirteen, at my bar mitzvah, since I wasn't friends with any girls, I couldn't have a dance. So I got a magician to saw me in half with a chainsaw. That was my dream come true. I have been really obsessed with horror movies since I was a kid. I think that this was because when I was growing up and you missed a movie in the theaters, you would never see it again. We had no cable television and no VCRs. The horror movies I loved, like *Mother's Day* [1980], I would see ads for in the newspaper and knew they would never be shown on television, as they were way too graphic and disgusting. So it became an obsession for me to see these films. I'd look at the ads and wonder what was happening in these films. I was eleven or twelve years old when VCRs were available, and for a period of about twenty years after that I have saturated myself watching non-stop movies.

What were your parents like?

Actually my parents are unbelievably supportive. My dad is a psychoanalyst and my mother is an artist. When I was eight years old, me and my father would watch movies. Every time I saw the credits and saw who it was produced by, I would say, "I want to be a producer." My dad was like, "You don't want to be a producer; they have to make the money," so I asked my dad what the director does, and he said that the director gets to *spend* the money. Then I was like, "Okay, I wanna be a director!" I was obsessed with horror movies, and my parents just used to watch movies with me and my brothers. We would watch movies like *The Texas Chain Saw Massacre* [1974]. Any movie I wanted to watch my parents were fine with, and look what happened. Look at the mess I became.

How long did Cabin Fever *take to get from script to screen?*

Eight years. I wrote the first draft in 1995, after I graduated from NYU Film School in 1994. There is an obsession in film school that you have to be a director right when you graduate. I wrote it and re-wrote it with my friend Randy Pearlstein. I was so used to just grabbing a camera, grabbing my friends, going to the woods, and shooting that I really thought it would be the same situation filming *Cabin Fever*. In fact, it was a nightmare. I couldn't get anyone to give me any money. I kept sending scripts over and over to Miramax, Paramount, and they all passed. I was working in New York at the time in production, and over the course of six years I worked on one hundred different movies. In 1999, I moved to L.A. specifically to get *Cabin Fever* made. I had to. I didn't come from a film family, so I had to make myself indispensable. I picked up a lot of contacts along the way until eventually I found a team of producers who knew people with money, and we convinced them to help us make *Cabin Fever*.

How difficult is it to draw inspiration from the films you love but at the same time be original?

I had to find that balance. I hate movies that rip off other movies, but at the same time I love it when you see a horror movie that looks like another film. When I see *Mulholland Drive* [2001] and I see the car from *Sunset Boulevard* [1949] in the background, I know that David Lynch loves that movie. I really wanted to have fun with *Cabin Fever* and pay tribute to my favorite films. I felt that as long as the deaths were original—like the leg shaving or the fingering or the harmonica in the throat—I could get away with paying tribute. I wanted people to know that this film was made by a horror fan and that he understands what makes them great. Hopefully people won't see *Cabin Fever* as a rip-off.

A lot of horror movies have been taken seriously. Do you think your humor works against Cabin Fever *or compliments it?*

I think that it compliments it. The key to making it work is that the kids always have to take the situation seriously, that it's never a joke. They have to be far into trying to get out of the situation and trying to get help that they cannot make fun of it. It's interesting to watch *Cabin Fever* in different age groups. When the audience is thirty, they are laughing hysterically. Teenage audiences are silent. You can see that they were terrified.

The special effects in the film are great. How much of the budget went on special effects?

A very small amount. I knew this company KNB Effects from when I was working with David Lynch. They did *Mulholland Drive* for him. At the time we shot the movie during the summer of 2001, everyone was worried that there was going to be a writers' strike, so a lot of movies got rushed into production. Nothing was shooting when we started, and I had very little money to shoot this film, but I wanted it all to go into the effects. KNB gave me a good deal, as they knew me and we had a good time working with them.

In the wake of Cabin Fever, Wrong Turn *[2003], and* Blair Witch, *some of the communities have complained about how they are perceived in the film. What are your thoughts?*

No matter what people say, they love movie cameras. These communities love it. The people in the general store in the film—one is actually the mayor of the town. And the young girl selling lemonade at the end, her mother was like, "We are so excited to be a part of *Cabin Fever*. I can't wait to go and see it," and I am like, "Please don't! I want you to think I'm a nice guy!"

We filmed at a Boy Scout camp out of season. The scouts ran it in the summer, and when it's out of season, school groups still come by to visit. The head had given us permission to film, but wanted to bring groups down to see what we were doing. I tried to explain that this was a violent, disgusting movie, but he *still* wanted to bring kids by. Every time a group of kids would visit, there was always someone head to toe in blood screaming "Fuck! Fuck!" and they *loved* it. I would give a little introduction, and we had a great time.

There was this time when Rider Strong, who is on *Boy Meets World* [1993-2000], had a four-hour break and decided to go for a walk, still in his blood costume. This group of about thirty to forty eleven-year-old girls saw him and screamed. When they realized it was *Boy Meets World*, they chased him shouting, "Boy Meets World is hurt, we have to help him." Rider made it back to the set and we had to hide him until it was safe. People loved the blood and guts. I was very lucky.

How did you get in with David Lynch? What involvement did he have in Cabin Fever, *and what does he think of it?*

I met David ten years ago when I was in New York. David was going to write and direct a show for someone that I was working for, and they needed research doing. So I spent five to six years doing this. At the time I lived in New York, David was in L.A. I would visit him twice a year, and he would tell me what he wanted.

He called me in 1999 when I moved to L.A., and said, "Eli man, we're going on the Net"—davidlynch.com—"and it's gonna be *huge*. You're so organized with everything, I want you to chat with me. Here's the deal: we need rabbits. Get me rabbits." So I'd get them and they would be wrong. Anyway, David starts spouting out two hundred ideas and I'm trying to write everything down and outline what is now davidlynch.com. I'd go over to his house every day, grab a camera, sometimes DV, sometimes 35mm, and shoot crazy experiments.

So I said to David, "I have to get *Cabin Fever* made and I need your name on my movie as Executive Producer. If the movie sucks you can take it off." Once David put his name on it *Cabin Fever*, was considered an artsy film, a Lynchian film. I was having problems with money, and when you are making an independent movie, you have to play the game like chess, making strategic moves. I really needed his name, even if we took it off later. So in October 2001, David was named as Executive Producer. I told the investors that he could take his name off at any time, and all of a sudden David starts getting credited as the director of *Cabin Fever*. In May 2002, David is head of the Jury at the Cannes Film Festival, and so many people were like, "Tell us about *Cabin Fever* that you've directed." David was cool about this, but he said that it would follow my career for the rest of my life. Everyone will think that David directed *Cabin Fever*, yet I wrote it, produced it and directed it. David put his name on it to help get it made.

When David saw *Cabin Fever*, he thought it was great and said it didn't need his name anymore, I wouldn't have a problem selling it, and that I would be fine on my own. If David's name was still on the movie, every time that I attended a film festival people would ask about David and want to see David. It would have been sold in Europe as A David Lynch Film, and his name would have hurt me more than helped me. So all I did was put "Very Special Thanks to David" at the end of the credits. The investors were cool with this, as they loved the finished film, and they showed it to their kids who were like, "This is better than *American Pie*." When *Cabin Fever* was entered into the Toronto Film Festival, it didn't have David's name attached and we still got in. It was still the biggest sale. The two best things David Lynch did for my career was put his name on *Cabin Fever* and then take it off. I am still very close with David. He loves the movie. I think Deputy Winston is his favorite character.

Cabin Fever *reminds me of* The Crazies [1973], *where the people in a small town all go mad. Bearing in mind all the gruesomeness, was there anything you came up with or saw in other films that you wanted to replicate but felt was going too far?*

I feel that in a movie like this you can't go too far. There were some things that I wanted to do that I couldn't. In the leg-shaving scene I wanted to use an effect so that it looked like we were peeling a banana. But it would have had to have had a six-hour make-up session, and no one would buy that she would not notice this. We wanted to get the feeling that she was so lost in her own world and so upset that she wasn't thinking and on another planet. It got to the stage that if we went really gory, it would take people out of the movie. This was one of those instances. Budget-wise and timing-wise, we couldn't pull it off, but I didn't fight for this, and it would have been too ridiculous. With this film, and the deer, it is just so ridiculous, but I feel that if people are still in the theater at this point that they are going along with the ride.

Did you always want Rider Strong in the movie because of his heartthrob status?

I don't think of Rider Strong as a heartthrob. Rider's audience is ten-year-olds and their parents. He has a huge audience. The guy who gets a screwdriver in his ear was the world's biggest Rider Strong fan. When he found out he was in a film with Rider, he was like, "Oh my God, *Boy Meets World*. I'm gonna be in a film with *Boy Meets World*!" and I was like, "*Boy Meets World* is gonna stick a fucking screwdriver in your ear!" We were walking around a grocery store and saw this big guy and asked him if he wanted to be in our film. He was a schizo and recently released from a mental institute. He went mental when he saw Rider, took a Polaroid of him, and took it into restaurants. He was like, "Give me free food! I've made a film with *Boy Meets World*!" and it actually worked.

When we first wrote this movie, the part was going to Randy Pearlstein, and Rider was eleven years old. I knew who he was, but I had never watched *Boy Meets World*. Anyway, he auditioned and won the role. I had been auditioning for about five or six months, and I had a lot of TV actors wanting to do this, as it would break them out of how people see them. It's very difficult for TV actors to jump over to film. They can do it, but are people going to be willing to pay to see them when they have seen them for free? The fact I had never seen *Boy Meets World* worked to Rider's advantage. I love watching the show now, as I know Rider as the guy covered in blood.

What's the story behind the dog that got fired after just one day?

We had a dog that was cast at the last minute. Our prop guy told us he had found a dog that could be "the meanest motherfucker or your best friend." So we get this dog and its four hundred-pound female trainer. The dog was terrible. We tried to do shots with Cerina Vincent with blood on her legs, and the dog would just lick it off and fall asleep. He was meant to attack

Rider Strong, but the dog would just lick his face. And when we had Jordan Ladd in the shed, the dog was meant to eat her stomach but ended up just falling on her. It had Jordan in stitches. The trainer was scarier. She would be on the floor shouting, "Make me your bitch!" and growl at the dog. I just wanted to film her. She was scarier than anything, but the dog just had to go.

Anyway, we were losing time on the shoot and I was in a deep depression when the producer called to say she had found a dog. She thought it was a police attack dog but that it had done movies also. We got it on set and it was just this *evil* dog. The trainers told us that he had done movies but not on camera. It doesn't matter if a camera is there or not, he'll do what he does. So I started to ask the trainers to put the dog with the actors, and they said, "You ain't gonna put him with other people, are you? He's trained to do one thing and one thing only."

"What's that? Work with actors?"

"No. Kill."

I had to get everyone to meet the dog but not make eye contact with him, as we didn't want him keying in on us. We were all completely terrified of him. We could never have the dog and actors on screen together. When he is chasing Cerina, the entire crew hid behind trucks. The dog would just take off. Anyway, I'm the poor schmuck who had to pet the dog for an hour just so that it wouldn't kill me and so that we could film our scene. The dog just jumped up on me and started humping my leg. I just let the cameras roll and I would go with whatever the dog did. I wound up playing this part, as the person originally cast to play Justin couldn't handle the dog. Only I was brave enough.

What is your next project?

I'm making a film with Rich Kelly, who made *Donnie Darko* [2001]. He loved *Cabin Fever*, so it's great to work with him. We have so much in common. I'm on the same creative wavelength as this guy. I thought that *Donnie Darko* was a masterpiece. *Donnie Darko* is 99 percent funny and one percent *Evil Dead*, and *Cabin Fever* is 99 percent *Evil Dead* and one percent funny. Anyway, Rich and I are working together on a script. I have to write a Richard Matheson story, and we'll have total control over it. We're writing that now, and it's just great writing with a guy like this. I think that he is the best writer. He likes me because I can just throw in Scott Favor references and we make it a big joke. We sit there and try to make the most disturbing and most fucked up movie we can. We sit there laughing and saying, "Oh my God, this is so horrible. People are gonna *kill* us. This is gonna be so fuckin' beautiful!"

I've recently formed a company with two other filmmakers, Scott Spiegel, who wrote *Evil Dead II* [1987] and directed *From Dusk Till Dawn 2* [1999], and Boaz Yakin, who directed *Remember the Titans* [2000]. We have a company called Raw Nerve, and we're gonna make three balls-out disgusting horror movies a year. The idea is to pollute society as much as possible by making the most fucked up, controversial movies that we can.

Do you have any student films that you plan to release?

My student film has so many ridiculous copyright violations that it will be difficult to release. It's called *Restaurant Dogs* [1994], and it was like this McDonald's gang on a killing spree. My teachers were like, "What the fuck is this?" They would say that the films had to have a message. My message was that I want films to be entertaining from the start until the time the credits finish. I would hope to release it in an underground kind of way, because I could never officially sell it. I would get sued.

Have you planned a sequel for Cabin Fever?

I have been approached to make one. People seem to be mad for one. I am not rushing it though. *Blair Witch 2* [2000] was rushed, and it didn't do very well. I don't want to rush, as I don't want to make a bad movie just for the money. If I did make a sequel, it would probably be focused on Deputy Winston or something, rather than an exact copy of the storyline. But who knows?

2003

M. NIGHT SHYAMALAN and BRYCE DALLAS HOWARD
The Village

M. Night Shyamalan with Oscar winner Adrien Brody, just one of the actors making up the impressive ensemble cast of *The Village*. (Touchstone Pictures/Frank Masi)

Touchstone Pictures, 2004

THE PLAYERS: Ivy Walker, BRYCE DALLAS HOWARD; Lucius Hunt, JOAQUIN PHOENIX; Noah Percy, ADRIEN BRODY; Edward Walker, WILLIAM HURT; Alice Hunt, SIGOURNEY WEAVER; August Nicholson, BRENDAN GLEESON; Mrs. Clack, CHERRY JONES; Vivian Percy, CELIA WESTON; Robert Percy, JOHN CHRISTOPHER JONES; Victor, FRANK COLLISON; Tabitha Walker, JAYNE ATKINSON; Kitty Walker, JUDY GREER; Christop Crane, FRAN KRANZ; Finton Coin, MICHAEL PITT; Jamison, JESSE EISENBERG; Young Security Guard, CHARLIE HOFHEIMER; Man with the Raised Eyebrows, SCOTT SOWERS; Donald, ZACH WALL; Marybeth, PASCALE RENATE SMITH; 12 Year Old Boy, JORDAN BURT; Brown-Eyed Girl, JANE LOWE; 10 Year Old Boy, CHARLIE McDERMOTT; Young Man, ROBERT LENZI; Gerald, WILLEM ZUUR; Beatrice, LIZ STAUBER; Flustered Man, TIM MOYER; Oldest Walker Daughter, SYDNEY SHAPIRO; Middle Walker Daughter, MIA ROSE COLONA,; Youngest Walker Daughters, CHLOE WIECZKOWSKI, SYDNEY WIECZKOWSKI; Guard at Desk, M. NIGHT SHYAMALAN; Radio Announcer, JOHN RUSK; Those We Daren't Speak Of, JOEY ANAYA, KEVIN FOSTER.

CREDITS: *Writer, Director, and Producer*, M. Night Shyamalan; *producers*, Scott Rudin, Sam Mercer; *associate producer*, Jose L. Rodriguez; *director of photography*, Roger Deakins, ASC, BSC; *production designer*, Tom Foden; *editor*, Christopher Tellefsen, A.C.E.; *costume designer*, Ann Roth; *music*, James Newton Howard; *creature design*, Crash McCreery; *creature costumes*, Steve Johnson's Edge FX, Inc.; *special visual effects*, Syd Dutton, Bill Taylor; *visual effects supervisor*, Eric Brevig. Running time: 108 minutes.

> "The philosopher Bertrand Russell said, 'To conquer fear is the beginning of wisdom.' With this type of thinking, even in times of fear, daily life can continue. Fathers talk with their daughters. Sons fall in love. Friendships grow closer. How many times have we heard a parent reassure a child that 'there is nothing to be afraid of?'

> "But do these parents speak the truth? In *The Village*, the fear of the creatures in the woods—referred to as 'Those We Don't Speak Of'—threaten their community and the safety of the children.

> "The elders of the town have made a choice to co-exist with their community inside an isolated village. Cutting themselves off from the rest of the world, their fear of the creatures, and what other evils may exist beyond their town borders, gives them motivation to stay intact and safe with their loved ones."

Fear is the Unknown
M. Night Shyamalan and Bryce Dallas Howard on *The Village*

What was the inspiration for and the genesis of The Village?

M. Night Shyamalan: It was from being offered another movie. I was offered *Wuthering Heights*, so I went and re-read that book, which was an amazing experience, and I fell in love with this kind of knotted romance. It's a scary, Gothic story in its own way, which is why I think they offered it to me. They didn't offer me the script. They just offered me the book. They own the rights to the book, and they said, "Would you be interested in doing a version of *Wuthering Heights*?" There were actually actors attached and everything—wonderful, wonderful actors. That was there, but I wanted to do something original. I also had this *King Kong* idea of people that had rituals for dealing with a creature and they just incorporated them into their chores as if it was very normal. So the two ideas came together.

Given your family background, people might suppose that this is what you were born to do. Is that how it has been for you, or have you come via a circuitous route to starring in a film like The Village?

Bryce Dallas Howard: My Dad [Ron Howard] is a filmmaker and my Mom [Cheryl Howard] is a writer, so it seemed fairly reasonable to assume as the child of those two [that I would] somehow participate in this industry or at least in a business or livelihood that depended upon the imagination. My form of rebellion was to say, "No. I want to do forensic anthropology or law." I really gave it a good shot because I was just frustrated with all of the assumptions.

My imagination has always been so much stronger to me than my real life. That would have been a clear indication to most onlookers that a life in the arts or a life as an actor would be appropriate. I actually only admitted it to myself and my family when I was seventeen or eighteen years old and near adulthood. And even then I made a little loophole for myself where if I got into one school, I could try to be an actor, but it was the one school that also had a liberal arts education that was attached to it so I could double major.

Would you ever direct somebody else's script?

Shyamalan: It's really tempting because there is a lack of vulnerability that I would find very wonderful. Actually, I've been offered a lot of screenplays that are just fantastic. It's tempting to skip that eight months of torture and just go straight to, "Wow! This is how I can see it. You can have her come in this way," and all that stuff. Maybe a little bit I find it not courageous for me because it's the first thing that goes, usually. When you're a writer/director and you get offered a lot of wonderful, top screenplays, it's easier to let that side of you go. So I'm trying to fight that instinct a little bit. Even when I hear [people talk of] *The Village* opening to a big weekend, what I really wish they would say is something about originality in a summer marketplace.

Howard: It's a pretty standard compliment.

Shyamalan: If it made *money*?

Howard: That's a good dialogue to have. People associate a success with financial status.

You discuss making money as if it's some sort of bad thing.

Shyamalan: No, not at all. The idea is to always go for the thing that's risky. I'm in this situation and I want to be courageous and original. And original means you don't know what color movie you just saw. Unfortunately, I'm learning this: moviemaking is not a straight art form like painting or writing a novel or anything like that. That can be digested and interpreted and it's all good. This is so much about Starbucks coffee; give it to me, drink it, tastes great, I'm gone—especially since it takes two years to make each one of these. I don't mean anything by it: the money part is good, it's always judged on money, money, money.

    I remember when *Unbreakable* [2000] came out and people said, "Oh, it didn't do so well" and all that stuff, but *all* my movies have made money. That's important. It's my job to make money for the studio and I do that. And now every day someone comes up and says *Unbreakable* is their favorite movie. I think, *Where were you? Where were you? You were all just counting dollars!* So even now there's this dance between art and commerce, the Starbucks of my job—which I'm aware of—and the painting of my job. Sometimes I lean this way; sometimes I lean the other way.

How conscious are you of providing the surprise twist during the writing process and deciding when it comes in? And will the surprise one day be that there is no surprise?

Shyamalan: The surprise for me is that I didn't have it in the last movie and people think I *did* have it.

But Signs *was about a different thing altogether.*

Shyamalan: I didn't think of it that way at all. It was interesting coming off of *Signs* [2002], because I was thinking, *Well, that was a straight movie,* so the format in which I choose to tell *The Village* would be interesting. What's weird is that that's the way stories come to me, very naturally like that. If it was a story about me and you, I would be withholding something about you, immediately. You think, *He would be a great character because he has this motivation,* and then I think, *But I won't tell you that,* then I'll give you another part of his character. It comes like that and it's fun to think that way.

The negative part is that that's all that people are occupied with. All the gentleness of the movie is being overshadowed by the flashy cousin in the sequined vest who comes strutting in and takes the stage. In that respect, I don't know what to do. I approach it as a novelist in terms of saying, "I'm writing my next murder-mystery" or whatever it is. Agatha Christie can write thirty of them, but this is a very different art form for some reason. I don't know if art form is even the right way that I'm getting judged on it at this point. It's kind of a game or something. It's a tricky thing.

It's a craft thing. Even when I'm being manipulated as an audience member, I still want the experience.

Shyamalan: Yeah. Right, right. I *love* telling stories like that. I love it being multi-layered and coming at it from different angles and you don't understand its true emotional motivation until the very end. It isn't about a plot reveal but a true emotional expression. The story the picture is about is not clear until maybe you're in a car and you go, "Oh, this is about a group of people that were hurt and did this, and a counseling group, blah, blah, blah," that kind of thing. That's obviously not what you thought you were coming in to see.

There's a lot made of actors not being able to tell their loved ones about the script and having to FedEx pages back to Night when you get rewrites FedEx-ed to you. What can you tell us about the secrecy?

Howard: It's actually funny, because there *is* so much secrecy on a project like this, but it has never come from Night. He has never said, "This is *so* precious. Please keep it secret." It comes more from me and other people who've read the script. They would read it for the first time, and they would want others to experience the story the way in which I experienced the story: freshly. It's so unfortunate; scripts are released on the Internet quite often and they are reviewed. To me that's like if an artist has a blank canvas and a bunch of pots of paint and someone comes by and says, "That's not gonna be a good painting. I don't like those colors." You haven't *seen* the painting, for goodness sakes! I'm glad that there's this amount of secrecy, just so that people can form their own opinions of this art form that's become so popular.

Yeah, there is the FedEx-ing of pages back and forth. FedEx are very efficient! But Night, when he offered me this role—and I hadn't technically accepted it; he offered it to me and I said, "Well, of course I'll do it"—said, "No. Please go home and read it. There are a bunch of guys on the Internet who want this script [so] please don't give it to the Internet." But he never said, "Don't give it to the people that you love, don't give it to your agents, don't give it to your manager." When I read it, I didn't want to ruin it for my family and for my friends.

One of the elements that all four of your films possess is, if not the ability to scare the living daylights out of an audience, to at least deeply unsettle them. You seem like a nice, mild-mannered man. Where does that aspect come from? Are you tortured?

Shyamalan: [Laughs] No! I am intensely boring, so that creates a need to be exciting in other forms! For me, the ability to judge a director is from their tone. My favorite movie from last year is *Lost in Translation* [2002] because of its handle on tone. Sofia Coppola knew exactly the tone, and she held onto it from beginning to end. That's perfect direction.

My particular accent that I speak in is suspense, so if two people are having a conversation, my mind will immediately go to, *How do I do it in a way that creates a ticking clock in you?* even if it's a romantic scene or even a scary scene or an emotional scene. It's about defying expectations even in the littlest moment. That's what the great delivery of a line is—that Bryce delivered it in a way that you did not expect, you know? Or the music comes in a form you did not expect or not at the "right" time and the camera moves in a way you did not expect—it's starting to do something counter to what she's saying. If Bryce is saying, "I love you" and all that stuff, and the camera's pulling away from us, just gently, and it only starts on "I love you" and then it pulls away, that starts a tension. If the movie is about me, then I'm reacting: "Holy shit. How am I going to deal with this? My ground's starting to leave me." That's the opposite of what you think because right in her big moment, the camera is leaving us.

It's just finding the right moment because that heartbeat is the tension of the movie. That's why I find it so hard to put humor in [a movie], to be honest, and I really want to do humor more. It's because I find that it empties that tank of tension and I have to start all over again.

Hitchcock said if he'd made Cinderella, *they'd look for the body in the coach. Do you find that audiences come to your films expecting that level of suspense?*

Shyamalan: Yeah. That would be the singular thing: I hope that if they see the name and they have an attachment and they have an expectation, that it *not* be necessarily about a specific like a surprise ending, but more of a combination of originality and suspense. Those things are going to be there hopefully every time. Every single time.

You have put together a fascinating cast, but in a largely American ensemble, what made you put Brendan Gleeson in a role, very good though he is?

Shyamalan: Man, he is *so* great. He was in a couple of movies recently. I cast him off of *Gangs of New York* [2001] and *28 Days Later* [2002], in both of which I just adored him. Every time, you sympathize with him. He's committed and unique and he has this teddy bear thing—it's just a great addition to the group of elders. He brings such a wonderful color.

Was he the only actor you saw for that?

Shyamalan: Yes. And I let him keep his accent because that added the right flavor to the community, I thought.

Which directors have influenced you? And how and why did you start making Hitchcock-like appearances in your own films?

Shyamalan: So many directors. Sofia Coppola and everyone in my contemporaries like Quentin [Tarantino] and all these guys. They totally inspire me in everything. From people with a larger body of work, it would be Kubrick's formalism and that eerie way everything is centered. It feels very right. When Bryce comes in the door to find Lucius [played by Joaquin Phoenix], the door's in the center, she's in the center, and she comes in and everything goes wrong. When she says her speech, it's dead center, close-up. All that formalism feels very right to me. [I'm inspired by] specific movies like *Rosemary's Baby* [1968] and other things like that are really influential, or even *Being There* [1979]. Things that you wouldn't think of. It feels spot-on to me. Peter Weir's humanity that he brings to everything.

And the Hitchcock thing? It really has nothing to do with the Hitchcock thing. This particular one has its own constraints, as you know, and there is only one way that that would come to play out. But in *Signs*, I wanted to be a part of the storytelling. When I write, it is an emotional process. I'm really evoking the characters, and even when I talk to [the actors] it's a very emotional process about why I do it. When we sit down to have the first read-through, I and everybody else are crying. This isn't a job. It's a very, very serious expression of things that are important to me, and so it feels wonderful to have another outlet to do that if I can, up to a certain level. I wouldn't go past a supporting part because it really does affect the directing. You have to incorporate that into the schedule and all that stuff.

You seem to have a fascination with our fear of the dark—the audience's fear of the unknown. The Spanish filmmaker Alejandro Amenábar could trace his style back to a childhood fascination with Victorian ghost stories. That led to The Others [2001]. Where does your inspiration come from? Is it Victorian ghost stories like him, childhood stories told to you by your parents, or something else?

Shyamalan: They're both doctors. They never told me any stories. [Laughs] When you say fear of the unknown, fear *is* the unknown. The definition of fear is what you do not know. We fear what's in the other room. I don't know what's in the other room. We fear going to Seattle for a job because I don't know what Seattle's like. We fear being in a relationship because I don't know if she's a psycho! Fear is unknown, and it's genetically in us so that we are safe. We feel scared of the woods because we are not familiar with it, and that keeps you safe. As a human being, over the course of history, the people that aren't scared, that go into this thing and get mauled by a bear are not going to survive. All that stuff.

So it comes from making things that are familiar to you unfamiliar to you. So playing in your bedroom as a normal bedroom, until you realize that the phone is off the hook. You go nearer and you see there's broken glass. You look up. Now the room is unknown to you. It's no longer a familiar place. So you turn around and you find that kid naked in the middle of the room, and it's the beginning of *The Sixth Sense*. It's making everything that is familiar to you, unfamiliar.

I came home once from the mall when I was little with my dad and my sister. We drove into the driveway and the front door was open. That house was friggin' terrifying. Terrifying! The driveway was terrifying. I was like, "Let's get the hell out of here!" My dad goes in with the dog—my dog wouldn't hurt *anyone*, and my dad's about four feet, two inches. I'm like, "What's gonna happen here? This is a silly situation." But it was *terrifying* because it's your house and now it's unfamiliar to you. It's nicer for me. [I prefer] doing very gentle things to make you unfamiliar, as opposed to blood on the walls.

The unknown for you was the prospect of making a big movie like The Village. *Did you need to hype yourself up, or alternatively did you seek reassurance from your director that you could get what was needed from this part?*
Shyamalan: I can answer that one: heavy drug use!

Howard: [Laughs] I wasn't afraid. When it comes to my work, I don't operate from a place of fear because that is quite destructive and it would waste time. I got this role in May, we started filming in October, and I had a limited amount of time to prepare for this role. If I'd spent any amount of time being insecure, doubting my ability, or being nervous, that would have been disgraceful, especially with this opportunity that I was given and with this tremendous role that I was going to be allowed to play. I just felt very excited. And then also Night had this *insane* amount of faith in me. He cast me without auditioning me—just after watching an hour and a half production of a small play in New York. So it was my responsibility to have at least an ounce of that amount of faith in myself. But the day *after* we finished, I was quite anxious. The play was *As You Like It*. It was a small theater.

There was some controversy recently about a documentary [The Buried Secret of M. Night Shyamalan] *on the Sci-Fi channel. Can you give us your take on that and the controversy over whether it was real or faked?*

Shyamalan: I think what happened is that people stop on me to do a documentary or follow me around. All this reality TV business. They come and watch the filming and document the footage. As I pointed, out I'm quite boring and I thought—hopefully—that it would be very boring and uneventful. If something went wrong, I wouldn't show it to you. For instance, I wouldn't show me yelling at Bryce.

Howard: He's horrible!

Shyamalan: People kept coming to me with those [requests], and then this guy [director Nathaniel Kahn] and I talked. I said, "What if you do a documentary on me, but then you find out there's something supernatural about me that we keep hidden? And then you go on with the documentary." They said, "That's cool!" I thought that would be really fun. So we did that. I just kept shooting the movie. They came a couple of times and they shot [footage of] me. They did their own thing. A lot of it was real and some of it was not. It was really fun.

The trouble came in the way they marketed it. They went to a journalist and portrayed it as straight. The wiser way would have been to let five or six of you guys in on it and then have you write something. After that, though, it was all fine and dandy. Then my aunt called me and said, "I didn't know those things happened to you!" [Laughs] She called my mom, who was trying to explain it was all pretend. She was really upset.

Where do you hope your career will take you after The Village?

Howard: I just finished doing Lars Von Trier's movie. It's called *Manderlay* [2005]. It's the second film in his trilogy. His first was *Dogville* [2003]. After that, I don't know. Honestly, in many ways I feel like I'm doomed because I had this experience with Night and to follow that with a quite extraordinary experience with Lars—I don't know what I'm gonna do. And I'm nervous about it. I think about it every day. And it's not just the film. The filmmaking experience is very satisfying, and it can be with a lot of different filmmakers. I'm an actor. I like playing roles. But to work with a director who is an *angel*, it'll be hard to equal that.

Shyamalan: She's talking about Lars! [Laughs]

How did you get into the dynamic of playing a blind girl and to avoid making her into a gross caricature? Did you research it?

Howard: Yes. That was the first thing. Blindness constitutes a very small part of Ivy, but it was the thing that was most distant from my reality. I went to a place called The Lighthouse in New York City. It's an institution where they aid people who are visually impaired. The first thing that happened actually was that the head of one department came up to me and said, "I hope you enjoy your time here." Then she walked away. She was very pleasant. Then I noticed she was holding a cane in her hand. I hadn't realized during our dialogue that she was blind. I had never seen that before in a film, and I so I thought that was something that was very important: how do you play blindness where you are existing in an environment where there is no longer a handicap, no longer a disability—as in the case of Ivy Walker in *The Village*? Then the instructors took me through the entire script, because I was extremely skeptical of how this girl could do what she does. They said, "Yes, she does and she could do more," and they had a million examples. Then I had to spend a large majority of every day blindfolded because after wearing a blindfold for ninety minutes, your brain starts to rewire itself, so that was my rule: no less than ninety minutes. So there were a lot of thing that went into it. A lot of reading, watching other performances, seeing what spoke to me, what moved me and what didn't. It was very, very important to me that I did justice to that element of Ivy because if the audience didn't believe it—or if it wasn't believable, such as if she was stumbling around too much—it would have been a *big* problem.

Given that your father has enjoyed a long and varied career, did he offer you advice and, if so, did you take it?

Howard: It's unfortunate because the small amount of advice that my dad has given me about his profession I didn't take seriously when I should have. So now he's stopped giving me advice. And I say to him, "We're talking about when I was seven! I was an idiot." The one thing I have just learned more from example is that we can have very long careers that can extend to the day we die. And so there will be moments when you feel like you are experiencing failure or disappointment or, perhaps even worse, that you're disappointed in yourself and what you've done.

That that doesn't mean you should stop. That means you should try even harder. You should push it further and, perhaps because of failure, you are getting even closer to the ultimate goal. It terrifies me the position that I'm in right now, but that's a very, very good thing. That's what I've learned from my dad.

The Village focuses on family and the nature of community. How important is that for you?

Shyamalan: You try to write stuff that is important to you. *Signs* is obviously about family. They are all really about family in some form. Even when I think about aliens taking over the world, it's from the point of view of a family. It's that take on it that's interesting to me. Or about this bizarre world [in *The Village*], which is ultimately about creating a family environment. That's what really provokes me: dinner table conversations and the point of view of a family. Taking "B" subjects, having a very personal take on them, and treating it with reverence. That will be going on for a bit now.

2004

BARRY SONNENFELD and WILL SMITH
Men in Black

Barry Sonnenfeld and Will Smith enjoyed a fruitful 15-year collaboration on all three movies in the *Men in Black* series. Their relationship was based as much on humour and threats of violence as mutual respect… (Columbia Pictures)

MEN IN BLACK
Columbia Pictures, 1997

CAST: Kay, TOMMY LEE JONES; Jay, WILL SMITH; Laurel Weaver, LINDA FIORENTINO; Edgar, VINCENT D'ONOFRIO; Zed, RIP TORN; Jeebs, TONY SHALHOUB; Beatrice, SIOBHAN FALLON; Gentle Rosenburg, MIKE NUSSBAUM; Van Driver, JON GRIES; José, SERGIO CALDERÓN; Arquillian, CAREL STRUYCKEN; INS Agent Janus, FREDRIC LANE; Dee, RICHARD HAMILTON; 1st Lt. Jake Jensen, KENT FAULCON; Mikey, JOHN ALEXANDER; Perp, KEITH CAMPBELL; Zap-Em Man, KEN THORLEY; Mr. Redgick, PATRICK BREEN; Mrs. Redgick, BECKY ANN BAKER; Passport Officer, SEAN WHALEN; News Vendor, HARSH NAYYAR; Cop in Morgue, MICHAEL WILLIS; Police Inspector, WILLIE C. CARPENTER; Tow Truck Driver, PETER LINARI; Morgue Attendant, DAVID CROSS; MIB Agent B, CHARLES C. STEVENSON JR; Cook, BORIS LESKIN; INS Agents, STEVE RANKIN, ANDY PROSKY; NYPD Sergeant, MICHAEL GOLDFINGER; Security Guard, ALPHEUS MERCHANT; Mrs. Edelson, NORMA JEAN GROH; Baseball Player, BERNARD GILKEY; First Contact Aliens, SEAN PLUMMER, MICHAEL KALISKI; 2nd First Contact Alien, RICHARD ARTHUR; Alien Father, DEBBIE LEE CARRINGTON; Alien Son, VERNE TROYER; Scared Guy, MYKAL WAYNE WILLIAMS; Frank the Pug, TIM BLANEY; Rosenberg Alien, MARK SETRAKIAN; Worm Guys, BRAD ABRELL, THOM FOUNTAIN, CARL J. JOHNSON, DREW MASSEY.

CREDITS: *Director*, Barry Sonnenfeld; *producers*, Walter F. Parkes, Laurie MacDonald; *executive producer*, Steven Spielberg; *co-producer*, Graham Place; *associate producer*, Steven R. Molen; *screen story and screenplay*,

Ed Solomon, based on the Marvel comic by Lowell Cunningham; *director of photography*, Don Peterman, ASC; *production designer*, Bo Welch; *film editor*, Jim Miller; *costume designer*, Mary E. Vogt; *music*, Danny Elfman; *visual effects supervisor*, Eric Brevig; *alien make-up effects*, Rick Baker. Running time: 98 minutes.

> "Working for a highly-funded yet unofficial government agency, Kay and Jay are the Men in Black, providers of immigration services and regulators of all things alien on earth. They are our best, last, and only line of defense when close encounters get ugly. They are the best-kept secret in the universe. They work in secret and they dress in black. Protecting the earth from the scum of the universe."

Alien Movies are Hard to Figure Out
Barry Sonnenfeld and Will Smith on *Men in Black*

You were a cinematographer with the Coen brothers. When did you decide to become a director?

Barry Sonnenfeld: The whole point was to earn money to pay for the groceries. I was not looking to be a director. I was very happy as a cinematographer. I worked with Penny Marshall and the Coens and [Danny] De Vito and Rob Reiner and some other directors. Then one day, I was in Los Angeles shooting *Misery*, [1990] and Scott Rudin, who's a producer who does a lot of movies, sent me the script for *The Addams Family* [1991] and said, "You should direct. It's been turned down by Tim Burton and Terry Gilliam." Rudin's idea was you either get the best guys you can or get someone who might be new and either fail horribly or be inventive and original. And I failed horribly! I loved the Charles Addams drawings. I grew up with them. So I agreed to direct. But I had no interest in directing. It wasn't a plan.

*The Coens did three films with you—*Blood Simple *[1984],* Raising Arizona *[1987], and* Miller's Crossing *[1990]—that have a particular style. Was that you or was that the Coens?*

Sonnenfeld: It's entirely me! The Coens really wanted to learn a lot from me and then move on to their own [projects]. I was very happy to give them a nice foundation. [Laughs]

Did your appreciation of Charles Addams and his drawings have a bearing on the opening sequence of Men in Black?

Sonnenfeld: You know what? The drawings have given me a sense of scale and scope and a darkness. They really sum up my comedy style, both visually and as a funny, dark way into comedy. The guy who did the font, Pablo Ferro, also did both *Addams Family* movies and did my favorite movie ever, which is *Dr. Strangelove* [1964]. Basically, I just stole that font and paid them a lot of money to re-do it.

Is it true that the script of Men in Black *has been around for about four years?*

Barry Sonnenfeld: Oh, longer than that. These alien movies are hard to figure out. I was sent the script about four-and-a-half years ago, and I liked it very much because it just felt a little different. So while we were trying to figure out if we were going to make this movie or not, at the same time I was trying to get *Get Shorty* [1995] off the ground at a studio. And eventually, MGM agreed to make *Get Shorty*, I moved off *Men in Black*, they hired another director, they fired another director, [and] I finished *Get Shorty*. I ran into Barry Josephson, who was the Head of Production at Columbia, at a restaurant in Los Angeles, where he was having breakfast with Uma Thurman. I went up to Barry and said, "If you still want to wait for me I'm gonna be done with *Get Shorty* in six months."

Will Smith: The way I heard it was that he and his wife were lying in bed reading the script. She sat up in bed after she finished the script and screamed, "Will Smith!"

Sonnenfeld: And that had nothing to do with Will being in the movie. But as it turned out, the wife continued to yell "Will Smith!" in bed. I think she just loved the movie that much.

How late on did Tommy Lee Jones come into Men in Black?

Sonnenfeld: We wanted to cast him. I went into the studio and said, "Will Smith and Tommy Lee Jones." They said, "Tommy Lee Jones. Great," and they sign up Tommy. But of course that day, the number one and two movies didn't have Will in them. They had Keanu Reeves and Chris O'Donnell. I had to wait for those guys first, and then they didn't wanna be in the movie. So I waited around for Will.

You make the perfect screen team. What was it like on set, as there are stories that Tommy Lee Jones can be quite difficult at times?

Smith: You know, I think it's just you guys. We had a great time. Barry Sonnenfeld claims to be the best shoe kicker in the world. He claims he can put his shoe on the toe of his foot and kick it accurately anywhere within thirty yards. So one day, we set up a trashcan. Barry's kicking for an hour—nowhere near this trashcan. Tommy Lee Jones walks on the set, never opens his mouth and kinda observes what Barry's doing. Pulls his shoe off, onto the toe of his foot, kicks it thirty yards into the trash can, says, "Good morning, y'all. One y'all wanna go git that shoe for me, please?" [Laughs] Things like that happened all the time. We had a lot of fun.

What can you tell us about your working relationship with Steven Spielberg?

Sonnenfeld: Steven had asked me to direct *Casper* [1995] about four years ago, and I turned him down....

Smith: Nobody tells Steven no, Barry!

Sonnenfeld: I did, because I really didn't wanna work with Steven Spielberg at all! In fact, I was hired on *Men in Black* before Steven was involved in the project. And then they said, "Good news. Steven's gonna executive produce it!" And I thought, "Oh, great." I was scared. I knew that for the next three years, I would have somebody looking over my shoulder. It was horrible. So I said to Steven in pre-production, "You know, I just can't direct a Steven Spielberg movie. No one can but you." And he was great. He said, "I don't want you to direct as Steven Spielberg. I want you to direct a Barry Sonnenfeld movie." And I did.

    The great thing about Steven, especially in post-production, [was his attitude to] the creatures, which were done almost exclusively in the computer. [They] took a year to do and were very difficult and time-consuming. These guys [the computer effects personnel] don't really understand comedy performance. They understand pixels. And at some point in every shot, you'd say, "Now, tomorrow, what I'd like you to do...." and they'd say, "No, we're done with this shot. It can't get better. This is the way it is."

    And I'd say, "But it still doesn't look heavy enough."

"No, Barry. It will not get better. We're wasting time and money."

"You're sure?"

"IT WILL NOT GET BETTER!"

"Okay, I'm just gonna show it to Steven...."

"Oh, no, no, no, no! Wait, wait, wait!"

    Steven was like this eight hundred-pound gorilla whenever I needed him. And also when the studio wasn't sure that they wanted to spend more money, you'd go to Steven and you'd fight for your case. And he's very strict. He's like a strict dad. He says, "Well, can you do it this way?" Or "What about this?" And you'd work it out. Then he'd call the studio and say, "Give Barry $4 million more money." He was great.

How were you cast?

Smith: Steven Spielberg called me at home. I was sitting around in my underwear, and I didn't feel it was right to talk to Steven Spielberg in my underwear, so I got dressed. Then he sent a helicopter for me to bring me out to where he and Barry live. So we sat down and we talked. I knew it was Tommy Lee Jones and Barry and Steven. I call him "Steven." I knew it was ILM [Industrial Light & Magic] with the special effects, Rick Baker doing the make-up effects. It was a great team, and I wanted to be a part of that.

Sonnenfeld: Also, something that hasn't come out yet: it was over a year away from *ID4* [*Independence Day*, 1996] actually being released. And also, we didn't think we were making another summer blockbuster.

Smith: That's true also.

Was the ending always in the screenplay?

Sonnenfeld: If you're referring to the very last shot in the movie that pulls back and back and back, that was an idea I had one day, and I pitched it to Steven Spielberg, and he said it was great. For me, it sums up the whole movie, which is that you think you've seen one thing, but you're seeing something entirely different. I've never had enough money to do it. Then we screened the movie for the first time for Sony, and they loved the movie so much they started to give me all their money. At this point, the opening title sequence wasn't in the film. After they saw the movie, they gave me the go-ahead to do that. At one point, I was the director of *Forrest Gump* [1994]. So for me, the opening title sequence is my version of the feather with a little twist. It's as if the feather landed and some dog came over and urinated on it. [Laughs]

It was fun seeing Sly Stallone as an alien. What's his reaction been?

Sonnenfeld: I don't know. The truth is Stallone was the last one we put in there. I had all these other aliens. In fact, where Stallone was, I was, because I always like to put myself in some little place in the movie.

Smith: Another self-indulgent director! [Laughs]

Sonnenfeld: Exactly! So we showed it to the international guys at Columbia, and they said, "No one's gonna laugh at Tony Robbins," [the American life coach] who has a self-help infomercial, "or [fashion designer] Isaac Mizrahi. Can you get us Margaret Thatcher?" I said, "It's not funny in the States." So my agent had to find Stallone that day. I said, "Fred, get me Stallone," and he did. I don't know if he's seen the movie or not.

What are your views on whether there are aliens on earth and whether Sylvester Stallone might be among them?

Smith: I think there are enough strange and unexplained things that people say and do that it's highly possible that some people are from other places than here.

Sonnenfeld: They seem like they have a sense of humor. That's what the aliens can't duplicate. So that's why Michael Jackson—who we wanted very much to be in the movie—said no.

Smith: 'Cause he's actually an alien, so he couldn't make the move.

Sonnenfeld: Exactly.

You do a lot of throwing yourself around the place and performing stunts. How much did you do yourself, and did you get hurt?

Smith: Barry was very specific that he wanted me to do all of the stunts. We made Barry aware of a rule that my friends and I have, which we developed on *Bad Boys* [1995] with Michael Bay, because Michael was very serious about the actors doing all of the stunts [with] no stuntmen. He was always rushing; always rushing, and people were getting hurt. I said, "Mike, that's fine. I'll do all of the stunts, but at any moment that my buddy here realizes that I've been injured, he's been instructed to knock you the fuck out." That's what the rule was. And I thought it would be unfair to have that rule for Michael Bay and not have that rule for Barry. So we made Barry aware of it, and he said, "Okay. Listen, how about if you *do* get hurt, I don't have to get knocked the fuck out right *now*? Maybe later when I'm not looking; I think it would hurt a lot less." So we were able to do that.

Sonnenfeld: There was another problem, too. I knew that I wouldn't pay any attention to the stunt if I was worried about whether Tron [Smith's assistant Ernest "Tron" Anderson] was gonna stretch me.

Smith: That's the urban colloquialism: "stretch."

Sonnenfeld: "Slump" means kill. So I didn't wanna watch the take and then flee and look stupid. So I asked Will if this would be an okay amendment to the rule. And Will looked at me in all seriousness and said, "We'll let you know." [Laughs] We're right on a take. This is where Will gets kicked by the back leg of the alien we call Edgarbug and flies literally close to forty feet across the stage into a bunch of tabs. So we're ready to do the take, Will's getting wired up, and Tron comes behind me and whispers in my ear, "Will says it's okay." [Laughs] So I knew that I wasn't getting knocked out. It was just Will's way of making sure that I was making sure the stuntmen were doing their job properly. But because Will was doing the stunts, I was able to say "cut" and be on the stage and make it that much more exciting.

Smith: Because all of the stunts were aerial, it's a little easier than actually falling and all of that, so I didn't get hurt too bad. It was okay.

Sonnenfeld: Then there was the day when Tommy almost killed him.

Smith: Yeah, Tommy Lee almost killed me one day on the set. But he didn't *actually* kill me.

Sonnenfeld: So it's okay. And Tron didn't have to stretch me.

Smith: I was hanging out of a car. There's a scene where Tommy Lee pulls up and he says, "He's not leaving in a cab. Get in." So I go to get in and before I'm in the car, Tommy Lee starts driving off with me hanging out of the car.

Sonnenfeld: A grip actually stepped in front of the car making Tommy come to halt, and then Tommy started to yell at the grip, saying he had no right to that! [Laughs] But the funny thing is that Tommy and Will loved each other.

Smith: We do!

Sonnenfeld: It's about richness.

You've said before the film came out that you own the fourth of July.

Smith: Yeah, that's Big Willie Weekend!

On the basis of those weekends—this year and last year [with Independence Day*]—and the fact that you're now one of the hottest properties in Hollywood, everything seems to be linked with you. There's talk of* Ali *and* The Wild Wild West. *You seem to be in more films than it's possible to make.*

Smith: That's a good thing and—not a bad thing, but in choosing the films that I wanna do, [then] the big fourth of July blockbuster is exciting. [It's] really tempting to keep making those kinds of movies, but I wanna try other things and do different types of movies. *The Wild Wild West* is a film that Barry and I are looking to work on starting in April [1998]. Again, it's something to be different, to move away from that whole big summer blockbuster thing and do something that's gonna take a little more acting and preparation.

Sonnenfeld: You were doing a lot of acting [in *Men in Black*].

Smith: I was. But this is different.

Sonnenfeld: I've gotta disagree. The hardest acting is comedy.

Is George Clooney doing The Wild Wild West *with you?*

Smith: We're trying. He hasn't said yes yet, but we'd love to have George.

How did you get into music?

Smith: I was about eleven or twelve years old when I bought the first rap record. It was "Rapper's Delight" by The Sugarhill Gang. In listening to that, I appreciated the fun of it, and then there was a comedy in it also.

I enjoyed it. I just liked how it felt. It felt like something that I could do. From that point, I started writing raps and I started DJ-ing parties and stuff like that. It kind of evolved as a hobby gone mad.

Do you enjoy going back to your roots in music?

Smith: Yeah. I did two songs on the *MiB* soundtrack, and I just signed a new deal with Columbia Records. I've kinda been away from the music for about four years. Now with Columbia, they've actually got smart people working at it. They're good. So to have the opportunity to make some real records [is welcome]. I'm about six songs into my album. We'll be releasing sometime in late October.

Will the album be titled as you or the Fresh Prince?

Smith: That's interesting. People know me as the Fresh Prince, but I started that eleven years ago. And then on the album, everything was done really quickly, and they put "Will Smith" on the cover. So I don't know. People still call me Fresh Prince, but I'm gonna be whatever I need to be to keep making money!

One of the charms of Men in Black *is its brevity. For a summer blockbuster, it only runs about ninety minutes. Was that a deliberate move: to make it short?*

Sonnenfeld: That's how long the movie wanted to be. Here's the thing: most scripts are 120 pages, and most directors shoot a page a minute. That's the way those things tend to work out. But comedy needs to be paced very quickly. The script was just as long, but it's just that we had Will and Tommy and Linda and Vincent and everyone speak quickly. My main direction to any actor on any movie I've ever directed is "flatter and faster."

Smith: Yeah. Every take was, "Flatter and faster. Faster, faster! Come on! Don't wait for it." I was like, "Damn, Barry. Gimme a minute! I'm trying to feel the moment."

Sonnenfeld: I know. And that's the last thing you want from an actor. You don't ever want to see the acting, and if you give them any time to start to act, then the whole thing falls horribly apart. When I was growing up, movie times [at the cinema] were two, four, six, eight, ten. It was normal to have a ninety-minute movie, and I think most directors have become incredibly self-indulgent, where they fall in love with some shot. For me it's all about the story and telling the story as quickly as possible.

There's been a lot of talk about the Star Wars *reboot. What are you thoughts on that? Were you a fan as a kid? And have you been approached to be in the new ones?*

Smith: Star Wars was the most amazed that I've ever been in a movie theater. I might have been twelve years old or something like that, and I was just so completely shocked and amazed that they were able to do this on a movie screen. I haven't been approached, but I'd be more than interested if they came.

Sonnenfeld: They'll never approach Will because he gets too much of the gross now.

What was it like being slimed?

Smith: It was some sort of mass of cellulose with stuff they had mixed in. They would drop some noodles and [other] stuff in to kind of make it fleshy. But it's in your ears and in your nose and it's all in your hair for twelve hours a day for three days. And at the end of it—the thing with Barry, and the reason he's such a great director, is that he never allows you to be out there by yourself. He put himself in the position to be slimed also, just so he could experience what I had to experience.

Sonnenfeld: I put myself in the position to be slimed by not being able to run away from Will fast enough! He said, "Is this the last shot? No more? We're done with this slime?" I said, "Yes." He then tackles me to the ground and rolls around all over me.

Did the film go through the traditional preview process in the States?

Sonnenfeld: No. You see the problem is there were so many visual effects in this movie done with a computer that none of the effects were ready until very late. You never wanna preview a movie without the visual effects, or the audience gets taken out of the movie and starts to hoot and laugh and say, "Why did you waste my time?" So largely because the effects were very late in coming, there were only two previews. And they both were successful. I love that they missed some of the laughs. The Zucker brothers actually tape the screening and then transfer that screening to magnetic tape and basically crate a laugh track for their movie and stretch moments out so that the laughs die down. My feeling is, let 'em miss a laugh. Let 'em miss two laughs.

Given the success of the film, are you under pressure to develop a sequel?

Smith: Actually no one has approached us from the studio. It's really the fans and you guys [who are asking] "Are you planning it?" It took so much strength and so much energy and so much time to just get this one finished, we're kinda enjoying this one before we start thinking about the next one.

Would you do it?

Sonnenfeld: You would have to come up with a script that was *so* different that it almost felt like a different movie. You don't wanna just pump new aliens into the same situation again. That would be dreary.

Smith: My whole concept of movies is to never carry them alone. To always work with the best actors that you can work with, the best directors and the best producers that you can possibly work with. I'm not self-indulgent in that way. I just wanna make great movies. The next movie that I'm doing is *Enemy of the State* [1998] with Tony Scott. It isn't cast at this point, but I'm excited at who I can work with. It's not necessarily a buddy movie but just [about] having great people in the cast.

Sonnenfeld: When we were talking about *The Wild Wild West*, Will and Will's management team made it very clear to me that Will was only interested in doing it if there was an actor of equal or greater status than Will [involved]. And I think that that's adorable.

Kids are starting to see you as a role model. Do you feel pressure to act in a certain way?

Smith: The only real litmus test that I use about the work that I do and the way I behave is that I want my mom to not be embarrassed at work. How's my mom gonna feel if my record comes on the radio or if people see my movie? Is my mom gonna be embarrassed? I don't wanna get a spanking.

1997

QUENTIN TARANTINO
Grindhouse: Death Proof

Arguably the ultimate film buff working in movies today, Quentin Tarantino actively sought out Kurt Russell to play the psychotic Stuntman Mike in *Death Proof*, his portion of the *Grindhouse* double-bill experiment. Russell, says Tarantino, has been a star since childhood and represents "a breed of man that doesn't really exist anymore". (Dimension Films/Andrew Cooper)

Dimension Films, 2007

CAST: Stuntman Mike, KURT RUSSELL; Herself, ZOË BELL; Abernathy, ROSARIO DAWSON; Arlene, VANESSA FERLITO; Jungle Julia, SYDNEY POITIER; Kim, TRACIE THOMS; Pam, ROSE McGOWAN; Shanna, JORDAN LADD; Lee, MARY ELIZABETH WINSTEAD; Warren, QUENTIN TARANTINO; Marcy, MARCY HARRIELL; Dov, ELI ROTH; Nate, OMAR DOOM; Omar, MICHAEL BACALL; Lanna Frank, MONICA STAGGS; Jasper, JONATHAN LOUGHRAN; Punky Bruiser, MARTA MENDOZA; Tim the Bartender, TIM MURPHY; Venus Envy, MELISSA ARCARO; Earl McGraw, MICHAEL PARKS; Edgar McGraw, JAMES PARKS; Dr. Dakota Block (McGraw), MARLEY SHELTON; Counter Guy, NICKY KATT; Babysitter Twins, ELECTRA AVELLAN, ELISE AVELLAN; Peg, HELEN KIM; Juana, TINA RODRIGUEZ; Laquanda, KELLEY ROBINS; Lanna Frank Friends, EURLYNE EPPER, JAMIE L. DUNNO; Shanna Double, CHARLENE DLABAJ; Arlene Foot Double, SHANNON HAZLETT; Stuntman Mike Driving Double, BUDDY JOE HOOKER; Kim Stunt Driving Doubles, TRACY KEEHN DASHNAW, CHRISSY WEATHERSBY; Camera Car Driver, ALLAN KENT PADELFORD.

CREDITS: *Director,* Quentin Tarantino; *screenplay,* Quentin Tarantino; *producers,* Elizabeth Avellán, Robert Rodriguez, Erica Steinberg, Quentin Tarantino; *executive producers,* Bob Weinstein, Harvey Weinstein, Shannon McIntosh; *line producer/UPM,* Bill Scott; *California line producer,* James W. Skotchdopole; *associate producer,* Pilar Savone; *director of photography,* Quentin Tarantino; *production designers,* Steve Joyner; *costume designer,* Nina Proctor; *stunt coordinator,* Jeff Dashaw; *special make-up effects,* Greg Nicotero; Howard Berger; *editor,* Sally Menke; *visual effects producer,* Amber Kirsch; *art director,* Caylah Eddleblute; *special effects coordinator,* John McLeod; *department head make-up,* Tysuela Hill; *visual effects supervisor,* Ryan Tudhope. Running time: 114 minutes.

> "For Austin's hottest DJ, Jungle Julia, dusk offers an opportunity to unwind with two of her closest friends, Shanna and Arlene. This three fox posse sets out into the night, turning heads from Guero's to the Texas Chili Parlor. Not all of the attention is innocent. Covertly tracking their moves is Stuntman Mike, a scarred, weathered rebel who leers from behind the wheel of his muscle car. As the girls settle into their beers, Mike's weapon, a white-hot juggernaut, revs just feet away...."

Don't Cast 'Em Unless it's Right
Quentin Tarantino on *Death Proof*

It's many years now since Reservoir Dogs *[1992] came out. How does it feel to be a cult figure? Do you almost look on Quentin Tarantino as a different person now?*

Quentin Tarantino: No, I'm still always me. But, it's funny, this as a movie is the first time I've got that kind of question every once in a while. I've been thinking about it, too: I've actually been doing this for a little while now. I'm being completely sincere, but obviously I'm exaggerating [when I say] there's a little part of me that feels like I'm still the guy at the video store. Now, at the same time, this is my life. I'm not pinching myself like I was with *Reservoir Dogs*. I'm not waiting for it to all go away. *Man, is this a dream? No. This is my life and it's my profession and it's what I do.* I worked minimum wage for a decade. Well, now I've been making movies for over a decade. The last time I did a big UK tour was in '92. I was at the Glasgow Film Theatre. I was there before, and the woman who was there [in 1992] was there, and I remembered her. She showed me a picture of myself there then. [I thought], *Who the fuck is this guy? I was like that then?* My hair was so long.

Do you feel like you have grown up in the movies?

Yeah. Definitely. The answer to your question is yes. There would have been a process had I done anything, but I guess I have. The last few years have been kinda interesting, because part of the thing about it is that I've always been a student of directors' careers. You can usually look at any director's filmography and you can see where they went south. But you can also see where their tastes changed, where maybe their ambition changed. Maybe they got more ambition, maybe they got less.

When did the writer/directors stop being writer/directors and when did they just start directing other people's scripts? All that kinda stuff. You can see they had to work really hard, but now they're really successful, they don't have to work so hard. Now they work with their crew enough that they barely have to move their fat ass off the goddamn chair. All this kinda stuff you can see in their work. I'm always aware of this and I'm always asking myself certain questions. "Am I making it too easy on myself? Am I taking too much stuff for granted? Am I knowing too much? Is it better to be just a little bit more innocent?"

You can never know too much.

Well, you can a little bit. Say you have a flop, and say you have another flop. And you think, *Well, maybe I shouldn't do that anymore.* Maybe you kinda know too much now. Maybe it was better when you were just doing movies which you wanted to make.

Are you a slow worker? Is that the reason for your relatively limited output?

I was alluding to it before with my half-said analogy. Writer/directors come out, they do their first film, their second, their third, and there's this real voice there. But, you know what? It's hard fucking work to go back and start from square one every single time. That blank page doesn't give a damn what you've done before. It's like you're going to Mount Everest all over again, [starting] at the very bottom.

For a whole lot of people it's like, "Fuck that already! That's just too hard a world. Let me see what's out there. Let me read this book. Let me read these other scripts and either I can re-write it—because that would be easier and I could get more movies done—or at least I could talk the writer through what it is I wanna do and how I wanna shape the material." Then they get to make more money, they get to make many more movies than they would if they were starting from scratch. But then, all of a sudden, their voice just goes away. Now they're just a Hollywood director.

Will you always want to be a writer/director—a filmmaker directing his own stuff?

Yes. Writing is a little too hard for me to sit down and write a script for somebody else. I'm not saying that that would never happen to me. I really wish it could. I almost wish I could just sit down and write a script for this friend of mine or that friend of mine or a cool director or whoever. But I just can't. It's gotta really be all or nothing.

The only thing I can do is on certain friends of mine's scripts; I'll just give it a read. And as I'm reading it I'll have a pen with me, and if I just think of any funny lines, I'll write 'em down. If I just think of maybe what I think could be a better way to say something, I'll change the sentence. Or maybe I'll think, *This could be an interesting thing*, and I'll just kinda get lost and write a little scene, awright? Usually it's just back and forth, people talking. Then I'll give it back to them, and they can use whatever they wanna use or not.

What British films have you put on in your film festival in Austin over the years?

I've shown a few different British titles. Off the top of my head, in the first festival I showed *Twisted Nerve* [1968], *Cry of the Banshee* [1970]. I've always been a big fan of Douglas Hickox, and I showed my favorite movie of his, *Sitting Target* [1972], which has the greatest jailbreak in the history of cinema. I'm a huge fan of Douglas Hickox. I showed *Brannigan* [1975].

That's a terrible film!

It's fun! I like the pub fight.

I understand you like British pubs. Where did that come from?

It's kinda what you do when you're here, you know? My way of seeing a city is walking around, walking into a shop, getting lost, finding my way back. Usually I'll have a writing notepad with me, or a book. You walk around for a while until you get tired, then you go into a pub, sit down and have a beer and read for a while. I don't get anybody following me around.

The most I get is if somebody knows I'm at a hotel—this doesn't happen all the time—[so] I might have to sneak out the back because they might be waiting. Other than that it's just, "Hey, how're you doing?" Somebody will ask me for an autograph or they'll ask me for a picture. If I'm in the mind to do that, maybe it breaks the mood. Usually, especially during the daytime, it's not younger people in British pubs. It's older people.

Death Proof has been said to be a flop, but it could also be said that younger audiences haven't grasped the concept. What's your take on that?

The *Grindhouse* financial unsuccess in America. I actually think it is literally the fact that people don't want two movies in a night. You will notice, even when you go to revival houses that show double features, a lot of people clear out by the time the second movie shows. Part of them didn't understand it and, two, they just didn't want it! Harvey Weinstein said, "If you had one movie of three hours, that would have been better than the idea of two movies."

One of the things that me and Robert [Rodriguez] were thinking about that we thought would be cool was the idea of two for the price of one. People don't give a fuck how much movies cost anymore. They don't think about the price of a ticket. They just don't—especially young people. To prove it they go out and buy a DVD for $24—I'm using American money—that they've never even seen. So they don't give a shit about how much it costs. I think what people want, especially when you're talking about a weekend, is dinner and a movie. And if you fuck with their dinner, they're gonna do something else.

Kurt Russell is the latest addition to your repertory company. Do you have a hit list of people you want to work with?

It is true that when it comes to some of these older actors, I'm on the lookout. The only thing that's tempting about doing somebody else's script is that the average screenwriter tends to write more parts than I write in the average script. Even my *Pulp Fiction* [1994] script, which is a multi-character study, doesn't have zillions of characters in it. There's a few, and I just hang with them. Even something as big as *Kill Bill 1* and *2* [2003 and 2004], there's not that many speaking roles in the movie compared to just even an average movie.

Whenever I do read scripts—which I normally don't because I'm not looking and I'd rather spend that time reading a book—you can think about all these wonderful actors that you'd cast in this part or that part. I worked with John Saxon on *CSI*, and I'd love to work with him again and find a good role for him. I'd love to work with Robert Culp. I've always been a fan of his; I think he's terrific. I'd love to work with Jim Brown if I had the right role for him. That would be really cool. The actor James Bannister I've always really loved. He's old now, but he can still work out. That's something really neat.

Part of my thing, though, is that you don't cast 'em unless it's right, unless it seems right as rain. That's why they're gonna be so damn good when you do it with them. One thing they always bring up about the Kurt Russell thing, which is really fascinating and I think you'll appreciate, one of the things that is so fantastic about him being in the movie—and I have to say I hadn't thought about when I cast him—was he's so fucking natural. A lot of the guys that I was thinking about and who could be a great Stuntman Mike are just not around anymore. Ralph Meeker would have been a really good Stuntman Mike, or Cameron Mitchell, William Smith—he woulda been a fuckin' fantastic Stuntman Mike, awright? And the thing about it is there's nobody—and I mean *nobody*—of Kurt Russell's age that is still a legitimate leading man making Hollywood movies and that has worked in that Hollywood in the way he did.

He started working when he was four, and by twelve, he headed some TV series, *The Travels of Jamie McPheeters* [1963-64], and Charles Bronson was a semi-regular on that show. Not only that, but his dad was a cowboy character actor named Bing Russell. But the thing is that Hollywood doesn't exist anymore. Kurt Russell is the only movie star leading man in today's Hollywood that *knows* what that Hollywood is—at least at his age. To be that young—he's 55—but to actually work in Hollywood that long.

He's worked with all the stuntmen—he *knows* Stuntman Mike. Every stuntman has met a Stuntman Mike! Kurt knew one Stuntman Mike in particular, and he based a lot of his character on that. But not only that, except for *Vega$*, every TV he mentioned when Stuntman Mike went through his résumé, Kurt Russell did. He did *The High Chaparral*, he did two *Virginian*s, he's worked with William Smith—he worked with him on a *Laredo* [episode] and on the movie *The Mean Season* [1985]. He worked with Cameron Mitchell—he told me stories about Cameron Mitchell on the set of *The High Chaparral*. He's worked with all these guys and, not only that, they were *cool*.

We shot a little bit of it in Bilton, California, where Fess Parker lives. He's one of the big wine owners; the best pinot noir in the world comes out of that area of California. And Kurt Russell did a couple of *Daniel Boone*s! And so he took me and introduced me to Fess Parker. It's a different Hollywood and it's a breed of man that doesn't really exist anymore, and Kurt is *that*. And that's Stuntman Mike, you know what I mean? Everyone else would be trying to *play* it, conjure it up or bring it together. Kurt knows that guy. He knows those types of actors.

How will rape victims feel when they see the Rapist #1 doll in the shop?

The doll doesn't say Rapist #1. I just looked at the doll two seconds ago and I was like, "What the fuck are they talking about?" I really had to reach into my mind to think what the fuck they meant. And then I looked at the doll and it doesn't say anything like that.

It's just a doll of my character in the movie. It's not the Number #1 Rapist, it's Rapist #1, and that's not even written anywhere on the toy whatsoever. I'm never called that in the movie. It's a movie joke: that's my character's thing in the credit crawl. It's a movie joke about "Thug #1," "Thug #2." It's not on the toy whatsoever, so the answer to it is that a rape victim in a toyshop would not think anything. They'd think, *Hey, there's a doll of Quentin Tarantino.* That's my answer to the question.

The word rapist isn't anywhere on the doll. Everyone is bringing it up and no one knows exactly what their problem is. I've been all around the fucking world on this movie, and this is the only place this is happening. It's really tickling because everywhere I go, they talk about how it's a female empowerment movie! But this isn't even about *Death Proof!* It's about the fucking doll and they're wrong. I'm curious about where they got their information.

What can you tell me about The Inglourious Basterds?

It's probably gonna be the next thing I'm gonna do, but I'm probably gonna be writing it for about a year or so.

Is it a remake of The Dirty Dozen?

No, no, no. It's a script in that genre—that style of World War II movie. That's what I intend to do, but I still have to write it, and it has to be good. I have to like it. I have to keep being inspired. That's what I'm writing now, so we'll see.

2007

DAVID TWOHY
The Chronicles of Riddick

David Twohy, Alexa Davalos and Vin Diesel on *The Chronicles of Riddick*. Impressive DVD sales of *Pitch Black* led to a new adventure for our selfish, dark-hearted anti-hero. (Universal/Joseph Lederer)

THE CHRONICLES OF RIDDICK

Universal, 2004

CAST: Riddick, VIN DIESEL; Lord Marshal, COLM FEORE; Dame Vaako, THANDIE NEWTON; Aereon, JUDI DENCH; Vaako, KARL URBAN; Kyra, ALEXA DAVALOS; Purifier, LINUS ROACHE; The Guv, YORICK VAN WAGENINGEN; Toombs, NICK CHINLUND; Imam, KEITH DAVID; Irgun, MARK GIBBON; Toal, ROGER R. CROSS; Merc Pilot, TERRY CHEN; Eve Logan, CHRISTINA COX; Mercs, NIGEL VONAS, SHAWN REIS, FABIAN GUJRAL, TY OLSSON; Convicts, PETER WILLIAMS, DARCY LAURIE, JOHN MANN, P. ADRIEN DORVAL; Slam Boss, ALEXANDER KALUGIN; Slam Guards, DOUGLAS H. ARTHURS, VITALY KRAVCHENKO, RON SELMOUR, RAOUL GANEEV, MARK ACHESON, SHOHAN FELBER, BEN COTTON; Lajjun, KIM HAWTHORNE; Ziza, ALEXIS LLEWELLYN; Scales, CHARLES ZUCKERMANN; Scalp Taker, ANDY THOMPSON; Black Robed Meccan Cleric, CEDRIC DE SOUZA; Black Robed Clerics, AHMAD SHARMROU, STEFANO DIMATTEO; Coptic Cleric, MINA ERIAN MINA; Bump Pilot, JOHN PROWSE; Defense Minister, LORENA GALE; Helion Politicos, CHRISTOPHER HEYERDAHL, ROB DALY; Lead Meccan Officer, MICHASHA ARMSTRONG; Young Meccan Soldier, AARON DOUGLAS; Vault Officer, COLIN CORRIGAN; Shirah, KRISTIN LEHMAN.

CREDITS: *Written and directed by* David Twohy, based on characters created by Jim Wheat and Ken Wheat; *producers*, Scott Kroopf, Vin Diesel; *executive producers*, Ted Field, George Zakk, David Womark; *co-executive producer*, Tom Engleman; *associate producer*, Wendy Williams; *producer (director's cut)*, Camille Brown; *director of photography*, Hugh Johnson;

production design, Holger Gross; *music*, Graeme Revell; *editors*, Martin Hunter, Dennis Virkler, A.C.E.; *editor (director's cut)*, Tracy Adams; *costume design*, Ellen Mirojnick, Michael Dennison; *art direction*, Kevin Ishioka, Mark. W. Mansbridge, Sandi Tanaka; *visual effects supervisor*, Peter Chiang; *stunt coordinator*, Robert Brown; *fight choreographer*, Bradley James Allan. Running time: 119 minutes/134 minutes (director's cut).

> *"It is a dark time in the universe. Planet after planet is falling to an unholy army of Necromongers—conquering warriors who offer ravaged worlds a simple choice: convert or die. Those who refuse their rule hope in vain for someone or something that will slow the spread of Necromongers. But rebels are short-lived, and saviors, it seems, are in short supply. When things get bad, weary survivors turn to myths for comfort—murmured prophecies, vain hopes, legends of good vanquishing evil. But good isn't always the antidote to evil, and legends can be wrong. Sometimes the only way to stop evil is not with good, but with another kind of evil."*

People Like Their Bad Boys
David Twohy on *The Chronicles of Riddick*

What was the genesis of The Chronicles of Riddick? *Is it true you had the idea to make it even before* Pitch Black *was completed?*

David Twohy: Yeah. We had finished *Pitch Black*, and I actually sat down and wrote a small treatment for what a follow-up film could look like. I handed it to the studio—Universal—and they looked at it and said, "It's much too big and much too costly. By the way: *Pitch Black* [2000] did well, but it didn't do *that* well, so no. Go away. Darken our door no more!" So we did go away. About three years later, they looked at the numbers of DVDs they were selling for *Pitch Black*, and they realized it was doing very well in its after-market life. Even better than they would have expected from its theatrical release. That meant to them that it was catching on in a grass roots kind of way, that people were discovering the film and passing it on to a friend or telling their friends about it. And so it became more popular like that. And after only three-and-a-half years, the studio came back to us and said, "Didn't you have a treatment or something? Can we read that again?"

What is it about this character that you created that makes him so popular? Riddick is almost an iconic figure.

We think of him as an anti-hero, not a hero, because he thinks of himself first, not about other people first, in a very selfish and sometimes dark-hearted way. I guess you don't see a lot of that callousness displayed in the leads of mainstream American movies. It may be refreshing on that level for some people. And I think people like their bad boys, and Riddick is that.

Vin Diesel doesn't seem to be a man who's overly burdened with self-doubt. Can you describe the differences in him from Pitch Black *to* The Chronicles of Riddick, *and perhaps detail his increased involvement?*

It would be true that he has real investment in Riddick and in that character we go forward as co-creators. But he was very involved in the first one, too, [and] in that character, even though he was just one guy that we cast in a great succession of guys who came through our door. He had a lot of ideas even then about what Riddick should be like and how he should move. So as you might expect, yes, he is very involved in that. With the character of Riddick we do share a co-authorship approach.

He's become a bigger star via other movies since Pitch Black. *Have you seen a change in him?*

I guess it's manifested in that he is actually one of the producers of the film as well. That does not really mean that he's one of these producers who reads schedules and budgets and tries to keep us on schedule. He's more of a creative producer. He's there to help me protect the heartbeat of the character and the film, because on any big film, there's a lot of tidal forces that can sway a film this way or that way. A lot of things can pull at you creatively. So he helps me protect the film in that way, I guess. That's how he flexes his protesorial muscles.

What changes did you see in yourself between having a modest budget for Pitch Black *and not huge studio expectations to then getting a bigger toy box to play with and a lot more money with* The Chronicles of Riddick? *Did you feel a lot more pressure?*

You know, the funny thing is that to make a big movie, we do it in a very core way. It's just like making a small movie for me or for any other filmmaker. Our day is our day, and our day is comprised [around], "We've got to get this many scenes in this day." We break it down into shots and into setups. It is the same technical approach for me making a small movie, as it is a big movie. That said, there are just more people around me, more people talking in my ear, more questions that have to be answered. The great distraction in a movie like this is that I don't get enough time to spend with the actors because I've got eight hundred visual effects shots to pay attention to, I've got a great design side of the show to pay attention to, and all that can take me away from the heartbeat of the story or the actors. One way to solve it is that you sleep four hours instead of eight hours a night and you find those extra hours in the day. And that's not too far away from the truth of what happened on a big show like this. You can get stretched too thin; it is a danger that I face and that any director faces on a movie like this. But also being the screenwriter as well helps me [to] be able to answer the actors when they have questions about their character. I can answer them quickly.

What's your favorite aspect of the character, and were you able to expand it out in this film?

I guess because he was kind of a *tabula rasa* in the first film—we didn't know anything about his background or where he came from—we decided to go there and postulate. Part of the new mythology that we're introducing is that Riddick has a rich background that he's not fully aware of. He may be aware on a subconscious level, but he's not fully aware of it. So as he progresses forward in this story, so he's got to journey back a bit as well and understand about his Furyan origins. So it was about trying to develop a past for this guy, which he didn't have in the first film.

Will the international response determine whether there are more chronicles to come?

Very much so. Here [in the UK], Japan and Germany; all those are very important to us. As is the DVD. Ten years ago, it was true that on opening weekend, the studio knew exactly what they had. Sometimes they may wait until the second weekend, but they knew exactly what they had. They knew exactly if they wanted to pull the trigger on more films in a series. They can't say that anymore. *Pitch Black* is that case in point. We came out: "No, there won't be a sequel." Three years later: "All right, let's do a sequel." So in the same way, we are awaiting how well it does internationally and how well it does in November when we come out with the standard edition DVD and the director's cut of the DVD as well.

You must have a notion.

The difference is [that] if we are so fortunate as to have enough audience that would support another film, and we just don't know that yet. But if we do, [then] we know where we're going, as opposed to maybe a film series like Paramount's *Star Trek* [1979 onwards], for instance. They seem to be very reactive. They throw one film in the marketplace and it does well enough: "Oh, okay. Good. Let's make another. What do we do? Let's start from scratch all over again." If we are so fortunate as to make another, we know story-wise and character-wise where we go next.

What made you decide to cast Alexa Davalos, a newcomer, in the movie? What qualities did you see in her?

A lot of actors who auditioned for the role; it was really very tough. Tougher than maybe even you see on the screen. A lot of the actors had the ability to play tough, but you didn't really feel much for them or care much about them because they were *so* tough. That's all they were. Alexa starts out not really that; she starts out with a lot of sympathy and a certain softness. In the flashes of the toughness that she showed me, I thought we could get her there—that we could train her up and toughen her up. I think she's stepped up to that challenge.

So we began with somebody who was inherently sympathetic. She is that as a person and as an actor. Then we asked her to play this tougher role. It would be both sides of the character. For a lot of actors, it would be easy on the tough side, but they couldn't be sympathetic at the same time.

It was a surprise to see Judi Dench doing science fiction. How did you pitch it to her, and was she up for the challenge?

First of all, it was Vin's idea to get her. He had long thought of her, rightfully so, as one of our best actors, and "Wouldn't it be great if we could do a film with her someday?" I said, "Well, we have this Aereon role," who was very androgynous and written for neither sex, really. "We can offer that to her." I wanted to surround him with very good actors to challenge him to rise to that level. I said, "There are none better than Judi Dench. Let's start there." We sort of tag-teamed her. We went after her in different ways on different days. He would be sending her flowers and I would be coming to London and stopping by to see her stage show with Maggie Smith, and having a glass of champagne with her afterwards. And also, I just showed her an artist's concept of what the character would look like—very diaphanous and flowing, tall—and she responded to that. She responded to the picture: "Can you make me *seem* taller?" She was in a show with Maggie Smith, and even though they love each other, there's a little competition there. She's always been jealous of Maggie's slenderness, I guess.

It's a strongly Anglicized cast that includes Thandie Newton as Dame Vaako. What attracted you to her?

That aspect of it wasn't intentional. We were just going for the best available actors at a certain point. It turned out that Colm Feore, who's Canadian, not English, but we have Linus Roache, who is, and Thandie, who is Zimbabwean, I think. Why choose her? Her beauty and her talent. That's what attracted me to Thandie Newton. Just that. And she *got* the part. She understood it very well. I didn't audition her. We just offered it to her. It was a mutual coming together. Sometimes you pursue actors, like we pursued Judi. Sometimes they pursue you. This was mutual. I think she was circumspect about doing science fiction, and *Pitch Black* she didn't know. But once her agents read the script, they said, "You've got to read the script to understand it. It's a new deal and a whole new world. And you have a very interesting role."

2004

JAMES WATKINS, JANE GOLDMAN, and SUSAN HILL
The Woman in Black

A moody behind-the-scenes shot of Daniel Radcliffe and director James Watkins on *The Woman in Black*. Watkins describes Radcliffe's performance as exhibiting "a real sense of melancholy and loss". (Hammer/Nick Wall)

Hammer, 2012

CAST: Arthur Kipps, DANIEL RADCLIFFE; Daily, CIARÁN HINDS; Mrs. Daily, JANET McTEER; Jennet, LIZ WHITE; Mr. Bentley, ROGER ALLAM; Mr. Jerome, TIM McMULLAN; Nanny, JESSICA RAINE; Keckwick, DANIEL CERQUEIRA; Fisher, SHAUN DOOLEY; Mrs. Fisher, MARY STOCKLEY; PC Collins, DAVID BURKE; Stella Kipps, SOPHIE STUCKEY; Joseph Kipps, MISHA HANDLEY; Fisher Girls, EMMA SHOREY, MOLLY HARMON, ELLISA WALKER-REID; Nursemaid, LUCY MAY BARKER; Little Girl on Train, INDIRA AINGER; Doctor, ANDY ROBB; Victoria Hardy, ALEXIA OSBOURNE; Tom Hardy, ALFIE FIELD; Charlie Hardy, WILLIAM TOBIN; Gerald Hardy, VICTOR McGUIRE; Mrs. Jerome, CATHY SARA; Mrs. Drablow, ALISA KHAZNOVA; Nathaniel Drablow, ASHLEY FOSTER; Lucy Jerome, AOIFE DOHERTY; Nicholas Daily, SIDNEY JOHNSTON.

CREDITS: *Director*, James Watkins; *producers*, Richard Jackson, Simon Oakes, Brian Oliver; *co-producers*, Ben Holden, Paul Ritchie, Todd Thompson, Sean Wheelan; *line producer*, Vic David; *executive producers*, Tobin Armbrust, Neil Dunn, Guy East, Roy Lee, Xavier Marchand, Marc Schipper, Nigel Sinclair, Tyler Thompson; *assistant producer*, Jonathan

Hood; *screenplay*, Jane Goldman, based on the novel by Susan Hill; *music*, Marco Beltrami; *director of photography*, Tim Maurice-Jones; *editor*, Jon Harris; *production designer*, Kave Quinn; *art director*, Paul Ghirardani, Kate Grimble; *make-up/prosthetics supervisor*, Paul Hyett; *special effects supervisor*, Bob Hollow. Running time: 95 minutes.

> *"Young London solicitor Arthur Kipps is forced to leave his three-year-old son and travel to the remote village of Crythin Gifford to attend to the affairs of the recently deceased owner of Eel Marsh House. But when he arrives at the creepy old mansion, he discovers dark secrets in the villagers' past, and his sense of unease deepens when he glimpses a mysterious woman dressed all in black."*

Playing into Primal Fears
James Watkins, Jane Goldman, and Susan Hill on *The Woman in Black*

How did the project come to you?

Jane Goldman: Hammer approached me and asked if I'd be interested in adapting it. Being familiar with the material, it was an immediate "yes" from me. It was a very, very exciting prospect.

Were you familiar through the book or the play?

Goldman: Both. It was a wonderful story. Almost instantly I thought, *I would love to do that.* Every project is daunting in its own way before you start. That's the nature of adapting things. I guess I've been in a position of adapting things that are very beloved to their fans, and so that wasn't an entirely new position to be in. Certainly the point that Susan read the script and liked it and gave me her blessing was [good]. I then breathed a sigh of relief.

What was the dynamic from your perspective, and how happy were you to hand over the story to Hammer, Jane, James, and Daniel Radcliffe?

Susan Hill: I think I'm always happy to hand over because when you write a book, you finish it and you publish it. What you're basically saying is, "Go, little book, and seek your fortune. You're not mine any longer. You were mine when I was writing it—you were *only* mine—but now you're out there, other people have read you and you're going to seek your fortune. I may have a small amount of control over what you do in that if I really don't like the places you're going to go to late at night, I might haul you back." As far as films are concerned—just to skip the play for a minute—I think it was Ian McEwan said, "You either take the cash or you take control," which is a sort of way of saying, "Look, if you sell the film and you don't like it, well you've had the money, don't complain. If you don't want anybody else to touch it because you're afraid that they'll mess it up, don't sell it."

But the other thing is that the book is still there. If people go and see the film or they see the play and they don't like it or they don't think it works, then the book's still there. It's still there for me. They haven't taken it away—they haven't banned it because they've got the film. And I think, also, you've got to be able to trust other people. I know a lot of authors who've complained about films of their books, and it's because they haven't really understood what's happening. The same as with the play: they sort of expect it to be the book on the screen, the book on stage.

But it's not, because those are completely different mediums. They're being adapted for a different medium, and it would be a very bad film if it was the book being put on film in a stilted way—every single little tiny thing. That's not what any director wants to do, or screenwriter. They're adapting and interpreting it for their medium. I wouldn't want to be able to have control over that because I'm not a film writer, I don't know what's necessary, I don't have that skill.

So I was very, very happy when I heard that Jane was doing it, and I have seen some previous scripts of books of mine, and you think, *Oh God, why did they want the book in the first place? Why didn't they just go and write their own film?* I certainly knew Jane wouldn't do that, and when I read the script, I knew she hadn't done that. The one thing you do want is for them to retain the spirit of the book. That doesn't mean every character, every line, every scene. It means the spirit, so you don't turn this into a comedy because it's not what the book is about. But that's all, and really you're handing it over to people whose skills are different from yours, whose qualifications in their own medium are very high, and saying, "Okay, I trust you, do it. And if I don't like it, you've done what is your best, and who am I to complain?" So that really was it. So as soon as I saw Jane's script and the film, I thought, *Wow!*

James Watkins: Susan's been very generous. I think she's absolutely right. She's given us an enormous amount of freedom, but also at the same time as being there, so if we wanted to ask questions—we felt the pressure to honor the book and, exactly as Susan says, the *spirit* of the book. That's not necessarily, as Susan says, trying to do an absolutely literal line-by-line transposition onto the film negative. You can't do it. But the things that are wonderful in the book were in Jane's script, and hopefully we managed to transpose some of those onto the screen.

What were the biggest challenges in bringing it to the screen?

Goldman: Enhancing it. Any adaptation is taking something that is novel-shaped and turning it into something film-shaped, really. It's about pacing and the rhythm and the grammar of film that are different. But with such a wonderful story at the heart of it, in a sense that always makes it easier.

What makes a great ghost story?

Watkins: There's a great ghost, a great central character, it's very scary, it's very atmospheric. It has a deep understanding of what scares us. Obviously, Susan's read incredibly widely in the genre, knows and understands all of that amongst all the best—[Joseph Sheridan] Le Fanu, M.R. James—and really it shares with those a great location, and it plays into really primal fears. I think any film that sets out to scare you has to play into deep fears that resonate with everybody, whether those are fears of the dark or fears of being buried alive or fears of the water or fears of the dead. Fears of children. These are all fears that go back through literature, through history, and I think these are fears that Susan very much tapped into, but through craft managed to create a very rich and resonant story.

How did you select Daniel Radcliffe?

Watkins: We talked about Dan and we thought, *Ahh, that's interesting.* Obviously, we were aware of all the associations and connotations. So I met with Dan and we talked about the film and he'd read it. He just had such a strong and smart understanding of the character. Ultimately, as a director, that's what you're looking for. I thought it was just a really brilliant opportunity. People think they know Dan because they've got ten years of *Potter*, but he's playing a part, playing someone who's much younger than him, and here to really reinvent Dan but also to really land this character. In the film, Dan has this real sense of melancholy and loss. I think it's a really mature, adult performance from him. So when casting actors, you have a sense of *well, this might work,* and you meet them, explore it, talk about it, and see if you're seeing it in the same way. And if you are, you go on that journey together.

Did you ever have any reservations about the Pottermania?

Watkins: I was mindful of it. You'd be naïve not to be mindful of it but, that said, if you take Dan totally on face value in terms of his performance in the film, [then] I think he carries the film. I think he's very impressive. What's been very, very gratifying, actually, is the feedback that we've had [from] people—even people that don't like the *Potter* films—often saying, "Oh, we had this very strong image of Dan in one place, and he's totally in a different place."

Hill: He's grown up.

Watkins: His performance is in a different register, as it should be. It's a different role; it's a different type of film, the character. Dan is constantly trying to grow as an actor and you hope people give him that opportunity.

Did you feel the pressure to make a Hammer film, and did it constrain either of you?

Watkins: No. It wasn't even a thought, really. The pressure is to tell the story as the best it can be, rather than try and shoehorn it into the Hammer name. For me, the fact that it's got Hammer on the front of the film is a fun association, but if it had said "Hammer" on it and they had a Godawful script, that would not have been for me. I wouldn't have made the film.

Goldman: It's great fun to be part of British cinema history, but at the same time, I don't think that Hammer comes with any particular pressures these days—there's a whole generation who haven't heard of it, to be perfectly honest. The great thing about Hammer in their current incarnation is that they're very much allowing filmmakers to do their own thing, rather than being a brand.

Are you a big horror fan?

Goldman: Huge horror fan. Well, the *good* Hammer films, sure.

Watkins: We had a lot of chat about those. The good and the bad. There's a lot of good and there's a lot of bad.

Goldman: The *Quatermass* films [1955, 1957 and 1967] are wonderful. Yeah, I'm a huge horror fan, so it was exciting to see the logo come up.

What would you put on if you wanted to watch a good horror movie?

Goldman: Honestly, any horror movie. I love any. It's very, very hard to scare me, so I'm particularly impressed by anything that does scare me.

Watkins: Specific to this, we talked a lot about Japanese horror a lot, didn't we?

Goldman: Absolutely, yeah. I think we're both very inspired by [that]—we both love J-horror. But, you know, I'm not at all snobbish about horror. I will happily watch *Final Destination 5* [2011]. Love it! I just think there is room for all of these things.

Location filming took place at Halton Gill in Yorkshire. Why did you choose it? What did it give you, the actors, and the story?

Watkins: It really was this integrated sense of a village. It didn't need a fantastic amount of dressing. From a practical point of view, everything's sort of in the same place, so from a shooting point-of-view, it makes it cheaper and easier and faster. But from a pictorial point of view, it has a sense of scale, a sense of bleakness, a sense of the weather....

That's Yorkshire for you.

Watkins:... yeah! It was bloody freezing! [We shot in] November. It was cold. It was raining. The scene where we had the car with the mob around it, it was just raining all day, constantly. The thing about rain is that it rarely reads on film unless it's really, really hard. Film rain is so hard to make it real. Everyone was totally soaked through. But it just gives you that sense of [place]. Also, it's an antidote to American locations. I really wanted to get out and shoot British locations: there at Halton Gill, the causeway, the house, to have this sense of the iconography of a British landscape. This kind of bleak [feel], the train station, everything. There [in Yorkshire] it's actually quite a de-saturated, austere landscape, and remote—a complete otherness from London, I suppose. It was just a wonderful place. And also what was great is that you've got no phone signal there.

Hill: What was great about it—and I didn't set it in Yorkshire particularly; but I've never really said where I set it, so it could be anywhere. I certainly haven't had Yorkshire in mind, but I would love to have done, because as you know, I come from Yorkshire—but when I saw that place, I thought, *This is perfect*. I did know Halton Gill—I must have been a lot as a child—but if I'd known and thought of it, who knows what's been left in the residue of your mind from childhood? But it was just the perfect place. It just worked. When they said that's where they were going for the village, at first I thought, *Right, okay*. It is the remoteness as well, and that light. There's a light up there which is fantastic.

Watkins: Yeah, the way the moisture hangs in the sky gives it a really heavy, foreboding sense in terms of lighting it.

So we've got bleak, austere, foreboding, wet....

Goldman: ... and no phone signal!

You made the analogy that books are like children. Having seen the film and been on set, are you incredibly proud of your child?

Hill: Yes, but rather as when you see your adult children—and I've just had lunch with mine—and you think, *Who's this lovely person? Has she got anything to do with me at all?* It's a very strange sense, because once they've gone into the world and they've grown up and met other people and got jobs and been to places that you've never been to, suddenly they're an intimate part of you and couldn't exist without you, and yet they're other people's now. It's exactly the same in a way. They may turn into things you don't always like, they may have opinions you don't always have, they may wear clothes that you don't find suitable, but it doesn't matter because it's them. And yet there is still that funny feeling, there is that umbilical cord.

And I had it with the film. When I walked onto the set, particularly, there's that really strange feeling. And then seeing rushes of bits of Yorkshire and bits of the causeway, I thought, *Gosh. Wow. I thought of that first.* But again, it's not pride, it's just, *Gosh, yeah....* And it was a long time ago, as well. So it seems a long way. Thirty years. I'm very old. If it had been something I wrote a couple of years ago, it perhaps would seem much closer, and there's been the play, of course, since then, and so many different views of it that it has just had a little life of its own. I just watch it rolling on!

What was the original inspiration for it?

Hill: I wanted to write a ghost story because I loved them, and I needed to get right back to writing because my elder daughter was four or five and I hadn't really written anything of length since she was born. I just wrote bits and pieces because you don't when you've got a small child. And I wanted to get back to that. I must have been reading a ghost story and thought, *If I could do that....* And the real thing was that, first of all, I wanted to write it as a full-length ghost story.

Mostly, ghost stories are short, and people think they've got to be short to sustain the tension. They've got to have a punch and that's it. Having read *The Turn of the Screw* [1898] and *A Christmas Carol* [1843] again, I thought, *No. If you have an idea that will sustain the length—and you've got to give it a depth and a richness that you don't in the short story, and you've got to go into the characters much more deeply because you've got length—if you could do that, then maybe we'll have a revival*, because the ghost story felt it was fizzling out, really. Just the odd fan magazine put them in.

So I really settled down and thought, *What would I need to do? What does it need to have?* And the place—because places often come first with me—but I'd spent a lot of time in Suffolk writing in the winter. Behind the sea and the shingle beach there were marshes. And as soon as you come away from that shingle beach, which is making that shingly sound, it goes completely quiet. The wall just stops the sound. And walking across the marshes with just a little bit of a wind moaning, the reeds make that rattle-y sound. And if you walk across there at dusk, and the sun's setting and the sun sends the light across the water and it goes very steely, however hardened you are, you do tend to look behind you a bit. And I think that place was in my head.

I don't know where *she* came from, I really don't. I can't remember now. But it started with places, I'm sure, and then wanting to see if I could do the length, and hope that other people would do it as well. And actually, just lately people have started to write longer ghost stories, which is lovely. It's great. I feel like I've kick-started a revival.

Why do people still have a need to believe in the afterlife?

Hill: In a way, the ghost story doesn't really relate with me to [that]. I happen to be a Christian and an Anglican, but that kind of isn't really part of it. I think I would be interested in ghosts no matter what because I think the ghost story is on that edge that everybody finds interesting between life and death. And it's between darkness and light and it's between good and evil and it's all on that cusp.

If the ghost has a purpose—which they've got to, otherwise they're pointless, and there are plenty of pointless ghost stories: the headless man rides across the countryside and then he does it again. But in a fiction, you've got to have a point to them being there. I wondered why the play of *The Woman in Black* did so well in Japan, because they absolutely love it in Japan. Then they started loving it in India. And the film will go to all those places.

And I thought, *What? This is set in Edwardian England, London fog, no steam trains, Yorkshire landscape.* It's because the ghost story is absolutely part of every single culture, every oral storytelling tradition, every written [tradition]—ghost stories are there. So it doesn't really matter where it's set for them, the people in those countries respond to it straight away because, in India particularly, of this belief in the person after the death and the ghost and the return and the retribution or whatever. It's so much part of their everyday spirituality now—much more than here [in the UK]—that I think it is just a natural preoccupation, and it is fascinating. And you can do all sorts of things with it as well, which is the writer's point of view.

Do the scary bits in the film scare you, or do you know it's coming?

Hill: I still jump in the play, actually, sometimes! There were moments when I kind of did that [she puts her hands in front of her eyes] in the film with the dolls and one or two spooky sights, but not in general, obviously, because I knew what was coming. I didn't watch it the first time with any sense of waiting to see what it was going to do in terms of making me afraid. I very much wanted to see how each scene was put together, so it was almost a technical interest that slightly took away the edge. It didn't really; I just wanted to see what Jane and James had done. I knew what Jane had done, but obviously that had been on paper. Then to see it [on film], and then what Dan did. So it was a professional interest, if you like. I missed out on the [feeling of], *Is this going to frighten me?*

What are your fears in life?

Goldman: Real things? General anesthetic. That terrifies me, not in a rational way because I know it's super safe, but I think it's like being killed by lethal injection. It's a terrible phobia. And in folklore, doppelgangers. I find that notion really creepy.

Watkins: Really boringly, I'm scared of heights. Very high buildings.

There's a famous story about Ridley Scott shooting Alien [1979] *and the cast and crew wouldn't go on set when they weren't working because they were creeped out. Did that ever happen to you on* The Woman in Black?

Watkins: It's funny, at the end of the day, when they turn the lights off and you see the set in half darkness, you think, *I wouldn't want to spend the night in this house.* Kave Quinn, our production designer, has done a fantastic job and built a very atmospheric environment.

Hill: It is actually true in the theater. They don't like being on the set when the play's over and everybody's packed up. They've been having some very strange things going on in the theater because those stories get magnified, but there's no doubt that there's something odd. A lot of the stage crew [announce], "Gotta go, thank you. Goodnight! See you tomorrow!" because nobody wants to be the last [on stage].

2012

BEN WHEATLEY
Kill List

Director/co-writer Ben Wheatley on a night shoot for *Kill List*, a deliberately retro-styled chiller inspired by everything from *The Wicker Man* to *The Parallax View* by way of *The Killers* and *Race with the Devil*. (Optimum Releasing/Nick Gillespie)

Warp X/Rook Films, 2011

CAST: *Jay*, NEIL MASKELL; *Shel*, MYANNA BURING; *Sam*, HARRY SIMPSON; *Gal*, MICHAEL SMILEY; *Fiona*, EMMA FRYER; *The Client*, STRUAN RODGER; *Hotel Receptionist*, ESME FOLLEY; *Justin*, BEN CROMPTON; *Kiera*, GEMMA LISE THORNTON; *Stuart*, ROBIN HILL; *Hotel Waitress*, ZOE THOMAS; *The Priest*, GARETH TUNLEY; *Hotel Receptionist #2*, JAMELLE OLA; *The Librarian*, MARK KEMPNER; *The Doctor*, DAMIEN THOMAS; *Thorn Blindfold Woman*, LORA EVANS; *High Priest*, BOB HILL; *The Bride*, REBECCA HOLMES; *MP*, JAMES NICKERSON; *Father of the Bride*, DAVID BOWEN; *News Reader*, SARA DEE; *Radio Reporters*, ALICE LOWE, STEVE ORAM; *Procession Members*: TOM ADCOCK, CHAELYN ALLCOCK, JAMES BATESON, ALEX BLAKE, JOHN CHAPPELL, FRENCHIE COWLEY, GLYNN DAVIES, SHANE ZITZSIMMONS, KATYA GALIANA-PHILIP, BRIAN GAUGAN, LORNA GLADHILL, ALICE HARRAND, BIANCA HAY, KARL HALLIWELL, JOSH HONEYBOURNE, CIARAN HUMPHRIES, GARETH IAN JAMES, LUCIE JAMES, ALEX JANCZENIA, NIKI JONES, NICK LEA, ANN LOMAX, KEITH LOMAX, LAUREN MAILE-WILSON, DAVID MARES, JIMMY MAY, DAVE McKINLEY, RICHARD MILEHAM, JOSH MOORE, HANNAH MURTON, STEPHEN RAWNSLEY, HANNAH RENTON, SIMON SMITH, ANDY STIRLING, ANN TURNER, DENNIS TURNER, JANICE WORSLEY; Additional Cast: JENNIFER ANDREWS, KEN BIRCH, JANICE BIRD, EDWARD BOOTH, JOAN COOPER, LYNN COPPERFIELD, DAVID CHARLES DENWOOD, DAPHNE ELAND, SHARRON HARDY, PAT KELLY, NA-

DINE LLOYD, JOY PALMER, STEPHEN PRESTON, AAHID RASOOL, LEE STEELE, JOHN STRIKER, RICHARD STOCKS, LYN WESSON, STUART WEBB, DOROTHY WEBB.

CREDITS: *Director*, Ben Wheatley; *screenplay*, Amy Jump, Ben Wheatley; *producers*, Claire Jones, Andrew Starke; *co-producer*, Barry Ryan; *associate producer*, Ally Gipps; *executive producers*, Katherine Butler, Robin Gutch, Hugo Heppell, Mark Herbert; *music*, Jim Williams; *cinematography*, Laurie Rose; *editors*, Robin Hill, Amy Jump, Ben Wheatley; *production design*, David Butterworth; *art directors*, Nick Wilkinson, Julie Ann Horan; *make-up & hair design*, Fiona Lavin; *costume designer*, Lance Milligan *special make-up & prosthetics*, Mike Stringer— Hybrid Design; *special effects supervisor*, Ben Ashmore; *visual effects*, Big Buoy. Running time: 95 minutes.

> *"Eight months after a disastrous job in Kiev left him physically and mentally scarred, ex-soldier turned contract killer, Jay, is pressured by his partner, Gal, into taking a new assignment. As they descend into the dark and disturbing world of the contract, Jay begins to unravel once again—his fear and paranoia sending him deep into the heart of darkness."*

Folding Genres
Ben Wheatley on *Kill List*

Kill List *took me in a direction I didn't expect. I was reminded of Don Siegel's* The Killers *[1964] and Robin Hardy's* The Wicker Man *[1973]. What were your inspirations when you were writing the film?*

Ben Wheatley: It's always flattering to have comparisons. *The Killers* is a fabulous film. I'm a massive Don Siegel fan. And *Wicker Man*, equally. I've had a few *Wicker Man* comparisons. I think definitely I can't duck it because that whole construction from *The Wicker Man*—that you've been in a machine, in a trap slowly closing in on you but you didn't realize you'd been sent to it—that's a great idea. [It's] from *The Wicker Man*, but it's also an idea from *The Parallax View* [1974], Alan J. Pakula's movie, as well. That would be a touchstone for me. The strange ceremony stuff is kind of *Wicker Man*-ish, but I don't think it's specifically *Wicker Man*. I think it's something that is in it. The cultish elements that are in the film don't really resemble *The Wicker Man* cult, particularly. The Summerisle cult is almost benign in *The Wicker Man*, and good—even though Edward Woodward ends up getting murdered! I kind of support them in *Wicker Man*, but I'm not too sure I'm on the side of the people in *Kill List* so much. The idea of the two slightly down-at-heel [hit men] certainly recalls something like *The Killers*. But weirdly, the movie for me comes from other places as well. It's like *Race with the Devil* [1975], the film with Warren Oates and Peter Fonda where they're being chased by Satanists. It's that and *Wicker Man*, but from the perspective of remembering them and seeing them when I was a kid. When I watch those movies back now, they're suddenly not as scary as I remember them. I remember *Race with the Devil* being absolutely terrifying when I was little. I watched it again recently, and it was quite a silly film. I spent quite a lot of time in the library looking up books on Satanism. It was quite odd. It's that idea: little snippets of those movies, but remembered from about twenty years ago. I think if I go back and watch those films recently and think, *I really want to do a version of them*. I kind of picked them apart and took bits I wanted. It's a distant memory of it. But there's other stuff in there as well. In working with Neil Maskell and Michael Smiley and MyAnna Buring and Emma Fryer as well, I sat down and had a little hit list of people I really wanted to work with. The story was moved around to suit those people, and the script was written specifically for those actors. Their personalities changed and morphed the way that the story went.

In casting Neil Maskell and Michael Smiley, you've given them a platform and a springboard to really shine and break out.

I'd worked with everyone before that's in it, on different stuff. A lot of them are from a sketch show I did called *The Wrong Door* [2008], which was on BBC3. Neil, MyAnna, and Michael are all in that. I did a series called *Ideal* [2010], with Johnny Vegas, two series of that, which is where I worked with Emma Fryer and Ben Crompton. They're brilliant actors, and you wonder why they're not in more stuff. I looked Neil up on IMDB and saw that he'd been in a lot of these British crime films like *The Football Factory* [2004], *Rise of the Footsoldier* [2007], and *Bonded by Blood* [2010]. I thought that if he'd been in the '60s, he'd have been in *Get Carter* [1971] and *Performance* [1970]—in the background. MyAnna has been in *The Descent* [2005], *Doomsday* [2008], and *Lesbian Vampire Killers* [2009]. I imagined that back in the day she'd have been a Hammer actress. I started to have this idea that if you put them both together in the same movie, it would be like folding the genres together. They're representative of those different strands of British filmmaking.

You seem to be pretty firmly rooted in film lore. You know your cult movies. Was there any intention when you began this process to make a cult film?

There was the intention to make a horror film. I wanted to make it on my own terms—purely because I can't make a film any other way! [laughs] A cult thing is a double-edged sword, isn't it? Movies only end up as cult movies normally because they're just fucked at the box office and they're rediscovered later on. It's a dangerous game to intentionally try and make a cult film. I want it to be seen by as many people as possible, but then equally I understand it's a hard film. But I think there's a taste and an appetite for horror movies at the moment and has been over the last few years, but they're not getting necessarily served with stuff that's as smart as it could be. There's plenty of grim stuff about, but it's not stuff that gives the audience any respect for their intelligence. It's either massive blockbuster stuff or it's in that trend of torture porn, which is pretty dim underneath the bonnet. I wanted to make something that wouldn't tell the audience everything. They'd have to work at it a bit. Once they'd had a think about it, it would be rewarding.

Kill List *is a terrifically edgy film. The violence can take you by surprise. I'm not a prude, but the killing of the librarian had me choking on my popcorn. Were you in any way prepared to compromise on any of that, or did you write a script, stick to it, and compromise wasn't in your vocabulary?*

Pretty much. It's pretty important, that scene. There were a few key things behind it, one of which was it's about trust: do you trust the filmmaking? And if you pull something out of a hat like that, from that point on you don't know what's gonna happen. You've lost all trust in me, you think at any minute this film could go extremely nasty. Seen from that point on, any decision that they make could suddenly dip into that level of extreme violence. That really helps me because it means I can do things that are really innocuous, but you feel really scared of them. If you don't have that moment, then it lets you off the hook, if you like. If you'd handled that scene slightly differently, then it takes the foot off the accelerator and everyone isn't half as scared. I kind of got the idea from a film called *The Orphanage* [2007]. In that, they have that brilliant bit where they run the old woman over and she's on the floor. They pick her up and you think, *Oh, they're not going to show this*. They cut around it. Then they show a little bit of it. *Oh God*. Then they show a bit more. And they cut back to her a third time, and all her face is hanging off. And at that point you go, "Oh, GOD! This is so extreme." And at any point in that movie, from now on, they can go that far. It's very clever in that film because for the rest of the movie, you're terrified that they're gonna show the dead kid. That's how I felt, anyway. But then the film's really tasteful, really. But you're in this state of fear that they're gonna go all the way. That was the main thinking behind why we did that hammer thing. The other little side thought was this idea that hit men are like folk heroes, they are treated quite well in cinema. You've got your hit men in *Pulp Fiction* [1994]. It's a basic trope that they're kind of all right. They're not, and it's outrageous that people think of them as heroes. They're murderers, and they're even worse than serial killers because they get paid to do it. I wanted to lead the audience to this point of going, "Here we are. These are genre characters, but this is the reality of what they do."

There is conflict between Jay and Gal. One is business-like. The other is far more extreme. That notion of conflict versus loyalty is intriguing.

Your friends will do extreme things, and it's part of friendship to try and understand that stuff and cope with it. Gal doesn't give a fuck; that's the problem. He doesn't care that much morally about it. But there's also this idea that he's like Jay's minder. He doesn't really do any of the violence. He looks after Jay, who's like a kind of pit bull who he points in the right direction to do this stuff. In the same way that Shel is as well. They don't mind earning money off this guy. Jay is like the artisan—he's the talent, and they're the minders and the managers of this guy. Jay does go off the handle all the time; that's what's useful about him: he's absolutely extreme. But Gal doesn't have the imagination to go so fucking crazy as Jay does, but he has to pick up the pieces, calm him down, and look after him. That's kind of the root of their relationship. The hammer attack thing was also meant to be like this idea where you get guys with that *Daily Mail* thing: "If I ever got hold of a pedophile, I'd fucking murder them!" Well, okay, here we go: this is it. Not that it says anywhere in the film that that guy is a pedophile, but it's that kind of have-a-go-hero style, total misunderstanding of the way that violence goes both ways. You commit these things, but they look into you as much as you look into them.

What's your take on vigilantes?

I just think it's really complicated. That's why there's a legal system, because just going out and doing stuff ends up completely fucked up. If someone does something bad to you and you do something bad to them, then the other relations of the person that you've done over have got as much of a legitimate right to do you over. That's the whole basis of that tit-for-tat sectarian violence, isn't it? There's no end to it. And that's the whole point of the system, to stop that. There's a higher authority and you can arbitrate. If you go down that route, then it leads to chaos.

There is a vigilante aspect to the killing of the librarian. Yet Jay seems to be beyond all of that. You wind him up, let him go, and beggar the consequences. But that killing ratchets up the tension and takes audience expectations to a whole new level.

Yeah. It's a weird thing. And it's a physiological thing as well. It happened to me the first time I saw it. I saw it again at Frightfest the other day, and it happened there as well. You get this weird rush of adrenaline and fear in you when you see that violence. It doesn't go away—or at least it doesn't for me—for at least eight or nine minutes. You're into the next scene and you can almost feel your blood fizzing in your veins during that, and that's a really odd thing. The only other experience I've had like it, apart from being in pubs and seeing fights, is when you surf the net and you follow links and you end up looking at horrible execution footage or something like that—you see something that you really didn't wanna see. It's to do with the way that it's shot. It feels like it's shot in a language that's outside the language of normal cinema because there are no edits in it. You expect it to be cut. You can feel within it where the edits should be, and if you're watching a normal movie, there would be a cut as they raise the hammer. And when the hammer hit the head, you would cut to a close-up. You kind of expect that, and when you don't see it, it makes it doubly worse. And then, when he does it two more times, there's no way to escape. You've gone out of a film experience into some kind of reality, into a news experience. For me as a viewer, seeing that stuff is what really disturbs me.

The final sequence is left open-ended, allowing people to question what it was about. It might be considered brave or even foolish. Why did you make that decision?

I don't necessarily think it's open. You've gotta think why he reacts like that. What is the meaning of it? As with any bit of cinema, as you watch it, you gather the information on it: what does it mean? I've read lots of different reviews of how people have reacted to it, and it's a totally legitimate reaction as to whether it's satisfying or not. What I'd like to think is that the people who found it hard will think about it and come to their own conclusions. I want people to be thinking about the movie, about the ending, and working out what it all means. A lot of them have got it pretty on the ball—the reading that I was hoping for. The information is all there in the movie—to pull it together and work out what it all means. I had all this criticism from some people who think that the film is just made up on the spot and that the ending is tacked on because we didn't know what else to do. The whole film is completely structured—it all balances and it all works. Maybe it's a hard watch the first time around because it's jumping around so much. It needs a bit of thought to decipher it.

Where was it shot?

It was shot in and around Sheffield and a little bit in Harewood House [both in Yorkshire]. It's not meant to be a film that's set here in Sheffield. It looks very different, each place you go. It could double for lots of different places. It's kind of a road movie. They're travelling around, but obviously if you're a local, you'll spot a bunch of places.

Was it partly down to expediency and budget?

Yeah, sure. The funding was to do with Warp, but when we came here [to Sheffield], it totally made sense. It didn't compromise the shoot. It was brilliant. The locations and the unit base was all really good, and there was a lot of Warp infrastructure and support, so it made a lot of sense to shoot in Sheffield.

Warp Films are almost reinventing British film. They tackle edgy projects. What kind of an experience did you have with them?

They're very open and creatively pretty hands-off, but when they do make notes, they make absolute sense. We were pretty leery because we had come off of doing *Down Terrace* [2009], which we had complete control over. We paid for it ourselves, so we were a little bit tentative about working with another company. But they seemed like a really good fit straight away. And then there's [the] good thing of getting notes. First of all, you look at them and think, *I'm not fucking doing this!* but every bit of notes I got through Warp were brilliantly considered and clever and on the ball. I don't think there was anything that we didn't do in the end after talking to them about it. It was just really, really good, and we just came away from it all feeling good. You can't underestimate that. When you look at the roster of their movies, it's not a coincidence that they've done such good films. But it's about fostering a creative atmosphere and support. That counts for a lot. Sometimes things can be a bit controlling, and that's kind of crushing the feelings that you need to have to get the best work out of you.

There is a lot of talk about Kill List. *What does that mean for you and for future projects?*

On Friday we'll find out. This is the true test of it, and it's what the box office will be. The film has had the best critiques you can get. Optimum have been behind it, lots of posters, loads of really good PR, and they've done tons and tons of preview screenings, so I'm really happy. Then it's in the hands of the gods, isn't it? Everything seems like it's going in the right direction. All the reviews are pretty stellar, so fingers crossed. Then after that, we're in pre-production on another movie, so we'll start shooting in a month on a film called *Sightseers*, which is about a couple going caravanning. It's a bit of a comedy and it's kind of a real performance-led comedy. I took it because I really wanted to do something that was a bit lighter. It was very heavy doing *Kill List*. And the humor is really funny to do with such nice people. When you make something like *Kill List*, it makes you think twice, and you then might want to make something a bit more cheery! So we're going to do that. Then after that, there's another movie that we're filming, hopefully around April time, with Nick Frost, which again is another comedy. I didn't write *Sightseers*, but I've written this other one with Amy [Jump], my wife, who wrote *Kill List*. It's called *I, Macrobane*, which is a mad, knockabout, alternate reality comedy. Macro as in macrobiotic and bane as in wolfsbane. The title is the problem. I'm sure it'll get re-named before we can do it! It's kind of a big, bright, crazy, comedy thing, and after that, we're doing a sci-fi movie, which is in development at the moment. It's all looking really good. That's called *Freak Shift*.

I enjoyed Kill List *and I could have watched more.*

It's ninety minutes, man, and that's how long a film should be. We're working on a prequel. It's set during the English Civil War, though. [Laughs] I think it's gonna be good. You know ergot, the fungus on barley that makes you hallucinate? It's all about the ergot. Anyway, I'll leave you with that.

2011

EDGAR WRIGHT, SIMON PEGG, and NICK FROST
Hot Fuzz

Edgar Wright, director of *Hot Fuzz*, muses on what he calls "a deadly serious full-on cop movie set in these very parochial chocolate box settings." (Universal/Matt Nettheim)

Universal, 2007

CAST: Nicholas Angel, SIMON PEGG; PC Danny Butterman, NICK FROST; Inspector Frank Butterman, JIM BROADBENT; DS Andy Wainwright, PADDY CONSIDINE; Simon Skinner, TIMOTHY DALTON; Met Chief Inspector, BILL NIGHY; Joyce Cooper, BILLIE WHITELAW; Tom Weaver, EDWARD WOODWARD; Sergeant Turner, BILL BAILEY; Tim Messenger, ADAM BUXTON; PC Doris Thatcher, OLIVIA COLMAN; George Merchant, RON COOK; James Reaper, KENNETH CRANHAM; Mary Porter, JULIA DEAKIN; Sergeant Tony Fisher, KEVIN ELDON; Met Sergeant, MARTIN FREEMAN; Rev. Philip Shooter, PAUL FREEMAN; PC Bob Walker, KARL JOHNSON; Eve Draper, LUCY PUNCH; Leslie Tiller, ANNE REID; DC Andy Cartwright, RAFE SPALL; Martin Blower, DAVID THRELFALL; Roy Porter, PETER WIGHT; Dr. Robin Hatcher, STUART WILSON; "Not" Janine, ROBERT POPPER; Bob, JOE CORNISH; Dave, CHRIS WAITT; Bernard Cooper, ERIC MASON; Underage Drinkers, TOM STRODE WALTON, TROY WOOLLAN, RORY LOWINGS; Greg Prosser, TREVOR NICHOLS; Sheree Prosser, ELIZABETH ELVIN; Amanda Paver, LORRAINE HILTON; Butcher Brothers, KEVIN WILSON, NICHOLAS WILSON; Saxon, SAMPSON; The Living Statue, GRAHAM LOW; Annette Roper, PATRICIA FRANKLIN; Peter Ian Staker, STEPHEN MERCHANT; The Swan, ELVIS; Mr. Treacher, TIM

BARLOW; Peter Cocker, BEN McKAY; Michael Armstrong, RORY McCANN; Tina, ALICE LOWE; Arthur Webley, DAVID BRADLEY; Heston Services Clerk, COLIN MICHAEL CARMICHAEL; Mrs. Reaper, MARIA CHARLES; Aaron A. Aaronson, ALEXANDER KING. Uncredited: Janine, CATE BLANCHETT; Met Police Inspector, STEVE COOGAN; Thief Dressed as Santa, PETER JACKSON.

CREDITS: *Director*, Edgar Wright; *producers*, Nira Park, Tim Bevan, Eric Fellner; *screenplay*, Edgar Wright, Simon Pegg; *executive producer*, Natascha Wharton; *line producer*, Ronaldo Vasconcellos; *associate producer*, Karen Beever; *director of photography*, Jess Hall; *production designer*, Marcus Rowland; *editor*, Chris Dickens; *costume designer*, Annie Hardinge; *hair & make-up designer*, Jane Walker; *music*, David Arnold; *visual effects supervisor*, Richard Briscoe; *special effects lead supervisor*, Mike Kelt. Running time: 121 minutes.

> "Nicholas Angel is the finest police officer London has to offer, with an arrest record 400 percent higher than any other officer on the force. He's so good, he makes everyone else look bad. As a result, Angel's superiors send him to a place where his talents won't be quite so embarrassing—the sleepy and seemingly crime-free village of Sandford. With garden fêtes and neighborhood watch meetings replacing the action of the city, Angel struggles to adapt to his situation and finds himself partnered with Danny Butterman, an oafish but well meaning young constable. Just as all seems lost, a series of grisly accidents motivates Angel into action. Convinced of foul play, Angel realizes that Sandford may not be as idyllic as it seems. With his faithful new partner in tow, Angel fights to prove his instincts are correct and uncover the truth about Sandford. Is Angel simply losing his mind in the safest, sweetest village in Britain? Or is something far more sinister at work....?"

A Geek Conquest of the Universe
Edgar Wright, Simon Pegg, and Nick Frost on *Hot Fuzz*

I've just seen the film.

Simon Pegg: Are your ears still ringing?

Edgar Wright: It's the *loudest* film. Are you still in shock?

Is it hard to come up with a good second movie?

Wright: Level with us: is it better than *Fierce Creatures*?

Pegg: We were definitely aware of it, weren't we?

Wright: It's a weird thing, I suppose. It wasn't that *Shaun* arrived as a huge hit. It did pretty well at the cinema and then on DVD and then it did okay around the world. Over an eighteen-month period, it gathered a reputation, and during that period, we were trying to write the second film. It's definitely strange. There is an expectation there, which wasn't present before because aside from the *Spaced* fans, there was no real expectation of *Shaun of the Dead* [2004]. So it does make it kind of weird, and you can drive yourself crazy trying to second guess what people might want.

We've been in that position before, doing the second series of *Spaced* [1999-2001]. It can become very tricky [examining] what worked last time, what didn't, and what you want to do that's different again. More so than *Shaun* and *Spaced*, this is trying to go into another genre completely. We're trying to break new ground in a way, do characters that we haven't done before and subject matter that we haven't done before.

Pegg: And also out-do it, in a way. We should definitely try and do something that is grander in every way, so the film is, in a sense, an evolution from *Shaun of the Dead*. It's not like, *Well, that worked. Let's do it again.* Let's try and move it on slightly and create something that feels like an organic continuation of what we did in the first place.

Nick Frost: I like the idea of the chariot race in *III*.

Pegg: The Roman epic! Also, because we have quite a specific group of core fans, you always want to make people happy. You want people to not feel cheated and not think you're just resting on your laurels and making money. It's important to us that we do things that are good and that the people we respect like them. You're desperately in need of external validation.

What was the pitch on Hot Fuzz?

Pegg: That was the thing. *Shaun* was quite a simple pitch in a way: it was a romantic comedy with zombies. The tagline said it all. This couldn't have been our first film because it required a little bit more faith. You know what I mean?

Wright: You come up sometimes with little pithy descriptions to explain it—"Miss Marple directed by Tony Scott." Sometimes it works and it makes sense, but it's not the whole picture. In a way, the idea of doing a Bruckheimer-esque buddy-cop film in the countryside—that was the central conceit. We get to work in this very escapist genre that's set in a place that we know very well because me and Simon are from the West Country. So in a sense, there was a leap of faith with the script because sometimes a lot of the humor is derived from what's happening in the background on where it is. And even the accents, with it being a deadly serious full-on cop movie set in these very parochial chocolate box settings.

Such as Mr. Webley.

Wright: That came from a real anecdote as well. We interviewed a lot of police for the film, and one of them was a guy who transferred from Tower Hamlets to Wiltshire. When he was talking to some farmers in Wiltshire, he actually had to have another officer to translate. That's where that idea came from. When you hear an anecdote like that, you kind of think: *Idea for scene.* That was one of the first things we wrote because we thought, *That's got to be a funny scene.*

Simon and Nick have been accepted as a double-act. Is that fair and accurate?

Frost: I dunno. We work very well together. We've probably done more apart than we have together, but it just so happens that the things we do together are a lot better than the things I've done.

Pegg: Because it's a comedy, the term "double-act" seems more appropriate. You wouldn't really call De Niro and Pesci a double-act—not that I would ever compare ourselves to them at all—but with a straight drama, it's always just people working together.

Frost: But because *Hot Fuzz* is a comedy, then it is slightly more of that feel.

Pegg: We've known each other a very long time. We were friends before we were colleagues, so we bring our relationship to the roles. And with Edgar as well, it really counts being friends. Communication on set is a lot easier, and that's really, really important. Edgar brought up a point the other day that you'll sometimes read in a review that there was no chemistry between the lead players, and that's genuinely because they've never met before. They couldn't have that unspoken communication, and Nick and I do. I'm always really flattered when people say we're good on screen together, but half of me thinks, *It's just us*.

Frost: Yeah, we're not doing that much, really. Just saying our lines and us being how we are.

Pegg: It feels like it's over-complimenting, 'cause it is so easy and a lot of fun and we do arse around in real life. It's about bringing that to the screen.

Frost: All three of us, but especially Edgar, have a good strong work ethic. And just because we're mates, there's not that thing where you just come on and fuck around all day. Once you come on set and the camera turns over at eight, we're working all day. It's sometimes easy to get away with things with people you don't know, but because we're friends, we can't do that.

Pegg: Sometimes you watch films and you get the impression that they had more fun than you are having watching it. Perhaps it was just about messing around and making each other laugh on set. We don't ever want people feel that they're not invited to the party.

Where does the fun stop and the work begin?

Wright: In both cases, from my point of view—and slightly less so from Simon and Nick's—I love cop films and zombie films, and I've always wanted to make one of both. They're tough to make, especially trying to do action on a budget and shooting in the English weather. It was really tough. Several times during the making [of *Hot Fuzz*], I said, "This was supposed to be fun, making a cop film," and it never is, because it's really hard work. You come out with even more respect for a lot of the directors than I did before—people like Robert Rodriguez, Michael Mann, Tony Scott, even someone like Michael Bay. I wouldn't put him in the same league as the other three. You know what I'm saying. That said, it's easy to completely write him off, but you look at how those things are staged and you think, *There has to be something going on there to be able to make that kind of spectacle. Nobody just off the street could shoot those kinds of action scenes.*

Let's talk about the various references and the actors associated with them. Are you all channeling your inner nerd?

Frost: We try not to use the "n" word—the nerd word.

Pegg: It's "geek" now. It's positive again.

Wright: There was definitely an element in terms of the casting. Not giving too much away, but the thing with the casting was that we wanted the villagers to be all separately formidable presences. Certainly in a lot of cases, that was our theory. In the film, a lot of the cops are played by the more comedic actors and the villagers are played by the real heavyweight dramatic actors. That was definitely a logic, and a lot of those people were first choices—people we wanted to work with or see more of on the big screen. Billie [Whitelaw] and Edward [Woodward] have been away from the big screen for a while because they're in the later years of their careers. Someone like Paul Freeman, whenever you watch *Raiders of the Lost Ark* [1981], you think, *Fucking hell, Paul Freeman is amazing in that film*, and he was great in this. Stuart Wilson, whenever he's in a film—and he had a whole run of being in those Bruckheimer films—you watch thinking, *Stuart Wilson is in a different, better film.* A lot of those people, we wrote those things with them in mind, or at least people of that ilk. In 90 percent of cases, we got them. Timothy Dalton in a weird way—we didn't cast him as being Bond geeks, but instead for being one of the most underused villains of our time. I think of him in *The Rocketeer* [1991], or *Flash Gordon* [1980]. I know he ends up as a goodie in *Flash Gordon*, but Dalton makes a great baddie. Hopefully it comes across in the film, but he was having a whale of a time with us.

Did you have to attract them, or did they know you and come to you?

Wright: Some did. People like Jim Broadbent and Timothy Dalton were fans of *Shaun of the Dead*. I presume Edward or Billie hadn't seen it before they were approached, but they had certainly heard of it. In fact, Billie Whitelaw's son owned the flat that is Kate Ashfield's apartment in *Shaun of the Dead*. There was a strange connection.

Pegg: I remember Billie telling us that her son had said, "You should read this, Mum." And I remember Edward telling us that he'd turned down a cameo in Neil La Bute's *Wicker Man* [2006] but said yes to *Hot Fuzz*, which was lovely. All we could do was say, "Here's the script." With a lot of these people, you don't get them in to read; they either do it or they don't. It was nice to get that response back. Maybe it was because we had a calling card, or maybe because they liked the script. It was lucky. Jim Broadbent was funny because after *Shaun of the Dead*, he came up to us at the BAFTAs and, as we're shaking hands, he said, "I like *Shaun of the Dead*. Would you put me in one of your next films?" That's a comment you bank straight away, and as soon as you get back to your computer, you write, "Jim Broadbent walks into a room." That was sealed.

What about Martin Freeman and Steve Coogan at the beginning?

Pegg: We always thought of them for that.

Wright: They were always in there. On one hand, there is a joke in the novelty of the casting. It's as if they are the top brass, and with Bill Nighy, they are three of the best comic actors in the country. The idea of combining that into one joke and not particularly casting them for their names alone was key. They work hand-in-hand. They're all brilliant comic actors, and the idea of going up in age....

Pegg:... and trumping each other. *My God, it's him.* Then, *My God—it's him!* It's almost the same in what Nicholas is going through in terms of their status.

Wright: Steve said a funny thing, very much in jest, when we were casting, "Who's playing the chief inspector?" I said, "Bill Nighy." "So I'm between Martin Freeman and Bill Nighy? I can live with that."

Were you deliberately attempting to create your own ensemble?

Wright: It's weird. It would happen in TV on *Spaced* and stuff. The comedy community is very small, and people sometimes criticize things for being incestuous, but the truth of it is that there aren't actually that many brilliant comic actors. It's not as if they are few and far between, but there are not that many of them.

Pegg: And it's not as though they are actors.

Wright: The idea of a "rep" company is something I like, even going back as far as *Spaced* and *Shaun*. That's always what's fun. Yes, they are actors that you know, and obviously we write for Nick knowing he's playing that part. We write the part for him. We like the way that Tarantino works or Wes Anderson or the Coen Brothers work. They have a sense of theater.

Pegg: Always ever-growing. Always new people.

Wright: That's exciting. You're working with people that you know and love, but it's exciting having Paddy Considine because it throws in a new curveball.

Frost: There's a relaxed feel to working as well because you know you're going to go in and see our mate Martin Freeman or Bill or Jim Broadbent. There's none of that, *Oh fuck, I'm going to meet so-and-so today*. Well, at the beginning, maybe.

Pegg: Yeah. There were a lot of days where it was like, "You go in first," because Timothy was waiting to do his first rehearsals.

Frost: I spent two weeks after every conversation I had with Jim Broadbent walking away and in my own head saying, "You fucking IDIOT! How could you say that to him?"

Pegg: He had a man crush.

How easy or otherwise is it to keep your feet on the ground?

Pegg: I don't understand how anyone can take it in their stride, though; that's the thing. I don't know how you become immune to not finding it all wonderful and being very humbled by it. I worry that one day it might be something that I just go "yeah" at. For me, it's all still great.

Frost: We're massive fanboys as well.

Pegg: Yeah, we're fans of film, and it's amazing to be working in it. I'll never lose sight of that because I remember what it was like when I was a kid looking at it.

Frost: Also, we're surrounded by good, normal people. All our wives and girlfriends are normal, working people and our parents are fucking nice. If you get out of line, there is someone quite nearby who'll say you're being a dick.

How do you cope with kids recognizing you and generally becoming famous, cult faces?

Pegg: The big thing was having an action figure. As a collector myself—well, not a collector; I play with them....

Wright:... You play with yourself at home?

Pegg: I do! My wife's already bored with my talking action figure, which says a lot about me. I hope it's always surprising. And like Nick said, there'll always be somebody to take you down. And working with the likes of Billie and Edward and those people in their seventies who've been in the business for a long time and still so down to earth and so humble and so good to work with proves it's possible to stay that way.

Frost: Also, we're so close. It doesn't happen often, but if I was playing up, we're close enough to be able to say, "Come on, stop it." You don't get that all the time.

Wright: Also, we're not living in LA. That's where that solipsism goes off the end.

Frost: Once I lose ten stone and get my teeth done, watch out.

What sort of offers are you getting from the States? Is a move on the cards?

Frost: You can go and come back.

Wright: In this day and age that filmmaking has become truly international, the really stupid thing would be to move, buy a house in L.A., and then come back to make a film in Prague for a year.

Pegg: Or on the Isle of Man.

Wright: People are making stuff all around the world. In a weird way, people also don't make films in L.A. or New York that much anymore. It's in Canada, Australia, New Zealand, Prague, Luxembourg. Especially with the Internet age, it's very easy to be international and stuff. I don't see any reason to go, really.

Pegg: It's only if you want to work in TV, really—if you want to get a good series like *24*, something that's going to run for seven seasons, then you have to be there. That's the only reason to move to L.A. That's not what's interesting us at the moment.

What have you got lined up for film number three?

Pegg: Little crumbs flying around. We're going to sit down and have a chat about it at some point once all this dies down. The big mistake we made early on after *Shaun* was that the first thing we thought of was the title of *Hot Fuzz*. When we announced it, it became a thing, so everyone was going, "Where's *Hot Fuzz*?"—before it was even a fucking script!

Wright: We had a problem with that because it can create undue anticipation of something that we haven't figured out ourselves yet. Not that we didn't have the idea, but when we were writing, we were still doing press on *Shaun*. Simon was doing *Mission: Impossible* [2006]. I was doing some other things. Once you announce something, it allows people to say, "Where the fuck is it?" This time, until we're ready to unleash it, we'll keep quiet.

Pegg: It'll be fun in the way that information is so accessible, to keep the title back to the very last minute, almost until the poster is revealed.

Making Shaun *led to cameos in* Land of the Dead *[2005], for George A. Romero. Is anything more going to happen with him?*

Wright: Not specifically.

Pegg: We talked about a few things. I think the experience he had with *Land of the Dead*—when we were on set, there were always loads of people around the video, and you could feel him on edge. He was on edge a lot. That's why he's done *Diary [of the Dead,* 2007], which is a really stripped back [project]—just him and the minimum amount of people. It's like his own antidote to the experience on *Land*.

Wright: Diary of the Dead is another "dead" film. It's shot already.

Pegg: It's like *The Blair Witch Project* [1999] meets *Dawn of the Dead* [1979], which is a really crap way of describing it, but it's about a group of students who are out in the woods making a video documentary just as the crisis hits, so they pick it all up on their own cameras.

I can't wait to see it. I'm a Romero nut. Or nerd.

Wright: You're never too old to be a nerd! I mean that affectionately.

Pegg: We're trying a geek conquest of the universe. Films would be a lot better if everyone was a geek.

2007

Filmographies

Key: short (sh), documentary (doc)
Commercials, video games, and music videos are not included

ALEJANDRO AMENÁBAR (Born 1972)
Himenóptero (sh), 1992; Luna (sh), 1995; *Thesis*, 1996; *Abre los ojos/Open Your Eyes*, 1997; *The Others*, 2001; *The Sea Inside*, 2004; *Agora*, 2009; *Vale* (sh), 2015; *Regression*, 2015.

PAUL W.S. ANDERSON (Born 1965)
Shopping, 1994; *Mortal Kombat*, 1995; *Event Horizon*, 1997; *Soldier*, 1998; *Resident Evil*, 2002; *AVP: Alien vs. Predator*, 2004; *Death Race*, 2008; *Resident Evil: Afterlife*, 2010; *Resident Evil: Retribution*, 2010; *The Three Musketeers*, 2011; *Pompeii*, 2014.

LUC BESSON (Born 1959)
L'avant dernier (sh), 1981; *Le Dernier Combat/The Last Battle*, 1983; *Pull marine* (sh), 1984; *Subway*, 1985; *Le grand bleu/The Big Blue*, 1988; *La Femme Nikita*, 1990; *Atlantis* (doc), 1991; *De Serge Gainsbourg à Gainsbarre de 1958-1991* (doc, segment, "Mon legionnaire"), 1994; *Leon*, 1994; *The Fifth Element*, 1997; *The Messenger/Joan of Arc*, 1999; *Angel-A*, 2005; *Arthur and the Invisibles*, 2006; *Arthur and the Great Adventure*, 2009; *The Extraordinary Adventures of Adèle Blanc-Sec*, 2010; *Arthur 3: The War of the Two Worlds*, 2010; *The Lady*, 2011; *Lucy*, 2014.

DANNY BOYLE (Born 1956)
Shallow Grave, 1994; *Trainspotting*, 1995; *A Life Less Ordinary*, 1997; *The Beach*, 2000; *28 Days Later*, 2002; *Millions*, 2004; *Sunshine*, 2007; *Alien Love Triangle* (sh), 2008; *Slumdog Millionaire*, 2008; *127 Hours*, 2010; *Trance*, 2013; *Steve Jobs*, 2015.

TIM BURTON (Born 1958)
The Island of Doctor Agor (sh), 1971; *Doctor of Doom* (sh), 1979; *Stalk of the Celery Monster* (sh), 1979; *Vincent* (sh), 1982; *Luau* (sh), 1982; *Frankenweenie* (sh), 1984; *Pee-wee's Big Adventure*, 1985; *Beetlejuice*, 1988; *Batman*, 1989; *Edward Scissorhands*, 1990; *Batman Returns*, 1992; *Ed Wood*, 1994; *Conversations with Vincent* (doc, unfinished), 1994; *Mars Attacks!* 1996; *Sleepy Hollow*, 1999; *The World of Stainboy* (sh), 2000; *Planet of the Apes*, 2001; *Big Fish*, 2003; *Charlie and the Chocolate Factory*, 2005; *Corpse Bride*, 2005; *Sweeney Todd: The Demon Barber of Fleet Street*, 2007; *Alice in Wonderland*, 2010; *Dark Shadows*, 2012; *Frankenweenie*, 2012; *Big Eyes*, 2014; *Miss Peregrine's Home for Peculiar Children*, 2016.

JOHN CARPENTER (Born 1948)
Revenge of the Colossal Beasts (sh), 1962; *Terror from Space* (sh), 1963; *Warrior and the Demon* (sh), 1969; *Gorgo Versus Godzilla* (sh), 1969; *Gorgon, the Space Monster* (sh), 1969; *Dark Star*, 1974; *Assault on Precinct 13*, 1976; *Halloween*, 1978; *The Fog*, 1980; *Escape from New York*, 1981; *The Thing*, 1982; *Christine*, 1983; *Starman*, 1984; *Big Trouble in Little China*, 1986; *Prince of Darkness*, 1987; *They Live*, 1988; *Memoirs of an Invisible Man*, 1992; *In the Mouth of Madness*, 1994; *Village of the Damned*, 1995; *Escape from L.A.*, 1996; *Vampires*, 1998; *Ghosts of Mars*, 2001; *The Ward*, 2010.

WES CRAVEN (1939-2015)
The Last House on the Left, 1972; *The Fireworks Woman* (credited as "Abe Snake"), 1975; *The Hills Have Eyes*, 1977; *Deadly Blessing*, 1981; *Swamp Thing*, 1982; *Invitation to Hell*, 1984; *The Hills Have Eyes Part II*, 1984; *A Nightmare on Elm Street*, 1984; *Deadly Friend*, 1986; *The Serpent and the Rainbow*, 1988; *Shocker*, 1989; *The People Under the Stairs*, 1991; *Wes Craven's New Nightmare*, 1994; *Vampire in Brooklyn*, 1995; *Scream*, 1996; *Scream 2*, 1997; *Music of the Heart*, 1999; *Scream 3*, 2000; *Cursed*, 2005; *Red Eye*, 2005; *Paris, je t'aime* (segment, "Pere-Lachaise"), 2006; *My Soul to Take*, 2010; *Scream 4*, 2011.

ROLAND EMMERICH (Born 1955)
Wilde Witwe (sh), 1979; *Franzmann*, 1979; *Das Arche Noah Prinzip*, 1984; *Joey*, 1985; *Ghost Chase*, 1987; *Moon 44*, 1990; *Universal Soldier*, 1992; *Stargate*, 1994; *Independence Day*, 1996; *Godzilla*, 1998; *The Patriot*, 2000; *The Day After Tomorrow*, 2004; *10,000 BC*, 2008; *2012*, 2009;

Anonymous, 2011; *White House Down*, 2013; *Stonewall*, 2015; *Independence Day Resurgence*, 2016.

WILLIAM FRIEDKIN (Born 1935)
Good Times, 1967; *The Birthday Party*, 1968; *The Night They Raided Minsky's*, 1968; *The Boys in the Band*, 1970; *The French Connection*, 1971; *The Exorcist*, 1973; *Fritz Lang Interviewed by William Friedkin* (doc), 1974; *Sorcerer*, 1977; *The Brink's Job*, 1978; *Cruising*, 1980; *Deal of the Century*, 1983; *To Live and Die in L.A.*, 1985; *Rampage*, 1987; *The Guardian*, 1990; *Blue Chips*, 1994; *Jade*, 1995; *Rules of Engagement*, 2000; *The Hunted*, 2003; *Killer Joe*, 2011.

TERRY GILLIAM (Born 1940)
Storytime (sh), 1968; *Miracle of Flight* (sh), 1974; *Monty Python and the Holy Grail* (co-directed with Terry Jones), 1975; *Jabberwocky*, 1977; *Time Bandits*, 1981; *The Meaning of Life*, (co-directed with Terry Jones), 1983; *The Crimson Permanent Assurance* (sh), 1983; *Brazil*, 1985; *The Adventures of Baron Munchausen*, 1988; *The Fisher King*, 1991; *Twelve Monkeys*, 1995; *Fear and Loathing in Las Vegas*, 1998; *The Man Who Killed Don Quixote* (unfinished), 2000; *The Brothers Grimm*, 2005; *Tideland*, 2005; *The Imaginarium of Doctor Parnassus*, 2009; *The Legend of Hallowdega* (sh), 2010; *The Wholly Family* (sh), 2011; *The Zero Theorem*, 2013.

JON HARRIS (Born 1967)
The Descent: Part 2, 2009.
As editor: *Holiday Romance* (sh), 1998; *The Second Death* (sh), 2000; *Snatch*, 2000; *Ripley's Game*, 2002; *Occasional, Strong* (sh), 2002; *Dot the I*, 2003; *The Calcium Kid*, 2004; *Layer Cake*, 2004; *The Banker* (sh), 2004; *The Descent*, 2005; *Being Cyrus*, 2005; *Starter for 10*, 2006; *Stardust*, 2007; *The Pond* (sh), 2008; *Eden Lake*, 2008; *The Descent: Part 2*, 2009; *Kick-Ass*, 2010; *127 Hours*, 2010; *The Woman in Black*, 2012; *Trance*, 2013; *Christmas in a Day* (doc), 2013; *The Two Faces of January*, 2014; *Kingsman: The Secret Service*, 2014; *Bastille Day*, 2016.

FRANK HENENLOTTER (Born 1950)
Basket Case, 1982; *Brain Damage*, 1988; *Basket Case 2*, 1990; *Frankenhooker*, 1990; *Basket Case 3*, 1991; *Bad Biology*, 2008; *Herschell Gordon Lewis: The Godfather of Gore* (doc, co-directed with Jimmy Maslon,), 2010; *That's Sexploitation!* (doc), 2013; *Chasing Banksy*, 2015.

PETER JACKSON (Born 1961)
The Valley (sh), 1976; *Bad Taste*, 1987; *Meet the Feebles*, 1989; *Braindead*, 1992; *Heavenly Creatures*, 1994; *The Frighteners*, 1996; *The Lord of the Rings: The Fellowship of the Ring*, 2001; *The Lord of the Rings: The Two Towers*, 2002; *The Lord of the Rings: The Return of the King*, 2003; *King Kong*, 2005; *Crossing the Line* (sh), 2008; *The Lovely Bones*, 2009; *King Kong 360 3-D* (sh), 2010; *The Hobbit: An Unexpected Journey*, 2012; *The Hobbit: The Desolation of Smaug*, 2013; *The Hobbit: The Battle of the Five Armies*, 2014.

NEIL JORDAN (Born 1950)
Angel, 1982; *The Company of Wolves*, 1984; *Mona Lisa*, 1986; *High Spirits*, 1988; *We're No Angels*, 1989; *The Miracle*, 1991; *The Crying Game*, 1992; *Interview with the Vampire: The Vampire Chronicles*, 1994; *Michael Collins*, 1996; *The Butcher Boy*, 1997; *In Dreams*, 1999; *The End of the Affair*, 1999; *Not I* (sh), 2000; *The Good Thief*, 2002; *Breakfast on Pluto*, 2005; *The Brave One*, 2007; *Ondine*, 2009; *Byzantium*, 2012.

FRANCK KHALFOUN (Born 1968)
P2, 2007; *Wrong Turn at Tahoe*, 2009; *Maniac*, 2012; *i-Lived*, 2015; *Amityville: The Awakening/The Amityville Horror: The Lost Tapes*, 2016.

GEORGE LUCAS (Born 1944)
Look at Life (sh), 1965; *Herbie* (sh), 1966; *Freiheit* (sh, credited as "Lucas"), 1966; *1:42.08* (doc, sh), 1966; *Electronic Labyrinth THX 1138 4EB* (sh), 1967; *The Emperor* (doc, sh), 1967; *Anyone Lived in a Pretty How Town* (sh), 1967; *6-18-67* (doc, sh), 1967; *Filmmaker* (doc, sh), 1968; *The Making of "The Rain People"* (doc), 1969; *Bald: The Making of "THX 1138"* (doc, uncredited); *THX 1138*, 1971; *American Graffiti*, 1973; *Star Wars/Star Wars: Episode IV – A New Hope*, 1977; *Star Wars: Episode I – The Phantom Menace*, 1999; *Star Wars: Episode II – Attack of the Clones*, 2002; *Star Wars: Episode III – Revenge of the Sith*, 2005.

JAMES MANGOLD (Born 1963)
Heavy, 1995; *Cop Land*, 1997; *Girl, Interrupted*, 1999; *Kate & Leopold*, 2001; *Identity*, 2003; *Walk the Line*, 2005; *3:10 to Yuma*, 2007; *Knight and Day*, 2010; *The Wolverine*, 2013.

NEIL MARSHALL (Born 1970)
Dog Eat Dog (sh), 1994; *Combat* (sh), 1999; *Dog Soldiers*, 2002; *The De-*

scent, 2005; *Doomsday*, 2008; *The Descent: Part 2* (camcorder sequence, uncredited), 2009; *Centurion*, 2010; *Tales of Halloween* (segment, "Bad Seed"), 2015.

DANIEL MYRICK (Born 1963)
The Blair Witch Project (co-directed with Eduardo Sanchez), 1999; *The Strand*, 2007; *Believers*, 2007; *Solstice*, 2008; *The Objective*, 2008; *Under the Bed*, 2015.

CHRISTOPHER NOLAN (Born 1970)
Tarantella (sh), 1989; *Larceny* (sh), 1996; *Doodlebug* (sh), 1997; *Following*, 1998; *Memento*, 2000; *Insomnia*, 2002; *Batman Begins*, 2005; *The Prestige*, 2006; *The Dark Knight*, 2008; *Inception*, 2010; *The Dark Knight Rises*, 2012; *Interstellar*, 2014; *Quay* (sh), 2015; *Dunkirk*, 2017.

ANDRÉ ØVREDAL (Born 1973)
Future Murder (co-directed with Norman Lesperance), 2000; *Customer Support* (sh), 2009; *Trolljegeren/Troll Hunter*, 2010; *The Autopsy of Jane Doe*, 2015; *Tunnelen* (sh), 2015.

GEORGE A. ROMERO (Born 1940)
The Man from the Meteor (sh), 1954; *Gorilla* (sh), 1955; *Earthbottom* (sh), 1956; *Curly* (sh), 1958; *Slant* (sh), 1958; *Expostulations* (sh), 1962; *Night of the Living Dead/Night of the Flesh Eaters*, 1968; *There's Always Vanilla/The Affair*, 1971; *Jack's Wife/Hungry Wives/Season of the Witch*, 1972; *The Crazies/Code Name: Trixie*, 1973; *Spasmo/The Death Dealer* (inserts, uncredited), 1974; *Martin*, 1977; *Dawn of the Dead/Zombies – Dawn of the Dead*, 1978; *Knightriders*, 1981; *Creepshow*, 1982; *Day of the Dead*, 1985; *Monkey Shines*, 1988; *Two Evil Eyes* (segment, "The Facts in the Case of Mr. Valdemar"), 1990; *The Dark Half*, 1993; *Bruiser*, 2000; *Land of the Dead*, 2005; *Diary of the Dead*, 2007; *Survival of the Dead*, 2009.

ELI ROTH (Born 1972)
Restaurant Dogs (sh), 1994; *Cabin Fever*, 2002; *The Rotten Fruit* (sh), 2003; *Hostel*, 2005; *Hostel: Part II*, 2007; *Inglourious Basterds* (segment, "Nation's Pride" uncredited), 2009; *Stolz der Nation* (sh), 2009; *The Green Inferno*, 2013; *Knock Knock*, 2015.

EDUARDO SANCHEZ (Born 1968)
The Blair Witch Project (co-directed with Daniel Myrick), 1999; *Altered*, 2006; *Seventh Moon*, 2008; *ParaAbnormal*, 2009; *Lovely Molly*, 2011; *V/H/S/2* (segment, "A Ride in the Park"), 2013; *Four Corners of Fear* (sh), 2013; *Exists*, 2014.

M. NIGHT SHYAMALAN (Born 1970)
Praying with Anger, 1992; *Wide Awake*, 1998; *The Sixth Sense*, 1999; *Unbreakable*, 2000; *Signs*, 2002; *The Village*, 2004; *Lady in the Water*, 2006; *The Happening*, 2008; *The Last Airbender*, 2010; *After Earth*, 2013; *The Visit*, 2015.

BARRY SONNENFELD (Born 1953)
The Addams Family, 1991; *For Love or Money*, 1993; *Addams Family Values*, 1993; *Get Shorty*, 1995; *Men in Black*, 1997; *Wild Wild West*, 1999; *Big Trouble*, 2002; *Men in Black II*, 2002; *RV*, 2006; *Men in Black 3*, 2012; *Nine Lives*, 2016.

QUENTIN TARANTINO (Born 1963)
Love Birds in Bondage, (sh, unfinished), 1982; *My Best Friend's Birthday*, 1987; *Reservoir Dogs*, 1992; *Pulp Fiction*, 1994; *Four Rooms* (segment, "The Man from Hollywood"), 1995; *Jackie Brown*, 1997; *Kill Bill: Vol. 1*, 2003; *Kill Bill: Vol. 2*, 2004; *Sin City* (credited as "special guest director"), 2005; *Grindhouse: Death Proof*, 2007; *Inglourious Basterds*, 2009; *Django Unchained*, 2012; *The Hateful Eight*, 2015.

DAVID TWOHY (Born 1955)
Grand Tour: Disaster in Time, 1992; *The Arrival*, 1996; *Pitch Black*, 2000; *Below*, 2002; *The Chronicles of Riddick*, 2004; *A Perfect Getaway*, 2009; *Riddick*, 2013.

JAMES WATKINS (Born 1973)
Eden Lake, 2008; *The Woman in Black*, 2012; *Bastille Day*, 2016.

BEN WHEATLEY (Born 1972)
Rob Loves Kerry (sh), 2006; *Down Terrace*, 2009; *Kill List*, 2011; *Sightseers*, 2012; *The ABCs of Death* (segment, "U is for Unearthed"), 2012; *A Field in England*, 2013; *High-Rise*, 2015; *Free Fire*, 2016.

EDGAR WRIGHT (Born 1974)
Dead Right (sh), 1993; *A Fistful of Fingers*, 1995; *Shaun of the Dead*, 2004; *Hot Fuzz*, 2007; *Scott Pilgrim vs. the World*, 2010; *The World's End*, 2013; *Baby Driver*, 2017.

Sources

The interviews presented in this volume were conducted by the author personally and exclusively, via press conferences or round table gatherings. The majority previously appeared in truncated form in *The Yorkshire Post*. I am pleased to acknowledge them here.

Key
AI – author interview
PC – press conference
RT – round table

Alejandro Amenábar
 "Spectres at the feast," *The Yorkshire Post*, 11/2/01
 PC – 10/5/01.

Paul W.S. Anderson
 Previously unpublished.
 RT – Summer 2002.

Danny Boyle, Andrew Macdonald and Alex Garland
 "Dreams that became the ultimate nightmare," *The Yorkshire Post*, 11/1/02
 This interview was republished as "Apocalypse Here and Now: Danny Boyle surveys the wasteland," by the National Media Museum (UK) in *Archive* #17, (March 2010)
 PC – 10/6/02.

Tim Burton
 Previously unpublished.
 RT – 1/5/00.

John Carpenter
  A transcript of an interview compiled by the author and filmed by Mike Justice as an exclusive introduction to *The Thing*, which was screened in 70mm format as part of the 7th Fantastic Films Weekend, Bradford (6/13/08).
  "Horror master," *The Yorkshire Post*, 10/31/15
  AI – 4/2/08.

Wes Craven
  "Scream team," *The Yorkshire Post*, 4/28/00
  PC – April 2000.

Roland Emmerich, Dean Devlin, and James Spader
  Previously unpublished.
  PC – 1/5/95.

William Friedkin
  "The power and the gory," *The Yorkshire Post*, 10/30/98.
  PC – 10/1/98.

Terry Gilliam
  "Still wild at art," *The Yorkshire Post*, 4/19/96.
  PC – 1/26/96.

Jon Harris
  "Director's debut is a gruesome body of work," *The Yorkshire Post*, 12/11/09.
  PC – 10/2/09.

Frank Henenlotter
  "Creator of cult monster movie at Celluloid Screams," *The Yorkshire Post*, 10/18/13.
  AI – 10/14/13.

Peter Jackson
  Calendar Lunchtime Live, Yorkshire Television, tx: 12/20/02.
  PC – 12/8/01.
  AI for television – 12/8/01.

Neil Jordan and Stephen Woolley
"Interview with the Director: Neil Jordan in conversation with Tony Earnshaw," *Hammer Horror* #2, 2/95.
PC – Winter 1994.

Franck Khalfoun
This interview originally appeared on the now defunct allthingshorror.co.uk website in March 2013 written under the pseudonym "Marcus Spiker."
"How to remake a cult 80s horror movie," *The Yorkshire Post*, 3/15/13.
AI – 2/21/13.

George Lucas
"Shooting stars…" *The Yorkshire Post*, 7/16/99.
RT – 7/4/99.

James Mangold and Cathy Konrad
"A murderous case of mistaken identities," *The Yorkshire Post*, 6/13/03.
PC – 6/6/03.

Neil Marshall
Previously unpublished.
AI – 6/29/05.

Daniel Myrick and Eduardo Sanchez
"Witch guide to horror," *The Yorkshire Post*, 10/29/99.
PC – 10/7/99.

Christopher Nolan and Christian Bale
"How I saved the caped crusader," *The Yorkshire Post*, 6/17/05
PC – 6/13/05.

André Øvredal
"Childhood fears that spawned a monster hit," *The Yorkshire Post*, 9/9/11.
AI – 6/22/11.

George A. Romero
"The king of the zombies rises again," *The Yorkshire Post*, 9/23/05
PC – 8/19/05.

Eli Roth
"Horror in the blood," *The Yorkshire Post*, 10/10/03.
PC – 6/7/03.

M. Night Shyamalan and Bryce Dallas Howard
"Frightfully young and scarily talented," *The Yorkshire Post*, 8/19/04
RT – 8/9/04.

Barry Sonnenfeld and Will Smith
"Star quality," *The Yorkshire Post*, 8/1/97.
PC – 7/15/97.

Quentin Tarantino
"Where did America's favorite movie brat go wrong?" *The Yorkshire Post*, 9/21/07
AI – 9/11/07.

David Twohy
Previously unpublished.
PC – 8/9/04.

James Watkins, Jane Goldman, and Susan Hill
"The Woman in Black returns to life once again to haunt cinema screens," *The Yorkshire Post*, 2/6/12.
"An appointment with fear in the remote depths of the Dales," *The Yorkshire Post*, 2/6/12.
RT – 1/19/12.

Ben Wheatley
"More than gore to a thriller that breaks the rules," *The Yorkshire Post*, 9/2/11.
AI – 8/30/11.

Edgar Wright, Simon Pegg, and Nick Frost
"It's a fair cop for "movie nerds" now enjoying cult stardom," *The Yorkshire Post*, 2/16/07
AI – 2/7/07.

Index

20th Century Fox 284
24 (TV show) 380
28 Days Later (film) 46-55, 283, 309

A
Abre los ojos (film) 8, 11
Ackerman, Forrest J. xiii
Addams, Charles 319
Addams Family, The (film) 319
Aereon (character) 346
Aja, Alexandre 189-190
Albany, New York xiii
Ali (film) 325
Alice in Wonderland (novel) 18
Alice Through the Looking Glass (novel) 18
Alien (film) 21, 23, 81, 141, 211, 227, 228, 293, 359
Alien 3 (film) 21
Alien Love Triangle (film) 54-55
Aliens (film) 21, 22-23
Allen, David 225
Allen, Woody 173
Alligator People, The (film) 152
Almodovar, Pedro 43
Altman, Robert 282
Amadeus (film) 205
Amenábar, Alejandro **4**, 4-13, 310, 383, 391
American Graffiti (film) 202
American McGee's Alice (video game) 18-19, 23,
American Pie (film) 297
American Zoetrope 205
Anderson, Ernest "Tron" 324
Anderson, Paul W.S. **14**, 14-29, 383, 391

Anderson, Wes 378
Apocalypse Now (film) 163
Argento, Asia 285
Argento, Dario 285
Armageddon (film) 86
Arquette, David 83, 84, 85
Arrupe, Father Pedro 113
Artisan 243, 244, 245, 249, 251
Ashfield, Kate 377
Ashley, Ted 116
Assault on Precinct 13 (film) 22
Astounding Science-Fiction (magazine) 73
As You Like It (play) 312
Audsley, Mick 124

B
Bad Biology (film) 154
Bad Boys (film) 323
Bad News Bears, The (film) 73
Baker, Rick 322
Bale, Christian 254-266, 393
Ballard, J.G. 51
Bannister, James 336
Barrymore, Drew 83
Basket Case (film) 144-158
Batman (character) 258-259, 260, 261, 262-263, 265, 266
Batman (film) 67, 68
Batman (TV show) 126, 258
Batman Begins (film) 254-266
Battle of Hastings (projected film) 233
Bava, Mario 62
Bay, Michael 323, 376
Bean, Sean **160**
Beatles, The 165

395

Before I Wake (projected film) 284
Being There (film) 310
Belial (character) 155-156
Bell, Keith 227
Bell Witch, Tennessee 246
Bermingham, Thomas 112
Besson, Luc xiv, **30**, 30-44, 383
Bianchi, Kenneth 214
Big Daddy (character) 287
Bilton, California 337
Birthday Girl (film) 8
Birthday Party, The (film) 112
Black Hawk Down (film) 52
Blair, Linda 107-108
Blair, Tony 246
Blair Witch Project, The (film) 60-61, 236-252, 273, 293, 381
Blatty, William Peter 107, 108, 110-111
Blood Simple (film) 319
Blue John Caves, Derbyshire 139
Bolt, Jeremy 26
Bonded by Blood (film) 364
Bonnard, Pierre 113
Book of Shadows: Blair Witch 2 (film) 251, 300
Book of the Dead (book) 289
Boorman, John 165, 173
Bottin, Rob 73-74
Bourne Woods, London 139
Boyens, Philippa 160-169
Boyle, Danny **46**, 46-55, 383, 391
Boy Meets World (TV show) 296, 298
Brain Damage (film) 154
Bram Stoker's Dracula (film) 180
Branagh, Kenneth 55
Brando, Marlon 264
Brannigan (film) 335
Braveheart (film) 122
Brazil (film) 122, 123
Brides of Dracula, The (film) 151
Bridges, Jeff 127
Bridgewater, Stephen 127
Broadbent, Jim 377, 378
Brody, Adrien **302**
Bronson, Charles 337
Brown, Jim 336
Bruckheimer, Jerry 376
Bruiser (film) 282, 284

Buried Secret of M. Night Shyamalan, The (TV documentary) 312
Buring, MyAnna 363, 364
Burkittsville, Maryland 245
Burstyn, Ellen 108, 109
Burton, Barry (character) 22
Burton, Tim xiii, **56**, 56-68, 319, 384, 391
Butler, Rhett (character) 174

C

Cabin Fever (film) 290-300
Cabinet of Dr. Caligari, The (film) 152
Cage, Nicolas 66-67
Caine, Michael 260, 262
Cameron, James 22-23, 183
Campbell, John 73
Campbell, Neve xiii, 76-88
CanalPlus 93, 282
Canton, Mark 283-284, 285, 286
Carolco 93
Carpenter, John xiii, 2, 22-23, **70**, 70-75, 217, 228-229, 384, 392
Carter, Sarah (character) 137-138, 142-143, 231
Carton, Sydney (character) 122, 128-129
Casper (film) 321
Castle, William 151
Catwoman (projected film) 68
Celador Films 226, 234
Cenote Caves, Mexico 139
Changeling, The (film) 9, 81
Channel Islands 7, 8,
Christie, Agatha 9, 307
Christmas Carol, A (story) 357
Chronicles of Riddick, The (film) 340-347
Cimino, Michael 184
Cinderella (story) 309
Cinefantastique (magazine) 75
Circus of Horrors (film) 151
Claudia (character) 176, 181
Clayton, Jack 9,
Cleasby, Emma 233
Clooney, George 325
Close Encounters of the Third Kind (film) 228
Cobb, Lee J. 109

Coen Brothers, The 319, 378
Cohen, Harry 247
Cold and Dark (film) 229
Collins, Michael 185
Colson, Christian 135, 136, 141
Columbia 320, 323
Columbus, Chris 276, 284
Combat (short film) 234-235
Company of Wolves, The (film) 178
Considine, Paddy 378
Coogan, Steve 377, 378
Cooney, Michael 211, 212, 213, 216
Cop Land (film) 215
Copperfield, David 289
Coppola, Francis Ford 115-116, 199, 205
Coppola, Sofia 308-309, 310
Cops (TV show) 242
Corman, Roger xiii,
Costner, Kevin 184
Cox, Courteney 84, 85
Craft, The (film) 86
Craven, Wes xiii, **76**, 76-88, 228-229, 384, 392
Crazies, The (film) 297
Creepshow (film) 283
Croft, Lara (character) 26, 28
Crompton, Ben 364
Crosby, Bing 59
Crowe, Cameron 10,
Cruise, Tom 8, 10, 11-12, 29, 174, 175-176
Cruise/Wagner 8, 29
Crumb, George 110
Crying Game, The (film) 178, 179
Cry of the Banshee (film) 335
CSI (TV show) 336
Culp, Robert 336
Cundey, Dean 74
Curse of the Fly (film) 152
Curtis, Jamie Lee 86
Cusack, John **208**, 212, 214-215, 219
Cutthroat Island (film) 128

D

Dallas, Korben (character) 38
Dalton, Timothy 376-377
Daniel Boone (TV show) 337

Dark Blood (film) 176
Davalos, Alexa **340**, 346
Davidson, Jaye 99-100
Davis, Jack 283
Dawn of the Dead (film) 23, 51, 281, 287-288, 381
  Dawn of the Dead (remake) 281
Dawson's Creek (TV show) 79
Day Mars Invaded Earth, The (film) 152
Day of the Dead (film) 23, 281, 282, 288
Daytrippers, The (film) 50
de Lioncourt, Lestat (character) 175-176, 181, 184, 185
de Pointe du Lac, Louis (character) 181, 184
De Caunes, Antoine 42-43
De Niro, Robert 27, 375
De Palma, Brian 173
De Vito, Danny 319
Dead Calm (film) 211, 217
Death Proof (film) 330-338
Defective Detective, The (projected film) 130
Delgado, Rob 182-183
Deliverance (film) 227, 228, 232
Dench, Judi 346
Depp, Johnny 63-64, 65
Descent, The (film) xiv, 2, 137, 139-140, 222-235, 364
Descent: Part 2, The (film) 132-143
Descent: Part 3, The (projected film) 143
Devlin, Dean 90-103, 392
Digital Domain 182-183
Diamond Dead (projected film) 285
Diary of the Dead (film) 381
Die Hard (film) 233
Diesel, Vin **340**,
Dirty Dozen, The (film) 338
Dirty Pretty Things (film) 226
Disney, Walt 59, 130
Dog Eat Dog (short film) 234
Dog Soldiers (film) 137, 225, 228, 229, 232-233, 234, 273
Dog Soldiers 2 (suggested sequel) 226
Dogville (film) 312
Dollymount, Ireland 184
Donahue, Heather 239, 246

Donner, Richard 261, 263-264
Donnie Darko (film) 299
D'Onofrio, Vincent 326
Doomsday (film) 364
Down Terrace (film) 368
Dr. Strangelove (film) 206, 319
Dr. Who and the Daleks (film) xiii
Dream of a Beast, The (novel) 183
Drought, The (novel) 51
Drowning Mona (film) 86
Dublin, Ireland 184
Dunst, Kirsten 177-178, 181
Duvall, Clea 215
Duvall, Shelley 217

E

Eagle's Nest, The (projected film) 233, 235
Ealing, London 139
EC Comics 282-283, 289
Eccleston, Christopher 54
Eden Lake (film) 135, 136-137
Edward Scissorhands (film) 63, 68
Ed Wood (film) 60, 64
El Cid (film) 96
Emmerich, Roland **90**, 90-103, 384-385, 392
Empire of Lights, The (painting) 110
Enemy of the State (film) 328
English Patient, The (film) 205
E.T. – the Extra-Terrestrial (film) 75
Eurotrash (TV show) 42-43
Event Horizon (film) 24
Evil Dead, The (film) 293, 299
Evil Dead II (film) 300
Exorcist, The (novel) 107, 110-111
Exorcist, The (film) xiv, 19-20, 81, 104-117, 227, 242, 293
Exorcist II: The Heretic (film) 115
Exorcist III (film) 115, 117
Exorcist IV (projected film) 250-251

F

Farnham, Surrey 139
Favor, Scott 299
Fellini, Federico 44
Feore, Colm 347
Ferretti, Dante 179

Ferro, Pablo 319
Field in England, A (film)
Fierce Creatures (film) 373
Fifth Element, The (film) 30-44
Figg, Christopher 225
Final Destination 5 (film) 355
Fiorentino, Linda 326
Fishburne, Lawrence 24
Fisher King, The (film) 122, 124
Flash Gordon (film) 377
Fog, The (film) 229
Foley, Scott 84
Football Factory, The (film) 364
Fonda, Peter 363
Ford, Glenn 264
Foree, Ken 287
Forman, Milos 217
Forrest Gump (film) 322
Fountain Society (novel)
Four Rooms (film) 54
Frank (character) 192-193
Frankenheimer, John
Frankenhooker (film) 155
Frankenstein (film) 180, 227
Freak Shift (projected film) 369
Freeman, Martin 377, 378
Freeman, Morgan 260, 262
Freeman, Paul 376
French Connection, The (film) 115
Fresh Prince (character) 326
Friedkin, William xiv, 2, **104**, 104-117, 385, 392
Friedman, Mark 93
From Dusk Till Dawn 2 (film) 300
Frost, Nick 369, 370-381, 394
Fryer, Emma 363
Fulci, Lucio 23

G

Gambon, Michael 64
Gangs of New York (film) 309
Garland, Alex 46-55, 391
Gaultier, Jean-Paul 30-44
Gaumont 34
Geffen, David 173, 179, 184-185
Geffen Company, The 175
Georgetown, Washington 110-111
Get Carter (film) 364

Index | 399

Get Shorty (film) 320
Gibson, Mel 122, 128-129
Gilliam, Terry xiv, **118**, 118-130, 319, 385, 392
Giraud, Jean (see: Moebius)
Girl, Interrupted (film) 215, 217
Gladiator (film) 139
Gleeson, Brendan 53-54, 309-310
Godfather, The (film) 115, 116
Godfather II, The (film) 115
Goldman, Jane 348-359, 394
Gorshin, Frank 124, 125-126
Gough, Michael 62, 65
Grant, Hugh 27
Grau, Jorge 52
Griffiths, Richard 64
Grindhouse (film double-bill) 330-338
Grisham, John 25
Grosse Pointe Blank (film) 215

H
Hackman, Gene 264
Hale, Gregg 239, 240
Hallenbeck, Bruce G. xiii, xii, xiii-xiv
Halloween (film) 22, 229
Halton Gill, Yorkshire 355-356
Hamlet (play) 41-42
Hammer Film Productions 61, 62, 156-157, 351, 354-355, 364
Hammer Horror (magazine) 393
Hanks, Tom 129
Hard Day's Night, A (film) 206
Hardy, Robin 363
Harlin, Renny 128
Harris, Jon **132**, 132-143, 385, 392
Harryhausen, Ray 288
Harry Potter (film series) 55, 164
Hartley, Richard 285
Haunting, The (film) 9, 13,
Hawks, Howard 73, 228
Heart of Love (projected movie) 250, 251
Heavy (film) 215
Heavy Metal (magazine) 33
Hellraiser (film) 225
Hemmings, Lindy 258
Henenlotter, Frank **144**, 144-158, 385, 392

Henriksen, Lance 84
Henry: Portrait of a Serial Killer (film) 242
Henze, Hans Werner 110
Herrmann, Bernard 44, 125
Hess, Rudolf 233
Heston, Charlton 96
Hickox, Douglas 335
High Chapparal, The (TV show) 337
Hill, Susan 348-359, 394
Hitchcock, Alfred 13, 44, 94, 125, 211, 217, 309, 310
Hitler, Adolf 40
Hood, Robin (character) 180
Hopper, Dennis 286
Horrors of the Black Museum (film) 62, 151
Hoskins, Bob 202
Hot Fuzz (film) 370-381
Hot Zone (book) 53
House of the Damned (film) 152
Howard, Bryce Dallas 302-314, 394
Howard, Cheryl 305
Howard, Ron 305-306, 313-314
Howling, The (film) 74
Hunchback of Notre Dame, The (projected film) 130
Hyett, Paul 229-230

I
I Am Legend (novel) 50, 51, 284-285
Ice Age (film) 27
Ideal (TV series) 364
Identity (film) 208-221
Ievins, Edgar 147, 148-149
I Know What You Did Last Summer (film) 242
I, Macrobane (projected film) 369
Impact Pictures 29
Impostor (film) 54
Inch, Rob 65, 66
Independence Day (film) 322, 325
Indiana Jones (film series) 96, 202, 228, 268
Industrial Light and Magic (ILM) 322
Inglorious Bastards, The (projected film) 338
Innocents, The (film) 9, 12, 13,

In Search Of... (TV show) 239
Interview with the Vampire: The Vampire Chronicles (film) 170-185
Interview with the Vampire (novel) 173-174, 176, 178, 180-181, 182, 184, 185
Irving, Washington 59
Isaacs, Jason 17
Isaacson, Barry 122
I Spit on Your Grave (film) 227

J
Jackson, Daniel (character) 98-99
Jackson, Michael 323
Jackson, Peter xiv, **160**, 160-169, 386, 392
Jackson, Samuel L. **196**
Jack the Ripper 111
James, M.R. 9, 353
Jaws (film) 116, 227, 228
Jaye, Jina 9
Jespersen, Otto 272
Jetée, La (film) 123
Jinn, Qui-Gon (character) 205
Joker, The (character) 266
Jones, Duane 287
Jones, Jeffrey 65
Jones, Tommy Lee 320, 321, 322, 324-325, 326
Jordan, Neil **170**, 170-185, 386, 393
Josephson, Barry 320
Jovovich, Milla **14**, 17-18, 20-21, 27, 29, 35-36, 40
Julyan, David 140
Jumanji (film) 130
Jump, Amy 369
Juneau, Alaska 74-75
Jurassic Park (film) 52, 273, 274
Justice, Mike 392

K
Kahn, Nathaniel 312
Kaplan, Juno (character) 137-138, 230-231, 233
Karloff, Boris 180, 227
Kassar, Mario 93, 99-100
Kelly, Richard 299-300
Kersh, David 283

Khalfoun, Franck **186**, 186-194, 386, 393
Kidman, Nicole **4**, 8, 10, 11-12
Kieszlowski, Krzysztof 179
Kill Bill (film) 336
Killers, The (film) 360, 363
Kill List (film) xiv, 2,
Kinderman, Lieutenant (character) 109
King, Stephen 283, 289
King Kong (film) 305
Kittelsen, Theodor 274
KNB Effects 295
Knife in the Water (film) 211, 217
Konga (film) 62
Konrad, Cathy 208-221, 393
Kruger, Ehren 79
Kubrick, Stanley 310

L
La Bute, Neil 377
Ladd, Jordan 299
Lahr, Bert 111
Lancaster, Bill 73
Landau, Martin 64
Land of the Dead (film) xiii, 278-289, 381
Langmann, Thomas 189
Laredo (TV show) 337
Lasher (novel) 175
Lavasseur, Grégory 189-190
Laverty, Paul 52
Law, Jude 26
Lee, Christopher 61
Leguizamo, John **278**
Leigh, Mike 179
Leeloo (character) 35
Le Fanu, Joseph Sheridan 353
Legend of Boggy Creek, The (film) 239
Legend of Sleepy Hollow, The (story) 59
Leon (film) 41, 42
Leonard, Joshua 246
Leone, Sergio 44
Lesbian Vampire Killers (film) 364
Lifeboat (film) 211
Lighthouse, The 313
Liotta, Ray 215
Living Dead at Manchester Morgue, The (film) 52

Loach, Ken 52
Lord of the Rings, The (film series) 29, 164, 165, 168
Lord of the Rings: The Fellowship of the Ring, The (film) 160-169
Lord of the Rings: The Return of the King, The (film), 169
Lord of the Rings: The Two Towers, The (film) 160, 169
Lost in Translation (film) 308-309
Love Hewitt, Jennifer 242
Lucas, George **196**, 196-206, 386, 393
Lugosi, Bela 64
Luna (short film) 13
Lustig, William (Bill) 189
Lynch, David 295, 296-297

M
Macdonald, Andrew 46-55, 391
Macdonald, Shauna 142, 232
MacNeil, Regan (character) 107-108, 109, 114
Macpherson, Don
McCambridge, Mercedes 109
McEwan, Ian 351
McGinley, John C. 215
McKellen, Ian 166
McKidd, Kevin 226, 233
Machinist, The (film) 259, 265-266
Mad (magazine) 283
Mad Ghoul, The (film) 285
Magritte, René 110
Malloy, Daniel (character) 176-177
Manderlay (film) 312-313
Mangold, James **208**, 208-221, 386, 393
Maniac (film) 189, 190
Maniac (film remake) 186-194
Mann, Michael 376
Man with the X-Ray Eyes, The (film remake) 67-68
Marker, Chris 123, 125
Marshall, Neil xiv, 2, 137, 140-141, **222**, 222-235, 386-387, 393
Marshall, Penny 319
Mary Shelley's Frankenstein (film) 180
*M*A*S*H* (film) 282
Maskell, Neil 363, 364
Matheson, Richard 284, 299

Matrix, The (film) 12
Mean Season, The (film) 337
Medak, Peter 9
Meeker, Ralph 337
Mendoza, Natalie 232
Men in Black (film) 316-329
Men in Black 2 (film) 328
Merrin, Father (character) 109
Messiah (TV drama) 226
Métal Hurlant (see: *Heavy Metal*)
Metcalf, Laurie 85
Mézières, Jean-Claude 44
MGM 93, 217, 284
Miller, Jason 109
Miller's Crossing (film) 319
Mill Hill Medical Research Institute 265
Mimic (film) 54
Miramax 55, 80, 294
Mission: Impossible (film series) 380
Michael Collins (film) 184-185
Misery (film) 319
Mitchell, Cameron 337
Mizrahi, Isaac 323
Moebius 44
Molina, Alfred 215, 221
Mona Lisa (film) 179
Monty Python and the Holy Grail (film) 268, 271
Moore, Demi 41, 130
Morfitt, Darren 233
Morricone, Ennio 44
Mortal Kombat (film) 27, 28
Mortensen, Viggo 167
Mortimer, Emily 83-84
Mother's Day (film) 294
Motion Picture Alliance of America (MPAA) 281
Motion Picture Code 110
Moulin Rouge (film) 8, 9
Mozart, Wolfgang Amadeus 33
Mr. Shadow (projected film) 34
Mulder, Saskia 141
Mulholland Drive (film) 295
Mummy, The (film) 284
Murphy, Eddie 27
Music of Chance, The (film) 101
Music of the Heart (film) 87-88
Myrick, Daniel **236**, 236-252, 387, 393

N

Neeson, Liam 129, 262
Netherlands Film Festival 176
New Line Cinema 165, 284
New Orleans, Louisiana 153-154, 174, 179-180
Newton, Thandie 346-347
Nicola, Father John 112-113
Nichols, Mike 179
Nicholson, Jack 266
Nicotero, Greg 288-289
Nightmare Before Christmas, The (film) 66
Nightmare on Elm Street, A (film) 79-80
Night of the Demon (film) 274
Night of the Flesh Eaters (film; see: '*Night of the Living Dead*')
Night of the Living Dead (film) xiii, 281, 282, 284-285, 287
Night of the Living Dead (remake) 287
Night They Raided Minsky's, The (film) 111
Nighy, Bill 377-378
Nolan, Christopher xiv, **254**, 254-266, 387, 393
Norske Folkeeventyr (book) 274
Norwegian Folk Tales (book; see '*Norske Folkeeventyr*')
Notting Hill (film) 27
Novak, Kim 125
Nyby, Christian 289
NYU Film School 294

O

O'Donnell, Chris 320
O'Malley, William 112
Oates, Warren 363
Oldman, Gary 40, 41-42, 262
Omega Man, The (film) 21, 22, 51
Omen, The (film) 227, 242
On the Beach (film) 51
One Flew Over the Cuckoo's Nest (film) 217
Only Angels Have Wings (film) 228
Open Your Eyes (film) 8, 10, 12
Orphanage, The (film) 365
Osborne, Barrie 163
Others, The (film) 4-13, 211, 293, 310
Others 2, The (suggested film) 13
Outland (film) 293

Outpost (projected film) 233, 234
Øvredal, André **268**, 268-276, 387, 393

P

Pakula, Alan J. 363
Panic (film) 86
Parallax View, The (film) 360, 363
Paramount Pictures 29, 294, 345
Park, Ray 66
Parker, Fess 337
Party of Five (TV series) 86-87
Pathé 234
Pearlstein, Randy 298
Peckinpah, Sam 228
Peeping Tom (film) 194
Pegg, Simon 370-381, 394
Penderecki, Krzysztof 110
People magazine 175
Peoples, David 122, 123, 125, 128
Peoples, Janet 123, 125, 128
Performance (film) 364
Pertwee, Sean 233
Pesci, Joe 375
Philadelphia (film) 129
Phoenix, Joaquin 310
Phoenix, River 176-177
Pilote (magazine) 33
Pinewood Studios 139, 261
Pinkett-Smith, Jada 83
Pinter, Harold 112
Pitch Black (film) 340, 343-344, 345, 347
Pitt, Brad 126, 176, 177-178
Plummer, Christopher 126-127
Poe, Edgar Allan xiii
Polanski, Roman 173
Powell, Michael 194
Powell, Sandy 179
Prescott, Sidney (character) 82, 83, 84, 85-86
Preston, Richard 53
Price, Vincent xiii, 67-68
Prinze Jr, Freddie 242
Proust, Marcel 182
Psycho (film) 115, 180, 217
Psycho (remake) 115, 217
Pulp Fiction (film) 336, 365
Puzo, Mario 115-116

Q

Quasimodo (character) 130
Quatermass (film series) 354
Quinn, Kave 359

R

Ra (character) 99-100
Race with the Devil (film) 360, 363
Radcliffe, Daniel **348**, 351, 353-354, 358
Raiders of the Lost Ark (film) 202, 261, 376
Raising Arizona (film) 319
Razorback (film) 273
Rear Window (film) 211
Rebecca (film) 9
Reeves, Keanu 320
Reindeer Games (film) 79
Reiner, Rob 319
Remains of the Day, The (film) 233
Remember the Titans (film) 300
Repulsion (film) 81
Reservoir Dogs (film) 333
Resident Evil (film) 14-29
Resident Evil 2 (film) 29
Resident Evil 2: The Game (video game) 19, 21, 22
Restaurant Dogs (short film) 300
Ricci, Christina 64
Rice, Anne 174, 175, 178, 182, 184
Riddick, Richard B. (character) 343-344
Ridley, Judith 287
Rimmer, Ben 265
Ring, The (film) 293
Rio Bravo (film) 228
Rise of the Footsoldier (film) 364
Roache, Linus 347
Robbins, Tony 323
Robinson, Edward G. 174
Rocketeer, The (film) 377
Rocky Horror Picture Show, The (film) 285
Rodriguez, Michelle 18
Rodriguez, Robert 336, 376
Romero, George A. xiii, 2, 22-23, 24, 51, **278**, 278-289, 381, 387, 393
Rope (film) 211
Rosemary's Baby (film) 81, 110, 310
Rosses Point, Ireland 184
Rota, Nino 44
Roth, Eli **290**, 290-300, 387, 394
Roven, Chuck 122
Rubinstein, Richard P. 283
Rudin, Scott 319
Rumsfeld, Donald 286
Russell, Bing 337
Russell, Kurt 97, 102, **300**, 336-337

S

Salmon, Colin 18
Salt, Debbie (character) 85
Sanchez, Eduardo **236**, 236-252, 388, 393
San Francisco, California 201, 205
Saving Private Ryan (film) 53
Savini, Tom 287, 288
Saxon, John 336
Schindler's List (film) 129
Schwarzenegger, Arnold 93-94
Scott, Ridley 141, 359
Scott, Tony 328, 374, 376
Scream (film) 79, 86, 225, 242
Scream 2 (film) 82-83, 84
Scream 3 (film) xiv, 76-88
Screen Gems 211
Seattle, Washington 311
Serial Murder (book) 213, 214
Serra, Eric 44
Seven (film) 126
Seven Days to Noon (film) 51
Seven Samurai (film) 206
Shaun of the Dead (film) 283, 373-374, 377, 380, 381
Sheffield, Yorkshire 139
Shepperton Studios 261
Shining, The (film) 211, 217, 227, 228, 242
Shock Theater (TV package) xiii
Shopping (film) 26
Shostakovich, Dmitri 110
Showtime (film) 27
Shyamalan, M. Night **302**, 302-314, 388, 394
Siegel, Don 363
Sightseers (film) 369
Signs (film) 307, 310, 314
Silence of the Lambs, The (film) 180
Silent Hill (video game) 25
Silver Spring, Maryland 110-111
Simkin, Margery 125-126

Sinise, Gary 54
Sitting Target (film) 335
Sixth Sense, The (film) 12-13, 81, 311
Skellington, Jack (character) 66
Skywalker, Luke (character) 203
Slater, Christian 176-177
Sleepy Hollow (film) xiii, 56-68
Sluizer, George 176
Smith, Maggie 346
Smiley, Michael 363, 364
Smith, Paul 226-227
Smith, Will **316**, 316-329, 394
Smith, William 337
Soderbergh, Steven 55
Solo, Han (character) 203
Sonnenfeld, Barry **316**, 316-329, 388, 394
Spaced (TV show) 373, 378
Spader, James 90-103, 392
Spartacus (film) 96
Speedwell Cavern, Derbyshire 139
Spider-man (film) 225
Spiegel, Scott 300
Spielberg, Steven 44, 173, 179, 202, 228, 321-322
Spinell, Joe 190
Split Screen (TV show) 248
Stallone, Sylvester 93-94, 322-323
Stardust (film) 135
Stargate (film) 90-103
Star Trek (film series) 203, 345
Star Wars (film) 94, 96, 164, 199, 202, 203-204, 205, 252, 261, 327
Star Wars: Episode I – The Phantom Menace (film) 66, 196-206, 327
Star Wars: Episode II – Attack of the Clones (film) 225
Stern, Aaron 110
Stewart, British Columbia 74-75
Stewart, Donald 73
Stoker, Bram 182
Stowe, Madeleine 123-124, 125
Stravinsky, Igor 110
Streep, Meryl 87-88
Streiner, Russell 287
Strong, Rider 296, 298, 299
Stuntman Mike (character) **330**, 337
Sugarhill Gang, The 325-326
Sunrise with Sea Monster (novel) 183

Sunset Boulevard (film) 295
Superman (unrealised film) 66-67
Superman: The Movie (film) 261
Survivors (TV series) 50
Swayze, John Cameron 289
Sweet Sixteen (film) 52
Sykes, Eric 8-9

T
Tale of Two Cities, A (projected film) 122, 128-129
Tales from the Crypt (comic) 283
Tarantino, Quentin 310, **300**, 330-338, 378, 388, 394
Taylor, Richard 163
Tenant, The (film) 81
Terminator, The (film) 123
Texas Chain Saw Massacre, The (film) 81, 227, 294
That Championship Season (play) 109
Thatcher, Margaret 323
Thing, The (film) xiii, 70-75, 211, 217, 229, 392
Thing from Another World, The (film) 73, 289
Three to Tango (film) 86
Thurman, Uma 320
Time (magazine) 117, 245
Time Warner 117
Tingler, The (film) 151
To Kill a Mockingbird (film) 9
Tolkien, J.R.R. 164, 167, 169
Tomb Raider (film) 22, 26, 27-28
Townsend, Stuart 167
Toy Story (film) 27
Travels of Jamie McPheeters, The (TV show) 337
Troll Hunter (film) 268-276
Truman Show, The (film) 128
Tucker, Chris 36
Turn of the Screw, The (story) 9, 357
Twelve Monkeys (film) 118-130
Twisted Nerve (film) 335
Twohy, David **340**, 340-347, 388, 394

U
Unbreakable (film) 306-307
Unforgiven (film) 122

Universal Pictures 27, 62, 73, 122, 284, 285, 289
Universal Soldier (film) 93
University of Central Florida 239
Unzipped (documentary) 43

V
Vader, Darth (character) 264
Valentine, Jill (character) 22
Van Hentenryck, Kevin 150, 153, 154-155, 156
Van Sant, Gus 217
Vanilla Sky (film) 8
Vega$ (TV show) 337
Vegas, Johnny 364
Velvet Goldmine (film) 265
Vertigo (film) 125
Village, The (film) 302-314
Vincent, Cerina 298-299
Virginian, The (TV show) 337
Von Daniken, Erich 94
Von Sydow, Max 109
Von Trier, Lars 312-313

W
Walken, Christopher 65, 66
Walker, Ivy (character) 313
Walsh, Fran 164
War and Peace (novel) 173
WarGames (film) 21
War of the Worlds, The (novel) 228
War of the Worlds, The (radio drama) 247-248
Warner Bros. 116, 117, 179, 261
Warp Films 368
Watchmen (projected film) 130
Wayne, Bruce (character) 258-259
Wayne, Jeff 228
Watkins, James 136, **348**, 348-359, 388, 394
Webley, Mr. (character) 374
Weinstein, Bob 80
Weir, Peter 310
Welles, Orson 247
Werenskiold, Erik Theodor 274
West, Adam 258
Wheatley, Ben xiv, 2, **360**, 360-369, 388, 394

Whitelaw, Billie 376, 377, 379
White Palace (film) 95
Who Framed Roger Rabbit (film) 128
Who Goes There? (short story) 73
Wicker Man, The (film) 360, 363
Wicker Man, The (remake) 377
Wild Wild West, The (projected film) 325, 328
Williams, John 44
Williams, Michael 246
Williamson, Kevin 79
Willis, Bruce 35-36, 37, 38-39, 41, **118**, 122, 123-124, 126-127, 129, 130
Wilson, Stuart 376
Winston, Stan 182-183
Wizard of Oz, The (film) 217
Woman in Black, The (novel) 357
Woman in Black, The (film) 348-359
Wood, Elijah 186, 190, 191, 193
Wood, Wallace 283
Woods Movie, The (film; see: 'Blair Witch Project, The')
Woodward, Edward 363, 376, 377, 379
Woolley, Stephen 170-185, 393
Wright, Edgar **370**, 370-381, 389, 394
Writers Guild of America 178
Wrong Door, The (TV show) 364
Wrong Turn (film) 295
Wuthering Heights (projected film) 305

X
X-Men (film) 26

Y
Yakin, Boaz 300
Yorkshire Post, The (newspaper) 1-2, 391-394

Z
Zaentz, Saul 205
Zombie Flesh Eaters (film) 227
Zombies: Dawn of the Dead (film; see 'Dawn of the Dead')
Zorg (character) 40, 44
Zucker Brothers, The 328

www.ingramcontent.com/pod-product-compliance
Lightning Source LLC
Chambersburg PA
CBHW050831230426
43667CB00012B/1962